An Intellectual
History of Cannibalism

An Intellectual
History of Cannibalism

Cătălin Avramescu

TRANSLATED BY Alistair Ian Blyth

PRINCETON UNIVERSITY PRESS   PRINCETON AND OXFORD

Originally published as Filozoful Crud: O Istorie a Canibalismului, copyright © 2003 by
Humanitas, Bucharest, Romania
English-language translation copyright © 2009 by Princeton University Press
Published by Princeton University Press, 41 William Street, Princeton, New Jersey 08540
In the United Kingdom: Princeton University Press, 6 Oxford Street, Woodstock,
Oxfordshire OX20 1TW

All Rights Reserved

Library of Congress Cataloging-in-Publication Data

Avramescu, Cătălin, 1967–
[Filozoful crud. English]
An intellectual history of cannibalism / Cătălin Avramescu ; translated by
Alistair Ian Blyth.
p. cm.
Includes bibliographical references (p. 317) and index.
ISBN 978-0-691-13327-0 (hardcover : alk. paper)   1. Cannibalism—philosophy.
2. Cannibalism—history.   I. Title.
GN409.A87 2009
394'.909—dc22   2008030488

British Library Cataloging-in-Publication Data is available

Publication of this book has been aided by a grant from the Romanian Cultural Institute

This book has been composed in Sabon
Printed on acid-free paper. ∞
press.princeton.edu
Printed in the United States of America
1 3 5 7 9 10 8 6 4 2

INSTITUTUL
CULTURAL
R O M Â N

CONTENTS

LIST OF ILLUSTRATIONS

ACKNOWLEDGMENTS

Work on this book began at the Institute for Advanced Study in the Humanities (Edinburgh). Professor Peter Jones, the Director of the Institute, was a gracious host, and I have warm memories of my colleagues there. Since then, I have been a visiting fellow and pursued my research on this project in the following departments and institutions: the William Andrews Clark Memorial Library/UCLA Center for Seventeenth & Eighteenth Century Studies, the Department of Social and Moral Philosophy at the University of Helsinki, the Sigurdur Nordal Institute (Reykjavik), the Netherlands Institute for Advanced Study in the Humanities and Social Science (Wassenaar), the Herzog August Bibliothek (Wolfenbüttel), the Institut für Geschichte (Vienna University), and the Facoltá di Lettere e Filosofia (University of Ferrara). I also had the privilege of working in the national libraries of Austria, Finland, Iceland, and Scotland, as well as in the university libraries of Leiden, Trent, and UCLA. I hereby thank them all, as I thank many others not named here, while adding that none of these institutions or persons is responsible for any errors in the present work.

I am grateful for financial assistance during these years from the Mellon Foundation, the Lise Meitner fellowship program of Austria, and the Marie Curie fellowship program of the European Union.

A special word of gratitude is due to Professor Gabriel Liiceanu, the editor of the first, Romanian edition of this book, and to Alistair Ian Blyth, the translator who struggled with my prose. The work of translation was supported by a subvention from the Romanian Cultural Institute. New research for this revised English version was facilitated by a fellowship at the New Europe College/Institute for Advanced Study (Bucharest) and sustained by the Rector, Professor Andrei Pleşu.

I owe a different order of thanks to my wife, Adina, to whom I should dedicate so much more than this book.

INTRODUCTION

A AND B, THE TWO PHILOSOPHERS whose dialogue opens Denis Diderot's work *Supplement to the Voyage of Bougainville. . . on the Inconvenience of Attaching Moral Ideas to certain Physical Actions which they do not Presuppose* (1772), review the recent discoveries in the South Seas, on which occasion they find themselves confronted with a situation requiring special consideration. Will an island situated in the midst of natural abundance, with a limited surface area (a league in diameter, as the text specifies) and whose inhabitants have arrived there almost by miracle, be able to sustain population growth? What will happen, asks B, when the people begin to multiply?[1] For A, the answer is clear: they will begin to exterminate and eat one another. It is possible, continues A, that, due to this type of situation, anthropophagy may have appeared at a very ancient date and would thus be "insular in origin."[2] Hence there results the necessity and the source of cruel customs, such as infanticide, human sacrifice, castration, and infibulation, which arose in order to halt unsustainable population growth. Diderot qualifies these as "so many customs of a necessary and bizarre cruelty, whose cause has been lost in the night of time and which drive philosophers to distraction."[3]

Amateurs of metaphysics might wonder why we have found it fitting to torture the public with an analysis of oddities occurring on real or imaginary islands of the past. In the context of eighteenth-century theories, however, the discussion between A and B seems unremarkable at first sight. The primitive anthropophagi of exotic lands, the origins of religious worship and fanaticism in the necessities of natural existence, the obsession with population growth within a given territory: these are all tried and tested subjects of the Enlightenment. The significance of the theory that cannibalism is insular in origin will come to light only if we distance ourselves from the text and view it in relation to the type of science it sets out to employ, namely "natural history," in the sense in which this term was understood during Diderot's epoch. The anthropophagi of the Lancer Islands are placed in a situation that is at the intersection of two major theories. On the one hand, they are necessary products of natural history. The combination of limited natural abundance and the tendency to multiply cannot logically be prolonged except as far as a point at which the accumulation of bodies must generate reciprocal consumption. On the other hand, however, it is precisely the fact that anthropophagi are cultivated by the philosophic imagination in the isolation of the island-laboratory which proves that the nature of cannibalism is not an element of natural history understood as a universal genus.

The discussion between A and B captures the cannibal at a crossroads, at a precarious point in history when access to him becomes opaque and the way he is understood radically altered. Beyond this point, the anthropophagus will become the creature we know today: a product of particular circumstances. Extreme hunger, extinct customs in regions now invaded by tourists, and the manifestations of a profoundly deranged mind: all these are glimmers of a causality once described by distinct sciences. The anthropophagous nation has been reduced to a sad rabble of eccentrics, who each separately lead a tortured existence within a small ecological niche, incapable of constituting any starting point for the articulation of a moral philosophy.

Having ended up as functionaries who know very well where their next meal is coming from, the philosophers of our times teach us one or another version of utilitarianism, moral relativism, or juridical positivism. Sensible to the pleasures of the no longer topical, I have elected to present the reader with a study about a period of the past during which the eater of human flesh made his atrocious hegemony felt within the bounds of the science of natural law. The debate between A and B allows us to contemplate, at least as a possibility, a situation in which the cannibal was an original subject of universal history. If true, then the cannibal is one of the great forgotten figures of philosophy, and the story of man and his obligations, as these were seen by the philosophers of the past, would be incomplete without him.

This history of cannibalism can be reconstructed as three successive stages, part historical and part conceptual. In the first, the cannibal is viewed as a creature from the perspective of natural law. In the second, the cannibal becomes the diabolical retort in which the flux of particles confounds the calculations of theologians and metaphysicians. The third stage is that at which we seem to have arrived today, when the cannibal is a creature of circumstances and education. Natural law, materialism, and anthropological relativism are the three major contexts that impose a division in the history of the cannibal's passage through thought and which are, in their turn, clarified by his presence.

Nevertheless, the present work is not one that is primarily historical. First of all because it is in no way a history of cannibalistic practices. Of course, the instances of verifiable anthropology have sometimes left their traces in the ideal productions of the philosophers. However, whether cannibals existed or not is a fact of marginal importance. My cannibal is in the first place a scholarly creature, a personage who animates theoretical texts, and only to a lesser extent, if at all, is he a subject for the anthropology of the aberrant.

Before anything else, this book is about us and our world. What I have attempted to explain is not just the way in which anthropophagy was treated by the sciences of natural law but above all the general mystery of the disappearance of those theories. This disappearance has a significance of a philosophical order, since it is within its space that we now think about good and evil.

Together with the sanguine figure of the cannibal disappears a style of philosophical argument, leaving behind an imagination that is the poorer. But what is fundamental is the fact that a world of arguments, values, and sensibilities become inaccessible or unclear to us once their point of articulation is exiled from the field of reflection.

The anthropophagus was an unyielding creature who brought to light the law of a harsh and profound nature. As such, perhaps he has something to tell us about ourselves, the people of a time in which nature has become merely an occasion for the picturesque. In relation to us, the subjects of technologically mediated organization, the cannibal of the state of nature allows us to explore this impossible dimension, to traverse the crystalline sphere of the political.

In his strangeness, the cannibal is sovereign over a species of freedom. His story is one that casts light on the origins of the modern state and the boundaries of modern civilization, and weighs up their right to existence. Let us listen to this cannibal, for his voice comes from beyond, whence we too come and whither we shall perhaps never arrive again.

CHAPTER ONE

A Hobbesian Life Raft

Eugene Delacroix, *The Shipwreck of Don Juan*

THE THEATER OF NATURAL LAW

IN WHAT IS PERHAPS THE most concise and most ignored characterization of his scientific method, Thomas Hobbes argues in *Leviathan* (1651) that "examples prove nothing."[1] What Hobbes is signaling here is a profound difference, in nature rather than style, between the political science whose inventor he had declared himself to be in *De cive* (1642) and the moral philosophy of his predecessors. As early as 1630, Hobbes had elaborated the idea of a human science understood as one that was universal and rational, modeled according to the principles of Euclidean geometry. This is a science of rational deductions, systematically and logically drawn from a number of axioms. It does not wholly dispense with experience, but rather reduces it to a restricted set of observations that admit no contradiction, such as the observation that men fear each other. The necessity of this new branch of science is, for Hobbes, dual. On the one hand, it flows from the nature of the body politic, which is an artificial construct, resulting from the will of individuals. This means that it is not a part of nature and cannot be deduced based on the natural sentiments of sociability. Hence political science must set out from definitions rather than empirical facts. On the other hand, the deductive science of man and of the body politic is opposed to an idea of political discourse that Hobbes regards as profoundly suspect, namely the tradition of "rhetoric," a term whereby he includes ancient philosophy and history, together with their modern interpretations.[2] He sees this science as one of vague or erroneous representations, capable of fostering dissension as regards the most fundamental principles of morality. In contrast with the "rhetoric" of classical authors, Hobbes proposes an axiomatically ordered science, similar to physics and mathematics, a science of universal relevance, in which "examples" at most have the scope of clarifying certain aspects and revealing certain implications of the theory.

Hobbes's idea of science, which has some scholastic antecedents, was particularly influential in the seventeenth and eighteenth centuries, when political philosophers began to cultivate a style of argument that notably distanced itself from the moralists of literary extraction. Spinoza is one of the first to adhere to this doctrine, with a work in which ethics is "demonstrated geometrically" (*more geometrico*). The list of authors from this period who elaborate abstract works, ostensibly conceived as scientific, is long, and includes names as diverse as Cambridge Platonist Henry More; Richard Cumberland, author of *De legibus naturae* (1672) and a prominent critic of Hobbes; Francis Hutcheson; and William King.

What these thinkers reject is the concept of moral discourse taken as a sum of particular experiences. This is also the moral philosophy here with us today, one where examples have a value which is either negative in essence, that of "falsifying" a general principle, or which is positive only in a marginal, illustrative sense.

Today, against the backdrop of an impoverishment of the moral imagination, it is difficult for us to grasp that, in the seventeenth century, the dominant formula of moral philosophy was nonetheless different. Up to the point when the abstract science of man and of society entered the scene, there had been a number of other sciences for which imagination and example were the primal matter around which discourse was constructed. Even after the new scientific canons are accepted, the rupture between the latter and what we have here designated as the classical style of moral argument is not sudden. Hobbes himself deviates from his own principle. He must have thought that examples, ultimately, prove something, otherwise *Leviathan* would have been a considerably shorter book. In his writings, as well as in the writings of most other philosophers of the scientific style, there are numerous examples with a moral value. The necessity by virtue of which they are mentioned and discussed is complex.

By the early eighteenth century, one of the major forums for discourse about morals was the science of casuistry. This discipline is a collection of "cases," collated in treatises that group them by categories and discuss them separately, in connection with the relevant authorities. In England it was illustrated by authors like William Perkins (*Armilla aurea*, 1590), William Ames (*De conscientia*, 1630), Robert Sanderson (*De juramenti promissorii obligatione*, 1647), Joseph Hall (*Decisions of diverse Practicall Cases of Conscience*, 1649), or Jeremy Taylor (*Ductor dubitantium*, 1660). Casuistry is a science of examples, in which the beginning and end of the research is the particular rather than the general: a "practical" science in the Aristotelian sense of the term. In the epoch during which the modern scientific model is in formation, casuistry is an obligatory interlocutor. Scientific authors write within a space saturated by the conventions and vocabulary of casuistry. Casuistic arguments and influence partly explain why the social philosophy of the eighteenth century is one in which examples remain central to the order of demonstration.[3]

However, more profound is the fact that it is the very nature of the knowledge of man in general that demands examples. It is not too great an exaggeration to say that, for classical and early modern man, "to know" means to imagine, to dispose of a set of adequate images. The juxtaposition of a series of images is what forms the gallery of science, up until the great censorship of the imagination heralded by the conventions of modern science and discourse.[4] Up until that moment, the humanities were organized around ideas that probably originated from the Greek sophists, after which they were systematized by the theory of argumentation and Aristotelian categories, before being handed down by the Skeptics and the tradition of the Roman rhetoricians.

These influences explain why knowledge of the world and of humans ends up being conceived during the Renaissance as a species of theater. The scholar and the reader are seen as spectators who contemplate a show, a "theater of the world" (*theatrum mundi*). The metaphor of the theater is a model of scientific discourse. The term *theater* begins to be employed in the titles of works that are summary expositions of vast subjects.[5] Applied knowledge also begins to explore the virtues of theatricality. In the sixteenth century the first "theaters of anatomy" appear in Paris and Leiden, while numerous collections of natural curiosities from the same period are designated "theaters of nature."[6] In the seventeenth century, William Petty says of a "Theatre for Anatomy" that it is "(without Metaphor) a Temple of God."[7] In 1630, Jean-Pierre Camus describes the world as "an amphitheatre soaked in blood." Because evil men outnumber the good, it is necessary to inspire fear and terror in the former by presenting the punishments fixed by law for those who transgress.[8] In *The Natural History of Religion*, Hume writes: "We are placed in this world, as in a great theatre, where the true springs and causes of every event are entirely concealed from us."[9]

In the eighteenth century, the theater is also the place where the ingeniousness glorified by the new mechanical philosophy finds fertile ground for presentation. Fascinated by the new techniques of miraculous movement, the baroque theatrical producer draws on a series of mechanisms to automate the performance. On the stage, which now begins to be illuminated with artificial light, an allegory of movement in society and the world is performed. In the dialogue *A Plurality of Worlds*, French philosopher Bernard Fontenelle (1657–1757) is just one of the many authors to compare the curious machines of the theater to those of the universe.[10] The baroque also cultivates a taste for the spectacle of human cruelty and suffering. Pleasure and pain are mutually necessary: there is no pleasure without pain, and any satisfaction is compensated with suffering in the natural order.[11] Something concerning the influence of the theatrical model is also said by the fact that even contestation of the theater, which Jean-Jacques Rousseau will expound in the *Lettre à d'Alembert sur les spectacles*, is possible only insofar as there is a profound connection between theater and the human nature: "The stage is a tableau of the human passions, whose germ is to be found in all hearts."[12]

A theatrically organized system of images, the science of the baroque is animated by the central passion of curiosity. Aristotle had already remarked, in the *Metaphysics*, that wonder is the first impulse toward philosophy: "Due to the fact that they have wondered, men now begin, as they have always begun, to philosophize."[13] In the seventeenth and eighteenth centuries, curiosity is removed from the catalogue of vices and elevated to the rank of primary passion. In *The Spectacle of Nature*, Noël-Antoine Pluche argues that of all the means that can be employed to teach young people to think "there are none whose effects are more certain and more enduring that curiosity."[14] The spectacle of nature is one that the divinity has particularly intended for the instruction of man. In nature, man has the opportunity and the duty to decipher a providential order. If we content ourselves to observe nature without understanding the plan of the Creator, Pluche believes, we shall be no better than the savage who looks at a clock manufactured in Europe without understanding what use its mechanism serves. "The whole of nature is a magnificent clock whose mechanism functions only in order to teach us something completely different to that which can be observed at first glance."[15]

Curiosity is not merely a passion, but also an object of research. The science of the classical age is, more than any other, a collection of curiosities. Many treatises of the period include in their titles references to "curiosities," highlighting moral and natural philosophy's fascination for the grotesque and bizarre during the Renaissance and the baroque periods.

Up until the eighteenth century, when science succeeds, at least at a conceptual level, in making intelligible and plausible Francis Bacon's ideal of complete mastery of reality, the wider world is viewed through the lens of a system of fundamental oppositions between city and nature. This system of oppositions is epistemologically guided by "dialectics," a science that proceeds by overturning its initial object in order to distinguish its hidden nature and its relation to its opposite in the universal balance of creatures. The dialectical structure of the world commences from the pinnacle of the celestial hierarchy, where God and His monkey, the Devil, are to be found, and continues to the very base of the pyramid of beings.

Thus beyond the boundaries of the premodern city extends an inverted world, the opposite of civilization, peopled by grotesque figures, inverted images of civic man. The boundary of the republic is the symbolic limit whence begins another world, announced by such constructions as the *Rabenstein* (Ravens' Rock): the scaffold on which the ritual execution of capital punishment took place in German cities, the place where those who broke the laws of man and of nature were killed and their remains were left impaled on pitchforks.[16] This was the limit beyond which evil nature became visible, whence it came and whither it was summoned to return.

The state of nature invoked by the philosophers, prior to being a thought experiment of modern science or a historical hypothesis, is part of this fundamental inversion, a grotesque theater of lawless figures. It is a carnival in which all the hierarchies of civic order dissolve in criminal confusion. Hence the description of the state of nature as a generalized war, a war of all against all, a war in which anything goes.

This is the natural anarchy against whose background the central figure of our narrative takes shape: the anthropophagus. Among the diabolical creatures unleashed by anti–civil freedom, the cannibal is an eminent presence. The idea according to which the absence of supreme power leads to a state of chaos characterized by cannibalism is common. In a seventeenth-century sermon, we learn: "Take Sovereignty from the face of the earth and you turne it into a Cockpit. Men would become cut-throats and Canibals one unto another. We should have a very hell upon earth, and the face of it covered with blood, as it was once with water."[17] In *The Right of War and Peace* (1625), Hugo Grotius approvingly cites what he claims is a Hebrew proverb: "If there were no Sovereign Power, we should swallow up one another alive." The same idea, he asserts, is also to be found in the writings of Saint John Chrysostom.[18] In Thomas Malthus's *An Essay on the Principle of Population* (1803 edition), American Indians, who live in a state of nature, are said to war with each other continually, like predatory beasts, killing and eating each other. In the islands of the South Seas, things are even worse: "The state of perpetual hostility, in which the different tribes of these people live with each other, seems to be even more striking than among the savages of any part of America; and their custom of eating human flesh, and even their relish for that kind of food are established beyond a possibility of doubt."[19]

When, in the late eighteenth century, a band of anthropophagous Gypsies horrifies Vienna, we witness one of the last incursions of these extraordinary creatures into the space of civilization, creatures that once populated broad swathes of the geographic imagination.[20] Pigmies or giants, talking birds, tribes with strange customs, Gog and Magog, dog-headed or single-legged people: this is the raw material of the science that lies behind the dissertations about the theater of natural law. It is a species of geography, but in contrast to common physical geography it is sooner a speculative geography, concerned with describing and explaining bizarre inversions beyond the boundaries of common understanding, whence stretch regions in which civilized individuality is doomed to perish.

Of all the inverted species, the cannibal is the object of a veritable fixation. In ancient literature, there are frequent mentions of anthropophagi, from Homer and Strabo to the Roman historians. The most influential accounts were those contained in the *Histories* of Herodotus. The margins of the world known to the Greek author are peopled with numerous cannibal nations, such as the Mesogetae. When one of them nears the end of his life, his relatives kill him, and then prepare his flesh for a banquet. They reckon such a fate to be the most fortunate and also believe that people who die of illness are not good enough to eat, but only to bury, an eventuality that causes them to mourn.[21] Also in the environs of the Black Sea, when a Scythian warrior slays a foe for the first time, he drinks his blood. The Scythians make their clothes and even the quivers for their arrows from the skin of their enemies, and drinking cups from their skulls. Some flay their victims and stretch the skin over a frame.[22]

In the Middle Ages, the Crusades were an occasion to import extreme images into the European imagination. In a late-twelfth-century *chanson de geste*, in which the events of the First Crusade are described, the army of the legendary King Tafur, an ally of the Christians, is presented as a mob of barefoot, primitive savages, armed with clubs. The crusaders are astonished to discover that the savages prefer human flesh to that of nightingales stuffed with spices and are fearful that they themselves might be cooked and eaten.[23] Richard the Lionheart is portrayed in some chronicles as a cannibal who gobbles up the flesh of a Saracen at a banquet. In the same period, a chief source of information about nations with strange customs is the book of Marco Polo. In Asia, there are nations that hold marriages between the dead, others that kidnap foreigners and hold them to ransom, while the king of another land goes naked, exactly like his subjects. In the kingdom of Felech, in the island of Java Minor, the natives eat the flesh of all kinds of animals and are by no means adverse to human flesh.[24]

The crucial event that generated the emergence of a mass of geographic literature treating cannibalism was the discovery of the Americas. The term *cannibal* dates from this epoch and probably originates from the word *cariba* ("bold"), a label the Arawak Indians applied to themselves. In the early sixteenth century, Peter the Martyr, in *De novo orbe*, launched an image that would have an extraordinary career. He claimed that the anthropophagi of the Americas impregnate their women in order to ensure that, from the fruit of their wombs, they will have fresh meat. This topic, probably inspired by the Island of the Lotus-Eaters, where Odysseus and his men are fattened in order to be eaten, influenced another work widely read up to the eighteenth century: *A Journey to the Land of Brazil, otherwise called America* (1578) by Jean de Léry (1534–1613). De Léry claims that the savages give their captives to their daughters. The daughters then fatten them like pigs, before butchering them for the feast.[25] According to de Léry, the Caribs have a simple religion, which ignores God. In the *General History of Spain*, Jesuit Juan de Mariana (1536–1613) presents us with a standard image of the American Indians: they practice human sacrifice and sometimes eat the flesh; they are polygamous sodomites who more often than not go naked.[26] In the same century, another key opus to propound cannibal images and myths was that written by Sebastian Münster (1489–1552). Between 1544 and 1650, his *Cosmographia* went through forty-two editions in six languages.

Through the question of the origin of the American Indians, erudite scholars of the sixteenth to eighteenth centuries rapidly linked the geographic literature about the savages of the New World to the literature of antiquity. The savages in question, they discovered, did not seem to have been mentioned in the Bible or any of the ancient sources, which thus threw into doubt the interpretation or even relevance of these texts. The anthropophagy of the Americans was regarded by some scholars as significant in the clarification of their origins. Jean de Laet, director of the Dutch East Indies Company and author of a work about the American Indians (1640), believed that they must have been the descendants of the Scythians, since both nations were anthropophagi. This idea was adopted in the eighteenth century by French Jesuit François-Xavier Charlevoix (1682–1716), who traveled to the Americas as part of a geographical expedition. Joseph-François Lafitau (1685–1740), a French missionary to Canada, argues that terms such as *Scythia* and *Thrace* are too vague, and he therefore attempts to offer a more precise location. He agrees that the customs of the Americans prove they are descended from the ancient peoples of Europe. His analysis situates the ancestors of the Indians among the barbarous nations that once inhabited continental Greece and the islands of the Aegean Sea. The method he pursues consists of a comparison of Indian customs with those mentioned by ancient historians. The Indians of Illinois wrap their dead in raw buffalo hide and suspend them from trees, exactly the same as the inhabitants of ancient Colchis used to do, while others sacrifice children, the same as the Canaanites, who made burnt offerings to Moloch.

In the seventeenth century, a leading chronicle of cannibal behavior is the work of Spanish historian Garcilasso de Vega (1539–1617), *The History of the Inca Kings of Peru* (1608). Quoted by Algernon Sidney,

John Locke, and Samuel von Pufendorf, the book was also probably known to Hobbes. In 1746, Formey, secretary of the Berlin Academy, mentions it in *Conseils pour former une Bibliothèque peu nombreuse, mais choisie*, among the travel books that any cultivated person ought to possess.[27] According to Garcilasso, there were two "epochs" in the history of the peoples of the Andes: the age of the civilizing Inca kings, subsequent to a primitive and savage age, which still persisted in those mountain regions whither the power of the Inca kings had not reached. This was the part of the book that so much inflamed the imagination of European readers of the seventeenth and eighteenth centuries, with its account of the perfect, rational, and frugal order imposed in the Inca state.

The eighteenth century is the heyday of travel accounts, whether real or imaginary. Among the latter, containing numerous references to cannibalism, can be numbered Daniel Defoe's *Robinson Crusoe*, which Rousseau, in *Émile*, argued was "the most felicitous treatise of natural education" (le plus heureux traité de l'éducation naturelle) and the first book his pupil ought to read.[28] Robinson lives in a state of nature, where permanent terror arises from the possibility that others may be cannibals. Before building himself a fortification, he finds it difficult to sleep, for fear of being devoured. In the late eighteenth century, Diderot's article on the "Caraibes" (an article referred to in the entry on "Anthropophages" in the *Encyclopédie*) reveals that the perception of the anthropophagus had not changed in its essentials. The Caribs, according to Diderot, are savages of the Antilles Islands. "They are generally sad, brooding and lazy, but with a sound constitution, commonly living to a hundred. They go naked; they have olive skin. They do not swaddle their children, who, by the age of four months, crawl on all fours, and acquiring the habit, can run in this fashion, when they are older, as quickly as any European on two legs. They have many wives, who are not at all jealous of each other. . . . They give birth without pangs. . . . They eat their prisoners on spits, and send morsels to their friends. . . . When one of them dies, they kill his black, to serve him in the other world."[29]

One of the most important contributions to the eighteenth-century debate on cannibals was that made by Cornelius de Pauw. In his *Philosophical Researches on the Greeks* (1788), he argues that there are many savage nations who live by rapine and subject to no man, such as the Bedouins of Turkey and the Kurds of Persia. Some of these nations are anthropophagous, forming enclaves in the midst of civilized nations, such as the man-eaters of Gujarat or what might be a tribe of Aromanians in Greece, who, in their accesses of fanatical fury, devoured many

Muslims. They committed so many massacres and excesses that the governors of the land banished them in 1676.

The geography of morals and moral philosophy are two aspects of the same discourse. This is first because travel literature is a primary source of images and subjects for reflection on moral norms. In the *Rhetoric*, Aristotle argues that travel to various climes is useful in the legislative work, because from it we can learn the "laws of nations."[30] In the *New Organon* (lib. 1, cap. 84), Bacon hails the contribution of geographical discoveries to the progress of philosophy: "Many things in nature have come to light and been discovered as a result of long voyages and travels (which have been more frequent in our time), and they are capable of bringing a new light in philosophy. Indeed it would be a disgrace to mankind if wide areas of the physical globe, of land, sea and stars, have been opened up and explored in our time while the boundaries of the intellectual globe were confined to the discoveries and narrow limits of the ancients."[31] In part due to the influence of Bacon, the Royal Society viewed the knowledge accumulated during voyages as an indispensable component for the progress of the new sciences. In *Some Thoughts concerning Reading and Study for a Gentleman* (1703), Locke argues that geography and travel books are absolutely necessary. He gives a long list of works, beginning with Hakluyt and Purchas. At the beginning of the eighteenth century, *The Tatler* describes how "there are no books which I more delight in than in travels, especially those that describe remote countries, and give the writer an opportunity of showing his parts without incurring any danger of being examined or contradicted."[32]

There is also another, more profound reason, which links travel literature to moral science and the science of the body politic. Many of these texts, especially the modern ones, are written with a critical intention. They propound subjects and arguments lifted from the speculations of the moral philosophers. Frequently, these texts are themselves the support for and source of such arguments.

The theory of climate is one of these. It is first mentioned by ancient authors. In *De ira*, Seneca argues that those who live in the frozen North are savage in temper, like wild beasts, and are susceptible to outbursts of fury.[33] In the passage in question, Seneca does not directly discuss cannibalism, but he makes a triangular link between climate, the extreme passion of fury, and anarchy, a link that we shall later discover in accounts of the freedom of the savages. Nations that are like lions and wolves, he argues, enjoy the freedom of the wild. They cannot be subjected to any authority and are unable to exercise any kind of political domination. The nations that are capable of living under governance are only those that live in a moderate climate.

In one of the main sources for the theory of climate, *The Six Books of the Commonweale* (1576) by Jean Bodin, we learn that the nations of the south are crueler and more vengeful than those of the north, who in turn are more vengeful than the peaceful nations that are lucky enough to dwell in the temperate zone. The Brazilians, for example, are not only content to eat the flesh of their enemies, but also bathe their children in their blood. Geographical position causes there to be more lunatics in the southern than in the northern hemisphere. In his turn, Garcilasso de Vega attempts an explanation inspired by the scholarly literature circulating in early modern Europe: the "fury" of consuming human flesh is stronger in the Indians living in hot climes than in colder regions. Pierre Petit's *Historic Treatise on the Amazons* (1718) attempts to show that nations of fierce Amazons really existed in the harsh climate around the Black Sea. In *Recherches philosophiques sur les Américains*, de Pauw describes the funeral rituals of the Iroquois Indians and the Tungus, who suspend their dead from trees. The cause is double: ignorance (they do not know how to cremate their dead) and climate (the ground is frozen). De Pauw here inserts a critique of Christianity. In contrast to the religion of the Romans, which recommended cremation of the dead, Christianity "has contributed nothing to the general reform of this part of our morals."[34]

Ancient and modern history, travel literature, and the geography of morals are all genres that permeable boundaries separate from the moral theory of the classical and modern philosophers. They form a complex in which geographical expressions are often merely a vehicle for theoretical arguments.

AN ENCYCLOPEDIA OF BIZARRE CUSTOMS

One of the forms taken by the dissertations of moral geography is that which we might name, in the absence of any established term, the "encyclopedia of bizarre customs." It is sometimes found within self-contained works, such as that of Boemus (*The Customs, Laws, and Usages of All Nations*, 1558) or Jean-Nicholas Demeunier (*The Spirit of the Traditions and Customs of Nations*, 1776). However, it most frequently occurs as an insert within broader works. It is an encyclopedia because it takes the form of an exhaustive and systematic enumeration of extreme laws and customs. Typically, such a list includes strange funeral rites, atrocious punishments, exceptional marital arrangements, curious sexual habits, eccentric forms of religious worship, and disgusting culinary practices. Cannibalism is a recurring item in such lists, if not the central piece. One of the sources for this genre of dissertation may have been the list of funeral customs which Cicero tells us was compiled by Chrysippus.

The presence of this encyclopedia interests us because it is connected, at a philosophical level, to the debate about the universality of natural law. If we leave aside the hypothesis of its divine origin, there are two major definitions of natural law in the period from classical antiquity to the eighteenth century. The former sees the law of nature as a natural principle of human action and knowledge. This broad definition conceals a remarkable variety of conceptions. *Corpus juris civilis* presents natural law as common to man and beast: "*Jus naturale* is what nature has taught all animals, because it is not a law specific to mankind, but is common to all animals on land and sea and to all birds. From this law derives the union of man and woman that we name marriage, the procreation of children and their education. We indeed see that other animals may also be regarded as knowledgeable of this law."[35] The law of nature is seen by writers such as Saint Augustine, Saint Thomas Aquinas, and Pufendorf as a principle of justice, a genus of sentiment, implanted in man by God and capable of being known by rational means. The classical expression of this concept is that provided by Cicero and had an echo as late as Blackstone and Hamilton: natural law is inscribed on the human heart by the finger of divinity.

The second great definition of natural law treats it as a kind of universal agreement between human beings. The law of nature may thus be known by observing what is common to the laws and customs of nations, the principles that any society is obliged to respect. And in this case also, it is Cicero who provides a canonical expression for the theory. In *De republica*, he defines natural law as "right reasoning, in accordance with nature, dispersed to all nations."[36] Positive laws cannot contradict it; a decision of the authorities cannot excuse us from respecting it. It admits of no exceptions or particularities: "There shall not be one law of Rome and another of Athens, one now and another later; but all nations shall always be subject to this eternal and unchanging law."

However we might decide to consider it, natural law is, in both cases, universal. This is a characteristic that it is not overlooked by any author. From the first occurrences, in the pre-Socratic period, of the expression "natural law," down to modern authors, the law of nature is seen as eternal and universal, in contrast to human laws, based on local authority and on convention.

The presence of the encyclopedia of bizarre customs in the context of the discussion of natural law suggests to us that classical and early modern authors were aware that the diversity of customs raises a particular problem. If natural law is consented to by all nations, then where is it to be found? If natural law is inscribed by God on the human heart, then how can it be that so many men seem to ignore it, practicing what reason teaches us are crimes against nature? These authors lucidly perceive this apparent contrast between the unity of the law of nature and the variety of morals. In contrast to some modern authors, however, they do not extract a negative argument from this, but rather attempt to explain the fact from the perspective of a conception of natural law.

In *The Apology to Raimond Sebond*, Michel de Montaigne discusses the diversity of the customs of nations as a possible objection against the relevance of natural law. The only argument whereby the philosophers might reveal what these laws are would be "the universality of their acceptance. What nature has in truth ordained to us we of course follow based on unanimous consent."[37] However, there is no law in existence that has not been contradicted by not just one but by many nations. Theft, "license for all kind of luxuries" (*licence à toutes sortes de voluptez*), incest and, of course, cannibalism are the examples given by Montaigne. "There is nothing more horrible to imagine than to eat one's father."[38] However, nations that practiced this custom believed that they were performing an act of piety, incorporating the marrow of the dead within the living and somehow bringing them back to life through the "transmutation" of their digested flesh. In this context of eccentric opinions, the doctrines of the philosophers are also mentioned, because "even the healthiest philosophy suffers from licenses that are far from the common use, and excessive."[39] Some have argued for public brothels and communal women; Diogenes masturbated in public. However, Montaigne does not deny the existence of natural law: "It is to be believed that there are natural laws [for man], just as there are seen to be for other creatures; but they have been lost in us" due to the inconstancy and vanity of reason.[40]

In *De jure naturae et gentium* (1672), Pufendorf makes recourse to the authority of the encyclopedia of extreme customs in order to reject the idea according to which natural law is to be discovered in the mutual consent of nations, or at least of all civilized nations. It is absurd to take as a foundation of natural law the mutual consent of those who most often violate it. In any case, there is no one who knows the customs of all the nations on earth or even their names. It is in vain that one claims the mutual consent of the civilized nations is sufficient, and we may ignore the opinions of barbarians. Is there any nation that would recognize itself as barbarian? And what nation would be so proud as to demand that other nations should be guided by the beliefs of the former? Even if there were mutual consent of nations, experience teaches us that there are more stupid people than clever people. Some nations might agree to respect certain things, but this does not prove anything other than that natural law allows them, rather than positively prescribes them.

In order to demonstrate that there is no supranational understanding of natural law, Pufendorf enumerates a variety of contradictory and unacceptable customs. Cannibalism figures at the head of this list of aberrations, ahead of other outrages such as incest. The Scythians ate human flesh and murdered their children "under a religious Pretence" (the sources cited are Plutarch, Aristotle, Eusebius, and Diogenes Laertius). The Tibareni in Cappadocia "threw their Ancient Persons down Precipices." The laws of the Parthians and Armenians absolve those who kill their wife, daughter, son, childless brother, or unmarried sister. Ancient Greek men were "scandalously addicted to [the] unnatural Vice" of "Pollution with the Male Sex." The Indians perform their conjugal duties in public. In many parts of Egypt "for Women to prostitute themselves was look'd on as a Creditable Profession." The Stoic philosophers "held it to be no irrational Practice either to frequent the Stews, or to maintain one's self by Pimping." The Persians marry their own mothers, the Egyptians their own sisters; such relations were approved by Zeno and Chrysippus. Plato allowed the "Community of Wives." Some barbarous nations feed on human flesh, a custom approved by the Stoics. The Amazons deliberately crippled any male progeny. The Spartans punished thieves not for stealing but for allowing themselves to be caught. A law of Solon allowed infants to be exposed. The thieves in Abyssinia present part of their booty to the king, "keeping the rest without Scandal for their own use."[41]

In *Essays on the Law of Nature* (1663–64), Locke devotes a number of pages to the exposition of strange customs, many taken from ancient historians. There was a custom in Sardinia whereby children club their parents to death once they have reached old age. Other tribes expose their children or demand that widows die along with their husbands. The inhabitants of Soldania Bay and some nations of Brazil "worship no God at all."[42] All this serves to show, Locke argues, that "natural law can in no wise be inferred from the general consent to be found among men."[43] Travel literature demonstrates that the law of nature is not "written in the hearts of men." If it were, it would be practiced by those who have no learned men, govern themselves according to nature, and are "least spoiled by arbitrary moral customs," which is to say by tribes of savages. However, the latter repeatedly violate natural law by their customs, Locke argues, "since among most of them there appears not the slightest track of piety, merciful feeling, fidelity, chastity, and the rest of the virtues; but rather they spend their life wretchedly among robberies, thefts, debaucheries, and murders."[44]

For many authors of the school of natural law, whether classical or modern, the catalogue of contradictory and aberrant customs is not sufficient proof that the definitions of natural law should be amended. In *Sketches of the History of Man*, Henry Home Lord Kames argues that the variety of customs does not demonstrate that there is no "consensus in morals, but only that the latter have not always been perfect.[45] The universality of natural law is also defended by Jean-Jacques Burlamaqui, in *Principes du droit naturel* (1751). According to the Swiss philosopher, the Creator has endowed us with discernment of good and evil, with "a sentiment or taste for virtue and justice" (*un sentiment ou un goût de vertu & de justice*). However, there are some who contest the reality of these sentiments on the grounds that there are savage nations who appear to possess no such sense of virtue. Burlamaqui is nevertheless more optimistic. He believes that even such savage nations have traces of this sense of good. If there are some who seem not to possess it, he explains, this is because we do not know enough about their *moeurs*. Or perhaps it is because they have become brutalized (*abrutis*), falling into an "abuse contrary to these principles, while not positively rejecting them" (*non en les rejettent positivement*) due to the effect of some prejudice that prevails above their sense of good. There are savages, he argues, that eat their captive enemies, believing that this is the rule of war (*le droit de la guerre*), and because they are able to slay them there is nothing to stop them from profiting by their flesh (*profitent de leur chair*). It is therefore a mistaken notion of natural law that impels savages to cannibalism. Anthropophagy is based on an epistemological deficiency. However, it is merely an error resting on an otherwise solid moral foundation: "The same savages . . . possess amongst themselves law and rules, good faith is no less esteemed there than in other parts, and a grateful heart receives no fewer eulogies from them than from us."[46]

The reason for which the philosophers of natural law do not automatically extract relativist concepts from the encyclopedia of mores is twofold. Firstly, it is because they make a net distinction between the stipulations of natural law and those of civil law. Ideally, civil law (political, municipal, or positive law are three other terms used to designate this) shall be based on natural law or, at least, should not contravene it. In reality, however, many laws and customs are not in conformity with natural law, but this does not at all mean that natural law exhausts its reality beneath this variety of deviations from it. The diversity of customs does not contravene the idea that natural law is universal, because deviations are ultimately the result of convention rather than nature.

More profoundly, however, the philosophers of natural law react to the problem of the diversity of customs and to the omnipresence of crimes against nature with a theory of the fragility of the cognitive faculties or of the perversity of the human will. Man, from this viewpoint, is unable clearly to know natural law because his reason is clouded by something else, by passions as a rule, which cause him to refuse to listen to the dictates of this reason. The diffusion of crimes against nature is compatible with the unity of natural law, within the context of a conception of human depravity.

The visit of Carneades to Rome in 155 BC was awaited with much interest on the part of the studious young, who crowded in their hundreds to hear the two speeches given by the Greek philosopher. The audience was shocked to hear Carneades speaking with great eloquence in favor of justice on the first day, and then, with equal skill, against it on the next. Cato the Censor was so scandalized that he demanded that all philosophers should be expelled from Rome, in order to prevent them corrupting the youth. The repercussions of these two speeches have been felt down the centuries. In one of the *Essays on Natural Law*, Locke argues against those who uphold that there is no natural law and that the only thing that can justify a given action is individual utility. The target of his attack is the philosophy of Carneades, whom he claims had an intellect so sharp that he caused very many to adopt his doctrine and to proclaim that "natural liberty be vindicated" to the detriment of positive or divine laws. However, "this most harmful opinion," Locke believes, has been "opposed by the more rational part of men."[47]

The speeches of Carneades put forward a fundamental definition of the theoretic approach of classic moral philosophy. To a considerable extent, this approach is based on specific cases. The origin of the standard analyses that occur in modern natural law is to be found in the theories of the Greek Cynics and Stoics. One of those who furnished later authors with a model for these discussions is Carneades. In *Divinae institutiones*, Lactantius tells us that Carneades argued that "there is no natural law" and that men seek only their own advantage. In some situations, one cannot be just without placing one's own life in peril. Two of the examples Carneades put forward would find their place in eighteenth-century tracts of moral philosophy. The first is that of the plank over which two shipwrecked sailors fight, as the plank is only capable of keeping one of them afloat. The second is that of the man who is fleeing from an enemy and finds himself having to fell an innocent man in order to take his horse. The conclusion of Carneades is that in these two cases each man is justified in pursuing his own conservation.

Lactantius disagrees: according to the latter, Carneades has perverted the notion of justice. In both cases, a just man would choose to die rather than kill another.[48]

We do not have an exact knowledge of the content of Carneades' speeches, and thus we cannot know whether he touched on the problem of cannibalism. However, this is a possibility. Anthropophagy had been discussed by Greek philosophers prior to Carneades. Diogenes the Cynic wrote a work named *The Republic*, where, along with cannibalism, other customs that would later be discussed in the same context are commended: homosexuality, incest, rape, prostitution, nudity, pacifism, penury, and the sharing of women.[49] Chrysippus argues that observation of the way in which animals live proves that there is no custom which is misplaced or which lacks any foundation in nature. Zeno of Citium, the founder of the Cynic school, was also supposed to have advocated the eating of the flesh of dead parents.

Even without having dealt with the specific issue of cannibalism, the two speeches of Carneades tell us something essential about the method of the philosophy of natural law. Carneades spoke in support of one thesis one day, and against it the next, thereby creating a paradoxical situation, within whose limits a genus of moral truth awaits discovery. It is precisely this genus of theoretical situation that intervenes when the anthropophagus is summoned to appear within the framework of the science of natural law.

Regardless of whatever recent reconstructions the theory of natural law might claim, the classical philosophers never derived their formulations from a naïve idea of reason or sociability. In a world of corrupt and passionate beings, to descry the outlines of such a law becomes a delicate operation, which brings to bear considerable theoretical resources. Perhaps nothing makes this law more visible than the extreme presence of the anthropophagus. However, the anthropophagus, like Carneades, is the wielder of a dialectical knowledge. On the one hand, he is the eminent incarnation of a crime against nature. On the other hand, in the case in which anthropophagy is excused by absolute necessity, the cannibal is the very man of nature, and as such is governed by the laws of nature. The anthropophagus therefore causes a double exposure of the law of nature: first of all negatively, as a deviation from it, and then positively, as a representative of it. The paradox is the royal road whereby the cannibal enters the history of philosophy.

In that case, as Blaise Pascal would say, we must choose. One group of philosophers, setting out from the idea that it is impossible to excuse crimes against nature, argue that anthropophagy is unjust, even in the situation of absolute necessity. Aristotle, in *The Nicomachian Ethics*, argues that some acts must not be committed, even under torture.[50] In *De republica*, Cicero writes that natural law derives from Divinity, and that he who does not abide by it becomes estranged from the divine. If he ignores his own human nature, the sinner will thereby incur "the heaviest punishment, even if he escapes all those other things that are generally recognized as punishments. . . . There is no one who would not rather choose to die than to be turned into an animal as long as he still possesses a human mind; and even more wretched is to have the mind of a beast in the body of a man."[51]

However, another philosophical camp discovers that, in certain situations, anthropophagy is legitimate. Johann Gottlieb Heineccius observes that "there is no doubt but that they are excusable, who in extreme hunger and want have recourse to any food, even to the flesh of dead men." He argues that we are here dealing with "a contest between two duties towards ourselves; of two physical evils, death and detestable food, the least ought to be chosen." But it is not excusable for a starving man to kill another "that he may prolong a little his own miserable life by eating his flesh." "However direful and imperious the necessity of long hunger may be," concludes the German professor of jurisprudence, "it does not give us a right to another's life that we ourselves may be saved, because here the condition and necessity of both persons are equal."[52]

One of the most sophisticated analyses of the legitimacy of cannibalism is that of Pufendorf, in chapter 6 ("On the Right and Favor of Necessity") of volume 2 of the *De jure naturae et gentium*. God cannot impose laws that are so inviolable that to obey them would cost us our lives. Thus believed the seven brothers in the Book of Maccabees about the flesh of the suckling pig, thinking that, if they ate it, they would thereby abjure the true religion. In contrast to God, the authors of positive laws, those whose purpose is the safety and advantage of humans, must bear in view human weakness, as well as the irresistible inclination to flee all that causes us to perish. This is why we suppose that the state of necessity is tacitly excepted from the majority of laws, at least positive laws. As regards affirmative natural laws, that is, those that proscribe us from doing a certain thing, we must have the occasion, means, and power to act. But, in the case of absolute necessity, we do not have any of these and it would be something impossible, or else above the typical resolution of the human spirit, for us to do what is proscribed by natural law. If there is nothing in the nature of the thing in question that forbids our action then we are exempted by necessity.

This exemption by necessity has its limits. If our action comes into conflict with respect for the divine majesty, then it is absolutely forbidden.

Since God can cause us a harm far greater than natural death, it follows that we must suffer this death rather than cause Him an affront. In a manner that recalls Pascal, Pufendorf writes that reason shows us that it is "probable" that we would lose our life in favor of an infinitely more considerable good. As regards the mutual duties of man, some laws, as Pufendorf argues, refer to a humanly established fact and they do not therefore cover cases of extreme necessity.

After thereby establishing in general terms the justness of the recourse to the foundation of necessity, Pufendorf goes on to examine "particular cases." After mentioning the question of suicide and that of mutilation, he moves on to the thorny problem of cannibalism. In certain circumstances, the latter is acceptable under the species of natural law. "To feed on Man's Flesh in the desperate Extremity of Famine, when no other Sustenance can be procur'd, is a lamentable in deed [sic], but not a sinful expedient."[53] The true problem intervenes when we must discover whether nature authorizes such sustenance in "those instance when in Distress and Want of all Provisions, Men have been kill'd to preserve their Fellows, either by Compulsion and against their Consent, or else by the Determination of Lot." On the one hand, the law that condemns homicide seems to condemn such a barbaric form of sustenance. On the other hand, the despair of those who have arrived at such a pressing hunger and the inevitable death of all, if one of them is not sacrificed in order to save the others, seems to allow recourse to this grim expedient.

The arguments relative to anthropophagy will remain a central part of modern doctrines of natural law until the moment at which they begin to diffuse into the sphere of political action. In his project for a *Declaration of the Rights of Man and of the Citizen* of 1789, Jean Paul Marat, (who was also a doctor of medicine who had practiced vivisection), observes that when man lacks those things necessary for life, he has the right to "seize" from another that surplus which the latter enjoys. This is an idea that is almost universally accepted in medieval and modern political philosophy, although Marat here extrapolates a consequence that would seem unprecedented were we to ignore the presence of the cannibal in the discourse of *jus naturalis*. The one stricken by need has the right to seize from the other even those things necessary, "and rather than die of hunger he has the right to kill him and to devour his flesh still twitching with life. . . . In order to preserve his life, man has the right to assault the property, liberty and even life of his fellows. In order to escape oppression, he has the right to oppress, to reduce others to slavery or to massacre them . . . he is doing nothing more than to cede to an irresistible inclination, implanted in his soul by the author of his being."[54] The theories of the legitimacy of cannibalism have therefore covered the entire spectrum of opinions, from the inflexibility of divine commandments to the revolutionary consequences of late-Enlightenment *jus naturalis*.

CANNIBALS ADRIFT

In 1884, three British mariners were inculpated for murder and having been found guilty they were sentenced to hang. What makes their case (*The Crown v. Dudley and Stevens*) interesting in terms of legal history is the fact that the three were convicted of a murder for which, a century earlier, they would have enjoyed immunity before the civil courts. Having survived the shipwreck of the vessel *Mignonette*, the three, impelled by hunger, killed and ate a midshipman together with whom they were adrift on a life raft.[55]

In another case, in 1737, a number of English mariners were accused of homicide because they had eaten one of the comrades following a shipwreck. The judge amnestied them, recognizing that their crime had been absolved by inevitable necessity. Handed down in Latin, the sentence shows that the judge avoided imposing his authority in a matter where natural law took precedence. In *The Law of Nature and Nations*, Pufendorf had already mentioned that the two English shipwreck survivors who had eaten a third in a lifeboat were cleared by a judge when they reached shore. He does not explain on what grounds the decision was taken, but the context allows us to believe that it was a question of the doctrine of natural necessity.

The decision of the court in 1884 as well as the arguments during appeal (the sentence was amended, and the perpetrators released after a short time) show how the categories of political and of natural law are drawn into a dispute whose stakes are the establishment of jurisdiction over a territory where nature's constitution holds sway. In the nineteenth century, the open sea is annexed to the domain of positive law. The expanse of the sea had up to then also been a domain where the will of a sovereign authority was exerted. In the seventeenth century, Grotius and Selden were the protagonists of a polemic about the right to rule the waves.[56] John Selden's work *Mare Clausum* (1635) had established that the sea might be an object for appropriation: a doctrine to which sovereigns occasionally made recourse in order to claim a right of access or exclusive use over a portion of the ocean. In opposition to this, Grotius, in *Mare Liberum* (1609), argues that the sea belongs to those domains whose very nature excludes any ownership other than the common ownership of all mankind.[57] This kind of argument, however, concerns only the strategic and commercial presence on the sea. Free or otherwise, the blue sea is, up until the nineteenth century, not a background against which civil offences are visible.

The institution of legal authority over the ocean is a process in which Britain plays a central role. In the eighteenth and nineteenth centuries, Britain found itself in a unique position. The possessor of a world empire, Britannia ruled the waves. Fleet, ports, and colonies, and the entire movement of people and goods over the ocean were now situated within a territory where there existed a sovereign power that could impose laws and cause sentences to be executed. The British naval empire was the space in which a precise system of maritime law began to be formulated, one that collided with the law of nature as it had been defined by legal experts and philosophers. The passing of the Merchant Shipping Act in 1854 eliminated the ambiguity about the nature of the valid jurisdiction in the case of shipwrecks. From now on, murders committed on rafts and lifeboats on the open sea will fall under the jurisdiction of the crown, whereas previously they had been regarded as outside the competence of positive law. Having previously been a corpus of precepts drawn from speculative reason, maritime law thus becomes increasingly British in its content. British jurists discern this likeness between and superposition of natural and common law, a relation in which the initiative now belongs to national law. Blackstone deals with this topic in one chapter ("Of Offences against the Law of Nations") of the *Commentaries on the Laws of England* (1765–69). In the classical manner, he defines the law of nations as being a system of rationally derived rules "established by universal consent among the civilized inhabitants of the world." He goes on to argue that in England the law of nations "is adopted in its full extent by the common law and is held to be a part of the law of the land."

The case of *The Crown v. Dudley and Stephens* illustrates this complex evolution, in which civil authority ends up passing judgment in matters that formerly fell under the domain of natural law. But in doing so, it encounters a deviation from a rule that its categories only imperfectly comprehend. In the penal order, cannibalism had always had a peculiar, accessory status, an excess of cruelty whose nature the penal code had declined to explore. Cannibalism is not in itself an offence mentioned in the legal codices of the modern epoch.[58] In the civil space described by the laws of the land, cannibalism fades against the background of illegality. It is a transgression mentioned by legal theoreticians only in connection with the state of nature, where, by definition, civil laws hold no sway. For legal practitioners, a region of juridical chiaroscuro is to be found between the two forms.

We must therefore search for the clearly outlined protagonists of natural law prior to this moment in which juridical power is extended to the high seas. Up until the eighteenth century, the open sea belonged to the vast domain of natural law, and its sole sovereign was necessity. Robinson Crusoe was reduced to the state of man of nature thanks to the sea: "I was a Prisoner lock'd up with the eternal Bars and Bolts of the Ocean."[59] Caught by a current on his raft and in danger of being swept away, he realizes that his island is a paradise in comparison with the open sea.

The first personage in this grim gallery of aberrations from the maritime rule of natural law is the pirate. In a classic passage in *De Officiis*, Cicero argues that the pirate is not a "particular" foe, but a foe to all mankind, and therefore everyone has the right to wage war against him, beyond the boundaries of any particular jurisdiction.[60]

The second great occasion during which natural law dictates is the shipwreck. Ancient philosophers were the first to elaborate a sophisticated casuistry regarding the law applicable in such situations. Many of the images and solutions they invoke are commonplace in later literature, being recycled for the benefit of modern theories of natural law. For example, here is the case of the ship that is in danger of sinking during a storm and whose passengers must throw the cargo overboard in order to save themselves. If they cast overboard the goods belonging to a merchant, does the latter have the right to demand compensation from his fellow travelers once they reach shore? The arguments surrounding this case make up a major component of the theory of risk and insurance in the premodern period.[61] Then there is the equally famous case of the shipwreck survivor clinging to a plank. Does he possess any kind of property right over the plank, a right that excludes any other who might wish to snatch it away from him?

The entire casuistry of shipwrecks becomes highly important in the age of great sea voyages. It now overflows the bounds of systematic dissertations on law and finds new possibilities of expression in the novels and (real or imagined) travel diaries that illustrate the misfortunes of shipwreck survivors. This genre of literature becomes extremely popular in the seventeenth and eighteenth centuries, when images of desperate sailors saving themselves at the expense of their shipmates circulate widely. Cannibalism is a constant presence in such texts, which have a definite theoretical component. One of the most interesting examples of maritime literature is the book describing *The Voyages of Jean Struys in Moscovy, Tartary, Persia, India and Other Foreign Lands* (1682). Members of a group of European shipwreck survivors end up unable to sleep for fear that one might eat the other. In the end, one of them assumes the role of advocate for the anthropophagous order: "It is true that the law commands us to love our neighbor and that it forbids us to kill. However, nothing is closer to us than our own being."[62] Hence it clearly results that there exists a principle of conservation, which demands that we do all we can in order to preserve the being given to us by "Nature," reference to which indicates a certain sympathy for deism on the part of the speaker. In the world, he says, things occur in exactly the same way, with big fish eating little fish (probably a reference to Spinoza). Death is cruel, and we must avoid it if we have the means. Consequently, intones the voice of the one inclined to anthropophagy, why should we not oppose death with the sole obstacle that might still prevent it? And why should we not sacrifice the weaker among us, as "Nature" demands? This philippic closes with a challenge to his opponents to refute him. "False reasoning," argues another, "false principles. The interdiction to kill is formulated with such clarity by the law that no reasoning can exempt us from respecting it. The words *Thou shalt not kill* are clear and admit no exception. . . . If you wish to continue with this dastardly plan, you will become the foe of God and man."[63] The scholastic debate between the two castaways unveils to us a conflict between a traditional idea of natural law and a radical interpretation, influenced by Spinoza.

The most characteristic example of this literature is that of the raft of cannibals adrift. Subject to the cruelest necessity, they become the protagonists of a drama in which the major categories of natural law become visible, from the law of property to the question of cannibalism.

The *Historie de la Nouvelle France* (1609), by French lawyer Marc Lescarbot, is one of the first texts to evoke the lifeboat of shipwreck survivors. In desperation, they predictably decide that one of them must die in order to save the others. "And this was the thing that was done . . . the flesh . . . was divided equally among them all, a thing so horrible to relate that my quill falls from my hand."[64] His audience's taste is probably what allowed Lescarbot to find the courage to pick up his quill once more, for at the end of the book he relapses and presents other cannibals, this time a godless tribe of Indians.

This raft of shipwreck survivors is the thought experiment whereby a new theory is tested, one that is part of natural law, but which will ultimately give way to a decisive intervention on the part of civil law. We have seen that in the situation of shipwreck survivors crammed into a lifeboat, there is a conflict of fundamental rights. It is almost axiomatic for the law of nature that self-preservation, survival, is such a fundamental right, if not the fundamental right par excellence. However, the problem with this theory is that there are situations in which the right of one man is incompatible with the same right of another. The solutions to this problem are, as we have seen up to now, various. One of them consists in creatively interpreting this right and arguing for the existence of exceptions, at least in connection with the course of action that is recommended. Another theory is that according to which the primitive right to self-preservation cannot suspend the dictates of natural or divine law. The first theory has the disadvantage of dispatching us into a complex casuistry, which the authors of modern systems of natural law usually avoid, particularly from methodological motives. The second has the disadvantage of presupposing a multiplicity of fundamental principles, or too direct an intervention of the divine will in a construct that is usually intended to be secular. However, in the eighteenth century, Jean Barbeyrac was to place an alternative theory in circulation, one that avoided such difficulties.

His starting point is the raft of shipwreck victims that Pufendorf describes in *On the Duty of Man and Citizen according to Natural Law*. In the notes to his translation of Pufendorf, Barbeyrac intervenes in order to point out the existence of a contradiction between primitive rights. Whenever there is a conflict between the right to self-preservation of a number of men, he argues, in order to justify the precedence we accord ourselves to the detriment of others, it is necessary that that person with whom we find ourselves in "common danger" should not have any "particular right" over the means of salvation offered by Providence. "Thus, the one to whom the life raft belongs should not be thrown overboard, and nor is he obliged to draw lots."[65] It is clear, from the comparison with passages in Pufendorf, that Barbeyrac's opinion differs. Pufendorf does not accord such grace to the possessor of the craft, just as he does not consider, in the example of the plank disputed by two men floundering in the water, that there is any particular right which excludes a priori one of them from appropriating it, even in the situation in which the other loses his life when deprived of his plank. Commenting on the latter case, Barbeyrac argues that there is a "right of first occupancy, which excludes any pretensions on the part of others; the plank belongs [by right] to the one who has appropriated it."[66] In another case exhibited by Pufendorf, someone is fleeing from an enemy and encounters a child or an invalid on a "narrow road." In accordance with the teachings of the casuists, Pufendorf recommends that the fleeing man trample over the hapless man who bars his way. Barbeyrac does not think that things are so simple: "We must presuppose that it is a case of a public highway. For otherwise, the child or the cripple would be on their own property and thereby gain a particular right, which would prevent the one who is being chased from preferring his own conservation at another's expense."[67]

In order to understand Barbeyrac's arguments let us place his solutions in the context of the debates on the theory of natural law in the seventeenth and eighteenth centuries. The authors of the time argue, almost without exception, that natural law is the foundation of civil law, and consequently, at least in extreme situations, takes priority. Adam Smith is one of the first to introduce a notable correction, arguing, in the *Wealth of Nations* (1776), that civil property law is a perfect law which, at least prima facie, must take priority over considerations of necessity.[68] Barbeyrac does not, however, uphold that "particular" property law is what justifies the priority of one man before another, in matters of the right to self-preservation. However, his theory is not the orthodox theory of the philosophers and jurists of natural law who precede him. His idea as regards the exclusive "rights of prior occupancy," applied to the shipwreck survivor who takes possession of a plank, is a considerable variation in relation to John Locke, who was probably his source when he speculated on this right. Locke, in *Two Treatises of Government*, had argued that there is an exclusive right of prior occupancy. But he had also argued that this is a right over the land, whose immediate purpose is cultivation, and taking possession of the land occurs in a situation of natural primitive abundance in such a way that sufficient land shall remain for others.[69] There is no question of any such thing for Barbeyrac, for whom the right of prior occupancy is exercised over the only present means for the conservation of life and for whom the right of self-preservation does not seem to possess the limits suggested by Locke. For Barbeyrac, the choice between two natural but incompatible rights is to be made by adding a specific, "particular" right. In other words, what are being compared are a simple natural right, on the one hand, and a mixed entity, on the other, a synthesis of natural and positive right. His logic is one of addition: natural law versus natural law plus a supplement.

His solution is as elegant as it is problematic. First, it does not seem sufficiently true to life when viewed in terms of the psychology of the agents of natural law. With disaster imminent, under the pressure of mortal fear, how is it still possible to obey such a "particular" law, especially if obeying it leads to an outcome so baneful, so contrary to the instinct of self-preservation? We can now see that what is marginalized in Barbeyrac's discussion is precisely the element that accompanies the theories about the knowledge of the principles of natural law. For a majority of authors, knowledge of the postulates of natural law by means of the lights of reason is only a part of the narrative. Another part is that of the human affections, desires, impulses, passions, and instincts. In their legitimate incarnation, these are also in contact with natural law.

The right to self-preservation is not one that is abstract, but rather manifests itself as desire, impulse, passion, and inclination toward the conservation of life. Minimizing this dimension of the natural passions, Barbeyrac seems to wish to convince his reader that the shipwreck survivors would respectfully speculate on the right to private property, after which they would resignedly throw themselves into the water.

Another important consequence of this theory is the marginalization, in the general economy of the philosophy of natural law, of the theory of the state of nature. For Barbeyrac's predecessors, such as Pufendorf, the state of nature is in principle opposed to the state of civil association: the law of nature takes precedence, from the point of view of the force of prescription. At least when they describe the transition from the state of civil association to the state of nature, Pufendorf and the other philosophers are in agreement: the necessity of the state of nature suspends the prescriptions of positive law. Humans thereby regain liberty and equality in the face of natural law. In Barbeyrac's schema, however, man no longer rediscovers this island of liberty, because the momentary dissolution of society does not absolutely dissolve all civil obligations, which will remain as an immutable supplement to the natural law of individuals. The shipwreck survivors, the fugitives, the starving, the cannibals: all these agents of desperation will be left to bear, in their simulated flight from the bounds of social order, the chains of civil obligations.

For Christian Wolff, the discussion about the raft of shipwreck survivors is prefaced by a clarification of some postulates of natural law. If there is an irresistible necessity, then, according to natural law, which includes this tacit exception, we are excused. However, as long as there are means to resist an inevitable obstacle, the law preserves its obligatory force. When danger threatens us and another equally, we are obliged to think first of ourselves. In general, all our duties to others include this exception, that we must set precedence on our own interests, when they enter into conflict with those of another. If there is a contradiction between what we owe ourselves or others and what we owe God, then the duty to the divinity takes precedence, even at the cost of our life. As long as we preserve the use of reason, we do not possess the right to commit deeds contrary to that which we owe God.[70]

A tome entitled *Questions de droit naturel* (1762), by Swiss jurist Emmerich de Vattel (1714–67), is probably the last important work in the tradition of natural law that systematically discusses the problem of anthropophagy.[71] His commentaries regarding what we should do in order to save ourselves in cases of necessity contain the obligatory references concerning the distinction between actions illicit in themselves and those illicit by convention on the one hand, and between alienable and inalienable rights on the other. In the manner in which we have seen to be intensively practiced in the school of natural law, the cannibal is summoned to illumine the outlines of these distinctions. Here we find the celebrated question of whether necessity can cause an otherwise illicit action to become licit. It is ultimately an interrogation of the origin, nature, and consequences of the object of natural law. Vattel proceeds in the consecrated manner, illumining the rule with the aid of the exception. Two cases: the first is the common case in which a man kills an aggressor in order to save his own life. The second is that in which a man is forced to kill another in order to feed on the latter's flesh in circumstances of extreme hunger. Necessity weighs equally on the protagonists in both situations. However, there is a principle, argues Vattel, which is not brought to light by Wolff, namely that it is not permissible to do harm to another, to act against his established rights.[72]

The difficulty that looms in the path down which Vattel wishes to lead the text is that this principle must conserve its general validity under circumstances in which there is an extreme event, such as necessary anthropophagy. If we accept that necessity—evident and unproblematic in the case of killing the aggressor—can excuse an action that is illicit in itself, then on the basis of this reasoning we must also tackle the aberration of forced cannibalism, since it is directed by the same natural and legal resorts.

Vattel's solution is quite novel, although it seems to be argued in a traditional manner. He argues, first, that the idea that we have a right to do anything in order to fulfill our obligations (including our obligation to preserve our life) presupposes that the actions to which we make recourse are not, in their turn and in themselves, absolutely illegitimate. Obviously, this would confront us with a paradox, because we are faced with the need to order absolute and incompatible duties. One of the solutions, as we have seen, is to examine the nature of rights and duties, in order to find exceptions to or defects in their perfection, which would allow us to insert them within a hierarchy. A second solution, which we have already seen outlined in the eighteenth century, consists in a negation of the natural character of rights or vices. Vattel, however, attempts, in criticizing the position of Wolff, to avoid both solutions, employing a theoretical construct that aims to conserve the absolute character of natural rights and, at the same time, not to expose itself to the paradoxes of extreme necessity.

The case of the aggressor killed in legitimate defense is resolved without difficulty, because it is situated outside the total guarantee of his right to life, by virtue of the fact that he places the life of another in imminent danger. In the case of the innocent in danger of disappearing inside the belly of a starving man, it is likewise clear that he has a right that cannot be suspended by his antagonist. In the name of natural equality, the philosophy of natural law thus refuses to lift the guarantees accorded to the life of the innocent in favor of the symmetrical right of another innocent. However, Vattel refuses to shatter this symmetry by introducing a dynamic element into the structure of rights and obligations visible in the case of tragic collective starvation. He argues that it would be permissible to eat human flesh in the case in which one of the starving consented to sacrifice himself for the preservation of others. Vattel here passes over two difficulties in silence. The first is to what extent forced consent is valid consent. The second, which is, in its turn, a classic objection, is whether actions that are in themselves bad (*mala per se*) can be made licit by a pact. However, Vattel has quite a different agenda, so that for the time being he is content to argue merely that if consent exists, he cannot see any reason why the sacrifice should not be accepted. He declines to pose the question of the legal basis on which such acceptance should be allowed, and whether it allows significant exceptions, such as the situation of children or women, whose free consent cannot be assumed. Nor does he examine the consequence and legitimacy of cannibalism in the probably more realistic hypothesis in which the victims of hunger might not have in their midst a character generous enough to consent to become a martyr to extreme gastronomy.

THE LOTTERY OF HUNGER

A subject that frequently occurs in discussions of cannibalism in general and of maritime cannibalism in particular is that of the lotteries held by those who find themselves in an extreme situation in order to choose who among them is to be sacrificed. It is possible that such a sailor's tradition may have existed. It is not cannibalism in itself that is the crime of which the sailors of the *Mignonette* are guilty. A moral monstrosity, it is not yet translatable into the language of the penal code. As such, it is merely an aberrant episode, without adverse and specific judicial consequences. No doctrine of necessity is called into account, because the deed of which the sailors are accused is not that they have murdered someone in order not to die of starvation. It is a stipulation of natural law that is employed to uphold the authority of the civil judge. What they are accused of by the court of the first instance, the identified grounds of their guilt, is the fact that they failed to draw lots to decide on the victim. Instead of doing so, they killed the weakest of their number. A similar case is that of the *United States v. Holmes*.

Here, the captain of the ship ordered, in an emergency, that male passengers be thrown overboard. The judge was of the opinion that the victims should have been chosen by lot.[73]

The sources and significance of the lottery episode on the raft must sooner be sought in the very same literature of natural law. The lottery is a procedure that is frequently discussed by philosophers, and its occurrence must signal to us the presence of a complex theoretical analysis. It is not a procedure whose legitimacy can be explained simply. Up until the eighteenth century, the lottery gave rise to vehement debate, and its justification in divine and natural law was far from being assured. Numerous theologians condemn lotteries as an affront to the divine will. First, because drawing lots seems a way of forcing God to "show His hand," as a card player might say, of forcing Him to reveal His intentions for the future. Then, because drawing lots and fortune telling are associated with pagan and idolatrous practices, such as the Roman haruspices. Last, because gambling is an occasion for many abuses, from enrichment without labor to laziness and blasphemy. Another complication, of a political and legal nature, is the right to organize a lottery. This right is usually recognized only by the public authorities, and private lotteries are viewed with suspicion or hostility.

On the other hand, however, the drawing of lots had been associated, since antiquity, with a perfectly equitable procedure. In ancient Greece, democracy was a political regime in which offices were equally distributed, in other words by the drawing of lots and only rarely as a result of public election. The desperate men who draw lots to choose which of them shall be eaten thereby make recourse to a primitive form of democracy, where perfect equality dominates.

In the *Journeys of Jean Struys*, most of those shipwrecked agree that extreme necessity knows no law, and declare that they will eat one of their number. It is demanded that the choice of victim should be made according to the principles of natural equality: "He proposed that they should draw lots, so that none of the company should be exempt, and further told them that the one whom the Heavens should destine by lot should be deemed worthy to die."[74] In the *Histoire et Description Générale de la Nouvelle France* (1744) by Jesuit Pierre François Xavier de Charlevoix, a veritable encyclopedia of tales about cannibalism, we learn how a French colony in Florida was reduced to extreme starvation. In this state of desperation, one told the others that they could all be saved by the sacrifice of one of their number. This proposal was not only not rejected in horror but was even applauded. They were on the point of agreeing to draw lots to determine who would be eaten when one of their number declared that he wished to hasten his death, which he saw as inevitable, in order to prolong the lives of his fellows for a few more days. "He was taken at his word and then killed on the spot, without putting up the least resistance. They did not waste a single drop of his blood." The blood was hungrily drunk and the body chopped into pieces and shared equally.[75]

In natural law, the legitimacy of the lottery derives from the fact that it is based on a contract. It belongs to the great class of contracts in which chance intervenes, the best-known example of which is the insurance contract. Since participation in a lottery is an understanding between parties, some authors regard it as a legitimate means of ensuring the transfer of rights and property.

Between these two subjects, those of democracy and the contract, there is, of course, a solid alliance. In natural law, democracy is sometimes considered to be a regime based on a contract of association, known as a "social contract," which is supposed to be the original of all other types of civil association. The starving men in the lifeboat who draw lots to determine which of them survives form a kind of association that shares with contractual democracy more than just its form. Analysis of their association reveals the same elements as an analysis of the genesis of political society: primitive equality, the right to self-preservation, the right to execute natural law, and the transfer of these rights on the basis of mutual consent. The raft of cannibals is, in natural law, a model of the body politic.

The first references to the drawing of lots to determine who should be eaten show that the ritual also used to be practiced on dry land. Herodotus describes how, during the expedition of Cambyses, the soldiers ran out of provisions. They were forced to eat their pack animals, until no more were left. Had the Persian king been a more rational leader, Herodotus remarks, he would have led his troops back and given up the fight. However, he gave orders for the march to continue, and the army continued to deteriorate. The soldiers began to eat grass in order to survive. "But once they reached the desert, some of them did something even more terrible. They drew lots to choose which man out of ten they should eat."[76] On hearing this, Cambyses realized that his authority was in danger of crumbling beneath the pressure of necessity, and he gave the order to retreat, abandoning the expedition.

The age of great voyages reveals the lottery on the high seas. In *The Law of Nature and Nations*, Pufendorf presents the case of a raft with three English sailors, who drew lots to decide which of them should serve as food for the others. Ziegler, a commentator on Grotius, argues Pufendorf, would have held that they were guilty of a great sin because they had plotted the death of one of their number, and each had even plotted his own death, thereby imperiling the salvation of their souls in order to save their bodies. They ought not to have set such little price on their lives that they were willing to sacrifice themselves in order to quell another's hunger. And they ought not to have killed their fellows in order to sate their stomachs.

Pufendorf does not agree with this solution. It cannot be said, he comments, that the sailors plotted the death of one of their fellows, under the pretext of drawing lots. Had they not done so, they would have perished wretchedly along with him, and thus they had nothing to fear for the salvation of their souls. It would mean that we do not cling to life if we wished to prolong it effortlessly and without necessity, and we do not warrant to be considered as having betrayed ourselves when we lose it intentionally in such a situation of necessity. There is no cruelty on the part of those who accept such a sacrifice. Nor is there any on the part of the victim, who allows himself to be killed for the common good and who suffers less by receiving the mortal blow than he who is reduced to the sad necessity of plunging the dagger into his comrade's chest.[77]

However, Heineccius holds that Pufendorf is mistaken. No one has the right to take another's life, not even in cases of extreme necessity. As for the consent the shipwrecked sailors may have given to participate in the human-flesh lottery, this is invalid. "For none hath a right to take away another's life. And he who consents to his own murder is as guilty as he who kills himself or another. Ziegler justly asserts 'That none ought so far to despise his own life, as to throw it away to satisfy another's hunger, nor ought others to attack their neighbour's life to quell their own cravings.'"[78]

Wolff argues that when an incurable disease afflicts a limb, it is permissible for us to amputate it, and we are even obligated to do so, because given the choice between a certain loss and an event whose success is doubtful, we must prefer the latter. This is one of the bases on which he judges what happens on the raft of shipwrecked sailors. In this case, the sacrifice of one of them would be a certain evil, but the salvation of all would be an uncertain event. It is clear that Wolff is inverting the terms of the equation as this is usually presented: the death of all is a certain outcome, whereas the evil that might befall each individual is uncertain. This allows him to draw the conclusion that, in the extreme absence of food, it is not permissible to kill another, either by force or after drawing lots, in order for the others to feed on his flesh.[79]

For Vattel, the consequence of this negation is absurd. If Wolff were right, then we would all die of hunger. However, there are many "contrary practices, even ones mentioned by our author," which contradict him.[80] When a town is attacked, is it not permissible, even laudable, that a part of the citizens should go forth and repel the enemy, even at the risk of dying on the field of battle? Shall we not say of them that they have a right to their own lives? Hunger, Vattel goes on to say, is a most cruel foe, who threatens all those on the raft. By drawing lots, each exposes himself to death, for the salvation of his fellows and for his own good, "if he finds himself among the fortunate ones" who do not draw the short straw. This policy, he argues, is in better harmony with our duties to ourselves and with our duties to others than the decision to allow all to die of hunger.

Vattel's comparison, whereby he believes he has resolved the tension on the raft, is not necessarily surprising. In the late eighteenth century, classical concepts of heroism were already in ruins, at least for some of the philosophers of social progress. From this viewpoint, to die for one's country, weapon in hand, covered in glory, seems perfectly comparable to consenting to be roasted on a spit. This comparison is also made possible by another transformation, for which Vattel is by no means responsible, because it is effectively complete before he begins to elaborate his arguments. The parallel between the body politic (or the church) and a ship has a venerable history, which goes back before early Christianity to Plato. In the seventeenth and eighteenth centuries, however, such a comparison acquires a strictly utilitarian content. What Vattel retains from the old metaphor of the ship is a community of limited if not infranatural interests. This is an example congruent with the new vision of the political order intensely cultivated during the Enlightenment: that of an association based on necessity and inspired by pragmatic considerations. From this angle, it was predictable that ancient patriotism would no longer be perceived as personal attachment to a leader or familial association, or as a religious, historical, or anthropological engagement (one in the name of honor, for example). For Vattel, the forced anarchy of desperation on the raft has the following essential characteristic in common with the body politic, in whose name ancient *philia* is invited to abandon the stage: namely that it is variable based on the simple impulses of the passion for self-preservation.

From the horizon of the modern intellectual, Vattel is now free to rewrite the details of the prescriptions of natural law. While it is true that prescriptive [*préceptive*] law must bow to prohibitive law, it is no less true that there are also "many exceptions." One of my duties is to shield my body from injuries, and another of my duties is to save others from any danger in which they might find themselves. However, I cannot perform the latter duty without exposing myself to "light injury," so the duty to myself is not that which should take precedence. Likewise, the law forbids me from damaging the goods of others, something that is undoubtedly just in general. However, if I see a man being attacked by a wild beast, it is undoubtedly permitted that I trample another's field in order to come to the aid of the victim. How could the law forbid such a thing?

From enunciating particular exceptions, Vattel goes on to enunciate more general rules. We must always choose the greater good, or the lesser evil, while taking into account things in their complexity, "with all their connections and with all their consequences and interdependencies. We must do so because the decision cannot be based only on the present case, regarded in itself and independently of its consequences in the world."[81] A classical philosopher might also subscribe to the imperative of the Swiss jurist, probably adding, however, that the present "happiness" of filling our stomach with one of our peers ought not make us lose sight of our values and aims as human beings, even if the difficulties of the moment thrust these beyond the horizon of our imminent interests. What is significant in Vattel is the link he establishes, during the course of his argument, between law in the state of nature and political law. In this comparison, made possible by the presence of the cannibal, the relations between the law of nature and political law will be found to have been transformed.

The raft of shipwreck survivors is the laboratory where Vattel distills the new ingredients of law. He mentions another case proposed by Wolff, namely that of whether, on an overladen raft, the stronger have the right to throw the weaker overboard. Is it not the same situation, he wonders, as the one in which the stronger eat the weaker from dire necessity? "To throw a man into the sea or to eat him are no different from the point of view of the evil done to that man. I see no essential difference between these two cases. Both in the one case and in the other, the stronger takes the life of the weaker in order to conserve his own."[82] Possibly, but the question was precisely what would cause such recourse to brute force to be legitimate. We have seen that in the tradition of natural law, this question has received different answers, from Seneca onward. However, Vattel prefers to consider his solution as self-evident and to move on to an adjustment of the data of the problem itself. In order to see who remains on the raft and who is cast into the sea, a drawing of lots is allowed. Why then, he argues, should it not be allowed, in the circumstances of a dire lack of provisions, for lots to be drawn, by common consent, "in order to decide who perishes, and thereby saves the others, leaving them his flesh as food?" One logical difficulty is that Vattel furtively leads the reader from a description of a Hobbesian universe, in which the strong throw the weak off the raft without debate (*sans autre forme de procès*), to one in which the passengers of the raft now deliberate, in a contractualist manner, on the common good and organize a kind of lottery.

The most important element Vattel introduces into the debate on cannibalism might be signaled by one of his reservations. He argues that acceptance of the lottery depends on a condition, namely the presumption that the extreme solution of anthropophagy is the only means of salvation available to the unfortunates on the raft: "As long as there is hope, we must undoubtedly delay recourse to such a horrible expedient." Such would seem to have been the case of the Dutch captain who, after his ship had exploded on the high seas, managed to persuade his men not to eat one of their shipmates. They then all managed to reach shore before being reduced to "cruel extremity." In other words, it is the presence, in proximity to the state of nature, of another territory, of civilization and material abundance, that suspends the conscience of man as a subject of natural law.

In order better to understand the quality of Vattel's position, let us elucidate this inverted relationship between the state of nature on the one hand, in which, at the limit, cannibalism is licit, and the state of political association on the other hand, a state that is used, as we have seen, to clarify one of the principles of the law of nature. The key to the reading is to be found in the discussion of nature and the limits of sovereign power. One of the problems of absolutism was that it is permeable to the consequences of an extended natural law. The absolute sovereign would receive, by virtue of a certain understanding of natural law, a limitless capacity to dispose of his subjects, which would authorize him—as proven by reason and the experience of exotic peoples—to cannibalize them. For Locke, this is an absurd and unacceptable consequence. Vattel, however, sites the entities familiar to the natural law analysis of cannibalism within exactly the opposite order. In this context, he does not commence from natural authority, in order to elucidate nature and the limits of political authority, but proceeds in the opposite direction, setting out from the constitution and the functioning of political sovereignty, in order to derive the limits of natural authority. This attempt is surprising not only because of its epistemological order but also because, at the close of the analysis, we rediscover the traditional entity of the cannibal, invested with his natural rights as recognized by the majority of classical philosophers, but having set out from a moderate and modern conception of political sovereignty, which rejects the component of tyranny.

The limit of sovereign power is, for Vattel, to be sought in the tacit reserve of absolute necessity. The prince is free to exercise his legislative

and executive powers, but only on the general and universal condition
that he has the public good in view. "The people," argues the Swiss philosopher, "are subject to the prince's judgement as regards the adminis-
tration of the state. However, no one can rely on another's judgement
except as regards matters that are the object of divergent opinions, not
those that are indisputable. If I have promised to obey the orders of a
governor, does that mean I am obliged to allow him to do anything,
even if he wants to cast me into the sea or to kill me?"[83]

On the political raft, it seems that the strongest does not quite possess
all the rights, and what was evident, a hundred pages earlier, in the state
of nature is no longer so clear in the civil state. But if Vattel keeps natural law apart from civil law, and rejects the spontaneous derivation of
the one from the other, he does so merely because he is getting ready to
attribute to limited and constitutional sovereign power the rather special right to dispose of the lives of citizens.

This right is not despotic, at least not in the terms in which classical
political science understands despotism. Following reasoning probably
inspired by Locke, he argues that government is established for the
common good of society and not for the good of those who exercise it.
Despotism is not a form of government, and therefore the people cannot confer despotic authority on anyone. Even if we were to presuppose that the people could do this, it would not at all obligate future
generations. Finally, the people have the right, if they have the means,
to "arrest" a prince whose actions stray from the good of the state.[84]
Thus the sovereign qua natural person does not have the right to oblit-
erate any of his subjects who remain within the limits of their political
freedom.

But if this right does not spring from the natural qualities of the sovereign it is derived from the very constitution of the body politic. Vattel's demonstration is contained in those passages where he discusses
another "difficulty" of natural law, namely, whether the sovereign has
the right to sacrifice an innocent citizen for the good of the state.[85] This,
he admits, is a very difficult and delicate question. If Wolff was right to
say that we do not dispose of our own life, then whence derives the
power of a regent or society to dispose of the life of an innocent? Indeed, not even necessity excuses acts that are absolutely illicit in themselves, and such actions are forbidden by an immutable law. But if we
accept the principle in this form, it is clear that we arrive at an absurdity: namely the whole of society would perish in the case in which
none of its members decided (as would be likely, or at least highly probable) to sacrifice himself, in the name of his right to self-preservation.
How can we resolve this difficulty? Vattel wonders.

His solution is a systematic secularization of Pascal's wager. In virtue of a probable reward, I subject myself to a calculated risk. Let us therefore admit that each has consented in advance to be sacrificed in the case in which he exposes the public, by his existence, to a lethal danger. This does not mean, Vattel argues, that I directly accept to lay down my life, but only that I expose myself to a danger that, at least in advance, seems uncertain. "Because society is based on a solid foundation . . . every citizen must be ready to lay down his life for its salvation. Therefore it is permissible and advantageous that each should consent, when he becomes a member of society, to be sacrificed for it, if necessity demands it. The good that the citizens thereby procure is present and certain [*présent et certain*], and the danger to which they [each individually] expose themselves is far-off and very uncertain [*très éloigné et très incertain*]."[86]

This is the right to dispose of individual lives that Vattel derives from his analysis of the body politic and which he then transfers to the small republic adrift that is the raft of shipwrecked sailors. That it is not a matter of natural primitive law, directly attached to the private subject of the philosophy of natural law, is also apparent from Vattel's speculations regarding the duty of the person of the sovereign in the situation where such a dilemma as that above might confront the state. In this case, he argues, it is the prince himself who ought to lay down his life first, and this would be a laudable and heroic action. Where the modern political order is tested to its extreme limit, Vattel puts forward not a sovereign who devours his subjects but, on the contrary, one who is swallowed by the body politic in the name of the latter's right to survival.

It only remains for us to hope that among the shipwrecked sailors there will not be one of a different philosophical bent, one who will have read Jean Barbeyrac rather than Vattel. In *The Duties of Man and the Citizen*, his commentaries on the treatise of Pufendorf, Barbeyrac argues that one of the two conditions in which it is not permissible to exercise the right to self-preservation directly is when the person with whom we find ourselves in competition is infinitely more useful to society. In this case of necessity, Barbeyrac argues, a subject must sacrifice his life in order to save that of his prince, above all if it is a case of a good prince. If among the few survivors of the shipwreck there should happen to be the owner of the lifeboat (another condition imposed by Barbeyrac), it means that the subject would stand a very real chance of rapidly becoming a martyr to natural law.

We are now capable of appreciating the nature of the revision that Vattel introduces into the analysis of the classical topic of cannibalism. The natural law that directs the actions of the subjects of the state of nature is amended and elucidated by the appeal to political law. In his analysis, civil law is a presence that explains, corrects, and lends its substance to primitive rights. Vattel's cannibal is only momentary and accidental, a creation of nature; he is, ultimately, a civil subject. On the horizon, the Hobbesian lifeboat glimpses the port of the *Leviathan*.

CHAPTER TWO

The Tortures and Fate of the Body

Theodore de Bry, *Sick Person Killed and Roasted*

SUFFERING IN MODERATION

THE NATURE OF THE RIGHT TO punish those who break the law did not pose any fundamental problems for the ancient Greeks or Romans. In Plato's *Laws*, we find an encyclopedic proposal for the reform of punishments, but the nature of the punitive right in itself is not placed under discussion.[1] It is probable that, in the ancient republics, the right to punish did not constitute an object of philosophical discussion because of the participatory and traditional nature of authority. In the *Crito*, Socrates accepts and upholds the legitimacy of the sentence handed down against him. According to him, a citizen has the evident obligation to respect the decisions of the city-state. In the period of the late Roman Empire, the sovereign's right to punish was not intensely questioned because he was seen as a mirror of divinity and because criminal sentencing and punishment depended, in practice, on lower magistrates. It was not until the Middle Ages that matters changed radically. From this period a theory originates about authority's right to punish, which would be current until the eighteenth century, when the great reform of penal punishments in the West inscribed the terms of the problem anew.

Although we should view any generalizations with caution, we may nevertheless claim that the premodern period is one in which the punishment of lawless acts during peacetime was the principal task of the sovereign. The monarch is seen as supreme judge, which means that he is recognized as having a specific right, that of deciding the life and death of his subjects. This is the "right of the sword" (*jus gladii*), which Christian political and theological doctrines treat with particular attention.[2] By the end of the seventeenth century, the theory of the right to punish will have included the power of execution as a central element. In Locke's *Two Treatises of Government*, political power is taken as "a right of making laws, with penalties of death, and consequently all less penalties."[3] Hence it results that the right of life and death is regarded as a foundation that allows the derivation of the sovereign's wider right to act. The right to punish is, indeed, the hard core of the discussion on civil authority until the eighteenth century.

The debate about who is invested with the right to punish, about the origin of this right, and about the legal procedures that must be abided by is complicated by the political and social situation in the medieval and Renaissance West. In the Roman period, the emperor was the wielder of a supreme power (*imperium*) that also included the quintessence of judicial power, and in the aristocratic republics of antiquity customary right and popular consent appeared as sufficient foundations of punishment. But in the Middle Ages there begin to appear a series of institutions that contend for the domain of the right to punish. One of the first controversies surrounds the question of whether the supreme pontiff has temporal as well as spiritual power, more precisely whether he has any effective right over political sovereigns. But even without the great dispute between popes and emperors, the stage was further complicated by a host of other actors. Local nobles also claimed separate jurisdictions; the guilds and free cities in their turn possessed their own legal institutions, and to all these can be added countless local customary laws.

Between these major institutions, conflicts were inevitable, such as the one that occurred in 1476 at Regensburg, when the burgers and the emperor contended for jurisdiction over a group of Jews arrested on suspicion of ritual murder and cannibalism. Friedrich III, discerning a usurpation of imperial rights in the local procedures, ordered the city council to free those under arrest. The city's opposition brought down on it the accusation of rebellion and a suspension of civic freedoms, including that to apply capital punishment. In reply, the worthies of Regensburg, inspired by canon law and the republican ideology of the northern Italian cities, declared that the emperor had no right to meddle in the course of communal justice, and that the Jews did not belong to him as subjects in the first place, but to the Christian community in general.[4]

This is the almost anarchic backdrop against which jurists and philosophers attempt to impose order. The simplification and rationalization of law has two major components. The first is the rediscovery of the authority of a single formula of law, in essence that of Roman law. This is what happens, beginning in the eleventh century, in the milieu of Italian jurists; its initial signification is that of legitimizing imperial power. The second consists in the stipulation of a right whereby the possessor of supreme power expounds laws, now seen as acts of his personal will. The sovereign, whether individual or (more rarely) collective, begins to be the focal point in which an entire system of punitive justice is concentrated. The latter, as Foucault shows in *Discipline and Punish* (*Surveillir et punir*, 1975), at a given moment ends up being conceived as an activation and restoration of the personal power of the sovereign. Bearing in mind the multitude of jurisdictions and principalities in Europe at that time, this idea brings with it profound consequences. The traditional immunities and privileges of subjects begin to be dissolved by a punitive right that the theoreticians of sovereignty compare with the absolute power of God.

At the center of the discussion resides the form that punition takes. Namely what is allowed and against which accused—in practical terms, this means the enunciation of a solemn discourse about corporal ordeal.

And by definition, this ordeal, whence is extracted the legitimacy of all other forms of punishment, is execution.

The racks of the body: this is the field on which part of the battle about the political right to punish is fought. What exactly the state is allowed to dictate against the condemned was and remains a subject of controversy. In the premodern period, when the symbolism of power is much more sophisticated than the monochrome punition of the nineteenth century, the stakes wagered on the details are considerable.

Modern readers of Machiavelli are shocked by the advice he formulates, in *The Prince*, to use cruelty in moderation, depending on the circumstances. However, from the point of view of readers contemporary with the Italian philosopher, the issue was merely one of a choice of terms. The art of premodern penal punishment is precisely the ability rationally to dose suffering. There is a kind of optimal "middle term" for judicially sanctioned agony. Too little, and the prince has no authority. Too much, and he is transformed into a bloodthirsty tyrant. This is the period in which political regimes are categorized according to the severity of the punishments they mete out. The general opinion is that tyranny (or despotism) is the cruelest regime, while a monarchy tempered by an aristocracy can practice a just degree of pain. An illustration from a thirteenth-century French manuscript of Aristotle's *Politics* presents a hierarchy of bad regimes—tyranny-oligarchy-democracy—deduced on the basis of the cruelty of the punishments practiced by each.

Hence one of the major conclusions of the theory of the right to punish: excess means tyranny, and tyranny, as we know, is illegitimate. The tyrant will be struck down by the wrath of God and, according to some authors, the wrath of men. The boundaries of the right to punish are therefore those between political legitimacy and illegitimacy, the line between the monarchical glory and the call to tyrannicide. Arbitrary power is recognizable, up until the eighteenth century, by the fact that it imposes arbitrary and excessive punishment. Phalaris, the tyrant of Syracuse, who roasted his enemies inside a red-hot bronze bull, is one of the prototypes of a literature that dwells on political cruelty. This perception of tyranny as an excess of the right to punish also explains the interdiction stipulated by Amendment VIII of the Constitution of the United States against "cruel and unusual punishment." Asiatic despotism is the great transgressor of the rational punitive right. In Asia, Europeans are appalled to discover agonizing punishments. In Persia, Jean Struys comes on a white slave attempting to flee: recaptured, he is flayed alive and his skin hung from a wall.[5] Impalement is the great specialty of the Oriental despot. Herodotus (3.159) tells of story of Darius impaling three thousand Babylonians; the medieval prince Vlad Dracula is shown in German drawings organizing mass impalements as a form of collective punishment. Toward the end of the Enlightenment, the knout is another symbol of punitive excesses, this time originating in Russia.[6]

The distinguishing mark of bad royalty is the transgression of divine, natural, and civil law. In this process, the tyrant is transformed into a curious creature: a rebel against God, nature, humanity, and the body politic. When it is necessary to lend the tyrant a face or give him a voice, he is compared to a bloodthirsty beast or an exotic despot. In both cases, the standard move is that of lowering him to the rank of anthropophagus.

There is another direction in which the theory of the right to punish confronts anthropophagy. Let us return to the question of the nature of the right to punish. Whence does the sovereign possess this right? The reply of philosophers, from at least as early as the eighteenth century, is that it is a right transferred from the "people." The sovereign is the custodian of a right that initially belonged to someone else. Thus there was a period in which the right to punish was invested in individuals rather than in a sovereign. However, this is the state of nature, in which each has the right to punish breaches of the natural law, a right of execution unlimited by worldly authority. How could it be possible for it not to be abused? Hence two types of account. The first is the portrait of the bloodthirsty despot. The second is that of the savage. In both cases, speculative geography and history become a reservoir of images and of problems. Both despot and natural man are proven transgressors of the rational right to punish. In the epoch of the people's regimes, a third figure is joined to this somber couple: the man of the crowd. Beginning in the late eighteenth century, he will enjoy a brief period of glory. Ignorant and brutal, he is a relative of natural man, whom he will sometimes surpass in his cruelty. The man of the crowd is fundamentally an inhabitant of the state of nature resulting from the violent decomposition of political order, and the law by virtue of which popular justice acts is as cruel as the law of savage nature. During the French Revolution, there are numerous accounts of the atrocities of the Parisian crowd, as well as accounts in which acts of cannibalism are mentioned.[7]

Part of the political controversies of the seventeenth and eighteenth century will gravitate around these figures of the abuse of power. The theory of sovereignty will have to execute a deft maneuver in order to delimit the boundaries of legitimate power. On the one hand, it has to attach a right over life and death to the person of the sovereign. On the other hand, it has to explain and keep at a distance the savage tyrant and the man of nature. This is why the rational analysis of punishments becomes an important subject of the political philosophy of the period.

Its scope is that of legitimizing a right to punish that is comprehensive, efficient, and proper to the sovereign. This presupposes the denunciation of punitive excess and the elaboration of an idea of penal reform in which punishments are modernized.

Montaigne is one of the first authors to advance a critique of the cruelty of punishments. In his *Essays* we find the example of a *voievod* (lord) of Transylvania who ordered that a prisoner be bound naked and then tortured in every shape and form, while the other prisoners were deprived of food and drink so that they would be forced to eat their comrade. "The Savages," he writes, "do not so much offend me in roasting and eating the Bodies of the Dead, as they do who torment and persecute the Living. . . . For my Part, even in Justice itself, all that exceeds a simple Death, appears to me perfect Cruelty; especially in us, who ought to have Regard to their Souls, to dismiss them in a good and calm Condition: Which cannot be, when we have discompos'd them by insufferable Torments."[8]

However, not all are prepared to see in the savage a favorable term of comparison. Numerous references to primitives highlight the savagery of their punishments. Lescarbot reveals how Champlain, a French explorer of North America in the seventeenth century, proposes to the savages that he put a tortured prisoner out of his misery with a bolt from his harquebus. The humanitarian spirit of the Frenchman does not, however, prevent the anthropophagous denouement. The victim is dismembered, his innards are cast into a lake, and his heart is ripped out, chopped up, and given to the other prisoners to eat.[9] The civilized nations of Asia too are viewed, following accounts of the travelers, with skepticism and repulsion precisely for the reputation of harshness attached to the penal systems of countries like Japan or China.

Opposition to corporal punishments involving mutilation or death is not proper only to modern philosophers. It is also known in antiquity; in ancient Rome, *saevitia* (savage cruelty) is probably the most pejorative of the terms that could be applied to an emperor.[10] In the Middle Ages, there was a hostility to atrocities of the scaffold that culminated in the founding of religious associations that set out to minister to the condemned, not only in their final moments but also postmortem.[11] The soul of the condemned must not despair because of pain, losing hope in divine justice. Such was the argument employed prior to Montaigne by Jean de Gerson (1363–1429), a theologian of the University of Paris, who demanded of the king of France the attendance of a confessor at the scaffold and the shortening of torments.

Philosophers, however, are more interested in remaining within the bounds of a rational and historical analysis of the nature and limits of the right to punish. In his commentary on Pufendorf's *Law of Nature and Nations*, Barbeyrac comments on Locke's theory of the right to punish. He admits that in the state of nature each is entitled to "execute" the natural law, but this power, as he defines it, is not absolute or arbitrary. He who kills with premeditation deserves to be destroyed like lions, tigers, or other ferocious beasts with which we can cultivate no social relations. In conclusion, the interest of society is that which authorizes us to punish in the state of nature. As for the limits that must be imposed on this right to punish, Barbeyrac argues that if we punish with too great a cruelty we shall do more harm than good. It is not permissible that we should be led by passion to punish a transgression excessively. When someone tramples the laws of nature underfoot, the laws that God has given to man and that are the rules of equity and reason, he becomes the enemy of the human kingdom. Since each has the right to guard that human society be maintained, it follows that anyone has the right to punish, guided by the light of calm reasoning.[12]

These are the theoretical premises for a critique of punitive excesses, which will become an important philosophical genre in the Age of Enlightenment. In *Sketches on the History of Man*, Lord Kames argues that the punishments of European nations are excessively cruel. In the Middle Ages, for example, the hand of a person caught stealing from the lead-mines at Derby used to be nailed to a table, "and in that state he was left without meat or drink, having no means for freedom but to employ one hand to cut off the other." Kames comments that, although the barbarity of the English people at the time made harsh punishments necessary, the punishment in question transcended severity and was nothing but "brutal cruelty."[13] The modern nations of Europe and Russia too, he shows, have horrific punishments. All these accounts are in the chapter that deals with the "progress of manners." Torture, that supposed "criterion of truth" (*critère de vérité*), as the marquis of Beccaria (1738–94) argues in his *Treatise of Crimes and Punishments* (*Dei delitti e delle pene*), a text on penal reform influential during the Enlightenment that argued for the abolition of capital punishment on utilitarian grounds, is a "custom worthy only of cannibals."[14]

Consequently, in the seventeenth century a call for moderation in penal punishments makes itself heard. Corporal tortures are replaced with prison or deportation overseas, to savage and inhospitable lands. The deported are reintegrated into the state of nature whose inhabitants they became by right when they did not heed civil law. In these lands, they are neighbors with a series of other figures of anomie, including savage cannibals. One of the earliest justifications of deportation as a form of penal punishment was that which emphasized the presence of anthropophagi. One of the first to propose such a measure was French monk Émeric Crucé (1590–1648) in *The New Cineus* (1623). He argues that one cause of war is the existence of men who leave their country in order to seek war in other parts. However, the world was not created for those who know nothing else except to do evil. They should be banished and "all be sent to the Cannibals and Savages, who have nothing of man but the face."[15] In his travel essays, François la Mothe le Vayer (1585–1672) claims that in France there is a multitude of persons that justice condemns for their crimes. They might be sent, depending on what crime each had committed, to uninhabited places, to dwell among inhuman savages and even cannibals. Such an exiling of criminals could be practiced not only in Australia, he argues, but also in any other part of the world, on condition that the danger to which they are exposed should be no greater than the punishment deserved by the guilty. Consequently, those who equip long-distance ships should be obliged to take one or two of these criminals, leave them in the appointed places and draw up a written statement. Other ships should then be instructed to visit those places from time to time in order to learn what had become of the exiles.[16]

What the penal reformers of the Enlightenment demand above all is the marginalization of physical tortures. Atrocious punishments and torture are condemned, and for the first time the legitimacy and utility of the death penalty begins to be questioned. The first abolitionist text is probably a fictional journey to America, *The Adventures of Jacques Massé* (1710) of Tyssot de Patot, where the hero discovers, uniquely, a land where the death penalty has been abolished and punishments consist of forced labor; the work also contains a eulogy to the philosophy of Descartes.

This does not mean that the curious crowd no longer gathers around the scaffold. However, what takes place there begins to be less and less bloody theater and more and more a cold, rapid and efficient execution of criminal justice, culminating with the introduction of the guillotine. It is a gradual process. The medieval scaffold was never, in principle, a place of unbridled passions. Capital punishment and the tortures that preceded it had their logic, in which the final moment was established with precision, according to symbolic and moral considerations. Gradually, two not necessarily connected things occur. On the one hand, the moment of death is concealed.[17] For example, in seventeenth-century Holland, the condemned are strangled behind a screen, before their bodies are subjected to the rest of the punishment in public view. In nineteenth-century France, the guillotine begins to be erected in public places furtively, at the crack of dawn, so that only the most decidedly curious can come to watch. Later, it will be completely concealed behind prison walls. On the other hand, legal atrocities, primarily the forms of bodily mutilation, become less and less tolerable to onlookers. This is also valid for the nonlethal forms of mutilation: flogging, branding, amputation of ears. The combined result of these developments is the discreet withdrawal from the urban landscape, by the end of the eighteenth century, of the scaffold and the gallows. The latter had often been elaborate structures, from which the corpses (or pieces of the corpses) of those executed were hung. Their ubiquity was also suggested by the fact that they were landmarks for wayfarers, rather like milestones.

Cruelty does not merely vanish from the sentiments of the Enlightenment public. On the contrary, in the eighteenth century we may even detect an increased interest in some of the agonies of the body. Except that the theater of this new and morbid interest is sooner to be found in the domestic sphere. In particular, sexual suffering seems to be a subject that fascinates. "Make me suffer even more," a nun asks her lover, in the *Letters of the Portuguese Nun* (1669). This is the moment in which there is a considerable heightening of interest in extreme sexual practices, an interest that will culminate in the work of Sade.

In this context, torture no longer relates to the grim realities of penal justice and the fate of the soul, but becomes rather a question of manners. In 1753, Jane Collier publishes *An Essay on the Art of Ingeniously Tormenting*; the title might give us a mistaken idea of the contents of the book, which is nothing more than a satire which sets out to teach women how to annoy their husbands and servants.

Against the backdrop of these revisions in mores, the dismemberment of a human body is no longer a spectacle worthy of a civilized nation. And it is not only a question of human bodies. In the Middle Ages, the butcher was a neighbor who carried on his activities in the communal courtyard or even in the middle of the street. Urban modernization banishes him to the abattoir, where we now find him as a wage laborer. Bleeding flesh and its production are ever more difficult to observe. As cannibalism is hard to dissociate from a perception of bodily dismemberment, the question arises whether these developments are of such a nature as to thrust anthropophagy into the shadows.

It is not at all apparent whether there is a simple answer. Repulsion at the cruelties of the flesh was, undoubtedly, a force that sent the cannibal to the underground of collective representations. On the other hand, however, the contrast with the new state of sensibility turns the cannibal into an exceptional figure. Once the executioner has been transformed into a public functionary, there is one other personage alone who still shares with the cannibal the domain of bodily disposal: the physician.

Surgery is the figure of modernity that displaces punitive practices as a method of the extreme visibility of the body. And the extreme figure of the medical macabre is the performer of autopsies, in connection with whom a new and sinister folklore appears. He is one of the two extremities of a continuum, which is legal in its significance but medical in its content. At the other extremity is the sadistic criminal, an urban cannibal in his most violent incarnation. Between them and uniting them there is an entire nebula of suspect figures, which provide the object of sensationalistic literature and journalism.[18] What they have in common is that they are city-dwellers, who are no longer struck by social stigma, who are no longer part of a separate order, like medieval executioners. The twilight of tortures and civilization of manners eliminated the spectacle of bleeding flesh, but they coincided with the transformation of the cannibal into a citizen. Their rhythms will no longer be the rhythms of nature or penal ceremony, but those of labor and *loisir*.

At the end of the eighteenth century, according to Foucault, we witness a rethinking of deviancy, a process in which the vast domain of modern abnormality is formed. One of its main figures will be that of the moral monster, a personage who first manifests himself during the revolutionary period as political monster. Here we are dealing with three main formulae of abnormality. The first is the primordial political monster, the tyrant, who became the template of all the others. Louis XVI was, in the revolutionary imagination, the transgressor par excellence. The second is the popular monster, multifarious, violent, and bloodthirsty. At this period, popular violence indeed takes shocking forms, and accusations of cannibalism are frequent. Setting out from these, the figure of the modern criminal takes shape, springing up in the margins of theories of the social contract. Thus the criminal is a product of regression to the state of nature, because he has broken the social contract. The savage reemerges in the form of the criminal, as Foucault argues in *Les Anormaux*. The sources of this new figure are the anthropophagus, or popular monster, and the perpetrator of incest, or princely monster. These two serve as a grid of intelligibility and means of access to a number of disciplines, especially anthropology and criminal psychiatry.[19]

This schema is as interesting as it is debatable. The political monster that Foucault believes was born of the upheavals of the French Revolution has a venerable history. Cannibalistic and incestuous, this is still Plato's tyrant. That the people or the crowd can manifest themselves more bloodily than a band of cannibal Indians intoxicated by the desire for revenge was an idea that was also studied in prerevolutionary texts.

In *The Social System*, Paul-Henri Dietrich Baron d'Holbach (1723–89) argues that the man of the crowd is entirely an authentic savage capable of any excess. In *Sketches of the History of Man*, Kames relates that in Burgundy in 1348, during an uprising the peasants roasted a noble on a spit and then, after raping his wife and daughters, forced them to eat his flesh, after which they were killed. In the *Second Treatise of Government*, John Locke also describes the delinquent as a reversion to bestiality. According to Locke, the criminal, in renouncing natural law, has declared war against all mankind, and therefore "may be destroyed as a lion or tiger, one of those wild beasts with whom men can have no society nor security."[20] In *Principes du droit politique* (1751), Burlamaqui also argues that he who renounces the natural law becomes a dangerous enemy of the human kingdom.

The link between criminal and beast also occurs in penal history under the symbolic form of casting the condemned to wild beasts (*damnatio ad bestias*). This was one of the standard punishments in ancient Rome and was reserved for murderers and slaves. Of Caligula, Suetonius affirms that he was so passionate about the spectacle of those torn to pieces in the arena that, after the condemned had been dispatched, he gave the order for spectators in the stands also to be cast to the beasts after their tongues had been cut out to silence them. The last time this punishment was officially applied in Europe was probably in Germany during the eighteenth century, when a number of Polish bear-handlers were sentenced to be torn to pieces by their own animals.

What occurs in the French Revolution is nothing more than an irruption of anterior symbols. It is highly likely that Foucault is right in that the figure of the abnormal is the point of intersection for a number of new domains of knowledge. However, what he seems not to observe is that, at the same time, the obsolescence of classical representations of the cannibal is what signals and accompanies not only the genesis but also the decline or disappearance of certain domains of scholarly knowledge: natural law, the moral geography of the seventeenth and eighteenth centuries, and the theory of the social contract. The comparison between bestiality and the transgressor of the social pact does not wait for the epoch of Revolution; it has medieval origins and will reappear in Locke and Rousseau. It is true that authors prior to the late eighteenth century do not systematically describe transgressions against civil law as a moral and physical degeneration. However, nor is there any need to do so from their perspective. Until the seventeenth century, a theory of the passions with a theological substratum is that which does away with the need for the figure of the degenerate, because it is the background against which the figure of the sinner is outlined.

THE RIGHT OF BURIAL

Privation of funerary rites was a form of punishment known to most societies. It occurs in Jewish religious texts, where it is mentioned as a punishment for apostates; in Homer's *Iliad*; and in Sophocles' *Antigone*, which includes the first occurrence of the expression "natural law" in the speech whereby the interment of an unburied body is justified. The Romans resorted frequently to the denial of burial as a legal punishment. In the Christian period, the interdiction of funerary rites is documented as an extreme supplement to punition. In the year 177, a number of Christians from Lyon are condemned by the Roman authorities to be executed in the local arena. Their death does not, however, put an end to the punitive ritual. The bodies are cast to the dogs, and the remains are guarded day and night to prevent the Christians from removing them for burial. Up until the eighteenth century, the severest punishments are those in which the ritual shattering of the body continues after the moment of death. Witchcraft is punished by burning at the stake and scattering of the ashes, while regicide or treason give occasion for elaborate spectacles in which the body of the condemned is cut up into pieces that are then exhibited in different places. Even the more common punishment of hanging is sometimes supplemented by leaving the body suspended in the noose until it completely rots. Thomas More's utopians punish those who commit suicide without the permission of the Senate by forbidding burial or cremation of their bodies: "He that killeth himself before that the priests and the council have allowed the cause of his death, him as unworthy either to be buried or with fire to be consumed, they cast unburied into some stinking marsh."[21]

Privation of burial attains such preeminence in the West due to the Christian doctrine of resurrection. During the religious persecutions of the year 177, Roman authorities made a calculated attempt to present the Christians overwhelming evidence of the impossibility of the resurrection of the body. The Christians were prevented from burying the bodies of their martyrs. After lying exposed for six days, the corpses were cremated and the ashes cast into the River Rhone, in order to leave not a single relic. The Christians' persecutors were convinced that thereby they would cause them to despair in the possibility of resurrection.

Along with such extreme forms of punishment, the theologians still have to elucidate the consequences, which appear similar, of privation of burial in the case of those who die in shipwrecks or are devoured by marine creatures, by beasts, or by birds. The answer of some of the Church Fathers to these difficulties is to negate the necessity of funerary rites for resurrection of the body. In *The City of God*, Saint Augustine argues that absence of burial does not matter for a Christian. "We have assurance that the ravenous beasts will not hinder the resurrection of bodies of which not a single hair of the head will perish."[22] Decent funerals and a proper burial, with a procession of mourners, are "a consolation to the living rather than help to the departed." The doctrine of the resurrection of the flesh causes the metaphysical concern for funeral rites to be superfluous: "Christians have the promise that their bodies and all their limbs will be restored and renewed, in an instant, not only from the earth, but also from the remotest hiding-places in the other elements into which their dead bodies passed into disintegration."[23] For Augustine, corpses are buried only as an act of piety, in order to affirm our belief in resurrection.

Saint Augustine and the martyrs continue an ancient philosophic tradition of scorn for the fate of the body postmortem. Diogenes the Cynic demanded that corpses should be left to the birds and wild beasts, in order to be of use to them, arguing that it was better for the body to serve as food for other creatures than to be allowed to decompose. Anaxagoras, asked by his friends on his deathbed whether he wished for his body to be buried in his native place, Clazomenae, assured them that "the descent to Hades is much the same from whatever place we start."[24] In the *Tusculan Disputations*, Cicero recalls Theodorus of Cyrene, who, when threatened with crucifixion by the tyrant Lysimachus, answered the latter with the following words: "I pray you threaten your courtiers with such atrocities. To Theodotus it is all the same whether he rots in the earth or in the air."[25]

However, such opinions were marginal, even among the contemporaries of the Cynics and the Stoics. Slowly and partly due to changes in fashion rather than in the ideology of the afterlife, burial replaces cremation in the late Roman Empire.[26] Jurists agree that the laws recognize the right to burial. Justinian's *Digest* argues that the right to burial is stronger than the right of property: "It is in the public interest, so that bodies should not remain unburied, that the strict principle [of the right of property] should be ignored . . . because the higher of these principles is that which serves the interest of religion."[27] In the seventeenth century, this kind of stipulation is also to be found in civil law. French jurist Jean Domat, author of *The Civil Law in its Natural Order*, argues that the violation of graves, as an insult to the dead, in the interests of theft, or for other forbidden purposes, is a form of sacrilege. How serious such crimes are can be deduced from the fact that immediately after them Domat mentions the worst of all possible crimes, that of lese majesty.

Philosophers and theologians also speak of the right to burial. A discussion of legislation regarding burial is to be found in Plato's *Laws*, and a philosophical analysis of funerary laws in book II of Cicero's *Laws*. In a passage in which opposing sentiments are fused, Seneca questions the reasons behind the practice of burial:

> Let us presuppose that we had found the body of a man's father in a remote spot and buried it. We have not done any good, either to the man in question, for whom the manner in which he rots is unimportant, or to the son. For what can he gain by this act? However, I shall tell you what the latter has gained. In using me as his instrument, he has fulfilled a traditional and necessary duty. . . . Nevertheless, this act becomes a benefit only if I have fulfilled it not from a sense of pity or of humanity that has impelled me to conceal the corpse of another, but because I have recognized the body and supposed that I am doing a service to the son. However, if I have cast earth upon an unknown corpse, then by this act I have not created any debt to any man, I have acted only as any other man, with humanity.[28]

Lactantius argues that the greatest work of piety is to bury strangers and the poor.[29] Even Saint Augustine, in *De cura pro mortuis*, shows that each man has a "natural love" for his own flesh that makes him fear for the eventuality that it might remain unburied.[30] Hugo Grotius dedicates an entire chapter in *Of the Rights of War and Peace* (1625) to a discussion of the "right of burial." He concludes that this is a right that cannot be refused even to enemies, whether private or public. One of his references is to the Greek poet Moschion, who attributed the reason for burying the dead "to the Savage Cruelty of the Giants, who us'd to devour the dead Bodies of Men, the Abolition whereof is signified by Burial."[31] In *Discours sur l'origine et fondemens de l'inégalité parmi les hommes*, Rousseau makes the right to burial an instinct. That the impulse to bury the dead is natural is proven by the fact that even some animals bury their own kind. "An animal does not without disquiet pass by a dead animal of its species."[32]

There is therefore a broad current of opinion which establishes that there is a duty and a right, be it civil or natural, to burial. The problem is the justification of this right. The possibility that it might be a strictly civil right does not overly preoccupy philosophers until the eighteenth century, because it was not until then that civil laws were viewed as being founded on natural law, while burial was regarded as a religious rather than a civil act. However, if there is a natural right to burial it means that it must be common to the majority of nations. But now the difficulties begin, because philosophers and travelers observe that not all nations seem to adhere to the same funerary standards. Some have strange and atrocious customs, while others seem to despise the very idea of funerals. This contrast is all the more apparent to the theologians and philosophers of Christendom given that they recognize only two forms of funeral rite: Christian burial and Graeco-Roman cremation.

Thus there appears a genre of philosophic discourse regarding mortuary customs, which, as a rule, commences with a catalogue of the most extravagant of these practices, where anthropophagy is the most extreme case. From Cicero we learn that Chrysippus collected a multitude of strange customs, but the facts "are so repugnant that speech flees and shrinks from it." In Hyrcania, the populace rear dogs in order for them to devour the corpses of their masters when they die; each man keeps as many dogs as his rank and wealth allow.[33] In the *Histories* of Herodotus, we discover that in the North there is a tribe named the Issedones, who prepare a meal using a mixture of the flesh of the deceased and that of the beasts of his flock. The skull of the dead man is cleaned, gilded and used as an object in religious worship, during the annual feasts held in honor of the departed. "Each son proceeds in this way with his father, exactly the same as the Greeks in their festivals for the dead."[34] The cannibals mentioned by Jean Struys do not bury their dead, but preserve them for "a better use." In reply to those who reproach them for eating the flesh of their fellows, they rationalize their custom by saying that it is opinion and habit that cause a thing to be good or bad and that no one who follows these lights can sin. In *Petits traités en forme de Lettres*, La Mothe le Vayer mentions the custom of some American Indians who pound up the bones of their parents and mix the powder into a potion. In *The Law of Nature and Nations*, Pufendorf includes an exhaustive list of astonishing rituals, from which cannibalism is not lacking. The travel literature of the Enlightenment also reveals the existence of strange customs. Lafitau dedicates considerable space to the question of burial in *Moeurs des sauvages amériquains comparées aux moeurs des premiers temps*. Like the Scythians and most of the barbarian tribes of former times, many Indians are cannibals and do not grant the deceased any other grave than the stomach, he asserts. In volume 2 of the work, there is a chapter on the customs of the Indies: mummification, the smoking of corpses, human sacrifice, and processions during which the dead are carried on the backs of the living.

In such conditions, the obvious question is whether there is a natural right to sepulture. And presupposing that there is such a right, does this prescribe burial, as Christians know it, as the only acceptable form? These questions especially arise in connection with anthropophagy. On the one hand, the consumption of a body by anthropophagi seems to be the most absolute privation of burial. On the other hand, as early as the ancient sources, some peoples justify anthropophagy as a substitute for interment, advancing arguments that justify consumption of the deceased as an act of piety. Finally, another question posed by the theory of the natural law of sepulture is that regarding the theological or juridical consequences arising from denial of civilized sepulture.

The discovery of cannibalism and the funerary rites of the New World occasioned debates about the right to burial, on which rested considerable political stakes.[35] One ingenious treatment of the subject is to be found in a work entitled *On Dietary Laws* (1538), written by Francisco de Vitoria, a leading Spanish scholastic of the day and major exponent of the theory of the just war. According to the latter, burial is a right recognized by natural law.[36] However, this law would be broken if the practice of eating human flesh were to be admitted. Moreover, cannibalism would arise as an injustice (*iniuria*) to the resurrection of the body, because human bodies would be mingled one with another. Finally, to bury the dead is an act of compassion, whereas to deprive them of burial is a lack of piety. To the extent that they are anthropophagi, the Indians of America thereby become guilty of crimes against nature.

The right to sepulture is also a subject present in treatises of modern natural law. Pufendorf observes that the right to sepulture is part of the duties of humanity. Barbeyrac notes, however, that such a thing is rather hard to sustain, as long as Pufendorf himself enumerates a series of funerary customs among the most aberrant. This variety does not lead Barbeyrac to deny the existence of a universal law of sepulture, but merely to suppose that the latter has not been judiciously explained. According to him, if a thing is not advantageous to human society in general, then it is forbidden by natural law, even if there are peoples who practice it. Such is the case of theft for the Spartans and adultery for the Mesagetes. Furthermore, Barbeyrac employs the traditional model of discussion about burial. It is human not to leave our corpses to putrefy in the sun or to be devoured by animals, because this is a gruesome spectacle for the living and produces a baleful effect (*dommage réel*), by affecting the air, most injurious to the health. Even the most indifferent persons must bury the dead for this reason. Some, such as Thomasius, discussed the laws that forbid sepulture as a punishment for certain crimes and argued that a dead person feels nothing. However, it is possible to cause someone harm even in this state, as in the case of a child in its mother's womb or a madman, without either of them being aware of this thing. We are told that the dead no longer have being, but reason has no absolute certitude as to this, as the continued existence of the soul is sufficient possibility. Even leaving aside the immortality of the soul, do those who calumny the dead not sin thereby? Privation of sepulture is a cause for just war on the part of the relatives or friends of the dead, while the right of war does not extend to privation of burial for enemies, which would be a barbaric cruelty.[37]

Not all authors present primitive peoples as sinners against nature and God in their funerary customs. Marco Polo writes about a kingdom in Asia where people gather around a sick man, suffocate him, chop him into pieces, cook him, and eat him at a feast to which the friends and neighbors of the deceased are invited. This account was obviously inspired by Herodotus, but Marco Polo throws in a few details that are to have a notable career. His anthropophagi believe that if a man's sickness is allowed to take its course then his flesh will be transformed into worms, after which they will die of hunger, something which would cause great sufferings to the soul. They bury the bones with care, so that they will not be disturbed by wild beasts.[38] Lafitau claims that the majority of Indian savages nevertheless bury their dead, the same as Christian peoples. For the Americans, privation of sepulture is an infamy and cruel punishment. They guard their cemeteries so that not even wild beasts can dig up their dead. But how does it stand with the strange customs presented by Lafitau? These do not originate in a fundamental perversion of nature, but rather in the Indians' mistaken idea of certain virtues. It is true, Lafitau admits, that there are nations which kill and eat their old folk, but they imagine that they are thereby doing them a good. This is badly understood piety, he admits, "but it is a piety nonetheless colored by a certain shadow of reason," because they believe that such sepulture is more honorable than being abandoned as prey to worms and putrefaction.[39]

In the case of La Mothe le Vayer, the discussion of the right to sepulture leads him to denounce excesses of funerary refinement. In *Petits traités en forme de Lettres* he advances a series of radical theses. However fine a grave might seem from the outside it is still a receptacle of putrefaction. Philosophers have shown, against the popular opinion, which upholds that sepulture is honorable, that there are peoples who abandon the bodies of their dead to wild animals. And in this respect, the middle term between two extremes, of which Aristotle also speaks, is the best, according to the French philosopher. There should not be too much ostentation at funerals. The custom in Turkey and China, which requires that cemeteries should lie outside the towns, is commendable. Physicians who do not wish to endanger the health of the living by forbidding burials in church are laudable in their intentions, which are sometimes wrongly interpreted, he claims.

Against the background of growing atheism in the seventeenth and eighteenth centuries, it is not surprising that some radical writers direct their attacks against the traditional theories of sepulture. In his posthumously published *États et empires de la Lune* (1657), libertine French thinker Cyrano de Bergerac describes a funeral procession for someone who had been condemned to die a natural death twenty years previously.[40] The terrestrial visitor is amazed, but a Lunar local assures him that burial is a grave punishment. It is clear that de Bergerac's intention was, ultimately, to write about Christian funerary writes from a comparative perspective. When someone grows old on the Moon, he calls an assembly of his friends to vote on his death. We are dealing with a form of inverted contractualism, where the scope of the pact is not the conservation of its members but precisely ratification of the renunciation of the right to life. After approval has been obtained, a party is held the next day, at which each person invited is seated according to rank. The dearest friends of the victim, after tenderly kissing the latter, plunge a dagger into his heart. The lover, we further learn, does not draw the dagger out of the wound and does not part his lips from those of his comrade until he is dead. It is therefore a species of stoicism with homosexual overtones. After the dagger is withdrawn, the lover closes the wound with his mouth and drinks the blood, sucking until there is not a drop left. The dead man is laid in his bed, where others subject him to the same treatment. Once they are sated, they hold an orgy, at which each comrade is brought, for four or five hours, a girl of sixteen or seventeen. The party then continues for another few days, during which time they feed only on the raw flesh of the dead man. The purpose of this strange ritual is to recover the substance of the dead friend, whom it is supposed might be reborn, following the embraces to which the cannibals devote themselves.

In the Age of Enlightenment, the philosophers return to Earth with attacks directed against the right to sepulture. In *Recherches philosophiques sur les américains, ou Mémoires interessants pour servir à l'histoire de l'Espèce humaine* (1771 edition), Cornelius de Pauw argues that this right is based only on the sentiments of the living. The manner in which "the gross elements and matter of a being deprived of its intrinsic organization decompose is undoubtedly an indifferent action in itself." There is, our philosopher thinks, no difference whether "worms, Iroquois or cannibals gnaw a corpse."[41] The article "Flesh" in the *Yverdon Encyclopaedia* seems to plagiarize de Pauw. Funeral rituals have a role, but one that is psychological. Some actions, though indifferent in reality,

cease to be so in the context of civil or social order. In this case, legislators must take into account the fact that people are guided more by
prejudices than by laws. For this reason they have prescribed that the
dead should be respected, because, ultimately, the living must be respected, and the dead are an image of the living in the eyes of the many.
Enlightenment philosophy, in its struggle against prejudice, accepts a
residue of irrationality, as long as it translates into the system of public
utility. Adopting arguments he probably finds in de Pauw, Brissot de
Warville claims that it might seem strange to a savage that we bury the
"bleeding corpses" of our enemies rather than eating them. According to
Warville, savages have a natural right to the corpses of the slain similar
to that of crows and worms. In the last instance, it is utility that dictates
recourse to the dead body: "And why should they not feed themselves
[with corpses]?" Organic molecules, explains Brissot, serve for nutrition and for the propagation of the species. A wolf will find in a wolf, a
man in a man, the organic molecules that alone maintain the animal
economy.[42]

In the article "Anthropophages" in the *Philosophical Dictionary*, Voltaire includes a discussion of burial that is at the same time a legitimization of cannibalism. In 1725, he claims, four savages were brought from
the Mississippi to Fontainbleau, and with whom "I had the honor to
converse" (*j'eus l'honneur de les entretenir*). From these rustic philosophers, the French savant wished to discover whether they had eaten
human beings. A "Lady of that country" (*une Dame du Pays*) answered
"very naively" (*très-naïvement*) that she had. "I seemed a little scandalized; she excused herself saying that it was better to eat your dead foe
than to leave him prey to the wild beasts and that the victors deserve to
have first choice."[43] We, in Europe, comments Voltaire, slay our fellows
and then leave them in "the kitchen of the crows and worms. Here is
the horror, here is the crime; what does it matter if, after you have been
slain, you are eaten by a soldier or by a dog or by a crow?"[44] The problem, as Voltaire sees it, is that in the civilized world we respect the dead
more than the living. "So-called civilized [*policées*] nations are right not
to put their vanquished enemies in the pot; for if it were permitted to
eat one's neighbors, one would soon be eating one's compatriots, which
would be a great inconvenience to the social virtues."[45]

The arguments of the Enlightenment philosophers are nothing more
than a rehearsal, within a modern context, of some of the theses hostile to
sepulture put forward by pagan philosophers or by the Church Fathers.
This is also evident in the transformations of the theory regarding the
human body as food for the worms, a subject obsessively recalled in the
Middle Ages and which now recurs in new forms. In the *Dialogues on*

Natural Religion, Hume argues that nature is a kind of Hobbesian universe, where

> a perpetual war is kindled amongst all living creatures. . . . The stronger prey upon the weaker, and keep them in perpetual terror and anxiety. The weaker too, in their turn, often prey upon the stronger. . . . Consider that innumerable race of insects, which are either bred on the body of each animal, or flying about infix their stings in him. These insects have others still less than themselves, which torment them. And thus on each hand, before and behind, above and below, every animal is surrounded with enemies, which incessantly seek his misery and destruction.[46]

Julien-Joseph Virey claims that nature is a scene of universal carnage, where creatures devour one another.[47] In an appendix to his work, he presents a terrifying vision of man as a mortal being whose most terrible enemies are the worms and parasites that devour him alive. These images of organisms parasitic on other organisms, to infinity, were clearly influenced by the discoveries allowed by the microscope.

Philosophical attacks on the right to sepulture were one of the reasons for which the latter was eliminated from the structures of natural law, even before that science entered into decline, in the nineteenth century. Another reason is the appearance of new attitudes to death. As Robert Favre argues, death lost its prestige in the eighteenth century. Images of death remain, but man is now more blasé toward them.[48] The cult associated with the cadaver begins to relax, as proven by a remark by Mercier, in *Tableau of Paris*: "As soon as anyone gives up the ghost, he is wrapped up warmly in his bed; those around him do nothing more than relieve themselves of his corpse." In *Robinson Crusoe*, the English castaway orders Friday to clear away the remains of a cannibal feast, gather them into a heap and burn them. Defoe does not explain why the remains were to be burned without ceremony rather than buried; it is possible that the absence of burial may have been deliberate, as it was a question of cannibal remains.

Modern, more pragmatic and expeditious, attitudes toward death and sepulture were prepared by the discourse of the philosophers, in which the problem of anthropophagy plays a central part and in which Stoic, Cynic, and patristic theories are recuperated. For Christian Wolff, as well as for the long casuistic tradition that precedes him, it is sometimes permissible to ignore the right to burial when the latter comes into conflict with the right to conservation of life. As Wolff argues, it is true that natural law does not allow anyone the right to kill anyone else in order to feed on the latter's flesh. This happens because natural law is supposed to include a commandment that forbids homicide. If there are human bodies that have not been killed with the intention of eating them, such as, for example, bodies on a battlefield, then "common natural law" does not forbid them being eaten, because they are ultimately a convenient food for us. But if any other food is lacking, no one can deny that the flesh of a person, in whose death we have not participated, cannot serve us as nourishment. On the other hand, we cannot eat the dead under the pretext that we thereby grant them sepulture.[49]

The treatment Wolff accords to the right to burial is quite typical. Although we cannot do harm to the dead properly speaking, we can sin against their memory or against the commitments we have made toward them.[50] We must remove corpses from places frequented by people and not treat them like the corpses of animals, leaving them to rot under the open sky. This right is universal and even our enemies must be granted it. It is permissible in accordance with natural law to cremate corpses, but positive law prescribes that we should bury them, because this is more convenient. On this point, Wolff inserts an argument which demonstrates that the right to sepulture has slid from the territory of natural law into that of civil law. Once it is established that corpses should be buried, Wolff argues that in the state of nature it is permissible to bury a dead body anywhere. However, once property has been established based on consensus, we must take dead bodies to places specially designated for sepulture.[51] Where such places are to be found is clearly an issue for political law. Once man has entered society, what was once merely a natural duty becomes an act animated by the will of a sovereign.

THE NATIONALIZATION OF CORPSES

In the eighteenth century a new doctrine, utilitarianism, appeared that dominated modern ethics. Historians of moral philosophy have described it as a theory based upon the "calculus of utility," which legitimizes norms depending on their social utility. In its turn, this calculus is possible because human moral physiology is reduced, at least by early utilitarianism, to a model of "pleasure and pain." Pain and pleasure are supposed to be two simple, opposing, and measurable sensations, whence the idea of a precise calculus of the consequences of human actions. Finally, utilitarianism is described as a secular doctrine, which acts a substitute for theologically inspired moral systems.

What the histories do not satisfactorily explain is the extraordinary success of utilitarianism. Argumentation based on utility, whether public or private, appears as long ago as antiquity. This species of argument becomes very attractive, of course, at the moment when, during the Enlightenment, a simple and efficient psychology emerges, based on Locke's theory of ideas. This is the period when a French school of utilitarianism develops, which puts forward radically secular arguments employing a simple model of the sensations.

The problem that needs to be elucidated is that of the relations between utilitarianism and the theories of natural law, before the decline of the latter. Indeed, the radical utilitarianism of the French sensualists forms in a medium in which the arguments of natural law have a well-defined status. If utilitarian justifications could be viewed as plausible, then this must have occurred during the course of an at least partial substitution for the traditional explanations of natural law.

While simple to describe in broad terms, this process is not without its complexities. Historians have presented it as the clash of two major systems, which is not entirely exact. First, the arguments that appeal to utility coexisted for a long time with those based on natural law. This is visible in the great jurists of natural law up to the close of the eighteenth century, when the orators and pamphleteers of the French Revolution uninhibitedly mixed the crudest utilitarianism with the exaltation of the laws of nature. In essence, there is no deeper motive for which a theory of utility ought to dispense with a notion of natural law. Actually, in the second half of the eighteenth century, the notion of a "natural law" is interpreted, in the field of moral philosophy, in a manner increasingly influenced by the natural sciences. This change takes place to the detriment of the traditional meaning, that of the dictate of reason. Now, the law of moral nature is assimilated to the laws of the mechanical universe, enabling this "scientific" version to coexist with, and even presuppose, a secular theory of the utility of human sensations. Following Bentham, who presented his version of utilitarianism in vehement opposition to the philosophy of natural law, many historians highlighted the opposition between natural law and utilitarianism.

This historical reconstruction of a net antagonism between two systems is not merely suspect because it loses sight of the real complexities of a historical evolution, but above all because it obscures much of its real significance. From the viewpoint of this utilitarianism sterilized for contemporary use, some of primitive utilitarianism's obsessions and objects of research are inaccessible to us. At its origins, utilitarianism can be seen as profoundly intimate with the arguments and objects of natural law. We must question the latter in order to reach the original intentions of the first philosophers of public utility.

However, if we turn our gaze from this theory of natural laws toward modern moral philosophy, a fundamental difference immediately becomes evident. The table of contents is very different for each. Here we are dealing not only with a difference in rhetoric but also one of essence. The objects, methods, and scope of preutilitarian moral philosophy are different.

We are dealing with a very general problem, which relates to a sound understanding of the history of ideas in general, and so we shall permit ourselves a short digression. Contemporary moral philosophy, insofar as there is such a thing, is constructed around "arguments." These arguments may be considered either in relative isolation, depending on their supposed logical merits, or in their "context," whether social or historical. The problem is that when we question the classical texts in this way, we lose sight of what is the keystone for any far-reaching interpretation: namely that they are systematic. Not absolutely all of them and to the same extent, but many of them, at least those written with a theoretical, scholarly aim, are systematic in their structure and references. The classical and early modern texts, therefore, possess an architecture that should be taken seriously. To pick "arguments" from here and there risks becoming an enterprise that falsifies not only the meaning of the classical texts but also might cut off our access to the moral truth toward which they would lead us.

Once we settle on regarding the structure of the classical texts with the proper attentiveness, we cannot fail to observe how different it is to that of today's professional writings in ethics. Indeed, it is not at all clear whether the latter have such a structure or whether they follow any eminent model. In the case of the classical texts, the structure, usually visible in the table of contents, is different not only in terms of the treatment of subjects, but above all in their selection. Before we can estimate the significance of isolated "arguments," this differentiation in the discursive universe must be understood.

With this we have returned to our problem. For two centuries, certain subjects have either not been dealt with by modern moral philosophy or else have acquired a perfectly marginal status. In contrast to the debate about the right to punish, about which it could be said that only its contents have changed, it is clear that the entire debate about the right of sepulture has vanished from among the identifiable concerns of the ethical philosophers.

How did this come about? Does it have any notable philosophic significance? The right to sepulture was, as we have seen, one of those subjects which, from the classical viewpoint, could be formulated only in the language of natural law. The silence of modern utilitarianism and contemporary moral philosophy as a whole should not merely be construed as an indication that some of the traditional problems are "outmoded" or have somehow been resolved. On the contrary, this silence must in its turn be explained in order to understand both its meaning and possibility. By virtue of what reasons was the right to sepulture removed from the contents of modern ethics? This question leads us toward a horizon of more general meanings. If we understand how this removal came about, then we shall be able to understand some of the deeper forces and intentions that lie at the origin of our current table of moral priorities.

We must avoid thinking that only a mutation of sensibilities might explain the discretion with which this right has been treated since the end of the Enlightenment. The modern age is one in which a fascination for the morbid is an element of mass culture. The disappearance of the subject matter of sepulture betrays something other than an implausible cultural taboo. The decline of philosophical discussions of the extreme implications of the right to punish and to sepulture is possible only as a decline or transformation in the idea of natural law, of the province to which they belong. The body of the condemned, of the martyr, and the corpse are parts of a discourse about natural law, whose arguments must either be ignored or confronted in order to reach the modern position. Thus it comes about that the history of the origins of utilitarianism are inseparable from the forgetting or revision of the classical arguments surrounding corpses and funerary anthropophagy.

A justification of cannibalism based on utility appears sporadically as early as the ancient texts. Herodotus describes Indians who are nomads and eaters of raw flesh. When one of them falls ill, whether man or woman, he or she is killed by his or her relatives, thus demonstrating that it is a sin for so much meat to go to waste because of illness. The sufferer is killed even if he denies he is ill, which seems to prove that the attraction of an extreme dinner depends on reasons more profound than the merely utilitarian. They also kill their old folk, although not many reach an advanced age, because they are killed and eaten at the first sign of illness.[52]

Also dating back a long way are the first references that reveal the body and sepulture as having entered into contact with an illicit regime of profit and utility. In a chapter entitled "On the Violation of Tombs and Graves" in *Historia de Gentibus Septentrionalibus*, Olaus Magnus reveals that, under the pretext of treasure hunting or prospecting for saltpeter, graves are opened. Our parents and forefathers would pale to see such a thing, he observes. Even pagan barbarians have the custom of respecting human remains, allowing them to lie in the earth, whereas this is savagery worthy only of dogs. Likewise, Lafitau claims that the conquistadors, in their greed, profane the tombs of the Indians in order to seek treasure. The Indians implored them to take the gold but to leave the human remains in peace. Such things occur, Lafitau believes, because these peoples have an idea of the resurrection of the dead.[53] Canonic law forbids the dismembering of corpses. In 1299, *Detestande feritatis*, a bull issued by Pope Boniface VIII, condemned the practice of chopping up the dead in order to bury them in a number of holy places simultaneously, and also the practice of dismembering and boiling down corpses in order to separate the bones that were to be brought back from the Crusades. Such practices are said to inspire horror in the faithful and outrage the ears.[54]

The idea according to which human cadavers in themselves might possess a measurable economic value is relatively recent, probably no earlier than the late eighteenth century.[55] Of course, there was the relative exception of relics and medical dissection. The Middle Ages knew and even tolerated the traffic in relics, and veritable specialized gangs practiced theft of the latter. However, here we are dealing with something that transcends the fragment of human body; it was something by no means regarded as ordinary. It is the residue of divinity that suspends natural putrefaction, and this is what is significant. The modern age introduces the ordinary corpse into the circuit of value. In Britain, this evolution is tied to strides forward in medical anatomy, in circumstances in which there is a deficit in the supply of bodies, due to legal restrictions regarding the quota of corpses of criminals that could annually be appropriated by the surgical guild. In the eighteenth century, dissection is employed as a multiplier of capital punishment, to be decided by sentencing judges. The fear that sentences of dissection seems to have induced in the condemned does not primarily come from the idea that the body might appear at the Last Judgment in a dismembered state, but above all from the fact that hanging was reputed not always to be lethal.[56]

In such circumstances, under the pressure of progress, the state organizes a legal space in which the human corpse acquires a precise utility.[57] In the eighteenth and nineteenth centuries, acts of Parliament establish the rights of the medical profession relative to dissections and address the problem of the private traffic in human corpses conducted by organized groups of "resurrectionists." The first regulations were interpreted against a background of class hostility. After the first Law of Anatomy was published in 1828, pensioners in poorhouses were panic-stricken, believing that they were destined for dissection after death. They also believed that they were being forced to become cannibals, being served a "'Natomy Soup" made from human remains and animals such as cats and donkeys. In 1832, another law on anatomy established that the bodies of the poor rather than those of criminals were to be destined for dissection. This perception reveals the lower classes' fear of dissection.

The association of such operations with anthropophagy had now arrived on European shores. A hundred years previously, Dominican missionary Jean-Baptiste Labat noted in his *Journey of the Knight Des Marchais to Guinea, the Neighboring Islands and to the Cayennes* (1731) that the Negroes regarded the whites as cannibals, as they were otherwise unable to explain why the white doctors made recourse to dissection. Labat protests that it is a useful operation, because otherwise it would be impossible to know the reasons for the deaths of so many black slaves. The latter preferred to jump overboard into the sea or to die of hunger rather than end up, as they believed, in a land where there were public butchers of human flesh. As regards the origin of these rumors, Labat speculates that they were launched by the white rivals of the French.[58]

The anatomical model becomes interesting in this period not only because it is the vehicle of a scientific certitude, but also because it announces a moral truth. Descartes' *Passions of the Soul* is an attempt to construct a science of morals on anatomical foundations. In the *Treatise of Human Nature*, Hume compares the moral philosopher with the anatomist who dissects bodies.[59] There is "something hideous," he admits, in the kind of things that these present.

Once the scientific and ethical implications of anatomy have been established in the eighteenth century, the process of the nationalization of corpses makes its debut. The human corpse becomes a resource within a system of power and knowledge specific to the modern bureaucratic state. In order for this to occur, it is necessary that some of the old sensibilities should be excised. In one of the rare legitimizations of dissection from before the eighteenth century, that found in the *Petits traités en forme de Lettres*, La Mothe Le Vayer does not appeal to utility or to natural law in order to defend dissection, but to the moral virtues. Saint Francis of Sales could not have given more proof of his compassion for others than when he left his body to the surgeons, in order for it to be useful in their instruction. A century later, the article "Cadaver" in the *Yverdon Encyclopaedia* (1771) underlines the scientific gain. The opening of corpses is most advantageous for the progress of medicine, as atheist and materialist philosopher "Monsieur La Mettrie" is supposed to have argued: a superficial examination is not enough, the viscera must be rummaged. This depth is coupled with an annexation of the anatomical art to the authority of the state, as opposed to the authority of tradition. The survival of mankind and progress in the art of healing are objects of such importance for "well-governed" (*bien policée*) society, the article goes on to say, that the priests ought not to receive corpses for burial except from the hands of the anatomist. The ecstatic author exclaims that there are countless phenomena of which we are ignorant and which we might overlook forever, because only the frequent dissection of corpses could reveal them. The article concludes with an observation which reveals that one of the classic postulates of natural law is on the verge of being corrected. Humans are concerned with their own survival, the author argues. This is hardly surprising, especially given that this is a common thesis of natural law. However, the article argues that this imperative is neglected by society. The state now begins to impose itself as a support and agent of rights traditionally attached to the individual or to traditional groups.

Christian Wolff also establishes that dissection is necessary and justified if it is performed in order to enhance knowledge of the structure of the human body and to prevent or heal maladies. What results is knowledge of the perfection of the Creator as revealed in his works, which leads to His greater glory.[60] The dissection of corpses is permissible from the point of view of nature, just as it is permissible for us to prepare anatomical materials or skeletons. There is nothing in all this that goes against the honor due to humanity. However, for Wolff, this right has its limits, because its excess contradicts the right to burial. After we have finished dissecting, he argues, we must bury those parts we do not intend to conserve. The two principles of the right hereby divide the body, properly speaking, and apportion the parts. By way of conclusion, Wolff adds that it is under no circumstances permissible to dissect living human beings.

The justification of dissection is just one of the elements of the process that dissolves the corpse of natural law in the acid of public utility. Another is the discovery of the practical utility of human body parts. In the article "Skin" in the *Encyclopédie* (1751), we find a recipe for tanning human skin. The latter can be prepared "in the same way as the skin of quadrupeds" (*comme celles des quadrupédes*). All that is needed is a mixture of salt, vitriol, and alum, into which the skin is introduced, after having been cleaned of fat. Monsieur Suë, a Paris surgeon, "donated to the cabinet of the king a pair of shoes made from human skin using the above procedure, which did not at all destroy the pores."[61] The procedure has the advantage of producing a material "of a firm consistency, quite smooth on the exterior surface, although the striations that surround the mamillas . . . seem more deeply etched than in the natural state; the exterior surface is uneven and . . . slightly wooly, because leaflets of membrane inevitably remain [attached]."[62]

The great ingredient of cannibal pharmacology is, until the late eighteenth century, the mummy. Its allegedly curative virtues were discovered in late antiquity and from the Renaissance mummy (*mumia*) found its way in apothecary shops; it was used as powder in the composition of various drugs (often in combination with other exotic substances like urine or *castoreum*), supposedly useful against ailments like coagulation of the blood. A lucrative trade in Egyptian mummy flourished in the Mediterranean basin, the mummified bodies of virgins being especially valued.[63] The article on "Mummy" in the French *Encyclopédie* cautions against forgeries. Unscrupulous Jewish merchants from Venice and Lyon use cadavers of the poor, dried in furnaces with a mixture of myrrh and other substances.[64]

The final step is a legitimization of cannibal incorporation based on the principles of the modern science of utility. In *Recherches philosophiques sur les américains*, de Pauw reveals that, during the times of the Catholic League disturbances, in Paris there was such famine that people ate bread made of ground up human bones, "in order to rebel to the extreme" (*pour désobéir jusqu' à la extrêmité*) against the best of kings. This foodstuff is supposed to have provoked a stomach ailment that killed off those who ate it faster than the hunger it was meant to alleviate. This fact, which an Iroquois would read with horror in the annals of France, does not, however, prove the thesis of "venomous particles" (*particules venimeuses*) in the humors of the human body, de Pauw believes. If the Parisians had eaten bread made from the bones of other animals the results would have been exactly the same. The ambassador of Roman Catholic Spain, that bastion of reaction to the Enlightenment philosophers, is supposed to have been the one who indicated this food resource to the League sympathizers, but he was "a denatured political thinker and a bad physician" (*un politique dénaturé & un mauvais physicien*). For de Pauw, it seems, the problem is not that men became cannibals, but that they did not have a healthy diet. Bone-meal bread is not morally but rather gastronomically defective. Happily, technical progress opens up the possibility of human substance being included in the nutritive circuit. An apparatus named *Le Digesteur*, invented by "the celebrate Papin," would, for de Pauw, be the "true means of extracting innocent nourishment from bone substance."[65]

Dissection, preparation, and anthropophagy: this is the shadowy zone in the history of utilitarianism, where a discourse on the human corpse is woven, one which avoids or corrects that of theology and natural law. Only after utilitarianism succeeds in referring to this extreme object will it be able to impose itself as a complete doctrine of utility, which might describe the entire sphere of human activities. The monument of this will to theoretical incorporation can be found in University College London. It is the famous "Auto-Icon," prepared according to the last will and testament of Jeremy Bentham, who demanded that after his death his mortal frame should be coated in wax, dressed in his usual attire, and seated on a chair inside a glass case. One of his acquaintances recalled that the philosopher was interested in his scalp being prepared in the manner of the New-Zealanders, in other words the Maori cannibals. Bentham's will also stipulates that his personal friends and other disciples should gather once a year to commemorate the founder of the system of greatest happiness in terms of morals and legislation. His executor is to transport the display cabinet containing the mummy to the room in which they meet. Tradition adds that Bentham's mummy takes part at sessions of the committee, where, in the case of a ballot, he always votes in favor of the motion.

CHAPTER THREE

Creatures of Evil

Schedel, *Liber chronicarum*

A RITUAL OF TORTURE

THE MAJORITY OF POLITICAL PHILOSOPHERS, ancient and modern, agree that natural man is a weak being. The nature and source of this weakness is a disputed question, but it is beyond any controversy for most of them that man in the state of nature is a vulnerable, incomplete being. It now matters very little whether this state is understood as a species of animality or whether it is painted in the attractive hues of a rustic utopia. However he might be designated, as man-animal, solitary castaway, or noble savage, natural man is imagined as having an essential lack in relation to the beasts. On the ladder of Creation, the latter are above him through brute force, senses, instincts, and anatomy. Nature is, in a profound sense, a collection of dangers and challenges amid which the primitive leads an existence that is if not precarious then at least insular, almost improbable. Hume captures this idea when he argues, in the *Treatise of Human Nature*, that man is the being in whom the "unnatural conjunction of infirmity and of necessity may be observed in its greatest perfection."[1] Voltaire, in *Essai sur les Moeurs et l'Esprit des Nations*, claims that carnivorous beasts would have exterminated a large part of mankind if the latter had not united in a society.[2]

There is a certain reason why this kind of man should be viewed by philosophers as a weak creature. One of their fundamental concerns, if not primary concern, is the nature of political association. Put simply, the fundamental question is: What is a body politic? However, this question demands—at least within the horizon of the classical humanities— to be elucidated in relation to the purpose of political association. We understand what a thing is by perceiving what it serves. In politics, it hence results that we must establish what need the *polis* answers. In order to achieve this, the favored method is that of proposing a state in which man can be seen as not belonging to the political order, precisely in order to extract the latter's reason for being, its surplus of utility. This means that the theory of the nature of the body politic must contain an account of the formation of this body, setting out from the state of nature populated either with isolated individuals or prepolitical entities.

However, were natural man not a weak being, were he able to confront all other creatures (and eventually his savage fellow men) as an equal, then his motives for emerging from the state of nature would be hard to descry. Were primitive man a self-sufficient creature, who could endure the same as any other natural species, what then would compel him toward civilization, at least toward one understood as being different in its nature to groups of social animals? He is condemned to bear a kind of stigma that somehow separates him from all other beings, or at least from those—the majority—who clearly do not live in any kind of organized state, and which marks him out for a political destiny. The absence of society is visibly inscribed in the nature of natural man.

The variety of conceptions of prepolitical man's frailty can be reduced to a general principle. Man is seen by classical philosophers as a being beset by need. In the *Republic*, Plato establishes that needs are those things that obligate men to associate with one another in a *polis*. Within the great world of need we may discern, also in very general terms, two broad tendencies. Firstly, we have an idea of a social sentiment that is proper to man. Man seeks his fellow man, he desires his presence, and he feels a certain pleasure in the fact that another man is close. Even his vices and vanities require others in order to be satisfied. We are here dealing with an ancient concept, formulated by Aristotle, among others, and then made canonical by the authority of Thomas Aquinas. According to the *Politics*, he who lives alone is either an animal or a god, but not a man.[3] This is why man cannot quite simply remain isolated, as such a state is alien to his nature.

On the other hand, there is another, grimmer kind of need, to which we can appeal in order to unite the social body. In its simple data, this is the irresistible desire for self-perpetuation. Here, what is at stake is a set of passions different to that invoked by the supporters of sentimental sociability. At the center of these passions is fear. Natural man is seen as dominated by fear and its various gradations from shyness to terror. Fear is interpreted as a fundamental passion of primitive anthropology. The classic locus of this kind of argument is, of course, Hobbes. Fear isolates man from nature and other men, who constitute for him nothing but a threat, and encloses him inside a circle in which he becomes visible as an individual being. But in the same immediate fear there is a common passion that places man in relation with other men, elevates him to the rank of member of an as yet negative society. Fear, in this theoretical context, that of the discussion about the formation of the social body, can be reconstructed as a productive relation. Driven by fear, natural man seeks an accommodation with others, whence will ultimately result civil society. The history of the establishment of society is, for Hobbes and other philosophers of the body politic, written in the key of a condemnable passion from the viewpoint of an ethics of virtue but acceptable in the framework of a philosophy of nature.

The dialectical movement from weakness to the birth of civil society is described by Lord Monboddo with reference to anthropophagy. Man is by his nature food for wild beasts; man is the "common prey of them all." By contrast, the Scottish philosopher believes that carnivores "do not prey upon one another; by which I mean, not only that a lion does not prey upon a lion, but that he does not prey upon a tiger, or wolf, or any other carnivorous beast, though of less size or strength, unless perhaps in cases of extreme necessity." Man's only advantage over wild animals is his "superior sagacity," which impels him to invent civil society, the arts and "that great instrument of social life, Language."[4]

But this conception of the philosophers regarding the character of natural man is not the only one to be found in the anthropological discourse of the seventeenth and eighteenth centuries. The primitive man constructed by the philosophers of natural law coexists with another man of nature, who above all populates the texts of travelers and historians. The characteristic problematic of the latter is his uncanny courage in the face of death and pain. This virtue is displayed in what is a classic picture of the literature and histories of the New World; the ritual torture of prisoners of war, a cruel ceremony that is described against the backdrop of a species of the state of nature, peopled with natural associations (families, clans, tribes). In the absence of a sovereign government to preserve the peace, the Indian tribes are engaged in a perpetual war of all against all, in which captured warriors are tortured before falling victim to the cannibalism of revenge.

William Robertson, in *The History of America* (1777) describes how "the prisoners are tied naked to a stake, but so as to be at liberty to move around it. All who are present, men women and children, rush upon them like furies. Every species of torture is applied that the rancour of revenge can invent . . . by avoiding industriously to hurt any vital part, they often prolong this scene of anguish for several days."[5] This scene is then followed by one "no less shocking." The Americans frequently devour the victims of their cruelty. It is well known that the New World is full of cannibals, as is the case in South America, where the tribes "seem studious to attach the captives to life, by supplying them with every enjoyment that can render it agreeable." Subsequently, they dispatch the victim with a single blow and "the women seize the body, and dress it for the feast."[6] Guillaume-Thomas Raynal, in *Histoire philosophique et politique des établissemens & du commerce des Européens dans les deux Indes*, gives an even more graphic description: some scorch the flesh of prisoners with strips of burning canvas; others tear out their fingernails; others cut off their fingers, which they fry and eat before their eyes.[7] According to Philippe de Longvilliers de Poincy, former governor of the French possessions in the Caribbean, some cut off strips of flesh and apply hot spices to the wounds. After that, the prisoner is killed, chopped into pieces, cooked, and eaten.[8] The Indians regard the flesh as delicious, and the women lick the spits. The fat of the enemy is stored in jars, and they drip it into their sauces at festive meals, in order to prolong, as long as possible, their revenge. Virey also describes how the savages subject their captives to every imaginable torment.[9]

Charlevoix's *Histoire et Description Générale de la Nouvelle France* contains one of the most exalted descriptions of the ritual.[10] The prisoners are forced to pass between two rows of savages, who beat them with clubs. Once they arrive in the village, they are taken from hut to hut. At one hut their fingernails are torn out, at another a finger is chopped off. An old man flays their flesh to the bone; a child stabs them; a woman whips them until her arms drop down in exhaustion. After that, a council is held, and the prisoners are distributed to the warriors. The Iroquois never set prisoners aside for the public. Some are adopted, others are enslaved, but the majority of them are killed. Those who are destined to die are well treated at first. It might be said that they are being fatted in order to be sacrificed to the god of war. They give them the names of their dead relatives; sometimes they give them their daughters as wives. When the moment of sacrifice arrives, these wives are transformed into furies, who scream and invoke the name of the one they wish to avenge. The whole village then gathers, for this is the death sentence.

Father Lafitau describes how the Indians bite off their victim's finger and smoke it in their tobacco pipes, and they make the victim have a puff.[11] The prisoner is tortured with burning brands, after which the tribe eats his roasted flesh. Sometimes they make him a bark shirt, which they set alight.[12] Sometimes they scalp him and then pour hot ashes or boiling water into his head.[13] Lescarbot describes how prisoners' nails are torn out, and hot coals are then applied to the fingertips and to the virile member. After that, they extract the nerves from their arms, twisting them around sticks. In *Histoire générale des Antilles habitées par les françois* (1654), Jean-Baptiste du Tertre asserts that the most astonishing thing is the fury with which the women bite the prisoner. The Indians, he believes, take the flesh left over from the feast home, where they share it with their friends and relatives.[14] James Adair, a trader and writer who lived among the Indians between 1735 and 1775, admits that the Indians' prisoners are treated with appalling cruelty. Tethering the prisoner to a stake by his neck, "they fix some tough clay on his head, to secure the scalp from blazing torches." From time to time, during the "furious onset" with their torches, "they pour over him a quantity of cold water, and allow him a proper time of respite, till his spirits recover and he is capable of suffering new tortures." Then the punishment, "which is always left to the women," resumes. When the victim has been rendered insensate, he is scalped and chopped into pieces, after which they "carry off all the exterior branches of the body (pudendis non exceptis) in shameful, and savage triumph."[15]

Cruel tortures inflicted on prisoners of war, followed by orgiastic cannibalism: this formula seems invariable in the travel literature. What is interesting to note in this entire outpouring of cruelty is the attitude of the victim. Robertson describes how "when the fatal sentence is intimated to them, they receive it with an unaltered countenance, raise their death-song, and prepare to suffer like men." Even during the most unimaginable tortures, "the victims continue to chant their death-song with a firm voice, they boast of their own exploits, they insult their tormentors for their want of skill in avenging their friends and relations, they warn them of the vengeance which awaits them, on account of their death, and excite their ferocity."[16] Raynal offers a similar image, in which the "hero" goads his persecutors, sometimes for as long as a week, after which he dies without them extracting so much as a groan from him.[17] To prove strength in such situations is the noblest triumph for a warrior. If one of the victims shows fear, he is killed on the spot, as being unworthy of a manly fate. Lafitau claims that under torture the prisoner insults his adversaries for not knowing how to do their job.[18] Charlevoix relates that a warrior says to his captive: "Be brave brother, for you are going to burn!" The latter "coldly" answers, "That is well, I thank thee."[19] He is then tethered to a stake, so that he can circle around it. He sings his death-song, gives an account of his brave deeds, while insulting his tormentors and urging them not to spare him. The elated prisoners of the Indians dance and utter the names of those they have killed or burned in their turn, especially those known to their captives. The manner in which they endure the harshest tortures would suggest that they enjoy them. In *The Theory of Moral Sentiments*, Adam Smith presents the victim of ritual torture in a similar way: "While he is hung by the shoulders over a slow fire, he derides his tormentors, and tells them with how much more ingenuity he himself had tormented such of their countrymen as had fallen into his hands." He converses with the "spectators," who "smoke tobacco, and amuse themselves with any common object, as if no such matter was going on." According to Smith, the victim is so absolutely insensible in the face of pain that he talks with his tormentors "upon all indifferent subjects, inquires after the news of the country, and seems indifferent about nothing but his own situation."[20] Adam Ferguson describes how a prisoner begs to die by fire rather than "'stabs of your knife," so "that those dogs, your allies, from beyond the seas [i.e. the palefaces], may learn to suffer like men.'"[21]

It is not a question here of resistance to physical pain. The American Indian is extraordinary in that his conscience seems immune to the disquiet that accompanies anticipation of torture and death. Cornelius de Pauw describes, in *Récherches philosophiques sur les américains*, how the savages of the New World possess a kind of indifference toward life and are not disturbed by the proximity of death. De Poincy believes that the prisoner goes alone, unbound and joyous to the place of execution, and seems to desire nothing more than death. He boasts that he and his fellows have tortured those of the enemy tribe more. He promises even more terrible torments for those of his captors who fall prisoner in their turn.[22] Adair describes how, while being tortured with burning brands, "the suffering warrior is not dismayed; with an insulting manly voice he sings the war song!"[23] Likewise, du Tertre believes that the prisoner confronts his executioners with a serene and constant countenance, insults them and spits on them. In the chapter "Of Cannibals" in the *Essays*, Montaigne presents ritual torture as he knew it from the books of Jean de Léry and André Thévet. The prisoner of war is killed and eaten, but "during the two or three Months, that they are kept they always appear with a chearful Countenance; importune their Master to make Haste to bring them to the Test; defy, rail at them, and reproach them with Cowardice. . . . And 'tis most certain, that to the very last Gasp, they never cease to defy them both in Word and Gesture." Montaigne even quotes a song, in which the prisoner boasts how those about to eat him will be eating their own ancestors: "He bids them *come all, and dine upon him, and welcome, for they shall withal eat their own Fathers, and Grandfathers, whose flesh has serv'd to feed and nourish him. Those muscles*, says he, *this Flesh, and these Veins, are your own.*"[24] This idea is repeated by de Poincy and then du Tertre.

The first mention of this Indian ritual in the scholarly literature, to be found in the work of de Léry (1578), places it in the context of the tale of the Indians who marry their daughters to prisoners of war, so that they can fatten them and eventually kill and eat them. The women of the tribe wash and scrub the corpse until it is white, cleansing it, as the French author says, like a suckling pig. The widow of the deceased, he claims, is the first to eat of the flesh. Prolonged tortures are not mentioned, but de Léry is convinced that the prisoner is well entertained until the moment of his death. However, in the eighteenth century, the scholarly literature will reach the firm conclusion that prisoners are subjected to gruesome tortures, which they endure with extraordinary courage, before being devoured.

Resistance to torture is not always attributed only to the American Indians. It seems to have been a recognized characteristic of primitive man and of barbarians in general. In the *General History of Spain*, by Juan de Mariana, a scholastic author of the sixteenth century, we learn that the old Spaniards (the name whereby he designates the Basques) were coarse, had ferocious manners, and resembled beasts more than men. They were so secretive that not even the most gruesome tortures were able to make them divulge a thing that had been entrusted to them.[25] In *Sketches of the History of Man*, Kames speaks of the incredible courage in the face of death displayed by the inhabitants of the Celebes, one of whom suffered a tiger "to lick the blood from his face, without shrinking, or turning away his eyes."[26] Ferguson claims (and Montaigne also mentions a similar story) that the Muslims are immune to pain in certain situations: they lacerate their flesh in order to win the hearts of their loves, and then gaily go to them, with their blood streaming, in order to show that they merit their esteem.[27] However, the anthropophagous finale to the ceremony of prisoner torture appears almost exclusively as a custom of the savages of America.

THE EXALTATION OF PAIN

What is it that produces this astonishing insensibility in the victims? Climate would seem to be the most convenient suspect. Montesquieu supports this theory, in book 14 of the *Spirit of Laws*, in which he argues that northern climates diminish the sensibility in the exterior fibers of the body: "The cold air tightens the external fibers of our body; this increases their energy, and aids the return of blood from the extremities to the heart: it reduces the length of these same fibers; it thereby further increases their strength."[28] Thus "you have to flay a Muscovite to make him feel anything."[29] It is also Montesquieu who explains the contradiction between the natural cowardice of the inhabitants of India, caused by the heat, and their atrocious actions, their barbaric punishments: "The Indians are naturally lacking in courage. . . . But how can this be squared with their atrocious acts, their customs, their barbaric punishments?"[30] Their vivid imagination, set in motion by the heat, is excessive and generates thousands of ideas of which they are more afraid than death itself. However, the theory of climate is not employed by the authors who speak of Indian ritual, just as the possibility of the savage's indifference might be explained by a thesis of Cartesian origin popularized by Malabranche, as regards the insensibility of brutes, seems to have passed unobserved. The explanations advanced by the authors who describe this ritual seem not necessarily to be connected to the major topics of the philosophical anthropology of the day.

The standard answer, advanced in travel literature, to the question of the nature of Indian prisoners' indifference to pain and death, is that the

harshness of savage life hardens the body and character. Another answer, related to the first, is to ascribe the power of endurance to the notions of honor prized by warlike nations: "Animated by those ideas,
they endure, without a groan, what it seems almost impossible that
human nature should sustain. They appear to be not only insensible of
pain, but to court it."[31] Education and honor: this is a formula that lik-
ens the cannibal Indians to some of the heroic peoples of the Old World,
especially the Spartans. The eighteenth century above all marks a proliferation of positive images of the political order of the Roman Republic
and of Sparta. The scope of the writers who circulate the myths of
Sparta and Rome is to criticize the corruption of the morals of contemporary monarchies.[32] The savage anthropophagus is sometimes invoked
against the backdrop of admiration for the archaic virtues of a Stoic education. Lescarbot believes that the Indians train themselves to resist
pain by using glowing coals, the same as the Romans and Spartans.
Robertson describes the trials which a young man had to endure before
becoming a warrior and observes that hunting and ceaseless war accustom the savage to strategy and the virtues of patience and secrecy. Adam
Smith also believes "every savage undergoes a sort of Spartan discipline,
and, by the necessity of his situation, is inured to every sort of hard-
ship."[33] Voltaire also refers favorably to "pretended savages [prétendus
sauvages]" in relation to the Spartans: "These Canadians were Spartans
in comparison with the rustics who vegetate in our villages."[34] Montaigne and Pascal also mention a story in which a Spartan boy, who
made no sign that anything had happened when a burning coal fell into
his sleeve, was burned to the bone. This idea was developed by Lafitau,
who claims to have seen with his own eyes a child of five or six, who,
scalded with boiling water in an accident, sang his death-song in spite
of the pains he was suffering.[35]

The chapters on Indian ritual in travel literature are part of a nebula
of texts that, beginning in antiquity, glorify resistance to pain. Primitive
Christianity, in particular, promoted defiance of pain as a supreme duty
of the believer, as a sign of divine benevolence. The Acts of the Martyrs
were probably the first set of texts that circulated the obsession with indifference to pain. Saint Lawrence, tied to a spit and roasted over a low
flame, tells the Roman magistrate to turn him over because that side
was ready. After he had been subjected to the flames on both sides,
he then told the man of law that he was roasted (*Coctum est!*) and to
taste him to see whether he was better raw or roasted. The geography
of the ancients was another source for these histories. Diodorus Siculus
describes the ikthyophagi of Arabia: they have no mercy on those who
suffer, they strangulate women and children without caring, "and even

when they succumb to the most extraordinary tortures, they remain calm, looking only at their wounds and inclining their heads at each blow."[36]

Another popular genre, which also presents examples of bravado in the face of death and torture, is "gallows literature." Up until the nineteenth century, capital punishment was a public ritual, and the reactions of the condemned (real or imaginary) had an especial importance. Sometimes, they give proof of extraordinary bravado. Aristocrats are portrayed as confronting death calmly, an attitude dictated by the code of honor. But even common criminals could rise above their condition. In the England of the seventeenth century, hangings were the occasion for a kind of carnival, where the main protagonist of the play is presented as attempting to profit from his status in order verbally to settle his accounts with the authorities. Montaigne relates the story of a man in Denmark who was condemned to lose his head, but when offered his life if he would marry, he "refused it, by Reason the Maid they offered him, had hollow Cheeks, and too sharp a Nose"; "another told the Hangman, he must not touch his Neck, for fear of making him laugh, he was so ticklish."[37] In Germany, a man sentenced to death shrugs indifferently on the scaffold; another eats with gusto the plums that the prosecutor had bought him before his turn came to be executed.[38]

Finally, a third genre detectable in this area is the literature concerning the attitudes of philosophers in the face of death. For a long period of time, philosophy was closely associated with the art of dying (ars moriendi).[39] The philosopher demonstrates his nature on his deathbed: fearless in the face of the terrors of death and unyielding to superstition. Indeed, a chapter in Montaigne's Essays is entitled "To study Philosophy is to learn to die." In a letter, Seneca mentions a man who did not interrupt his reading of a book while the surgeon operated upon him, an example also repeated by Montaigne, next to that, also from Seneca, of the philosopher who mocked his executioners in order to excite their cruelty. Hobbes is supposed to have admonished the dying Selden, when the latter called for a minister: "What, will you that hath wrote like a man, now dye like a woman?" Of Leibniz, it is told that he died an atheist, preoccupied in his final moments with the solution of a mathematical problem. Examples of philosophical fortitude in the face of death and pain form a parallel to the Acts of the Martyrs of the church and were a fundamental component of the image of philosophy as an occupation that forms a superior character. The spectacle of someone dying like a philosopher while delirious in a lunatic asylum would have to wait for the admirers of Nietzsche in order to be established as a genuine possibility.

With Montaigne, we are dealing with a fusion of these genres. In the *Essays* he wonders "how many Ordinary People [*personnes populaires*] do we see led to Execution, and that not to a simple Death, but mixt with Shame, and sometimes with grievous Torments, appear with such Assurance."[40] On their final journey, they are busy "settling their domestick Affaires, recommending them to their Friends, singing, preaching, and diverting the People so much, as sometimes to sally out into Jests, and to drink to their Companions, as well as Socrates."[41] Thus, there is no need to be a saint or a hero in order to face death courageously, Montaigne seems to be saying. He presents a short catalogue of such democratic courage, for example: "One that they were leading to the Gallows, told them they must not carry him through such a Street, lest a Merchant that lived there should arrest him by the Way for an old Debt."[42] There are even women who furnish examples of insensibility: "Who has not heard at Paris of her who caused her Face to be flea'd, only for the fresher Complexion of a new Skin? There are some who have drawn good and sound Teeth, to make their Voices more soft and sweet."[43] (Montaigne is here perhaps inspired by an episode involving Saint Jerome, who was credited with having filed his teeth in order better to pronounce the Holy Scriptures in Hebrew.) Others swallow "Sand, Ashes, and do their utmost to destroy their Stomachs, to get pale Complexions." Others, in order to give themselves a "Spanish" waist, endure "Tweaking and Bracing, 'till they have notches in their Sides, cut into the very Flesh, and sometimes to the Death."[44] Among the examples found in the *Essays*, some are inspired by history and travel literature. In one kingdom, wives joyfully burn themselves alive on the same pyres as their dead husbands. The inhabitants of a town besieged by Brutus display a frenetic desire to die.

All these examples indicate, according to Montaigne, the force of opinion. We are dealing here with a Skeptical and Stoic subject. Montaigne describes how Pyrrho, the forerunner of the Skeptic school, during a storm at sea, pointed out an unconcerned piglet to the terrified passengers. More frequently than philosophical education, religious ideas are responsible for the serene acceptance of pain and death. How many have not been killed in the wars between the Turks and the Greeks rather than submit to be converted? How many European flagellants have not lashed themselves to the bone? However, it is also Montaigne who accepts that besides opinion it is also nature itself that dictates our reactions. All living creatures tremble in the face of pain. Pain is, in fact, more terrible than death itself, as proven by the fact that many people prefer to die rather than be tortured. But again it is the "imagination" which, in anticipating death, gives us a more lively sense of pain.

Stoic and Spartan, impassable in the face of death and vehement with his persecutors, the primitive has the capacity to become the vehicle for subversive arguments. Raynal exclaims: "Fanatics of all vain and false religions, praise you now the fortitude of your martyrs! The natural savage effaces all your miracles!"[45] This possibility seems even to have moved a religious writer such as Jean de la Placette, who, in his *Moral Essays* (1716), admits that some men may successfully endure tortures such as those inflicted on the martyrs only from purely human causes and without any assistance from divine grace. Here, for example, are the pagan philosophers who resisted torture or threw themselves into the flames (Calanus and Peregrinus). Likewise, the women of India immolate themselves on the death of their husbands; last, as proven by the savages of the Americas, who are impaled on spits and roasted alive when captured, and who do not cease to sing until the moment they give up the ghost. Hence, claims Placette, it results that what the church demands of its martyrs is not impossible.[46] Lafitau essentially exposits the same theory. Prisoners who comport themselves with such heroism may be compared with the martyrs of the primitive church. What was for the latter the effect of grace and of miracle, for the Indians is, however, the effect of their nature and the force of their spirit.[47] For Henry More, the courage of unbelievers, motivated by the desire for glory or by superstition, demonstrates what true virtue is capable of.[48] According to Virey, the attitude of the victims of the ritual proves that men of nature are "heroes." What virtue, he exclaims, in comparison with modern peoples, who are effeminate and enfeebled.[49]

In *Recherches philosophiques sur les américains*, de Pauw puts forward a strictly scientific explanation of the fortitude to confront death that manifests itself in some peoples. Speaking of the Indian women who throw themselves on their husband's funeral pyre, he claims that they are drugged by the Brahmans with a potion whose secret he has discovered following the researches he has carried out on the subject. The potion in question contains a "powerful infusion of saffron" (*forte infusion de safran*), which is more potent than opium and other narcotics. The fact that the women are drugged by a "strategem of the Brahmans and Fakirs" explains the supposed gestures of joy with which the unfortunate creatures cast themselves onto the pyre. The American Indians, speculates de Pauw, also employ a similar procedure, drugging their victims with tobacco.[50]

However, this physiological theory is the exception. The rule is the exemplary image of the savage as a Spartan. Of course, this is important in relation to the general tendency of exalting the "noble savage" to the detriment of the excesses of Western civilization. Nevertheless, it is probably more worthy of our attention to the extent that it circulates a fundamental criticism of a certain seventeenth- and eighteenth-century political philosophy. The image of the savage who defies death is opposed to the notion of the state of nature as expounded by the theories of the social contract and by a part of the school of natural law. At least in the version of Thomas Hobbes, natural man is an individual endowed with essential timorousness. He can, of course, be aggressive, but in the end his incapacity to abide permanent danger on the part of others makes him—like any other denizen of the state of nature—demand peace. It is the moment of the famous pact for the foundation of society, in which individuals transfer the right over life and death to a sovereign. The fear of death and the desire for prosperity, passions which have led them to associate, are also at work in the framework of civil society, in order to keep them obedient to a sovereign.

The savage who views death with a strange indifference is anything but the timorous man of the state of nature. Not even the most terrifying torments, or the prospect of being eaten alive, can cause this savage to play the role in which some theories of natural law have cast him: that of fearing death. He can be malleable in other respects. He is cruel, he lives in the state of a permanent war of all against all, he has no government, he is poor, superstitious, and does not seem inclined to natural sociability. In all these things, the jurists and philosophers of natural law may recognize their creature. However, as regards the fear of death, a supposedly natural and essential impulse in the scenario of the generation and maintenance of political authority, the savage has other ideas. His "imagination," a capital dimension of the classical analysis of the motivation of political action, does not seem to be disturbed by the proximity of death. If the authors of the eighteenth century manage to keep their distance from the implications of Hobbes's theory, which they view with visible discomfort, this is due to the fact that the geographical literature consistently circulates an image of natural man that partially differs from that of the political philosophers.

Nor is the cruel Indian quite acceptable for theories of Aristotelian inspiration, which postulate a species of social sense in man and which do not construct their arguments by setting out from the passion of fear. For example, the savage manages the performance of contradicting Aristotle's theory of courage. According to the latter, courage is something contrary to ferocity. There are numerous tribes that do not miss a single opportunity to kill and even eat people, among which can also be numbered two tribes around the Black Sea, argues Aristotle. However, of the latter, as well as of the other nations that live from piracy, he does not believe that we can say that they possess courage.[51] Likewise, the gourmand sociability of the Indians is not quite comparable to the ideal of *philia*, which is claimed by Aristotelian ethics to unite the members of a *polis*. Whether this savage will have been grasped as opposite also to this class of arguments is of lesser importance. Political Aristotelianism was in any case in decline during the period, surviving above all through the pious commentaries of German university jurists. The new political philosophy of the seventeenth and eighteenth centuries is sooner contractualist.

In relation to this political science and the theory of natural rights to which it is allied, let us pose the question regarding the relevance of the theory of the savage advanced by travel literature. The latter lends to the theory of the contract part of its empirical matter, but the case of cruel ritual shows us that this generosity has its limits. The literature about the savage is a radical philosophical-historical genre, systematic and separate, which discovers a natural man other than the creature of the speculative philosophers. The two genres did not necessarily collide, but they each delimited their own space. This situation did not remain without consequences for the modern theory of the state of nature and the contract. Its capacity to present itself as a valid historical reconstruction was handicapped by this alterity of travel literature. Indeed, if the savage is as the travelers describe him, then it means either that the theory of the state of nature is erroneous, at least in some of its givens, or that the savage is not in a state of nature. The first variant implies a reconsideration of the relevance of the states of nature and of political association that have thence arisen. The second possibility materially impoverishes the theory of the contract and of natural right by depriving it of what might have been an ideal illustration of the state of nature.

The difficulties raised by the anthropology of the primitives can be avoided if the state of nature and the contract were sooner hypothetical situations, mental experiments. This is what David Hume recommends to the philosophers in *The Treatise of Human Nature*: "The state of nature, therefore, is to be regarded as a mere fiction, not unlike that of the golden age which poets have invented."[52] This concept, believes Hume, can be allowed only as "a mere philosophical fiction." From Kant down to Gauthier and Rawls in the twentieth century, this is the dominant interpretation of the theory of the contract. In this case, however, it diminishes its explicatory force, because it is no longer a reconstruction of the history of society. It is known that in the eighteenth and early nineteenth centuries, it was violently criticized, especially in England, in favor of a "historical" approach to political rights. What is now clearer is how it came to be vulnerable to such a critique, since from the beginning it was a theory not only of a hypothetical state, but also of a real state (albeit one also derivable as a logical hypothesis based on analysis). For a theory that is pressured into redefining itself only as a study of ideal conditions, travel literature can no longer function merely as a confirmation of the idea of the historicity of the sate of nature.

Within such a shift in the topography of human knowledge, the literature of the savage cannot in its turn remain unaffected. Indian ceremonial torture also poses problems for the new formulae of political science, which need to be neutralized or ignored, in the circumstances in which the ethics of Spartan republicanism or the logic of natural rights are no longer compatible with the spirit of these new sciences. This is why anthropophagy is an ingredient in the recipe of the victors' celebration whose presence begins to be questionable. In Charlevoix's book, we meet the case of a murderous orgy, described in minute detail, up to the moment when the prisoners are killed and burned. After the "crime," the tribe passes the night in revelry, but we do not find out whether the feast included human flesh. It is possible that this may have been an oversight: ultimately, Charlevoix does not hesitate to present numerous cases of cannibalism. However, Adam Ferguson, in *The History of Civil Society* (1767), mentions the ritual and the savages' phenomenal resistance to pain, without revealing that it culminates in a cannibal feast, perhaps because he believes that the majority of Indian prisoners did not end up being tortured but were rather adopted by the families of the victorious tribe and "came to share in all the privileges of a citizen."[53] Nor does Smith mention anthropophagy, although we have seen that he was familiar with the literature on the ordeals of the American Indians. The intervention of de Poincy occurs within other coordinates. He does not deny the presence of the cannibal, but he prepares the terrain for a minimization of the role of torments. According to him, the Caribs were formerly wont to torture their prisoners of war; but now they prefer to slay them with a single blow.[54] The case of Adair is also instructive, because here it is clear that the absence of the cannibal from the cruel ritual is intentional and is effectuated against the background of a selective reading of the classical sources. A brave warrior confronts his executioners, Adair informs us, telling them that he has tortured and slain many of their relatives in his turn, and how his nation "will force many of them to eat fire in revenge of his fate."[55] Of course, Montaigne's *Essays*, whence he may have taken this story, refer to the consumption of human flesh, a detail that does not at all fit with Adair's image of the American Indians.

But the most important inversion of philosophical perspective occurs at the general level of the general significance of savage ritual, a movement that heralds the evisceration of its profound meaning and its transformation into a satirical portrayal. The imminent torture of prisoners offers Voltaire occasion to mobilize a set of merely bourgeois passions. His novel *Candide, or Optimism* (1759) is known as a parody of Leibniz's idea of the best of all possible worlds. However, it also contains an episode whose theoretical content is well elucidated by its protagonists. Candide is captured by cannibals together with his servant Cacambo. Candide begs the latter to explain to the savages "how frightfully inhuman it is to cook people, and how little Christian" (*quelle est l'inhumanité affreuse de faire cuire des hommes, et combien cela est peu Chrétien*). Cacambo is evidently not convinced that his master's arguments will get very far with the cannibals, and so he makes recourse to a very creative translation:

> Sirs, said Cacambo, you reckon that today you will eat a Jesuit; that is very well done; nothing is more just than to treat one's enemies thus. In effect, natural law instructs us to kill our neighbor, and it is thus that things are done all over the world. If we do not exercise our right to eat him, it is because we have something else to put on the table; but you do not have the same resources as us; certainly, it is better to eat one's enemies, than to abandon the fruits of one's victory to the crows and ravens. But, Sirs, you do not wish to eat your friends. You think that you are going to put a Jesuit on the spit, but it is your defender, it is the enemy of your enemies you are going to roast.[56]

Our philosopher escapes from the cannibals' cauldron at the price of unbelief, justified, by a sophisticated irony, by the arguments of modern natural law. Cacambo shows the savages that his master has killed a Jesuit, and they find this discourse "très raisonnable." On this occasion, there will be no martyr, for the age of rustic Stoicism has passed.

THE DECLINE OF THE MONSTROUS RACES

Are cannibals human beings? That some humans have eaten the flesh of other humans is a fact that no one denies. However, the anthropophagy that historians recount is more often than not particular, the product of extreme circumstances: hunger, fury, religious enthusiasm. The individual must somehow leave the bounds of his species in order to touch forbidden nourishment. Having become a cannibal, he does not drag his own species behind him. As ordinary nourishment, human flesh seems intended for other species of creature. Ancient, medieval, and early modern sources tell us of savage nations of anthropophagi, who are described as collections of strange beings, hybrids between animal and man.[57] This step is explainable: only a race of monsters could lead an existence so alien to the rules of human life, and only for such a people could the rule of nature be inverted.

The typical image of the cannibal-monster was that of the cynocephalus. The first references to fantastic dog-headed peoples living in Asia date from the pre-Socratic period.[58] They then come to inspire the medieval imagination. Marco Polo discovers, on an island, anthropophagi with dog's heads. Columbus is the first to mention the presence of man-eaters in the New World, whom he claims have dog's heads—an idea adopted from Pliny, probably via a confusion with the Latin term *canis*.[59]

In their fight against superstition, the Enlightenment philosophers reject the idea that there are natural species of cannibals. Voltaire, in the *Essay on Morals*, claims that the existence of monsters is not impossible: "In hot countries apes have subjugated maidens." According to Herodotus, continues the philosopher from Ferney, in Egypt, a woman coupled with a goat in public. From this abominable union it is possible that monstrous beings were born, but "they have not influenced the human species, because, being like mules, which do not multiply, they were unable to denature other races."[60] In the article "Flesh" in the *Yverdon Encyclopaedia*, we read of Negroes in Guyana who possess the physiognomy of tigers and who are anthropophagous by instinct. When one of them is present on the slave ships, he rends the other prisoners. This might be surprising were it true, but it is contradicted by many persons whose authority is greater than that of M Roemer, comments the author of the article. Other scholars believed that anthropophagy was explicable based on variations in the teeth. Saint Jerome claims that Scottish anthropophagi have two rows of teeth. Thus human species with more teeth than others are supposed to be "carnassial" (Tartars, Chinese, Syrians). However, the most enlightened travelers have not encountered this phenomenon. It is true that in Matamba and in the Congo, in some tribes of cannibals, there was a custom of mutilating the teeth, which caused some superficial travelers to believe that the taste for human flesh comes from a multiplication of teeth, the author concludes.

Skepticism concerning the existence of monsters is not wholly unknown before the eighteenth century. A papal emissary to China in the fourteenth century argues, with reference to the Asiatic monsters described by travelers: "The truth . . . is that no such people do exist as nations, though there may be an individual monster here and there."[61] But doubt does not become a constant exercise until modern authors. It flows not only from a more critical observation of reality but also, and above all, from a theoretical viewpoint for which monstrosity becomes suspect against the backdrop of an integral philosophy of nature and society.

In the sixteenth century, Ambroise Paré, one of the fathers of modern surgery, had defined monsters as "things that appear against the course of nature" (it is true that some of the causes which, according to him, lead to the appearance of monsters are perfectly natural, for example, blows suffered by pregnant women).[62] However, in *De cive*, Hobbes turns the articulation of monstrosity with nature into a contingent relation. For Hobbes, what constitutes a monster is primarily a problem of the definition of terms, and the right to define legal notions is, according to him, the exclusive domain of sovereign authority. The moral monster is not therefore a matter for the competence of natural science. It is the state that decides who is a monster: "If a woman should give birth to a baby of unwonted shape, but the law forbids the killing of a human, the question arises of whether the newborn baby is human. It must therefore be asked, what is a human? No one doubts that it is the commonwealth that shall decide, and this without taking account of the Aristotelian definition, that man is a rational animal."[63] Why exactly the state should discount Aristotle is not entirely clear, but we may suppose that the latter is no longer needed now that the state has the more pragmatic theories of Hobbes.

The consequence of this critique is not the disappearance of the monster. During the Enlightenment, teratological galleries will remain an important category of the imagination. However, the monsters of modernity do not possess the same radical alterity of their classical and medieval predecessors but are rather the excrescence of an almost domestic world, mere deviations from the figures of normality. The sciences of physiognomy and criminology begin to describe, instead of sinners against God and nature, a constellation of degenerates, such as rapists. If, at the beginning of the nineteenth century, rape was (with some exceptions) a minor category of the common offences recognized by civil law, by the end of the same century we are already faced with the irruption of the type of the pathological rapist into the social imagination. The standard description: small in stature, robust, anomalies of the nose or genital organs, limited in intelligence, cranial deformations, an inveterate gambler. In the same period, another durable figure of fear appears: that of the serial killer.[64]

Among the exotic race of moral monsters, Devil worshippers occupy a place apart. In Christian iconography, the Devil was long the principal devourer of humans. Paintings of the Last Judgment depict sinners devoured by Hell, which is represented as an insatiable maw spewing flames. Alongside the demons, the worshippers of the Devil also take part in this monstrous feast. Marco Polo continually mentions idolatry when he refers to aberrant customs, among which is cannibalism.

America was above all the continent where the Devil was worshipped. Jesuit missionary José de Acosta presents the Incas and Mexicans as worshippers of Satan, who practice a cult that is a kind of inverted Christianity. In Mexico, there are monasteries of virgins dedicated to the Devil, where maidens are reared for sacrifice.[65] Discovering the rituals of the Aztecs, the Spaniards no longer have any doubt that they worship Satan, in honor of whom, as Acosta reveals, they shed infinite amounts of blood. Commenting on these accounts, Henry More asserts: "So *despightfully Cruel and Tyrannical* has the *Rule of the Devil* been in the New-found Pagan world." The peoples of Guyana and "other adjacent parts" not only sacrifice humans, "but some of them after feed on the sacrifice." In Florida, the Devil appears to them and "complains that he is thirsty: But nothing quenches his thirst but the bloud of men." In Peru, two hundred children were sacrificed at the coronation of the king. In Mexico, a boy or girl is drowned "to keep the Gods of the Lake company." In Mexico, "there is one nasty piece of Cruelty . . . which was the flaying of a Slave, and apparelling another man with his skin, who was to go dancing and leaping through all the houses and marketplaces of the City to beg money for the Idols; and they that refused to give, he was to give them a slap on the face with the bloudy corner of the skin."[66]

Belief in Satanic kingdoms makes More almost an exception among the philosophers and travelers of the late seventeenth century, when even in the New World the Devil seems to lose his appetite for human flesh. In Thomas Gage's book about his journey to New Spain (1648), the Aztec religion is described in terms that employ the traditional and visual symbolism of the Antichrist. An Aztec temple is built of the skulls of prisoners of war, a horrendous sight. However, there is not a word about cannibalism in this context. Describing another Aztec temple, Gage reveals that there an idol was discovered, made of the seeds of plants cultivated in that land and mixed with the blood of children and virgins, whose breasts are opened with a knife to extract the heart, which is then given as an offering to the god. After that, the idol is broken into pieces. The Aztecs then set about making another, but not before distributing pieces of the first to the people. This passage is dictated by a theory that circulated in the seventeenth and eighteenth centuries, which claimed that the anthropophagy of some of the nations of the Indies took merely symbolic forms. One example is de Pauw's work on the American Indians. The Peruvians, he claims, no longer make human sacrifices, but only draw off a little blood from a child, which they then offer to their god. This proves that, although they were originally anthropophagi, now they are civilized.[67]

After discovering a footprint on his island, Robinson Crusoe thinks that the Devil may have arrived to terrorize him. After rational reflection, he rejects this possibility as "inconsistent with the Thing itself, and with all the Notions we usually entertain of the Subtilty of the Devil." It must, he goes on, be a case of a "some more dangerous Creature," which is to say savage cannibals.[68] During the Enlightenment, the cannibal thus acquires one of the attributes of the Devil, that of being the incarnation of extreme evil. As for Satan, he will not survive the criticisms of the philosophers for long. Hobbes, in *Leviathan*, is one of the first to cast demonology into doubt, while, according to *The World De-witched* (1691), by Balthasar Bekker, there are few who might still be inclined to believe in his existence, at which point the representatives of the diabolical lose considerable influence over the learned imagination.[69]

For modern man, the monster is transformed from an ontological into a social or medical problem, and perceived in a minor key. Describing the "cyclops" brought into the world by a woman in 1755, a learned member of the Berlin Academy succinctly summarizes this new sensibility: "The generation of monsters by the human species is not such an extraordinary thing."[70] In *The Principles of Natural Law*, Burlamaqui allows the existence of moral monsters (*monstres de l'ordre moral*) but argues that these are very rare. In any case, he goes on, the fact of their existence has no theoretical consequences.[71] The coup-de-grace will be dealt by Johan Friedrich Blumenbach's *De Generis Humani Varietate Natura* (1775), which sets out to prove, from a scientific viewpoint, the unfoundedness of tales about monsters. According to Blumenbach, natural causes are sufficient explanation: what people have regarded as monsters were nothing more than normal humans, but afflicted with various diseases, such as skin conditions.[72]

From having been a moral category, the monster begins more and more to be perceived as an aesthetic category in the modern era. In *Émile*, Rousseau argues that modern man cultivates monstrosity. However, it is a domesticated monster to which he refers, more bizarre than terrifying, a mere deformity, such as garden plants or selectively bred dogs.[73] Contemplation of such creatures produces pleasure, not the anguish aroused by incursions of murderous races from beyond the bounds of civilization.

THE ANTHROPOPHAGOUS MENAGERIE

At the close of the seventeenth century, the cynocephalus is replaced by the orangutan at the limits of human identity. Philosophers and travelers are fascinated by the new beast, discovered in Java, which is suspected of being a kind of human, possibly the wild man spoken of by the sources of antiquity and theories of the state of nature.[74] The confusion that reigns in connection with this creature is perfectly illustrated by Cardinal de Polignac, who, on seeing an orangutan in a cage, addressed it as follows: "Speak, and I shall baptize thee!" In the *Essay on the Intellect*, Locke had already announced that a rational monkey would be part of natural law, exactly the same as a man.[75]

Intrigued by the possibility that this being might not be a monkey but rather the incarnation of primitive man, Rousseau inserts, in the *Discourse on the Origin of Inequality*, a long dissertation on the human race, in which he also speaks of the orangutan. He repeats a text from the *History of Voyages* about the orangutan of the East Indies, where we read, among other things, that they feed on fruit and never consume human flesh. Thus primitive man was not a cannibal. Rousseau is skeptical about those passages in the descriptions of travelers that do not agree with his image of natural man as a pacific creature. These travelers, he says, have not observed the facts carefully. At one point they write that orangutans attack the blacks who try to cross the forests where they live, and at another point they say that they do no harm to humans. More observations are necessary, Rousseau concludes. The "experiment" he allusively proposes, inspired by a passage about Buffon's ass, is that of crossing a man with an orangutan.[76]

Virey adopts from Rousseau the ideas as regards the similarity between primitive man and the orangutan, adding a dissertation on the classical sources of the hypothesis that the first humans were, like monkeys, frugivorous. According to Virey, man has been constituted by nature in such a way as to eat above all else vegetables.

Monboddo is one of the few Enlightenment philosophers who believes in the existence of monstrous races. "That there are men with tails," he asserts in *Of the Origin and Progress of Language*, "is a fact so well attested that I think it cannot be doubted."[77] They have recently been seen by a traveler to Nicobar, "where they act together in concert, particularly in attacking elephants."[78] Similarly, travelers to the South Seas have described a people "who had the nails of their fingers about an inch long, which served them for offensive arms."[79] On the New Guinea coast, there is a nation that use their teeth "as an offensive weapon; for, we are told, they bite those they attack, like dogs."[80] Nevertheless, for Monboddo, cannibalism does not spring from natural instinct, but is the work of education. This, he believes, is proven by the fact that beasts of prey do not eat their own kind.

Another incarnation of the wild man, which the Enlightenment public discovers in the very midst of Europe, is the wild child. The first celebrated case is that of Peter, discovered in Hamelin in 1724.[81] He was immediately regarded as a specimen of natural man by authors such as Daniel Defoe, in *Mere Nature Delineated* (1726), and then by Lord Monboddo, who, in 1784, considered him "a living example of the state of nature." In the notes to the *Discourse on the Origin of Inequality*, Rousseau displays a keen knowledge of a number of cases of wild children.[82] In 1755, naturalist and explorer Charles Marie de la Condamine publishes his observations on a wild girl found in a forest in France.[83] The classic case of the wild child is that of Victor of Aveyron, discovered in 1800. He appeared to be eleven or twelve years of age, walked upright, and was wearing the tatters of a shirt. But here any similarity with a human ended. Victor could not talk, but emitted only cries. In spite of the best efforts of the pedagogues and physicians of the day, he could not be accommodated to a human existence. As soon as he was discovered, he was treated by journalists and philosophers as a human in the state of nature. Having become a celebrity, the child was exhibited to the curious and even presented in the salon of Madame de Récamier. In his work from the Year 10, Virey includes a lengthy appendix on Victor, where he advances an argument inspired by Rousseau's *Émile*: this wild child ate little flesh, which would demonstrate, contrary to Helvétius, that man is by nature frugivorous rather than carnivorous. Not all the literature on wild children seems to favor this thesis. La Condamine argues that the little wild girl he saw could not for a long time break her habit of eating raw flesh and even living animals, whose blood she would suck. She is supposed to have hunted by sitting hidden in a tree and then jumping upon animals passing below.[84]

The wild child is an alternative to the robust and fearsome primitive cannibal. Once discovered, natural man will come to be understood more as a child whose development has been retarded than as a wild beast. This is an idea prepared by the speculative theory of the state of nature. Even before the eighteenth-century cases of wild children, Hobbes had said that the man of the state of nature was a "robust child." In *Principes du droit naturel* (1751), Burlamaqui asks us to imagine a child raised alone in the wilderness: "He would undeniably be the most wretched of all animals. We should see in him only weakness, ignorance and barbarity . . . and he would ever be in danger of perishing from hunger, cold, or in the jaws of a wild beast."[85] In another passage, he argues that such a child would be almost incapable of providing itself with those things necessary for survival; it is true, he adds, that on this occasion, the child would be "ferocious." In an influential report read before the Academy of Science in Paris, 1745, La Condamine also presents a somber picture of natural man, as represented by the American

Indians. Stupid, lazy, concerned only with the present moment, "they grow old without emerging from childhood, whose defects they conserve their entire lives . . . we cannot view without humility how man abandoned to simple nature, deprived of education and society, differs so little from a wild beast."[86]

The presence of the wild child thus upturned the terms of a possible relation between nature and culture. Races of savages were a threat to civilization or at least a dramatic demonstration of its limits. In distinction to the latter, the young, solitary savage reveals only the absence of society and its institutions, whose necessity is interpreted as society's duty to the savage part of the individuals of which it is comprised.

The disappearance of narratives about monstrous races and then those about natural man leaves in its wake two simpler representations. The first is that of the wild child, a creature lacking only in education and the company of other humans in order fully to be a part of humanity. The second is that of the animal, who, from the nineteenth century onward, will monopolize the space of anthropophagy in the natural state.

Here, it is not a question merely of the fact that some animals feed on human flesh. In itself, this is a common fact. However, at the dawn of the modern age, the animal becomes a participant in the great order of natural law. Sometimes, this translates into juridical responsibility for the beasts.[87] In the Middle Ages, there were cases in which animals were brought before the courts, tried, and sentenced. As late as the Napoleonic wars, in Hartlepool, the townsfolk executed a monkey, the sole survivor of a shipwreck, whom they suspected of being a French spy.[88] Some philosophers wonder not only whether humans have the right to eat the flesh of animals, but also whether animals have any right to eat the flesh of humans. For Pluche, the providential order explains the existence of carnivores. If animals died without being buried, he speculates, then the air would become fetid and infect us. This is why God created carnivores: "We may rightly name them a living *cloaca*, animal graves, which seek out and swallow all that is dangerous to us in excess." From argument to argument, Pluche ends up explaining anthropophagy. These beasts also eat us, and this happens because the Creator wished man to remain alert, wary of "surprises," and not indolent.[89]

The wolf was for a long time the common protagonist of anthropophagy. Cruel and sly, the wolf is more than a beast; it is, to use Jean de la Fontaine's expression, "the common enemy." To the wolf is connected not only an amorphous universe of fear. It is, perhaps more than any other creature apart from man, a social creature. The wolves that attack Robinson Crusoe in France after he has escaped from the island of cannibals are organized "all a Body, most of them in a Line, as regularly as an Army drawn up by experienc'd Officers."[90] The idea that wolves eat one another is commonplace. It appears in Aesop and Aelian, among others. The latter describes an elaborate ritual. In times of hunger, the wolves form a circle and chase one another. As soon as one of them grows dizzy and breaks the circle, the others fall upon it and eat it.

The wolf is also associated with rabies. A fatal disease before Pasteur, rabies was reputed to cause anthropophagy, as in that incident where a host served his guests with pork from a pig that had been bitten by a rabid dog: all those that ate of the "envenomed" meat became rabid, and then bit and rent each other.[91] Finally, the lycanthrope, that hybrid of man and wolf, is well known for its appetite for human flesh. In the sixteenth century, Jean Bodin, a great specialist on the subject of witchcraft, argues that there is a criterion that allows us to distinguish infallibly between genuine wolves and "diabolic lycanthropy." While the real wolf attacks sheep, the *loup-garou* has a predilection for human flesh. The courts were to take note, establishing burning at the stake for lycanthropy.

From the second half of the eighteenth century, the status of the wolf diminishes. The wolves that attack Baron von Münchausen in Poland jump over the man and fall directly on the sleigh horses. In the age of colonialism, other wild beasts replace the anthropophagous wolf. What distinguishes them from the wolf is that they are more primitive. They do not bring with them the disquieting mythology of the wolf's sociability, but rather are wild creatures with a taste for human flesh.[92] Reigning over all these beasts is the tiger. There now appears a hunting literature about feline man-eaters, and English aristocrats and officers outdo each other in collecting trophies of Indian tigers legendary for their number of human victims. Reduced to the level of pure animality, in the nineteenth century natural anthropophagy begins to be nothing more than the object of bloodthirsty entertainment.

The decline of the monstrous races, the disappearance of the Devil and of those tribes that worship him, the infantilization of natural man, and complete animalization: these are shifts whose effects make themselves felt within the theoretical sphere. At first, the elimination of monsters from the anthropophagous equation contributes to a consolidation of natural law. As long as cannibal tribes have a separate nature of their own, they do not necessarily rest under the same law as other nations. The universality of natural law cannot therefore be assured except on condition of the demonstration of a common nature. Only after the philosophers discover that anthropophagi are ultimately humans too can anthropophagy become a touchstone for natural law in general. And only after the massive fact of anthropophagy, which calls into question elementary notions regarding natural law and the nature of political association, can natural law constitute itself as a universal science.

Indeed, to the extent that natural law is a science of man, then at its origin rests the question regarding what this being is, or what he ought to be, by nature. If mankind is a collection of moral species, whose borders with animality or with the diabolical are permeable, then natural law can only reveal itself as a practical science, a collection of cases, not as a universal, rational, and deductive science, the ideal of the modern philosophers. It is only after mankind is discovered to be a universal genus that a true science of its law can be elaborated. Paradoxically, the latter is constructed, contrary to the modern philosophers' pretensions to originality, by setting out from classical cases. But the construction of a deductive science of man that would include such cases runs up against the fundamental alterity of anthropophagous tribes and of the legions of lycanthropes, devils, and social animals. In relation to the latter, the only natural law that can be conceived is one understood, in the sense given by Ulpian, as something common to man and beast, and eventually to hybrid and fantastic species, but not a universal science of the rights and duties of man qua man. Only after the nations of monsters have been either eliminated or elevated to the status of humans can anthropophagy appear as a problem wholly capable of being formulated by the theory of the natural rights of man. It is not merely a coincidence that the modern science of natural law was formed at the same time as the formation of modern perceptions about cannibalism.

However, it is also this evolution in the modern perception of cannibalism that then raises problems for natural law. This occurs because its main protagonist, natural man, begins to have less and less in common with the being around which some of its central cases have been constructed. Together with the simplification of the imagination signaled by the disappearance of the monstrous races, the wild child and the carnivorous animal are the extremes between which the image of the anthropophagus will dissolve, along with the science for which it was the messenger.

THE NATURAL CRIMINAL

As we know him from our own times, the natural criminal is someone who is mentally ill. Sensationalist journalism, the science of criminal psychology, and the imagery of popular culture present a modern anthropophagus who is, in essence, mentally alienated. Demented or schizophrenic, he is perceived above all in the image of the serial killer.

The consumption of human flesh is an irrational obsession, a perverse pleasure, in short, part of the delirium.

The figure of the criminal-anthropophagus raises considerable problems when he is evaluated against the background of the history of moral thought. An incarnation of anomie, he cannot by definition be the subject of an ethical discourse to coincide with the dynamic of his nature. He can, at most, be the object of a science of the good, but not as an agent of the latter. With the psychopath, philosophy has ceased to enunciate the moral truth of anthropophagy as natural inclination.

This silence must be explained in its sources and significations. It is a restriction of the field of moral philosophy that must either be legitimated or denounced. Before abandoning the cannibal to the criminologists and journalists, let us meditate for a moment on the fact that this gesture means that we must detach ourselves from an entire philosophical science of good and evil. In doing so, we enter the space of the sciences of the modern public, for which the anthropophagus-criminal is a clinical rather than a moral case. Anthropophagy may, of course, be of interest to moralists by its implications (the justness of society's reactions, the need for therapy) but not by its nature. The discourse on criminal cannibalism is, in principle, merely a discourse about madness.

The amoral identity of the cannibal psychopath is not a product of classical or modern moral philosophy. It is rather the result of their decomposition, at the end of the eighteenth century. In the nineteenth century, physicians and sensationalist writers will discover a type of criminal whose arrival had not been announced by the speculations of philosophers and theologians. He is, in essence, mentally ill. Coming from beyond moral philosophy, he is not recuperated by the latter as its agent.

The birth of this monster spurned by philosophy is significant precisely because it signals the elimination from the field of moral science of a series of subjects to the exclusive benefit of the madness/anthropophagy binary. However, whence does it derive its epistemological force? How did madness manage to annex the creature of natural liberty that was the cannibal?

Until the late eighteenth century, the cannibal and the madman were distinct personages. Madness, understood as a clinical category, does not figure among the reasons retained by philosophers and travelers in order to explain the diffusion of cannibalism. In historical accounts and judicial proceedings, the figure of the demented cannibal occasionally appears. However, the latter probably vehiculates a record of his own, because he is not the object of a systematic and separate science. The madman is a rare figure and thus it is problematic to capture him in a discourse other than that of the collection of oddities.

Until the appearance of positive psychology, madness opens toward cannibalism in two situations. The first is that of diabolic influence. This is an appendage to madness rather than a part of it. In court cases, anthropophagy is one of the signs of witchcraft. Numerous treatises on witchcraft and demonology mention anthropophagy among the gravest sins of the witches and sorcerers. In *De la démonomanie des sorcerers*, (1580), Jean Bodin claims that they murder children, especially unbaptized infants, after which they boil them in order to drink their humors and flesh. They consume the flesh of children,

> and of course drink their blood. . . . But one sees that it is a vile belief the Devil puts into the hearts of men in order to make them kill and devour each other, and destroy the human race. . . Now murder, according to the law of God and the laws of men, merits death. And those who eat human flesh, or have others eat it, also deserve death: as for example, a baker in Paris who made a business of making pies from the flesh of people hanged. He was burned, and his house razed to the ground.[93]

The second situation is that of the mad sovereign. It is a classical maxim that the perversion of high office leads to the most atrocious deviance. However, it is not madness as such, but rather sin that can be read behind the degradation of the raving king. The madman and the latter are contiguous at only one point, inasmuch as they have both lost their way and are hurtling into the void.

The cannibal may therefore have lost his mind, but the madman does not become a cannibal merely under the impulsion of his delirium. The anthropophagus is not one of the species in the garden of madness. He is the child of Sin. As a rule, in the classical texts, we are dealing with the mere lack of any connection between these two categories. But even when madness is discussed as a possible cause of anthropophagy, the scholars declare themselves skeptical. Vitoria argues that the American Indians are not mad, although he admits they are cannibals. Sepulveda is convinced that the Americans are mad and that is why they sin, but the madness to which he refers manifests itself only as atheism and worship of the Devil. Quite often, the cannibal is portrayed, up until the end of the Enlightenment, as a perfectly reasonable individual, and on more than one occasion he is the collocutor in a philosophical dialogue.

Why exactly anthropophagy does not constitute a species that might be annexed to madness is a rather obscure question. Certainly, before the late eighteenth century the anthropophagus could not have been "mentally ill" quite simply because the notion of "mental malady" did not exist, at least not in the modern, clinical sense. In the nineteenth century, at the same time as concepts of psychopathy begin to form, the image of a cannibal animated by a psychical malady will also take shape. However, this personage is not adopted from the portrait gallery of classical madness.

This portrait gallery is otherwise very extensive. First, in the seventeenth century, madness itself shares, together with other deviations from the rule, a space of therapeutic and disciplinary practices. The poor, lepers, those suffering from venereal diseases, and persons of questionable morals mix with the mad along the corridors of the hospices, houses of correction, and hospitals of the classical age.[94] The anthropophagus is not visible in this welter of the wretched. Maniacs, melancholics, hysterical women, nymphomaniacs, cretins—an entire Court of Miracles of the human spirit, where the cannibal has no place of his own. It is highly likely that in the records of some hospice we might also find proof that an anthropophagus was interned among them. The problem is that, until the beginning of the twentieth century, we are not dealing with a species of anthropophagy systematically classified as a malady of the mind. On the contrary, the categories that seem to anticipate our notions of extreme sadism, such as "dementia," do not invoke anthropophagy as a possible symptom.

Anthropophagy is not captured by the medical analysis of madness, either as a blatant fact or in its specific incarnations. This incapacity on the part of the science of mental maladies to improvise a discourse about the anthropophagus is most evident in the absence of any "psychiatric" consideration of cannibal tribes, of whose (a)moral excesses travelers and philosophers are very aware, but which they never site within the populations of madness.

This does not mean that a certain aberrant psychology is not at work among the savages. The latter are sometimes described in terms of behavioral pathology. Savages are lazy, indolent: a species of moral corruption that qualifies them for treatment in the workhouses of the white man, as in the Jesuit state of Paraguay. They are also frequently described in terms of the pathology of the passions. They are melancholy, indifferent to the point of stupor, debauched or impotent, addicted to tobacco and alcohol, and above all, "wrathful." All the foregoing are, of course, symptoms from the wider spectrum of madness. However, these savages and cannibals remain invisible to medical science. They are not a chapter in civil man's encyclopedia of clinical madness.

The cannibal's journey toward the light of medical science nevertheless begins here, from the great field of analysis of the passions. However, before he is subjected to medical science, he is part of the philosophical discourse on man. For classical authors, the latter is a dual being, a blend of reason and passion. These two forces that govern him are elementary because they originate from the two natures that make up man: spiritual and animal. As a passionate being, man is thus a species of animal.

These animal passions are what explain outbreaks of anthropophagy. The first to put forward an articulated theory concerning this process is Plato, in the context of the analysis of tyranny found in the *Republic*. The human psyche contains a profound stratum, whose existence is established in a manner that recalls later psychoanalytical theory, through observation of the desires that afflict us during sleep, when the other parts of the soul are dormant: "The beast-like and savage [part of the soul], replete with food and drink, leaps forth and thrusting off sleep seeks to emerge and satisfy its own urges; for you know that in such wise it is emboldened to do all things, as it is released and delivered from all shame and mindfulness. It does not shrink from laying hands and on having intercourse with a mother, or with anyone else, man, god or beast, it sullies itself with the blood of anything whatsoever, and abstains from no food whatsoever."[95] Here we find an association of ideas that will be frequent in learned theories of the cannibal, namely the association between the passion for human flesh and the ecstatic, brutal passion for sex.

The second major ancient source of ideas about anthropophagy being produced by passion is Stoicism. In *De ira*, Seneca examines the consequences of the passion of wrath. For the Roman Stoic, wrath is a species of malady whose consequences can be dramatic, as can be seen in the example of Cambyses' expedition, taken from Herodotus. His stubborn quarrel against the Ethiopians drives the Persian king into a reckless adventure, in which his soldiers are reduced to a nourishment crueler than hunger (*alimentum habuerunt fame saevius*) and draw lots to see who will die wretchedly and who will live more wretchedly (*sortirentur milites eius, quis male periret, quis peius viveret*).[96] Another episode related by Seneca is that in which Cambyses kills the son of a courtier and serves him up to his father. The latter, on being asked how he finds the flesh of his son, replies: "In the presence of a king any meal is agreeable."[97] (The same passage is also mentioned by Baron d'Holbach, in the *Social System*, to illustrate abyssal servility.) For Seneca, this shows how it is possible for a man to conceal the wrath provoked by such outrages.[98] This is an exercise in self-control that must, however, have a definite aim and not transform itself into the basest flattery. Seneca shows that he does not uphold that the subjects of tyrants should obey the orders of their "butchers" without opposition: "It is another question whether life merits this price." In the last instance, the road to freedom lies open, because man always has the option of suicide.

For Seneca, wrath leads to cruelty. A Roman noble gave the order that one of his slaves, who had broken a crystal cup, should be thrown into a vat of giant eels. On hearing this order, the emperor—rather surprisingly, given that the Roman emperors were hardened to such things—"was shocked by such an innovation in cruelty." Cruelty is also attacked by Seneca in *De clementia*: "Cruelty is an evil thing, most unsuited to man . . . because to find pleasure in the sight of blood and wounds and to leave aside the human aspect in order to change into a creature of the forest is the madness of a savage beast."[99] Such a man, the tyrant, drags behind him the hatred and punishment of the entire city.

In the age of discovery, this theory of fury begins to be employed in order to explain the anthropophagy of savages. In *On Cannibals*, Montaigne claims that it is not true, as is commonly held, that the American cannibals eat their prisoners out of hunger, as the ancient Sycthians did. The true cause is extreme revenge. Rochefort says that the savages of the Caribbean eat their enemies out of fury and a spirit of revenge, not because they enjoy their flesh. Some take their fury to such extremes that they even bite the stones that strike them on the leg or the arrows that wound them; the Canadians eat the fleas that bite them.[100] Du Tertre reveals that the savages of the Antilles do not consume human flesh because they are compelled by hunger or a taste for it, but because of the fury with which they avenge themselves on the vanquished. In any case, the majority of them fall ill after eating this "execrable" meal. Another explanation put forward in the same paragraph: they eat raw human flesh in order to give themselves courage. Those who eat the most are respected by the fellow members of their tribe.[101]

In the seventeenth and eighteenth centuries, the idea that men in the state of nature are "wrathful" is commonplace. William Robertson, in *The History of America*, describes how, in small communities "every man is touched with the injury or affront offered to the body of which he is a member, as if it were a personal attack upon his own honour or safety."[102] The savages "are not satisfied until they extirpate the community" of their enemies: "They fight not to conquer, but to destroy."[103] Such a desire for vengeance "is almost the only principle, which a savage instills in the minds of his children."[104] "With respect to their enemies, the rage of vengeance knows no bounds. When under the dominion of this passion, man becomes the most cruel of animals. He neither pities, nor forgives, nor spares."[105] According to Virey, anthropophagy is a product of the hatred the vanquished have accumulated against the vanquishers.[106] Lafitau writes about how some nations of South America eat the flesh of their enemies and then carry their skeletons into battle as a kind of standard, to give themselves courage and to terrify their enemies.[107]

The passion of rage also explains the origin of strange rituals. For de Poincy, some nations carry revenge even beyond death, and insult the insensible dead. Some Indians of Virginia wear a dried hand around their neck. Others, in the New Spain, wear parts of their massacred enemies as medallions. On an island near China (probably Formosa), a crown of skulls is woven with silk threads. The Chinese make cups from the skulls of the Spanish. When they dance in festivals, the Canadians and Mexicans wear the skins of those they have eaten. The Huancas, in Peru, make drums from this skin, believing it has the virtue of causing their enemies to flee.[108] Raynal argues that "it is revenge that gives savor to a food that a sense of humanity rejects." Some American Indians kill their enemies after "certain formalities" (by which Raynal means torture), after which they make flutes from the arm and leg bones, and necklaces from the teeth. Those maimed in battle are handsome in their eyes.[109]

In the eighteenth century, other passions will be added to rage in the catalogue of the urges that lead to anthropophagy. In *An Inquiry concerning the Principles of Morals* (1751), Hume argues that courage, a fundamental passion for warlike peoples, can be transformed into a vice, that of cruelty. The Scythians scalp their enemies and makes "towels" from their flayed skin, and "whoever has most of these towels is most esteem'd amongst them."[110] "Martial Bravery," comments Hume, "in that Nation as well as in many others, destroy'd the sentiments of Humanity; a Virtue surely much more useful and engaging." Hume's account seems to have been informed by Herodotus, who, among other things, writes that the Greek mercenaries in the Egyptian camp, who confront the expedition of Cambyses against the Ethiopians, drank the blood of a child before engaging the Persians.[111] An exaggerated sense of honor can lead to extreme gestures even on the part of refined nations, Kames believes. Excess of honor explains the "uncommon ferocity" of the Japanese: "In the midst of a large company at dinner, a young woman, straining to reach a plate, unwarily suffered wind to escape. Alarmed and confounded, she raised her breasts to her mouth, tore them with her teeth, and expired on the spot."[112] In the *Social System* (1773), D'Holbach upholds that an affliction named *ennui* is the true scourge of opulent nations and a tyrant over the rich. The term is almost untranslatable, because, for the moralists of the time, it designates not so much boredom as a total stupor and anguish, a suspension of the vital spirits. In order to escape such a distressing state, there is nothing that sufferers are not prepared to try. However, there is no course of action more mistaken than that of permanently amusing ourselves. The consequences of this pursuit of sensation are grim. A Mongol emperor, for example, mixed the blood of his prisoners in the mortar with which he built his palace.[113]

In the nineteenth century, the theory of the imbalance of the passions will undergo a shift in emphasis, which will detach the figure of the anthropophagus from his natural context and insert him in the narrow ecological niche of modern criminal psychopathology. While the classical theory of the passions unfolds its conceptual categories against the background of a notion of human nature in general or about natural man, at the close of the Enlightenment the interest of physicians and scholars focuses almost exclusively on civil man. It is as if the latter had a monopoly over nervous diseases. Virey believes that the majority of the maladies that afflict social man are nervous in origin, because our organs become more sensible due to our way of life.[114]

The decisive step in the transformation of the cannibal into a criminal madman is taken by the marquis de Sade. In the context of Sade's works, the discourse on cannibalism has a paradoxical status. The anthropophagy practiced by his characters is, as a rule, that of the unreflecting and unmediated sexual and criminal delirium about which twentieth-century psychiatry speaks. Sade's libertines gobble up pieces of women's breasts or hold orgiastic rituals in which patients and executioners eat human flesh together. In *120 Days of Sodom*, for example, the libertines make the unfortunate Aline eat her own roasted flesh, and a woman is devoured by a mouse introduced into her vagina. With a few exceptions, anthropophagy is not a subject in their delirious speeches of justification. Practically every type of crime, outrage, sin, and transgression are legitimized by Sade's characters, in what sometimes form genuine philosophical dissertations. Murder, blasphemy, rape, masturbation, sodomy, theft, ingratitude, prostitution—and the list could go on quite considerably—are the subjects of detailed exposition, in which Sade displays his considerable philosophical erudition with the aim of legitimizing aberration. Anthropophagy is usually absent from the list of these subjects of sadistic dissertation, in spite of it being mentioned frequently elsewhere.

Here we have Rodin, the murderous surgeon, providing arguments to his associate Rombeau for killing his own daughter for use in his cruel experiments. The right of parents to do as they will with their children has never been contested by any nation on earth, he claims. The theory of parents' absolute power over their progeny is well known from debates about the family and patriarchal power, and Sade's examples are typical in the context of his age—for instance, the Romans and Greeks exposed their children, and savages allowed abortion. We shall not follow de Sade's enumeration, whose only purpose seems to be that of compiling an encyclopedia of evil whereby to make the reader tremble at every page. What is more interesting here is for us to see that anthropophagy is missing from the list, for all that its inference from the absolute power over children was discussed by authors such as Locke, and the savages' custom of eating their progeny was frequently mentioned in the anthropological literature that Sade had read. In *Philosophy of the Boudoir*, the enumeration of the nations that accepted infanticide makes no reference to cannibalism, even though Sade's examples seem to have been taken from the classic works on the geography of anthropophagy. In the works of Sade, the anthropophagus ceases to be the source of a discourse on morality.

There are also exceptions, because Sade's thought nevertheless falls within the horizon of the classical disciplines. In *Juliette*—the most scandalous book ever written, according to Maurice Blanchot—Sade inserts a footnote in which he claims that human flesh is the best of foods in order to obtain an abundance and thickness of seminal matter. It is therefore the orgasm that lies on the horizon of sadistic anthropophagy. Nothing is more absurd, writes Sade, than our repugnance for such meat; once we taste it, it is impossible to desire any other. The close of the footnote refers to Cornelius de Pauw's *Recherches philosophiques sur les américains*. It seems that Sade's interest in the American savages led him back to the text of a lost *Dissertation on the Americans*. Mention of de Pauw's work also clarifies one of the sources of de Sade's sexual imagination. Outrages against women were a constant in the literature about primitive societies. Malthus describes how the savage kidnaps a woman from another tribe, "stupefies" her with blows of his club to her head and back, and drags her with one hand back to his dwelling, without taking any note of the rocks in his path. Beatings are commonplace, and for the American Indians, women have the status of beasts of burden.

Sade's perverse anthropophagus has obvious roots in previous descriptions of savage tribes. Sodomy, for example, was associated with anthropophagy early on. Speaking of the prevalence of the homosexual vice in America ("that shameful debauchery, which shocks nature and perverts the animal instinct"), Abbé Raynal reveals that it is due to a series of causes: climate, contempt for women and the servitude of the latter, inconstancy of taste, queerness, and the search for voluptuousness, "a thing more easily conceived than explained."[115] Lescarbot writes that the "girls in Brazil are permitted to prostitute themselves as soon as they are able." But the men seem unresponsive to the appetites of the former. Although prostitution and nudity ought to have made them more "amorous," they seem wholly indifferent to sex. The cause resides in the smoke of the plants they burn and which impede "venereal functions" (*les functions de Venus*).[116] Virey believes that the wives of the American savages cause them violent satyriasis by anointing their virile members with "caustic insects."[117]

At the centre of de Sade's delirium can be found the Russian Minsky, a hybrid figure, a cross between the criminal madman and the philosopher-cannibal. Of gigantic stature, he dwells within a subterranean fortress, which resembles an Aztec temple, decorated with skeletons and skulls. Minsky is an integral cannibal. According to his own admission, he feeds only on human flesh. His menu reveals that his tastes are rather diversified. For dessert, his guests are served, in white porcelain bowls, the freshest and best formed turds from the most beautiful bottoms in his seraglio.[118]

Beyond his minor inconsistencies, Minsky is important because he supplies a systematic justification of cannibalism. Minsky warns his libertine visitors that they will require much philosophy in order to understand him: "I know, I am a monster spewed out by nature to co-operate with her in the destruction she lays claim to."[119] Warned that a banquet of human flesh will follow, one of his guests argues that repulsion is born only of habit, that all flesh is nourishing and that there is nothing more extraordinary in eating a man than in eating a chicken.[120] After this summary elucidation of the question, they all wolf down the meal, in a dining room where the furniture is living (*meubles vivants*), being made up of groups of women arranged according to Minsky's instructions.

Minsky justifies anthropophagy in dissertations that seem to have been lifted from travel literature. The manners of Africans are more acceptable than the simple coarseness of the American, European cunning, and cynical Asiatic softness. "After I hunted men with the former, I drank and I ate with the latter, and I fully fucked the latter, I ate people together with the Africans. I have preserved all these tastes, and all that you see here are remains of people I have devoured."[121]

Another line of argumentation directly traverses the texts of the philosophers. Montesquieu is mistaken, in *Persian Letters*, claims the erudite cannibal, when he argues that the idea according to which justice depends on conventions is dangerous, because in this case no one would be safe.[122] Why should we conceal an essential truth from mankind? Only by becoming as unjust and as vicious as the others will we end up being safe from their snares. From moral philosophy we then move on to political philosophy. The rule of law is vicious and inferior to anarchy, according to Minsky, because men are only pure in the natural state. When they stray from the natural state, they degenerate. Comparative analysis of political regimes confirms this intuition, the giant believes. Rome conquered the world when it had cruel spectacles; when stupid Christian morality triumphed and the Romans became convinced that is worse to kill men than animals, Rome fell into slavery.

For Minsky, cannibalism appears as one component in a species of dark absolutism. I exercise all the rights of a sovereign, he says, I have tasted all the pleasures of despotism, I fear no one and live happily. For Minsky, the consumption of human flesh is at the centre of a physiological rather than political experience. He is a cannibal because this enhances his sexual potency. In *Juliette or the Prosperity of Vice*, cannibalism is on the way to being detached from the context of natural legislation in order to be attached to an exceptional physiology, in which sexual and murderous impulses merge. In the words of Minsky, he eats anything that fucks. And the appetite for fucking is sustained by human flesh. A perfect vicious circle. Minsky tells his guests that he ejaculates ten times a day and attributes this volume of seminal mass to the quantity of human flesh he consumes. Whoever tries this diet will assuredly triple his libidinous faculties, he claims.[123] Once you taste human flesh, you can eat no other flesh, because no other can compare to it.[124] The main thing at the beginning is to overcome your reservations (*les premières répugnances*). Ultimately, the discourse of the cruel philosopher is interrupted by the voice of delirium. This is the theoretical limit beyond which anthropophagy topples into the science about madness. Minsky howls horribly before ejaculating, and jets of sperm spurt as high as the ceiling. In his criminal delirium, this man in his evil nature marks the moment at which the anthropophagus no longer articulates anything except the dismembered truth of psychopathy.

CHAPTER FOUR

The Conquest of the Savages

Theodore de Bry, *Natives Accused of Sodomy Torn Apart by Dogs*

THE DIFFICULTIES OF EVANGELIZATION

IN 1492, ON A BEACH IN THE ANTILLES, Columbus asked a notary to read a proclamation in front of a group of Indians, whereby the latter were told they were to become subjects of the Spanish crown. It is highly unlikely that the Indians were able to grasp anything of what the official said;[1] from the European perspective, however, the scene was less bizarre than it seems to us today as Columbus was doing nothing more than formally observing the legal scruples without which his authority and that of his sovereign over the newly discovered territories might have been placed in question.[2]

Extending the political borders of the empire had a spiritual counterpart in the adoption of Christianity. As early as the Apostolic period, the Christian church discovered its missionary vocation, but not all nations seemed to be easily convinced of the need to convert.[3] This is why canon law begins to explore the question of the legitimacy of forced conversion, which is, as a rule, raised in connection with the Jews. In 1235, William of Rennes maintained that the children of the Jews could be baptized without their parents' consent. His argument set out from the idea that slaves do not possess any parental rights, by virtue of their servile status. William believed such rights devolved to the prince, which is also valid in the case of the Jews, who have a servile status before Christians. Soon, two separate camps form: one grouped around Thomas Aquinas, who, in *Summa theologiae*, argues that parental rights, like natural rights, cannot be subordinated to civil law; the other, represented by Duns Scotus, believed that forced baptism is justified by divine law, as a means necessary to the salvation of the soul.[4] In the late Middle Ages, the proliferation of debates about conversion is linked to the new status of Europe, which began to extend its rule over pagan and idolatrous lands and, on the other hand, to the influence of prophetic theories of history.

The more aggressive attitude of Christian theologians to the problem of conversion and of power relations between Christians and pagans was also motivated by a revision of the theories of property and sovereignty, for which there was a considerable interest in the scholastic period. In his treatise *On Ecclesiastical Power* (1302), Aegidius Romanus argued that nonbelievers and heretics are not worthy to own property, they cannot be entrusted with any authority, and none of their political institutions should be respected.[5] Such opinions, which are frequently found among the supporters of papalism,[6] are not elaborated in connection with the question of the colonization of savage lands but rather appear in the context of the struggle between the pope and European monarchs, or in connection with the Muslim lands during the Crusades. In the fourteenth and fifteenth centuries, however, Europe begins to extend its dominion over territories that are of a different nature to the infidel kingdoms. The peoples that the Portuguese discover in Africa seem to have no government worthy of the name and nor any admissible forms of religious worship. This is therefore a double outrage: against the law of nature and against the divine majesty. Lacking in any legitimate government, the savages are offered one that is recognized by the sovereign pontiff, on condition that the supreme aim of the action of the Christian princes should be the pious dissemination of religion. In 1436, King Duarte of Portugal asks papal permission to conquer the Canary Isles. He argues that the inhabitants of the islands live in savagery and therefore need a government. They are like the savages of the forest, not united by any common religion; they are not subject to the yoke of the law and live outside any social relations, like animals.[7]

As early as 1493, in the bull *Inter caetera*, Pope Alexander VI granted to the Spanish an exclusive right to spread Christianity in the Indies.[8] The New World, however, raises an especial difficulty in the path of evangelization. What was an exceptional situation now becomes the norm. In their majority, the inhabitants of America seem to be the kind of savages who live a dangerous life similar to that of animals. Graver still, and almost without precedent, they are guilty of monstrous sins, primarily cannibalism. The first question that demands to be solved is therefore whether these are men or subhuman beings, incapable of receiving the Gospels. For medieval theologians, to speak of a wild man meant to speak of a man with the soul of a beast, a man so degraded that not even the grace of God could secure his salvation.[9] In comparison with the period of primitive Christianity, when it was said that some apostles preached to anthropophagi and a cynocephalous saint is attested (Saint Christophoros), in the sixteenth century the attitude of the first authors to write about the Americans is very different.

Even after their quality as human beings has been admitted, the cannibalism of the inhabitants of the Indies is seen as incompatible with any kind of religious belief. Before Bayle issues his incendiary suggestion of a nation of virtuous atheists, and before the Jesuits suggest, in the mid-seventeenth century, that the Chinese have no religion, the American cannibals are regarded by some authors as nations of atheists. From his very first steps on American soil, on October 12, 1492, Columbus observed that it would be easy to convert the islanders to the Christian religion by love rather than force. On the very same day, however, he concludes that the natives have no religion. On November 1, he already has grounds for this intuition: he has not observed any of the captured Indians saying prayers. For the sensibility of the sixteenth century, this diagnosis is equivalent to an absolute condemnation. Without religion, the anthropophagi are packed off into the absolute alterity of total anarchy. In dealing with the Indians, any methods are allowable. Promulgated on December 27, 1526, the *Ordinances regarding the Discovery and Good Treatment of Indians* require Spanish captains who discover or conquer a new territory clearly to tell the Indians or inhabitants that they have been sent to teach them good customs, to discourage them from vices such as cannibalism, and to instruct them in the Christian religion.[10] In the seventeenth century, these opinions about the atheism of the savages persist. Contrary to Cicero, who argues that there is no nation, however savage, lacking in religion, Rochefort reveals that numerous savage tribes of the New World have no form of religion and respect no sovereign power.[11] In some regions of the Andes, claims Garcilasso, the natives do not hesitate to transform their stomachs into a grave even for their closest friends. When someone dies, he is eaten by the relatives, boiled or roasted, depending on whether the deceased was fat or thin. Afterward, they bury the bones with great ceremony, but without making any offering to God, because they know none.[12]

Some authors hold that the Indians nonetheless do have a kind of religion. Acosta believes that they have a certain knowledge of the divinity, even if their minds are ruled by superstitions and errors.[13] In the chapter on cannibals in the *Essays*, Montaigne argues that they believe in the eternity of souls and in punishments and rewards in the afterlife. Lescarbot is not decided on the matter of the Indians' beliefs. He claims that Christian theology cannot be explained to the savages, who do not have faith in God, idolize the Devil, and believe in dreams, which are nothing more than diabolical visions. On the other hand, the savages of Canada might easily be converted.

Whether the savages are capable by nature of accepting a religion is a question on which not only the legitimacy of missionary activity depends. One of the aims of the question is theological, that of clarifying the nature of the divine will. For writers of the seventeenth century, who build on scholastic antecedents, the divine will has two aspects—the general will that all men should be saved, and another, particular, will that some men should be damned.[14] If knowledge, however imperfect, of the articles necessary for salvation can be found even among the most fallen of men, then this would obviously illustrate the general and benevolent will of God. If, however, the nature of such men is opaque to the truths of faith, then it means that God has predestined some for sin and damnation. This theory is also connected to that of innate ideas. The existence of an innate idea of the Supreme Being and the worship due to Him would prove that the divine intention was that all should be saved.

The existence of anthropophagi—atheists and murderers—puts such speculations sorely to the test. The opinions of the learned are divided. In *Traité de la grâce générale*, Nicole argues that the knowledge of God is diffused amongst all nations, to differing degrees, including to the most barbarous of nations: the Samoyeds, Iroquois, and Caribs.[15] In *Écrits sur le systeme de la grâce générale*, Arnauld criticizes the argument of Nicole. According to the latter, the Iroquois, Brazilians, and Caribs might be enlightened by knowledge of the duties toward God; without this knowledge, he believes, the savages would not have the physical strength to respect the commandments of God. Arnauld believes that this notion of the savages' capacities is very implausible.[16] De Poincy claims, on the one hand, that the islanders have no religion of the Supreme Being. They believe only in spirits and hold that the idea of the resurrection of the flesh is nonsense. On the other hand, they allow the immortality of the soul, and some believe in transmigration. They have no knowledge of large numbers, and some Indians, in order to express the idea of a large number, scoop up a handful of sand, a comparison also found in the Holy Scriptures.[17] Father Jean-Baptiste du Tertre, who during thirty-five years managed to convert only twenty Indians, also reflects on the religion of the savages of the Antilles. Their harsh life and the privations they endure make the sufferings of the saints pale in comparison. What believers they would make! However, there are numerous difficulties in the path of their conversion, du Tertre reveals, not least the fact that the savages have been corrupted by the Europeans with whom they have come into contact. Another impediment is their religion, which is full of superstitions so absurd that it would be better not to name it a religion at all. Nevertheless, they believe in the immortality of the soul. The *History of the Filibuster Adventurers* reveals that the Caribs have no kind of religion; although they have rituals and sacrifices. They refuse to be converted, arguing that an omnipotent being such as God would have no need of them.[18] For Locke, the navigators' accounts leave no doubt: "Hath not navigation discovered, in these later ages, whole nations, at the bay of Soldania, in Brazil, in Boranday, and in the Caribbee islands, &c. amongst whom there was to be found no notion of God, no religion?"[19] Voltaire believes that the savage peoples adore random divinities or absolutely no God at all. For example, the "Kaffirs venerate an insect as their protector" (*Les Cafres prennent pour protecteur un insecte*).[20]

Beginning in the sixteenth century, a theory appears according to which a belief held by the tribes of the New World is supposed to have anticipated the Christianity preached by European missionaries. For Bartolome de las Casas, the Apostles must have made an attempt to evangelize America, whence the natives are even better suited than the Greek and Roman idolaters to receive the Gospel.[21] Garcilasso de la Vega holds that the Inca kings were the most "moderate" in the New World, and that their laws and customs were in conformity with reason and natural law. If historians have written that the Incas were cannibals it is because they have received false information and because they have confused the Incas with the Aztecs. In contrast to the latter, the Incas did not make human sacrifices and did not eat human flesh, which they regarded as repugnant.[22] His aim is to show that Inca society was prepared for conversion to Christianity, which was made possible by the arrival of the Spanish, because the Incas' beliefs and way of life were compatible with those of the Christian world. Thus even before the arrival of the Spanish they believed in the immortality of the soul and in universal resurrection. Some passages suggest that Garcilasso is trying to recycle, for the benefit of the rehabilitation of the Incas, the arguments of the Church Fathers. The Incas, he claims, believe in the resurrection, when bodies and souls shall rise from the grave. That is why they carefully preserve nails and hair, which they suppose they will need when their bodies rise from the earth to seek the fragments they lack. The stories about the Incas that put forward arguments connected to the problem of the body's integrity after the resurrection have such a suspect air as regards their authenticity that Garcilasso appears to fear being accused of inventing them. As for how the Incas arrived at such a miraculous coincidence, he argues that it is impossible to say.

In the eighteenth century, the most influential work to treat the problem of the religions of the barbarians of the Indies is *Moeurs des sauvages amériqains, comparées aux moeurs des premiers temps* (1724) by French Jesuit Lafitau.[23] One of the best proofs we have as to the existence of the divinity is that founded on the universality of the idea of God. However, some atheists argue that there are nations that know no God or which lack any religion. Of course, the privileged example is that of the American savages. This is why it is Lafitau's plan to counteract the arguments of these atheists by demonstrating that the Indians have a religion that presages Christianity. Thus he attempts to recuperate sacral and classical history, showing that Indian customs are in fact those of the peoples of antiquity. The sign of the cross, for example, is supposed to have been venerated in America before the arrival of the Europeans on those shores.

Such speculations regarding a religion similar to Christianity appear in relation to the preoccupation with deciphering the origins of the

American Indians.[24] If there was a single genesis of mankind, and above all if this was the genesis about which the Bible informs us, then it results that the American Indians must originate from the peoples of the Old World. How exactly was a hotly debated question, especially under the circumstances in which the geography of North America was still a mystery. Scholars from the sixteenth to eighteenth centuries attempt to elucidate the problem by calling on erudition, based on similarities between the customs and beliefs of the nations of the Bible and classical history and those of the Indians. Thus some believe that the latter are descended from the Scythians because both nations were cannibals, while others believe that the Indians are one of the lost Jewish tribes of the Old Testament. One of these authors is Hugo Grotius, who authored *De origine gentium Americanarum dissertatio* (1642).[25] During the Enlightenment, the ethnic origins of the Indians and the comparison of Christianity and savage religion become less interesting than the possibility that the Indians might practice a natural religion—a species of Deism. In the *Encyclopédie*, for example, Diderot claims that the savages of the Antilles know a form of religion, in which they combine God and the Devil, and believe in the immortality of the soul.

This is because in the eighteenth century, with the progress of more liberal attitudes in the subject of religion, the significance of cannibal atheism begins to fade. The fact that the anthropophagi are not Christians no longer crops up as anything more than proof of ignorance in one form or another. In *Principes du droit naturel et politique* (1751), Burlamaqui argues that the failure of the American Indians to acknowledge the teachings of Christianity is "involuntary and invincible" (*involuntaire & invincible*).[26] This is also apparent in Defoe's novel, which centers on the attempt to evangelize a savage. Friday, the cannibal saved by Robinson from the clutches of his anthropophagous enemies, proves easily convinced about God. However, other aspects of the Christian religion prove harder to digest: "I found it was not so easy to imprint right Notions in his Mind about the Devil, as it was about the Being of a God." In fact, the new convert proves to be an interlocutor so deft at grasping the difficulties of the Christian religion that Robinson Crusoe finds himself constrained to admit that he was "ill enough qualify'd for a Casuist, or a Solver of Difficulties."[27]

With the arrival of a Spaniard and Friday's father on the island, Robinson Crusoe emerges from the state of nature into which he had been cast in order to assume the position of sovereign: "My Island was now peopled, and I thought myself very rich in Subjects; and it was a merry Reflection which I frequently made, How like a king I looked. First, of all the whole Country was my own meer Property; so that I had an

undoubted Right of Dominion. Secondly, My People were perfectly subjected: I was absolute Lord and Lawgiver." The most remarkable thing
in this reverie inspired by the discourse of natural law is that Robinson
Crusoe decrees absolute religious tolerance in his kingdom: "We had
but three Subjects, and they were of different Religions. My man *Friday*
was a Protestant; his Father was a *Pagan* and a *Cannibal*; and the Spaniard was a *Papist*: However, I allow'd Liberty of Conscience throughout
my Dominions."[28]

The justification of missionary activity now begins to give way to a
more critical attitude toward the conversion of the Indians. Luigi Antonio
Muratori holds that anthropophagy is a rare phenomenon in America.
What inspires the greatest horror, he writes in *News from the Paraguay
Missions*, is that the "Indians feed on their own species. . . . In times
of peace, Indians, who live in Society together, mutually hunt, pursue,
and lay snares for one another, to satisfy their inhuman appetite." However, he goes on, "it must be owned, that many Indians in the midst of
infidelity have a horror of so unnatural a custom."[29] In general, the Indians do not eat their prisoners, but attempt to convince them to side
with them. Anthropophagi or not, this is not a problem for Muratori:
however barbarous they might be, there is in principle no obstacle to
their conversion. According to Muratori, it is the Europeans who are
guilty of the Indians' aversion to Christianity, due to the harshness of
their conduct. Thus Muratori claims that the Russians in Siberia, in
contrast to the Spaniards in America, have won over the natives to their
side: "The Muscovites engaged the Siberians so much with presents and
demonstrations of kindness, that they all voluntarily submitted to the
Emperor of Russia."[30] In the *Discours sur les origines de l'inégalité*,
Rousseau relates how hard it is to convert the savages to Christianity.
Those who hold that the savages are lacking in sufficient reason to be
able to adopt our ideas are mistaken, because the estimation of felicity
is not so much a problem of reason as much as sentiment. Rousseau is
content to provide "a single well attested example. . . . All the efforts of
the Dutch missionaries at the Cape of Good Hope have never been able
to convert a single Hottentot."[31] For authors of the eighteenth century,
conversion is no longer a necessary condition of felicity, and the anthropophagus may continue to live by his law.

THE SPANISH CONTROVERSY

At the beginning of the sixteenth century, skepticism regarding the legitimacy and necessity of conversion was still unknown. The evangelization

of the Indians was accepted by practically all jurists and theologians as a valid reason for Spain's intervention in the New World. The question of political dominion over the Indians was, however, very different. Not all the scholastics were convinced that the pope possessed any secular authority that might flow from his spiritual authority. This is why, for a number of authors, the evangelization of the Indians did not give the Spaniards any kind of right to occupy territories in America.

The debate is complicated by the abuses perpetrated by the first waves of colonists. The impact of these settlers on the Indians was immediately perceived as annihilating. In this situation, a number of Spanish clerics begin to formulate objections. The first was Antonio de Montesinos, a Dominican monk, who in 1511 preached an incendiary sermon before the authorities on the island of Hispaniola, in which he denounced the treatment applied to the Indians.[32] In *De Indiis*, Francisco de Vitoria argues that it is "not at all clear that the Christian faith has been announced and presented to the barbarians in such a way as for them to be obligated to believe under the threat of relapsing into sin. We have not heard of any kind of miracles or signs or any exemplary sainthood sufficient to convert them. On the contrary, I hear only of provocations, savage murders and a multitude of sinful acts."[33] The great advocate of the Indians during this period is Las Casas, thanks to whose influence the papal bull *Sublimis Deus*, of June 9, 1534, issued in favor of the Dominicans, rejects the idea that the natives of America can be deprived of their goods or freedom on the grounds that they are incapable of receiving baptism.

Those who uphold a right on the part of the Spaniards to subjugate the Indians are obligated to construct a theory as regards the incapacity of the natives of the New World to govern themselves alone. At the center of this theory stands the idea that the American Indians are "natural slaves," an idea that John Major derives from Aristotle and which had not been used to justify slavery in medieval Spain.[34] But why should these barbarians be slaves by nature? Because, say the upholders of this idea, they have a bestial manner of life, unsuited to human nature. The principal sign of this degradation is cannibalism.

The most formidable opponent of Las Casas and the friends of the Indians was Juan Gines de Sepulveda (1490–1573). *Democrates Secundus*, his text on the grounds for war against the Indians, remained in manuscript until the nineteenth century, as its publication was suppressed by the Dominican ecclesiastical censors, who were favorable to the ideas of Vitoria. However, he made his opinions heard in a famous confrontation with Las Casas in 1550, during a debate held in Valladolid. His theory reelaborates doctrine of just war advanced by the Christian casuists, especially Aquinas, and is bolstered by the idea of natural slavery. The inhuman customs of the American Indians, Sepulveda believes, prove that they are mad [*stulti*] and incapable of governing themselves with a view to virtue, the natural aim of the actions of civil man. They are warlike and idolatrous. They practice human sacrifice and hold "horrible feasts of human flesh" at the expense of innocent peoples. Gravest of all is the fact that they deny the existence of God, thereby living like beasts. Compared to the Spaniards, they are like children compared to adults or women to men.[35] To be conquered by a king as pious as that of Spain is a veritable boon for such peoples.[36] While the natural law of Christian charity obliges us to set them on the straight path from which they have strayed, it ought all the more to enjoin us to bring the countless pagans of the New World to the Christian religion. Last, natural laws are universal and can be known by all, whence it results that those peoples who choose to ignore them do not have the excuse of ignorance.[37] The Indian possesses, as a contemporary Spanish official declared, the same capacity to believe in God as a parrot.[38]

De procuranda indorum salute (1588), a treatise by José de Acosta, also cites the theory of natural slavery, with reference to the Indians of the Caribbean and Brazil. The latter live like wild beasts "with no law, no kings, and certainly no magistrates and no republic" (*sine lege, sine rege, sine certo magistrate et republica*).[39] These Indians consume human flesh and commit every venereal vice. There are therefore reasons why they should be occupied and converted, above all because Christians have the supreme right to make the Gospels known over all the earth. However, attention is called for, because the Spanish themselves, by their brutal conduct, have raised obstacles in the path of the evangelization of these peoples.[40]

The most systematic denunciation of the theories of natural slavery was formulated by Francisco de Vitoria (1485–1546), professor of theology at Salamanca, who, in 1538, gave a lecture *On Dietary Laws, or Self-Restraint*. The fundamental issue raised by Vitoria is whether natural law allows the eating of human flesh. In the scholastic manner, he furnishes a series of answers, objections, and proofs. Logic and history teach us that anthropophagy is contrary to natural laws. All "civilized" peoples regard it as something abominable, and what is universally regarded as evil is against natural law.

In *On Dietary Laws*, cannibalism is rejected from the viewpoint of both the law of nature and, inasmuch as it is a sacrificial act, Christian doctrine, which rejects human sacrifice. One logical argument seems to be that according to which no one can cede another the right to be killed and eaten, for the simple reason that the right to one's own life is nontransferable, as in the case of child victims, who would not even have been capable of alienating this right.

To the question of whether Christian princes have the right to declare war on the savages by virtue of the latter's transgressions against natural laws, Vitoria answers in the affirmative, adding that this may occur only as a last resort. Anthropophagy and human sacrifice are sufficient reasons to declare war against the Indians, but Christian princes cannot directly legitimize their actions based on the right of natural law. If they have any right to wage a just war against the American Indian anthropophagi, then this happens because human sacrifice and cannibalism are acts of injustice (*injuria*).[41]

If anthropophagy is illegitimate from the viewpoint of the law of nature, why then should the same law of nature not justify European intervention? More precisely, should not Christian princes simply assume the role of executors of the law of nature in the New World? Especially since in *De potestate civili* (*On Civil Power*), a discourse of 1528, Vitoria had argued that "the purpose and utility of public power are identical to those of human society itself."[42] The power of the sovereign "comes immediately from God himself," and in that sense "it is set up by God and by natural law."[43] In *De potestate civili*, however, Vitoria discusses the problem of sovereign illegitimacy from a distinct perspective: namely, that of the obedience Christians must accord Catholic sovereigns. The target of his arguments is the thesis of the theoreticians of resistance, the Lutherans and Calvinists, who hold that subjects have the right to revolt against him whom they, in their own conscience, regard as a "godless prince." This is why *De potestate civili* formulates a more agnostic position as regards the consequences of sins against natural law. In 1528, Vitoria argues the question of whether the imminence of a mortal sin is sufficient reason to reject the authority of a sovereign is not one that has been clarified, not even in the stipulations of divine law.[44] His response is thus to consider each case separately.

In the political order, outrages against natural law are not automatically translatable into a right to resistance or intervention. However, the question of anthropophagy is not exactly political. Vitoria nowhere holds that the established custom of anthropophagy might be useful or that it should be respected, while in *De potestate civili* he asserts that the laws which serve the purposes of a republic should be obeyed, even if they are laid down by a tyrant. This division then allows him to treat the question of the legal consequences of anthropophagy in a manner relatively independent of his statements in the discourse of 1528. In the latter, he had observed that the graver the sin the less subjects are obligated to obey their sovereign. At the level of nations, the latter cannot be allowed, in their turn, to ignore the "law of nations," because it has the sanction of the entire world.

Crimes against natural law in the New World are, according to Vitoria, an injustice to other men, and a precept of reason reveals to us that each person must defend the rights of the innocent. At this point, one of the premises of Vitoria's discourse becomes apparent, namely that not all but only some of the inhabitants of America may be guilty of anthropophagy, while others would be innocent victims, against whom hostilities cannot be declared. However, what is more important is something else, namely that the basis for intervention, as recognized by Vitoria, leaves room only for retributive justice. This means that the Christian prince must act for the reinstatement of an individual right and not by virtue of establishing a right of political domination, whereby he might substitute an eventual tyrannical authority. The European sovereign has the right to carry out acts of benevolence, which does not constitute, as such, grounds for setting up a political power in America.

Here we see that Vitoria's position severely limits the prerogatives of the Christian prince in the New World. At the end of the discourse on dietary laws, he announces that, regardless of the heading under which war was begun against the "barbarians," it is not legal for it to be waged any further than is legitimate for a war to be waged against Christians. In *De indiis*, he formulates critical reservations regarding another point in the agenda of the Spanish crown: the question of the forced baptism of the Indians. The latter are not at all mad. They are rational beings, as is evident if we judge by the fact that they live within a civil order (*ordo*), in other words, they have well-organized towns, marriages, magistrates and political leaders (*domini*), laws, crafts, and commerce, all of which indicate the use of reason.[45] The dominant image relative to the American Indians is now no longer one modeled after natural man. For Vitoria, the Indians are now nations with a civilization, one that is, of course, distinct, but no less veritable. American cannibalism can now be framed within just two different categories: either as an eccentric fact, an incarnation of anticivilization, or as an element of a social order. From the point of view of European order, the republics of the Americans are alien and offer a number of well-founded reasons for declaring a "just war": protection of converts and missionaries, defense of innocents against tyranny, and support of allies and friends. These motives reveal that between the Old and the New World there begins to be detected not so much an ontological fault line of natural sin as much as the space of communication and difference between civilizations. In a letter to Miguel de Arcos, written on November 8,

1534, Vitoria declares: "As for the case of Peru, I must tell you, after a lifetime of studies and long experience, that no business shocks me or embarrasses me more than the corrupt profits and affairs of the Indies. Their very mention freezes the blood in my veins. . . . Even if the emperor has just titles to conquer them, the Indians do not and cannot know this. They are most certainly innocents in this war."[46] Within Vitoria's horizons, crimes against nature are blurred by the violence with which the history of modern civilization is written.

THE PROTESTANT VERDICT

In the Protestant world and, to a certain extent, for those French writers inspired by anti-Spanish sentiments,[47] the justifications for occupation of Indian territories that cite crimes against nature committed by the Indians are known, but they are the exception rather than the rule. Richard Baxter, an important writer during the Civil War and Restoration, argues in *A Holy Commonwealth* (1659) that in the case in which "a poor barbarous Indian Nation, like the Canibals, would not consent to hear the Gospel, or suffer Preachers to come among them," then we should have the right to "force them to admit the Preachers" sent by the Europeans as, of course, "a work of Charity."[48] There are also moral scruples, according to Baxter: we must not injure them, but govern them; and we do not have the right to deprive them of their possessions. However, the majority of Protestant authors are not so much interested in justifying dispossession of the Indians as much as repeating the most violent accusations of Catholic authors, which they use in order to delegitimize Spanish authority in the New World and to illustrate the excesses of the Catholic powers. The modern theory of natural law, an almost exclusively Protestant creation, comprises numerous considerations of Spanish injustices. Like the Catholic supporters of a moderate stance toward the Indians, the problem the Protestant authors must solve is that of the signification of crimes against nature. Their initial arguments, like those of the Spanish critics, originate in fact from scholastic theories. In the *Short Discourse on Tyrannical Government*, William of Ockham refutes those who hold that nonbelievers cannot legitimately own property, conclude veritable contracts, or possess genuine political leadership in temporal affairs. His arguments are based on scriptural readings (Abraham, for example, recognizes the king of Sodom, even though the latter was an infidel), to which he adds interpretations of the Church Fathers and Papal Decretals. The opinion according to which nonbelievers have no just authority and no right of property is a "prejudice" for any mortal, Ockham argues. One of the consequences of this error would be that the children of pagans cannot legitimately inherit property, and this is against natural law and prejudices these children "before baptism." From an examination of the attributes of papal office, Ockham reaches the conclusion that the pope has no kind of temporal power over the Roman Emperor or over non-Christian princes and their subjects.[49]

Setting out from the scholastic arguments connected to the legitimacy of pagan authority, Grotius argues, in *Mare liberum*, that the idolatry of the Indians is compatible with a legitimate right of property. He also argues that the Americans are "skilled and hard-working," not "ferocious and stupid," so that the grounds invoked for their conquest are nothing more than impious pretexts.[50] Gradually, Protestant authors evolve toward modern, secular arguments. Pufendorf also argues against the conquest of America from the perspective of natural law. In the *Law of Nature and of Nations*, his target is Vitoria's theory, which he believes postulates a right on the part of the Spaniards to expropriate the Indians. According to Pufendorf, Vitoria holds that this entitlement is founded first on the society and commerce that men are obligated to maintain between them and therefore the Spaniards have the right to go to those countries and settle there, if they do no harm to the barbarians. However, communication between men cannot hinder an owner from granting or not granting another the right to use what belongs to him, protests Pufendorf. Foreigners do not have an unlimited right to travel and settle where they will; the local sovereign has the right to examine in what numbers and for what purposes they come. The second motive put forward by Vitoria is that the Spanish have the right to conduct commerce with the Indians, and that neither one nor the other can legitimately be hindered by their sovereign. However, this is a supposed freedom of commerce, on which limits may be placed when the good of the state demands. The third motive is that, if there are things that can be jointly owned in the lands of the barbarians, then the latter do not have the right to deny these things to the Spanish when they arrive to take possession of them. If others are allowed to prospect for gold, then the Spanish too must be allowed to do so. However, if I allow my neighbor to walk in my garden and pick some fruit, this does not mean I should allow another to cut down my trees and drive me out.[51]

In the second volume of the work, Pufendorf resumes his critique of the right to conquer. This time, his target is Francis Bacon, who argues that a custom such as the American Indians' custom of sacrificing humans to their divinities and eating their flesh is sufficient reason to declare war on them, as on people proscribed by nature herself. Here,

Pufendorf no longer argues with reference to the problem of expropriation, but with reference to the right to declare a just war. In order to decide this question, he writes, we must examine (1) whether a Christian prince may attack the Indians only because they feed on human flesh, or if they feed on those of the same religion, or if they feed on strangers. (2) In connection with the latter, we must distinguish whether they come to the Indies as enemies or corsairs, or as men who wish to travel honestly, without doing harm to others, or whether they have been cast away there by storms. Only in this case is it permissible to wage war against these peoples, if they have treated one of the prince's countrymen in a cruel and barbarous manner.

On this point, Barbeyrac inserts a footnote. If these anthropophagi eat only the flesh of people who have died from natural causes or who have been killed by others among them, however savage and barbarous such a practice might be, it does not justify that they should be attacked for this reason. Barbeyrac, it would seem, refuses to consider the fact that the anthropophagi infringe another natural right, that to sepulture. However, he admits that if they themselves kill other human beings in order to eat them, or if they sacrifice them to their idols, then this is a thing so cruel and contrary to humanity, so destructive to society and the human race, that we can only view as just and laudable any war that tends to abolish such a practice, even where those men practiced it only amongst themselves and spared strangers.[52]

Heineccius also believes that the occupation of America is abusive. He argues that one of the legitimate forms of property is that over the game in a territory that is not in any private possession. Hunting and fishing are thus "forms of occupancy" that "no one can deny." A people may claim for itself an exclusive right as regards those animals over which their "dominion" extends and from that moment it becomes unjust for anyone else to arrogate to himself the right to hunt that which has already been reserved by another. In another passage, he directly tackles the issue of the colonization of America, but using another kind of argument. Heineccius claims Grotius errs when he holds that crimes against nature committed by a nation, such as "if it worships idols, or eats human flesh," are just cause to wage war against that people. There is "absolutely no right to make war" in this case, our author argues. For, nations are in the state of nature one before the other and as long as a nation does not directly injure another by its actions, then it cannot be punished, because in the state of nature no one has any superior, and "none but a superior can punish a delinquent." This is why the Spaniards have no right to "punish the Mexicans for their crimes against nature," as even Spanish doctors in law have admitted.[53]

In Defoe, we find a complex discussion of the right to declare war on the cannibals. Discovering the remains of a cannibal feast on his island, Robinson can think only of nothing but how he "might destroy some of these Monsters in their cruel bloody Entertainment, and, if possible, save the Victim they should bring hither to destroy."[54] When these fear-inspired fantasies give way to "cooler and calmer Thoughts," Robinson asks himself on "what Authority or Call" he has the right "to pretend to be Judge and Executioner upon these Men as Criminals, upon whom Heaven had thought fit for so many ages to suffer, unpunish'd."[55] Employing a concept that also appears in Stoic literature, according to which the evil man's punishment is his own evil, Robinson argues that the cannibals are the "Executioners of [heaven's] Judgements upon one another."[56] He realizes that their actions do not concern him directly and that he therefore has no right "to engage in the Quarrel of that Blood, which they shed promiscuously one upon another." Although what they do to one another is "brutish and inhumane," Robinson realizes that the cannibals have done him "no Injury" (the term is juridical rather than moral). Only if attacked would he have the right to defend himself. Thus, his argument continues, he would be conducting himself like the Spaniards, who have committed "Barbarities" in America, under the pretext that the natives were "Idolaters and Barbarians, and had several bloody and barbarous Rites in their Customs, such as sacrificing humane Bodies to their Idols." In relation to the Spaniards, the Englishman believes, the Indians were "very innocent People," and the "rooting them out of the Country" was a "mere Butchery, a bloody and unnatural Piece of Cruelty, unjustifiable either to God or Man."[57] These arguments, to which he adds the possibility that the savages may return in greater numbers to seek him out and avenge themselves, make Robinson err on the side of caution: "As to the Crimes they were guilty of towards one another, I had nothing to do with them; they were national, and I ought to leave them to the Justice of God, who is the Governor of Nations, and knows how by national Punishments to make a just Retribution for national Offences; and to bring publick Judgements upon those who offend in publick Manner."[58] The language in which this decision is couched is saturated with concepts of natural law.

The effect of natural law arguments is complex. If Protestant writers managed to impose the idea that natural law does not authorize abuses against the Indians, even if the latter were guilty of crimes against nature, they were thereby left without a consecrated theoretic foundation, from the perspective of which the conquest of America might be justified. They are thus faced with a dilemma: either they admit that the Europeans have no rights over the Indians, or they seek other reasons for domination over them. The second option is explored by numerous authors, who begin to renounce the arguments based on natural law in favor ones that are pragmatic or economic. Charles de Rochefort is one of the many authors who claim, in the seventeenth and eighteenth centuries, that, in contrast to the Spanish, the French and the English have legitimately settled in the Antilles and Caribbean, through an understanding with the Indians' chiefs.[59] In the epoch of the Puritan colonies in America, the need to "civilize" or "pacify" the Indians, or else the fact that the latter did not cultivate the land as was fit, is among the favorite explanations that now occupy the space formed by the restriction of the arguments of the science of natural law.

GLORIFICATION OF THE PRIMITIVES

Later, the cannibal will be transformed, by a curious reversal, from victim to incarnation of a certain type of justice. One that is terrible, but not unrecognizable as such. Anthropophagy now begins to be regarded as a result, a reaction, or punishment for the brutality of the European colonists. In *Journeys to the Islands of America* (1722), Father Labat argues that cannibalism is somehow justified: "It is a wholly extraordinary act on the part of these peoples; it is rage that drives them to this excess, because they cannot fully avenge themselves upon the Europeans for the injustice done to them when they were driven from their lands except by killing them, when they catch them, with greater cruelty than is natural to them."[60]

The context in which this image of the avenging cannibal arises is one of discomfort about the justifications and effects of colonization, where the Old World takes the place of the New World on the playing board of history, usurping its attributes. Here we have Émeric Cruсé (Crucerius), a Parisian monk and author of the modern age's first treatise on eternal peace, *The New Cyneas* (1623), illustrating this possibility: "Let us fear that there happens to us what we have done to others. We do not know yet all the countries of the habitable earth. There is perhaps some people towards the Occident or the South who is preparing work for us. Who would have said one hundred and fifty years ago to the Americans that bearded men would soon come to conquer their country?"[61] There is a historical lesson that the Europe of divisions and religious wars ought to draw from the situation in the New World. The conquest of America would never have happened, Cruсé argues, if the states there had been pacific. However, their rulers "could not live content if they did not eat the bodies of their neighbours." Cannibalism is here a stylistic figure of territorial expansion. It is a sin against the nature of the body politic, according to the logic of this treatise, which can only be eliminated by a radical, new, and artificial measure, a form of contract between states: "Nothing can save an empire except a general peace of which the principal means consists in the limitation of monarchies, so that each Prince remains within the limits of the lands which he possesses at present."[62]

De Poincy describes the Caribs, who have been named "cannibals" or "anthropophagi," as living a simple, unprepossessing life. Of all peoples, they care the most for one another. What is more, something extraordinary for savages, they love cleanliness. They do not travel and they are not curious to find out about other lands. They are, however, curious about all that falls into their hands. They are moderate in their diet and have a passion for strong drink, something which, for a European of the seventeenth century, was probably not a cardinal vice. They receive strangers hospitably.

What else might be added to this list of virtues? Cannibalism, of course. De Poincy does not deny that the Caribs are cannibals, but he believes that this is a rare event, dictated by excessive revenge. Otherwise, the Caribs do not just eat any kind of flesh, and some are even vegetarians. Other barbarous nations of Asia and Africa "do also exceed the Caribbians in their inhumanity," and some are "more cruel than Tygers." They tie their prisoners to poles and chop them into pieces, after which they all feed, women and children included, on the raw flesh, which they devour "like so many Cormorants." The women "rub the ends of their Breasts with the blood of the Patient, that so their Children may suck it with their Milk."[63] As for the Caribs, they are not presented as sinners against nature. On the contrary, it is the cannibals who are given a voice in de Poincy's account. They reproach the Europeans for the injustice whereby they have driven them from their lands. Another text, *History of the Filibuster Adventurers*, argues that, while the Indians were guilty of sacrificing and eating people, the Spaniards were just as guilty of massacring the "wretches"; it is true that they have eliminated that "detestable custom," but they did so in the name of their own interests.[64]

Gradually, victimization of the savages gives way to glorification of the primitive man. At the modern origin of this current of thought lies Montaigne, who, in his essay *On Cannibals*, argues that their "wars are throughout noble and generous, and carry as much Excuse and fair Pretence, as their human Frailty is capable of; having with them no other Foundation, than the sole Jealousy of Virtue."[65] He compares the excesses of Western civilization with the cannibals' way of life, finding that the former is at least as bad. We are in the habit of condemning anything strange and incomprehensible to us as savage, but "we ought to call those wild, whose Natures we have chang'd by our Artifice, and diverted from the common Order."[66] The cannibal nations are, Montaigne believes, governed by the "Laws of Nature." Moreover, "what we now see in those Natives, does not only surpass all the Images with which the Poets have adorn'd the Golden Age, and all their Inventions in feigning a happy State of Man."[67] They have no vices, property, or illnesses. They enjoy a natural abundance of fish and meat, which they "eat without any other Cookery, than plain Boiling, Roasting, or Broiling," and they dance all day long.[68] Montaigne admits that the American savages kill their prisoners with excruciating torments before eating them. But that does not mean we should regard ourselves as their superiors: "I am not sorry that we should here take Notice of the barbarous Horror of so cruel an Action, but grieved that seeing so clearly into their Faults, we should be so blind to our own: For I conceive, there is more Barbarity in eating a Man alive, than when he is dead; in tearing a Body Limb from Limb, by Racks and Torments, that is yet in perfect Sense, in roasting it by Degrees, causing it to be bit and worried by Swine . . . under the Colour of Piety and Religion."[69]

Rochefort reproduces what he claims are discourses of the savages, in which they reproach the Europeans for usurping their rights, before launching into a eulogy of the primitives. The savage men and women of the Caribbean are beautiful, he believes.[70] Du Tertre holds that the Caribbean Indians are savage in name only. They are "the most contented, happiest, least vicious, most sociable, most sincere and least agitated of any nation upon earth. They are as nature has made them . . . they are all equal."[71] Rousseau, an attentive reader of Montaigne, argues that the savages of the Caribbean are happier than Europeans.[72]

The abbé Raynal's book is the most important eighteenth-century work to denounce the excesses of colonial occupation. It enjoyed notable success and was regarded as a subversive work and banned in France, following the first edition of 1770. Raynal denounces the occupation and the abuses perpetuated under religious pretexts, and which have led to the perpetuation of superstitions. According to the example of the Incas—he claims—the Jesuits have founded a theocratic government, but with an advantage owing to the Christian religion: the confessional. Instead of reducing crimes, confession aggravates them. Instead of eluding punishment, the guilty party comes begging for it on his knees. The severer and more public the punishment, the more it restores the calm of the conscience. Thus, punishment, which everywhere else terrifies the guilty, here consoles them.

In order to undermine the pretension to legitimacy of occupation and forced conversion, Raynal sees himself required to justify, at least up to a point, some of the questionable American customs. It is true, he admits, that Indian women resort to infanticide, but they have a well-founded reason selectively to kill baby girls at birth, in order to spare them from the tyranny of Indian males. The same argument will be found in Kames's *Sketches on the History of Man* (1776), where an Indian woman gives a philosophical speech justifying selective infanticide.

The main problem, however, is anthropophagy. The cruel customs of the anthropophagi are regarded by Raynal as a reservoir of virtue that has contributed to the natural liberty of the Indians. In Brazil, the heads of enemies slain in battle or sacrificed are carefully preserved, and are displayed as monuments of valor and victory. The heroes of these ferocious nations wear their exploits graven into their own limbs as marks of honor. The more disfigured they are the greater is their glory. Such mores did not predispose the Brazilians to bear the chains intended for them patiently, but what could they do against European firearms and discipline?[73]

The complete collapse of the traditional arguments regarding Europeans' rights to expropriate and convert the savages is followed by a movement to constitute new ideologies of liberation for slaves and colonies. This is a process in which the glorification of the savage plays an important role. From the perspective of the theories of natural law, the significance of this discourse is not easily defined. On the one hand, the noble savage and his extreme incarnation, the just cannibal, draw to scholarly attention what seems to be natural man. In the late eighteenth century, with the emergence of the cult of nature that culminates in romanticism, the noble savage will be propelled to the rank of hero of a culture of sensibility uncontaminated by the corruption of the modern world. However, in order to arrive there, a profound perception of natural law will have to be abandoned. In the texts of his admirers, the just savage emerges from the state of nature cleansed of all sins. However, the scholastics knew that in this state the sin against natural law is possible and visible. The good cannibal thus heralds a nature that, at a deeper level, is at peace with itself from the moral point of view, because its parts can no longer be guilty before one another. A sign of a future natural peace, the noble savage will become the agent of the idealists and radicals of the Enlightenment in a universal project of moral reform.

CHAPTER FIVE

The Predicaments of Identity

Hieronymus Bosch, detail from *The Last Judgment*

THE DEBATE ON THE RESURRECTION OF THE BODY

THE CYNIC PHILOSOPHER, WHO, in the year AD 180, had joined the crowd of curious onlookers at the trial of a Christian, reprimanded the latter: "Apollonius, reproach yourself; for all your subtle speech, you have wandered off the mark!"[1] What the accused had tried to do, seemingly without much success, was to convince his audience that the Christian idea of a martyr's death is not unlike the death of Socrates. The argument between the two raises a problem about the nature of the early doctrines of the martyrs and the persecutions to which they were subjected. The question of martyrdom in the Early Church has been analyzed from the perspective of its theological, legal, and historical implications. But the dialogue between Apollonius and the Cynic suggests that the differences between the martyrs and their adversaries were rather philosophical in nature. During the same period in which Apollonius confronts the Cynic, another future martyr, Prionius, disputes with an amateur philosopher: "At this, a bystander named Rufinius, one of those who had a reputation for superiority in rhetoric, said to him: 'Cease, Pionius, do not be a fool!' And Pionius answered him: 'Is this your rhetoric? Is this your literature? Even Socrates did not suffer thus from the Athenians. Were Socrates and Aristides and Anaxarchus and all the rest fools in your view because they practised philosophy and justice and courage?'" On this riposte, Rufinius has nothing to do but fall silent. In the *Acts of Phileas* (306), the Roman prefect expresses doubts concerning the philosophical abilities of Christ: "Perhaps you will say that he was superior even to Plato." Phileas: "Not only to Plato. He was more profound than any man. He convinced even philosophers . . . I am concerned for my soul. Christians are not the only ones who are concerned for their souls, pagans are, too. Take Socrates, for example. When he was being led to his death, even with his wife and children present, he did not turn back, but eagerly embraced death."[2]

A most unusual death, that is. Here it is not merely a question of the fact that the standard punitive procedures of the Romans included atrocities such as burning people alive or throwing them to wild beasts. In the case of the Christian martyrs, the authorities seem to have been particularly interested in applying exceptional punishments, due, on the one hand, to accusations of necromancy and cannibalism, and on the other, to the Christian doctrine of resurrection.

Why exactly the doctrine of the resurrection of the body produced such hostility is not clear. However, it was assured by a kind of strange complicity between the two groups. The authorities sometimes take unusual precautions to ensure the complete destruction of the martyr's body, eliminating any possibility of recovering the fragments. To this end, the arena emerges as a place of diabolical digestion, in which human bodies are masticated in the jaws of the Antichrist, only to be resurrected from their fragments at the imminent Last Judgment. Joyous that the Emperor Trajan had sentenced him to be devoured by wild beasts, Ignatius of Antioch announces that he will thereby disappear from the face of the earth more quickly, in order to reach God.[3]

In the second and third centuries, there were groups of Christians who professed an apocalyptic doctrine that centered on the idea of the resurrection of the flesh.[4] This idea is mentioned in the Bible, but during the period of the primitive church, it is put to the test by the practices of the persecutors. How the particles of a pulverized body might be conceived to reunite now ceases to be a purely speculative problem.

The first, instinctive reaction of Christian groups seems to have been carefully to gather all the remnants of martyred bodies. In the first martyrological texts, such as *The Martyrdom of St Polycarp* and *The Martyrdom of SS Carpus, Papylus and Agathonicê*, which describe events occurring in the middle of the second century, the Christians collect the remains, apparently without encountering any obstruction from the authorities. The remains of Polycarp are regarded as relics, "dearer to us than precious stones and finer than gold."

Things become complicated when the Romans resort to punishments that involve the pulverization of the body, such as in Lyon in the year 177. Sometimes, it is the Christians' excessive enthusiasm for relics that raises problems. *The Martyrdom of Bishop Fructuosus and his Deacons, Auguries and Eulogius* (259) reveals how the Christians gather the ashes of the martyrs during the night. It turns out that some fragments have not been recovered, and so one of the martyrs is forced to appear to his fellows postmortem, urging those who have, for love of him, removed pieces of him to return them forthwith.[5]

There were good reasons for the difficulties of resurrection to be regarded with special attention in the circles of the primitive church, which explains why the doctrine of resurrection is presented in the acts of the martyrs in a manner that incorporates the objections of opponents. Initially, it appears that the focus was on the miraculous resurrection of Christ. Paul's sermon before the Areopagus is received with a mix of surprise, hostility, and polite rejection by the philosophically minded Athenians.[6] In the following centuries, however, it is the more practical issue of the resurrection of the believers that comes to the forefront. The arguments are rapidly systematized in a series of treatises dedicated especially to the subject of resurrection. The first is the treatise

ascribed to Athenagoras, *De resurrectione*, probably written in the year
AD 180.[7] The subject of these treatises is the "resurrection of the flesh,"
not merely the resurrection of the "body." While, as regards the perpetuation of the soul, premises existed for agreement between the first
Christian apologists and their critics, as regards the resurrection of per-
ishable human matter the disagreements seem to have been acute. In the
fourth century, Augustine includes in *The City of God* a reply to the cal-
umnies with which nonbelievers treat Christian faith in the resurrection.
Dissertations on the difficulties of resurrection are then also presented
by the medieval theologians, for example in *Supplementum Tertiae Par-
tis, Q. 80, Art. 4* of Thomas Aquinas's *Summa theologiae*.

The early texts do not allow us to assert with any precision the identity of the critics of the theory of resurrection or what audience they addressed. It is possible that the first treatises on resurrection might have
served in the polemic against Docetism, which treated the body of Christ
as something metaphorical, and against Gnosticism, which argued for
renunciation of the body.[8] However, they sooner have the air of scrupu-
lously enumerating the logical difficulties of the idea of resurrection,
first of all in order to scatter all formulable doubt on the part of their
very authors. It is therefore conceivable that these were exercises whereby
the objections of an imaginary opponent were answered merely in order
to construct an unassailable case. But it is more likely that some of the
first arguments against resurrection might indeed have been formulated
in debates between pagan philosophers and the Christians of the second
and third centuries. For the former, the subject does not seem to have
been of decisive importance, because, perhaps with the exception of the
newly discovered and very concise *Epistle to Rheginus*, a Valentinian
tract on resurrection,[9] we do not have equivalent works in which this
topic is systematically developed. It is true, though, that some of the
works of the first critics of Christianity have completely disappeared or
have come down to us in very fragmentary form, in part due to the destruction of such books in the first centuries after Christianity triumphed
as an official religion. All that we know for certain is that there is an
asymmetry, which is difficult to explain, between the patristic discourse
on resurrection and that of the supposed critics of the idea. Athenagoras
attributes objections to the resurrection to certain unnamed persons
who otherwise have pretensions to spirit and wisdom. It is not clear
whether he is referring to an organized group of philosophers, because
he claims that these arguments are so simple and common that they
seem unassailable even to the wisest. Justin Martyr discusses objections
to the dogma of resurrection only to conclude that the doctrine is in fact
compatible with philosophical opinion. In a dialogue composed by one

of the first Christian apologists of the second century, Minucius Felix, a pagan critic mocks the Christian doctrine of the future life stating that it must produce abhorrence of the then widely practiced cremation; the Christian appears unconcerned.[10]

Whoever these critics might have been, the authors of the treatises on the resurrection of the flesh rigorously enumerate the objections to the dogma. The implications of anthropophagy raise the most serious doubts regarding the resurrection. In order to demonstrate the possibility of the resurrection, the authors of these treatises are obligated to mobilize an entire arsenal of theological and philosophic concepts against the cannibal. It is the massive authority of a theologian such as Augustine that assures us of the importance of anthropophagy in this debate. In *The City of God*, he recognizes that the most difficult problem for the doctrine of the resurrection of the body is that raised by the situation in which a starving man eats another. The question is in what body the man eaten will be resurrected, for his flesh has been converted into that of the man who has eaten him. Will his flesh be restored to him, or will it remain part of the cannibal who has assimilated it?[11]

The first line of defense of the theologians is to appeal to the absolute power of God. In the logic of the objections to the theory of resurrection, the flesh of the body to be resurrected disappears into the black hole that is the body of the cannibal. And only an infinite power can save the dogma of resurrection from being dissolved in the gastric juices of the anthropophagus.

In a certain sense, the intervention of an omnipotent being was programmed in advance. One of the objections to the resurrection regarded the improbability of the particles of the body being melded back together. The dead are transformed into ash, fragments of bone, and dust, which in their turn are scattered throughout the world, at random and without us knowing where to find them. To reunite these minute and countless fragments, all the atoms into which a body has been pulverized, is an extremely difficult undertaking. But it is not one that is impossible. The Christian apologists rapidly advance an argument that highlights two divine attributes: omniscience and omnipotence. As possessor of absolute knowledge, God knows precisely the position of each particle of each body, and as possessor of infinite power, he is capable of reassembling them at the Last Judgment, wherever they may be found. Athenagoras, for example, argues that God has both the power and the knowledge to command bodies to return to life; this assembly, he claims, will not occur at random, because not one of our remnants, however small, will have escaped the divine attention.[12] In the chapter "Of those abandoned to and devoured by wild beasts," in the *Dialogue between a Christian and a Pagan Philosopher*, the knowledge of God is brought into graphic relief: even if human bodies have been devoured, or mixed with water or earth, they conserve the precious matter of the flesh, which will then be sought out and restored by God, as though they had been marked with a "special dye." For Tatian, the entire matter of the body is always visible to God, even in the bellies of wild beasts.[13]

The being that throws this exercise of divine goodness, knowledge, and power into jeopardy is the anthropophagus. He is the only creature whose intervention alarms the authors of the treatises on the resurrection of the flesh, and the only one that designates limits to divine limitlessness. The aggression of this conceptual personage is one that possesses ontological significance. Beyond his defiance of natural law, the anthropophagus threatens to derail the divine plan of salvation, the universal recuperation of bodies.

In the order of exposition found in the treatises on resurrection, the first harbinger of difficulty is the animal that eats human flesh. This menagerie begins with the fish, probably because the Romans ate fish from the Tiber, into which the bodies of those killed in the games were thrown.[14] In another hypothesis, the animal is the beast of the arena, although the condemned were not as a rule eaten in front of the spectators, and cases of animals trained to eat people were rare and unusual. The flesh of the animals killed in the games was, however, sold or donated to the people, although this did not, of course, include the flesh of the carnivores.[15] Beyond such details, in the arena or in nature, the animal is the chasm in which the human body is pulverized. "Crushed and minced between cruel teeth" (Athenagoras), the corpse dissolves into the intimacy of a foreign body, that of the carnivore. Variations of this difficulty: a single human body might be shared between several animals. The latter, in their turn, may eat one another. A chemistry of absolute hazard, impossible to elucidate on a human scale. Restitution of atoms of matter to their rightful owner is possible only as a consequence of "the infinite power of God, guided by boundless goodness, Who will know how to distinguish and to extract from the body of carnivorous animals what once belonged to this unfortunate . . . even if the body has passed through many ferocious beasts, at the same time or successively."[16]

The second incarnation of the difficulty is that of the involuntary cannibal. We are sometimes dealing with an anthropophagous chain: a man eats an animal that has eaten a man etc.—a species of cannibalism by contamination. However, this is even more dangerous in the economy of resurrection. Imagine, Athenagoras's opponents argue, how many men die in shipwrecks. Their bodies serve to feed the fish in the sea. How many more are killed in war or public disasters, whose bodies remain unburied, prey to hungry beasts? In this case, when these "sad remains" have vanished into the body of animals of different species, who can separate such an alloy? This is further complicated by the fact that some of these animals are, in their turn, "good to eat." "Succulent pieces" of them end up on people's plates, and thence in their stomachs, nourishing them with their substance. Thus it is possible for a man to end up feeding other fellow men, with fragments of himself that have passed through animal bodies as though through a "store."

The third incarnation is that of the cannibal proper. An extreme figure, his mere invocation seems to inflame the discussion. Athenagoras: "At this moment there appear to us, amid lamentations, those parents who, in the clutches of cruel hunger or in accesses of madness or wrath, have devoured their own fruit, and others, even more wretched, the black evil of whose enemies has made them devour their children, presented to them as food and prepared with a care that brings shame upon mankind." In his *Summa*, Thomas Aquinas presents two cases even more troublesome. The first is that of the child of integral cannibals, who have fed only on human flesh. As the seminal fluid is produced, according to Aristotle, from a surplus of food,[17] then it results that this child has been conceived from a flesh that cannot belong to him at the resurrection. The second case is that of a cannibal who feeds only on human embryos that have arrived at the stage in which they have received a rational soul. These must contain the essential substance of the individual. But once consumed, they are transformed into the sperm of the father, who in conceiving a child will give life to a creature that will have adopted the essential substance of other beings. Macarius discovers an even more precocious cannibal: according to him, the fetus eats its mother in the womb.[18]

What is the difficulty that anthropophagy introduces into the schema of resurrection? Athenagoras: "After this exposition [of occasions of cannibalism] the critics think they are right to draw the conclusion that the resurrection cannot take place, because it is not possible for two men to be resurrected with the same flesh at the same time, and nor is it possible for the same limb to have two different masters. How can two bodies, which have successively been in possession of the same substance, appear in their entirety, without lacking a large part of themselves? In the end, either the disputed parts will be returned to their original owners, leaving a gap in the later owners, or they shall be fixed in the latter, leaving in this case an irreparable loss in the former."

The holes that anthropophagy bores into the speculative bodies of the dead mark a visible limit of the divine power. The difficulty revealed by the presence of cannibalism is therefore one that is logical and metaphysical: the simultaneity of bodies presupposed by the dogma of resurrection is contradicted by the passage of substances presupposed by anthropophagy. It is an extreme difficulty, in which ownership of matter is contested by two bodies with a definite and exclusive jurisdiction.

The first answer is to deny the possibility of cannibalism or at least to minimize its incidence. A tactic of economy: if anthropophagy is impossible, or almost impossible, to find, then there is no need for the difficulties of resurrection that these presuppose to gain an answer. Providence, believes Athenagoras, has prepared and designated each animal food according to its species. The anthropophagi, he claims, do not gain weight, but on the contrary lose weight until they die. For Tertullian, the whale that swallowed Jonah would have been able to digest the flesh of the prophet during the three days he stayed in its belly more efficiently than any grave, but it did not do so.[19] In the vision of the theologians, the intention of Providence is not that each creature should eat whatever food it can get hold of, no matter what its nature, because not everything can serve as nourishment. A universal lack of appetite for human flesh is therefore a characteristic of the providential order.

Then, it is a kind of selectivity intrinsic to the body that marginalizes anthropophagy. Contestable at the macroscopic scale, it is declared impossible at the microscopic scale. Particles of human flesh pass through the bodies of cannibals without being assimilated. Treatises on the resurrection of the flesh speculate on a providential anatomy. In the vision of Athenagoras, the first resort of this seems to be our natural repulsion for unnatural food: "It is sufficient to have examined for a little the nature and quality of foods and of those that eat them in order to observe that anything we swallow by force or against nature does not usually become profitable to the one that is placed in this situation. On the contrary, as soon as such meat, for which there is such a great antipathy, enters the space of the stomach, nature revolts and immediately eliminates it." Nausea thus has an eschatological virtue.

Even after human particles have been ingurgitated, the theologians establish that these follow a separate circuit. Here can be found the most powerful argument against cannibalism in the treatises on resurrection. By discriminating between an expendable and essential part of the body, the patristic authors attempt to shield God from any confrontation with the consequences of cannibal handiwork.

Let us presuppose, writes Athenagoras, that the foods forbidden by our constitution are nevertheless digested and assimilated. This is not a problem for the theory of resurrection, because what we wish to say when we assert that the body will be resurrected is that it will recover its bones and organs, the "essential parts," and not the liquid and dry matter that is to be found in the body, where the particles assimilated by the cannibal end up. It is therefore a double argument: on the one hand, selective assimilation of nonessential particles in the body of the cannibal; on the other hand, a postulated incorruptibility for some portions of bodily matter. Aquinas puts forward a similar doctrine, which he derives from Aristotle. The flesh consumed by the anthropophagus does not by its nature belong to the body in which it disappears. The flux of matter moves through bodies without defining them. In a town, the inhabitants come and go, but the "republic" remains the same; similarly, in a man, matter circulates without affecting his nature as an individual.

It is not only the principles of physiology that impose the separation and decanting of forbidden flesh. What keeps the human body apart from anthropophagous contamination is also a moral imperative. This is an argument that appeals to the necessity of coherence and moral order in the universe of man. If we were to accept that nature does not oppose us eating human flesh, argues Athenagoras, then it would be licit for us to tear each other apart, to eat one another, and to do "however many other things nature allows. How inconvenient it would be in such a system not only not to become anthropophagi . . . but also to relish the flesh of our closest relatives and to regard as the tastiest morsels those which we rip from the corpses of our closest friends or from those who most wish us well."[20] Cannibalism therefore presupposes such a supplement—in its turn unacceptable—which is that of cruelty. And this is not merely immoral, it is something that makes human society impossible, because it directly opposes, in Athenagoras's words, the principle of "affection" (*philia*), which, in the Stoic analysis, holds the social body together.

The metaphysical condition of the separation operated by God is the indestructibility of matter in the alimentary tract of the cannibal. Only once a principle of the conservation of matter has been accepted can divine analysis be conceivable. In *Enchiridion*, Augustine argues that the matter of the body is never destroyed, even if it becomes food for man or beast. In his treatise on the resurrection of the dead, Tertullian observes that many corpses have been conserved in good condition for hundreds of years, while the "bones of giants" (fossils) are proof that some parts of matter do not decompose.

Ultimately, however, the authors of the treatises on resurrection must concede a portion of matter to the cannibal. Confronted with the resilience of anthropophagous outrage, God must resign Himself to commanding a portion of matter, while leaving the rest to the cannibal. The opposition here is between matter and motion. God rules an essentially Parmenidean universe, while the cannibal is prince of a Heraclitean, dynamic realm. There is an entire flux of fluids and vapors over which he extends his authority. Delimitation of this exhaustible and uncontrolla-ble volume is one of the purposes of the treatises on the resurrection of the flesh. Athenagoras believes that nothing from all these materials—bile, air, and suchlike—permanently resides in the body during life. "Hence it results that the body can be resurrected without these materi-als, which in the new state would be perfectly useless to it and will in no way serve the blessed life we shall then enjoy."[21]

Augustine's solution, in *The City of God*, directly answers the diffi-culty of this most difficult of problems, namely to whom shall be re-stored at the resurrection a body that has become part of the body of another living man. Of the possible types of cannibalism, Augustine chooses to mention only that impelled by hunger. The flesh that was as-similated by the cannibal must be regarded as "borrowed." What hap-pens here is exactly the same as in the case of borrowed money, which must be returned to its owner. Of course, this leaves a gap in the body of the anthropophagus. Augustine replies to this objection using a principle of the conservation of matter. Of course, hunger has made the cannibal thinner, before eating human flesh. His body has been diminished by ex-haustion, but all the flesh that melted into the air can be brought back by the infinite power of God. A similar opinion occurs in Aquinas. The flesh swallowed by a cannibal belongs to his victim by right. Thus, there will be a lack in the cannibal's body at the resurrection, but this will be filled by the infinite power of God. As for the case of the children of ab-solute cannibals, they will receive a part of their being from others, be-cause although a part of the father's seed might originate in the essential substance of other men God will supplement the victim's deficiency.

The discussion of the cannibal in the treatises on resurrection is not merely about the body. The difficulties of the theory of resurrection re-flect not just the complexity of disengaging the particles of the body from the labyrinthine passage presupposed by anthropophagy. The can-nibal, as a conceptual person, is more dangerous than all the critics of Christianity because he claims for himself an extraordinary power over the circulation of atoms, upon which God will have to intervene with infinite power. Up until that moment, the anthropophagus is master of a world in which man, because he has a material body, is obligated to participate. If God will ultimately restore the natural position of parti-cles and bodies, this is a conclusion that the theory of resurrection will have to prove against the cannibal and one on which depends a funda-mental dogma of the Christian system. What is here at stake is the very possibility of salvation, and salvation is, in the patristic age, general, both of the flesh and of the soul. Without a body, the very salvation of the soul is threatened. The dissertation on the cannibal is therefore a reflection of a care for the soul. A mortal body pulverized for eternity in the earth or in the cannibal's innards no longer offers a corporeal target for the Last Judgment. Athenagoras explains this situation: "If God only recompenses the soul for all the good man has done, then it is clear that he is unjust to the body, because the body, after being party to all the trials that virtue has demanded of it, and after it has been in the service of the soul and of God, should have a share in the glory rightfully due to it." From the point of view of punishment, there is a similar dilemma: "We clearly see that God would wrong the soul by condemning it alone, in the absence of its accomplice, for the sins it has committed, for the most part only at the instigation of the body." Master over the great domain of natural corruption, where there reigns an injustice that threatens to contaminate the divine realm, the cannibal is a diabolical figure in the most profound sense, an anti-Divinity. After he has assimilated the body, the cannibal will dispute with God the soul of man.

THE EXPERIMENTS OF MECHANICAL SCIENCE

Up until the seventeenth century, the discussions about the resurrection of the body recapitulate the theories put forward during the time of the primitive church. With the appearance of mechanical science and atomism, however, the universe of reference changes fundamentally. From this moment, the circulation of particles of matter is, at least in principle, the object of an exact science. It is in the context of the new disciplines of physics or the chemistry of corpuscles that the difficulties of resurrection and its solutions will be reinterpreted. Resolution of the problem of resurrection now becomes part of a scientific project.

Hugo Grotius's *Treatise of the Truth of the Christian Religion* heralds this evolution. However many changes bodies might undergo, the matter of which they are formed always remains the same, and is capable of receiving different forms. To say that the resurrection is impossible means to argue that God is not omniscient, because he does not know the position of each particle that composed the human body and is not sufficiently powerful to reunite them. The metaphor Grotius uses in connection with the action of corporeal synthesis is a modern one: "But how could He not in this great Universe, where he is absolute Master, do that which we see Chemists do in their furnaces and in their instruments of their art, where after having destroyed a thing by dissolving it, they reproduce it by reuniting its parts?"[22]

The most redoubtable difficulty relative to resurrection is the traditional one brought forward by anthropophagy. Animals, after having fed on human flesh, might then be found on the table of another man, admits Grotius. Repeating an argument of patristic origin, he shows that the greater part of what we eat is not converted into our own substance, but into excrements or humors that are nothing but "accessory." Furthermore, God takes care that the substance of those animals that have fed on human flesh should not end up, through the effect of "a most particular providence [*une Providence encore plus particulière*]," being assimilated into the bodies of those that eat them. This process, argues Grotius, is similar to the passage of poisons and medicaments through the organism, substances which do not serve as nourishment. Moreover, nature dictates that "somehow" human flesh is not proper to our nourishment.

Grotius avoids discussion of the possibility of voluntary cannibalism. Whatever his motives might have been, this omission is promptly criticized in a translator's note to the Utrecht edition of 1692: "All the reasoning [regarding the impossibility of assimilating a cannibal meal] seems rather weak."[23] Grotius theory "supposes a miracle in the ordinary course of things."[24] Indeed, the explanations that will be constructed around cannibalism in the modern epoch will appropriate this element of the regularity of the course of nature, without recourse to a particular act of the Divine will. More than theology, natural philosophy is called on to discover the error of Grotius. The criterion of truth is now empirical: "One can be assured that experience destroys this supposition [that of nonassimilation] and that those of the Americans who feed on the flesh of their vanquished enemies are just as perfectly nourished by it as by any other foodstuff."[25]

In a series of sermons delivered in 1704 and 1705, in what became the Boyle Lectures, financed by Robert Boyle in order to combat atheism, Samuel Clarke, one of the defenders of the Newtonian system, discusses the dogma of the resurrection of the body. Clarke admits that this is not a doctrine that can be revealed based only on the light of reason and unaided by revelation. On the other hand, it is not contrary to reason. "The only real difficulty" identified by the preacher is that of cannibalism: "The supposition of one's body's being turned into the nourishment, and becoming part of the substance of another, so as that the same parts may equally belong to two bodies, to both of which it shall nevertheless be absolutely impossible that the same parts should be restored."[26] However, such an objection is, Clarke believes, a "great trifle." The solution is simple: to avoid the identity of the parts in question. "There does not at all appear any absolute necessity, that, to constitute the same body, there must be an exact restitution of all and only the same parts."[27]

Clarke does not believe that the supposition of a Providence that impedes the assimilation of the particles of one body by another, as advanced by Grotius, is necessary. In fact, it might even be false, as he gives us to understand. His argument makes appeal to the demonstrative powers of the cannibal: "It may be possible in nature for barbarous cannibals, if any such there be, to subsist for some time and live wholly upon one another."[28] Clarke sets the specter of absolute cannibalism in opposition to the flux of particles orchestrated by Providence.

The solution he puts forward is one based on the new science of nature. His instrument is the microscope: "No man can say it is improbable, (and they who have been most and best versed in microscopical observations think it more than probable,) that the original stamina, which contain all and every one of the solid parts and vessels of the body, not excepting even the minutest nerves and fibres, are themselves the entire body."[29] This is a repetition of the classical theory of the vital seed, but supported by the authority of the new scientific optics. The rest, Clarke claims, is nothing more than extraneous matter. This may be left to its anarchic flux, because the vital nucleus remains unaffected: "No confusion of bodies will be possible in nature."[30]

Clarke concludes by suggesting a program of scientific research to demonstrate the validity of this hypothesis of the body. Minute observations must be made concerning the way in which the body "unfolds itself by growth," the "impossibility of the body's extending itself, by any nourishment whatever, beyond that certain magnitude to which the original vessels are capable of being unfolded," and "the impossibility of restoring by any nourishment the smallest vessel or solid part of the body that has at any time happened to be mutilated by any accident; all which observations, often and carefully made, will seem very much to favour some such speculation as this."[31]

Samuel Clarke's sermons are significant in that they illustrate the flexibility of the new mechanical conception of nature. The difficulties implied by anthropophagy are so serious that he is required to amend the image of the body radically. In the eighteenth century, a conception of the body arises that considers it as a sum of the mechanical movements of its parts. This is the experimental body for philosophy: a system, a sum of trajectories, forces, and the mass of its elements. However, Clarke deviates from this model when he discusses a resuscitated body that is not the mere addition of elements among which the cannibal might sow confusion. He proposes an essentialist hypothesis, of classical extraction, formulated in a manner that will be acceptable to and testable by modern experimental science. That it is so is also shown by his approving references to patristic doctrines and to Saint Paul the Apostle. We

may imagine (there is here a marginal note to Origen) that just as there
is a "minute insensible seminal particle" in a grain of corn, which
evolves when the rest of the grain decays, "so our present mortal and
corruptible body may be but the *exuviae*, as it were, of some hidden and
at present insensible principle (possibly the present seat of the soul,)
which at the resurrection shall discover itself in its proper form."[32]

In *Some Physico-Theological Considerations about the Possibility of
the Resurrection* (1675), Robert Boyle identifies two objections that
might be brought against the theory of resurrection. The first: the human
corpse decomposes into countless fragments, which are scattered, corrupted, and then become part of other animals. The second objection is
the case of the cannibal, when resurrection might seem "much more impossible." One of the solutions he advances is a version of the incorruptible corpuscle. A human body is not like a brass or marble statue,
but is in perpetual flux; it grows from a "*corpusculum* no bigger than
an insect." The experiments of Sanctorius, the learned physician from
Padua, Boyle believes, prove to us that the greater part of the substance
of the human body is changed in a short time.[33] However, it is known
that the bones are of a "stable and lasting texture," as is proven by the
skulls and bones of those that history records as having died "an exceed-
ing long time ago."

Boyle's other demonstration places us directly in the universe of the
discourse of modern science. He sets out to provide experimental proof
of the reunion required for resurrection. Some solids are composed of
corpuscles, which preserve their nature even when combined with other
bodies. Such is the case of "metalline bodies."[34] Gold dissolved in aqua
regia resembles a "liquor" from which, after having been "dexterously
coagulated," a salt or vitriol appears. Boyle reveals that he has conducted such chemical experiments in order to clarify the idea of the resurrection of the body: "By another operation, I have taken pleasure to
make [gold] part of the fuel of a flame." In combination with another
mineral, it can be reduced to glass, and when precipitated with mercury
"it makes a glorious transparent powder."

The chemist is then seconded by the botanist. These transformations
observed in the study of metallic alloys are also to be found in animals
and plants. Butter sometimes has a different taste, depending on what
plants were growing in the pasture. The botany in question is not strictly
experimental, but rather literary: Hippocrates is supposed to have given
a child milk from an animal that had eaten *Elaterium*, which then found
its way into the liquid while preserving its medicinal properties. Therefore there are substances that have passed through many stomachs, without losing their nature and without exhausting their essential properties.

Boyle tells us of a man who lived on the coast of Ireland and could vouch that the pork tastes of fish there, so that strangers could not eat *them*; the cause was that the pigs were fed on shellfish. In the islands of the Caribbean, there is a fruit named Junipa, which lends a violet color to pork or the flesh of parrots and any other birds that feed on it. In America grows another fruit, well known to the English planters, which turns the urine red, so that those who eat it are easily able to convince others that they are "pissing blood."

Boyle's aim is to show that modern science, especially chemistry, can offer a model and an explanation of the divine operation of reuniting particles of matter. With scientific manipulation it is possible, he reveals, to extract particles from the mixture of which they are part, in such a way that those unfamiliar with the wonderful operations of nature will not believe it possible. These operations are not unknown to the "expert Chemists" who, for example, cause mercury to reappear from a crystalline sublimate.

Boyle's theses were elaborated in the context of the metaphysics of material corpuscles. He argues that matter is uniform in its nature, and in essence is only Prime Matter. The particles of a body are distinguished only by their motion, size, position, and so on, properties "that we are wont to call mechanical affections." An intelligent agent, such as we may presuppose the Divinity to be by nature, may watch the progress of a portion of matter "in its whole progress thro' the various forms it is made to put on, till it come to the end of its course or series of changes." The intelligent agent might then "lay hold of this portion of matter, clothed in its ultimate form, and, extricating it from any other parcels of matter wherewith it may be mingled, make it exchange its last mechanical properties for those which it had when this agent first began to watch it."[35] In this case, matter, regardless of the changes it has undergone, may become what it formerly was, thereby offering support to Divine omnipotence.

In order to illustrate this idea, Bolye proposes a thought experiment. Let us suppose that someone cuts a sphere of soft wax into two equal parts, and makes cylinders, cones, rings, spirals etc. from one of them. Mixing the other half with "paste," he makes "an appearance of cakes, vermicelli (as the Italians call paste squeezed through a perforated plate into the form of little worms), wafers, biscuits etc." After that, it will be possible to separate the wax from the dough, by dissolving it, and "reduce it in a mould to the same hemisphere it was before."[36] Another, more difficult example: "If you look upon precipitate carefully made *per se*, you would think that art has made a body extremely different from the common *mercury*." However, if we heat up the powder, we shall reproduce the mercury exactly as it was before we made the precipitate.

Boyle's enthusiasm for science is tempered by piousness. Although he has indicated several chemical methods of "recovering bodies from their various disguises," he admits to be "far from any desire it should be imagined that such ways were the only" that might be used in the resurrection. "Till chemistry and other parts of true natural philosophy be more thoroughly understood and farther promoted, it is probable that we can scarce now imagine what expedients to reproduce bodies a further discovery of the mysteries of art and nature may lead us mortals to." We cannot establish what means God will employ "since it is a part of the imperfection of inferior natures to have but an imperfect apprehension of the powers of one that is incomparably superior to them."[37]

Ultimately, for Boyle as well as Clarke, scientific certainty is translated only into moral probability.[38] What these scientists wish to do is merely demonstrate that the resurrection of the flesh is not in principle impossible; this possibility, in turn, being translated in a foundation of religious belief. Such a defensive position proves that in the modern epoch the dogma of resurrection is perceived against a background of growing hostility.

THEORIES OF PERSONAL IDENTITY

The difficulties of the resurrection of the flesh appeared so formidable that in the age of the first Christian apologists some advanced the thesis of a resurrection of a different kind of body than the natural one. In *Enchiridion*, Augustine accepts that the matter of bodies will be differently arranged at the resurrection, and that the bodies of the saints will be spiritual.[39] In the *Treatise of Principles*, Origen criticizes the narrow outlook and sterile arguments of those who attribute a wholly base and abject significance to the resurrection.[40] According to Origen, the literal doctrine of the resurrection of the flesh is wrong. The resurrected body is both the same and different to the deceased's body, just as a plant is the same and different to the seed from which it has grown. Origen puts forward a doctrine that will enjoy a remarkable career, according to which resurrected bodies are spiritual, purified of the corruption of the mortal frame. These spiritual bodies are so different to their earthly counterparts that it is possible, Origen believes, for them to be spherical.[41] The criticism of Origen includes, in fact, the acceptance of the validity of the "cannibal argument": "Just as the food which we eat is assimilated into our body and changes its characteristics, so also our bodies are transformed in carnivorous birds and beasts and become parts of their bodies; and again, when their bodies are eaten by men or by other animals, they are changed back again and become the bodies of men or of other animals."[42]

Porphyry's skepticism as to the possibility of resurrection will develop further along these lines.

> For often many have perished in the sea and their bodies have been consumed by fishes; many have been eaten by beasts and birds. How then can their bodies come back again? Let us briefly examine what we have said. For instance, suppose someone has been shipwrecked, and his body is eaten by mullets; they in turn were caught by some fishermen, who, after eating the fish, were killed and eaten by dogs; and when the dogs died they were completely consumed by crows and vultures. How then will the body of the man who suffered shipwreck be reassembled again after it has been eaten up by so many animals? And again, another has been consumed by fire, and another eaten by worms; how can such return into the existence which they had at first?[43]

To appeal to the divine omnipotence is not enough: "But you will tell me that this is possible for God. That is not true. . . . For not all things are possible." God is not omnipotent, according to Porphyry in the sense that he could do what is logically impossible.[44]

The Jewish medieval texts display a similar approach. Maimonides, in his *Treatise on Resurrection*, insists that resurrection is a miracle that will be performed by God alone, so why quarrel over the details now? Men have always been preoccupied with bodily resurrection, but this is due to the inability of the vulgar spirits to imagine "any firm existence other than of a body."[45] Before Maimonides, a Jewish sage of the ninth century, Saadia Gaon, already restricted the discussion on resurrection to the good and the righteous in a chapter of his influential treatise *Emunoth ve-Deoth* (Beliefs and Opinions). It is a miracle based on God's omnipotence and involves the reunion of the body with a soul that remains after death in a separate state.[46]

The origin of these sets of arguments and counterarguments regarding the possibility of the resurrection of the body could well be philosophical. According to Chadwick,[47] the debates of the early Christian apologists were decisively influenced by Epicureanism. It was Epicurus who claimed that gods did possess a human form. In the philosophical schools of the second century BC, then, the question became to what extent it could be said that gods have a similar existence to men. Epicurus believed that though gods have a similar form, they are nevertheless permanent. The solution is to imagine gods as a permanent stream of atoms occupying the same eternal form. In a work from the first century BC, Philodemus, an Epicurean philosopher, speculated that gods do not simply possess human form, they must even share other characteristics. They talk, they breathe, they sleep, and they could even talk to one another in Greek. The reaction was swift in competing philosophical circles. Sextus Empiricus pointed out that if gods could indeed talk, then they would have to share a similar anatomy (lungs and everything), which is absurd.[48] What Origen is attempting in his criticism of the thesis of bodily resurrection, demonstrates Chadwick, is simply to continue the arguments of the anti-Epicurean polemic of the Academy.

The theory of the resurrection of the flesh declines in the seventeenth and eighteenth centuries, in part due to the reiteration of classical difficulties, primarily that presupposed by anthropophagy. In the article on "Resurrection" in the *Encyclopédie*, we discover that the Christians believe in the resurrection of the flesh, but the philosophers have put forward two objections to this. In the first we see the cannibal as an ally of the struggle against superstition. The same matter should serve two or more bodies at the resurrection: "Otherwise, we have seen examples of men that eat other men, such as the Cannibals and other savages of the West Indies, who practice this thing with their prisoners."[49] Who has the right to the "common part" in this case? Some have answered this difficulty by arguing that not all matter can be assimilated by the human body; ingurgitated human flesh will be secreted and then stuck back on to its initial body by intervention of the divine power. However, for the Paris *coterie*, "Mr. Leibniz's answer seem the most solid."[50] What is essential to the body is an original *flamen*, which is to be found in the seed of the father, and which can be neither divided from nor added to another body. All the rest of the body is an addition of a "foreign substance" (*matière étrangère*). It results that there is ultimately no exact resuscitation of the body, therefore "the difficulty falls of itself, because it is based on nothing but a false hypothesis" (*la difficulté proposée tombe d'elle même, parce qu'elle n'est appuyée que sur une fausse hypothèse*). The second difficulty highlighted by the philosophers rests on "the latest discoveries that have been made regarding the animal economy" (*les dernières découvertes qu'on a faites sur l'économie animale*). The Enlightenment scholars reveal to us the novelty that the body is perpetually changing. No one has the same body as yesterday. Ergo, which body will be resuscitated and punished by divine justice at the Last Judgment? Happily, it is possible to answer these objections "based on the principles of Mr Locke"—"the personal identity of a rational being consists in its interior sentiment, in the power to consider itself [*soi-même*] as the same thing in different times and places."[51] It is this "personal identity" which, argues the author of the article, will be "the object of punishments and rewards."

In this enlightened version of the theory of resurrection, the task of God is simpler. All He has to do is on the one hand take into account a limited set of elementary particles, whose trajectories are not erased from the background of matter. On the other hand, He must become a psychologist, in order to examine the inner feelings of each person and apply His power to a fragment of them. Thus endowed with the capacity to read the minds of men, God might then be able to explain why the encyclopedists held no scruples in plagiarizing almost word for word the article on resurrection in the *Chambers Encylopaedia*.[52]

As can be seen from the article in the *Encyclopédie*, the difficulties do not disappear as soon as a strict theory of the resurrection of the flesh is abandoned. Spiritual or not, the resurrected body is problematic from the point of view of its personal identity. This objection had already been discussed by medieval theologians such as Thomas Aquinas. It is true that the discussions about the nature of personal identity are not exclusively bound to the problem of the identity of resurrected bodies, as is proven by Plato, for example. Whatever its sources, theological or philosophical, the question of the identity of a person becomes a subject associated with the discussion of resurrection at the same time as the emergence of Cartesianism and modern atomism.

In *An Explanation of the Grand Mystery of Godliness* (1660), Henry More argues that the doctrine of the resurrection of the dead is that most attacked by atheists, who thereby hope to destroy all the other articles of religion. According to More, "enthusiasts" have advanced a theory of the numerical nonidentity of the resurrected body. They argue that "the *Anthropophagi* or *Cannibals* are continually fed with mans flesh, as also they feed one upon another." How can it therefore be possible for a cannibal to have the same body at the resurrection? "For he will be left as bare of flesh, as the Crow was of feathers when every bird had pecked away what belonged unto themselves." The second objection shows that some men have not been buried but rather eaten by fish, while others have been burned or else rotted above ground, and their flesh has melted and dissolved into vapors. In the third place, they argue that the principle of the identity of bodies implies a contradiction, because the body has been partner "either in unlawfull pleasures or the laudable pains and labours of the Soul," but it has been transformed, it is no longer the same, like a flowing river. We do not have the same numerical body, but rather always acquire a new body. To claim that the same numerical body rises from the grave is an injustice, "for so shall the Body of an old man be punished for the sins of that Body he had when he was young."

More's answer mobilizes Plato's theory of the soul in the benefit of Christianity. The soul is unique and determines the identity of the individual. "There is no *stable Personality* of a man but what is in his Soul." Where there is the same soul, there is the same person. Those who are required to refer to the numerical identity of the body at the Last Judgment ignore the fact that the body is "utterly incapable of all sense and cogitation," a fact which has been determined by the "excellent philosopher Descartes." As regards the idea that the dead will rise from the grave, this is a prophetic and symbolic expression, although it is possible that this might really happen. Recent interpreters of the Scriptures argue that as in the case of the seed, at the resurrection God will give the soul a body different to that with which it was buried. We shall return to life in a "glorious" body," concludes More.[53]

Boyle inclines to a viewpoint close to the theory of the vital seed. There is no exact size at which the human body begins no longer to be the same. A minute portion of matter may sometimes serve as a support for this identity, as can be seen in the succession of the embryo in the uterus, the new-born child, the adult man, and the decrepit man of one hundred, all of whom are the same person, albeit of very different statures. In Boyle's opinion, even the theory of legal rights supports this perspective on identity: proof is provided by the crowning of kings and emperors in the womb and the sentencing to death of old criminals for murders committed in their youth.

The theory of the identity of glorious bodies is ultimately thrown into difficulty by the reality of anthropophagy. This time it is not merely a question of the individual anthropophagus, but of a vision of universal and involuntary anthropophagy. That involuntary cannibalism exists was something known as long ago as the patristic writers. However, the progress of the sciences amplifies the perception of the ubiquity of anthropophagy. Mechanical philosophy presents a universe in which particles move from one body to another, without the inhibitions proper to scholastic essences. Microscopic observations show that the universe contains an infinite number of particles that circulate in apparent chaos. The corpuscles of the flesh thereby reach every man. It is a reality discovered, among others, by Sir Thomas Brown, in *Religio medici* (1643):

All flesh is grass, is not only metaphorically, but literally, true; for all those creatures we behold are but the herbs of the field, digested into flesh in them, or more remotely carnified in our selves. Nay further, we are what we all abhor, Anthropophagi and Cannibals, devourers not only of men, but of our selves; and that not in an allegory, but a positive truth: for all this mass of flesh which we behold, came in at our mouths; this frame we look upon, hath been upon our trenchers; in brief, we have devour'd our selves.[54]

Confronted by a humanity that has wholly become a nation of cannibals, the exercise of the infinite power of God over the universe of physical movement is improbable, if not downright impossible. On the one hand, this leads to a doctrine of the "glorious body" and, on the other, to a circumscription of the domain of profound and secular physical disorder. Universal cannibalism is a thought-experiment that marks the boundaries of the modern physical world, just as Descartes' demon waylays the philosopher on the road to discovery of absolute subjectivity.

Thomas Burnet's *A Treatise concerning the State of Departed Souls, Before, and At, and After the Resurrection* abandons the theory of the resurrection of the flesh in order to salvage the theory of the resurrection of bodies. We are resurrected with a "glorious body," devoid of organs, not with a body made up of ordinary matter. Flesh and blood consist of particles whose essential properties will not be conserved in the incorruptible state that will follow the intervention of God. What determines the identity of the resurrected body is not the formula of its substantial composition, but the individual soul, which can be attached to any body, or to no body, without there being any question of another person.

Burnet's demonstration is a mixture of classical and modern arguments. "Our Bodies," he claims, "have no Stability, nor are they always the same, but are in perpetual Flux and Motion, and Mutation."[55] Thus, during the course of a lifetime, we have "six or seven different Bodies," and "perhaps, in one we have behaved ourselves well, and in another ill: How then shall impartial Justice be render'd to each of them?"[56]

In his *Treatise*, Burnet adapts some of the criticisms of resurrection to the advantage of revising Christian dogma. Here we have the problem, discussed by patristic authors such as Athenagoras, of whether the resurrection of bodies is an exercise worthy of the divine majesty. For Burnet, the entire enterprise is suspect because it results in a repulsive congregation: "How ill would the decrepit Body of an old Man, or the little helpless one of an Infant, become the Court of Heaven ... and either in the one or the other of these Bodies, the greater Part of human Kind expires."[57]

Burnet draws the main argument against the resurrection of the flesh from the new philosophy of the mechanical movement of matter. Corpses are pulverized into thousands of particles, which are "ingrafted into the Bodies of Animals, of Trees ... from which they cannot be easily be brought back again."[58] A correct notion of the nature of the resuscitated body causes the divine intervention no longer to have any object, because "'tis plainly of no Significance, that we should have the same Parts, either numerical or specifical . . . shall we dare to imploy the supreme Power of the Deity upon a Matter useless and insignificant?"[59]

It is not only pointless but downright impossible: "To collect the Dust and the Ashes of all human Carcasses from the Origin of the World to the End of it, then to reduce every one of them to its own Mass and its own Heap, and to work up and fashion that Heap a-new into its old Shape, and Size, and Bigness, would be the most astonishing of Miracles. But of such a Miracle, so manifold, and so useless, we have hitherto had no Example."[60]

Having thus inscribed God's omnipotence within the limits of utility and our capacity rationally to accept a phenomenon, Burnet arrives at the question of anthropophagy. For him, cannibalism is more of an ally in his demonstration. There are many persons, he argues, who doubt the possibility of resurrection: "Some Nations, say they, are *Anthropophagi*; they some of them feed upon others; and 'tis barely impossible that the same numerical Flesh can at the same Time be restor'd to several Bodies."[61] Burnet accepts the contrary implications of anthropophagy for the resurrection of the flesh. Moreover, he carries the argument even further: "But why do they mention some Nations? we are all of us ἀλληλοφάγοι [eaters of one another]; we all of us feed upon the Remains of each other; not indeed immediately, but after they have had some Transmutations into Herbs and Animals: in those Herbs and Animals we eat our Ancestors, or at least some minute Parts of them."[62]

The only hope for a theory of the resurrection of the flesh would be to transform the world into one huge mausoleum: "If the Ashes of every one, from the Beginning of the World, had been separately preserv'd in their own Urns or Coffins, or rather, if all Carcases had been converted into Mummy, and had so remain'd, for the greater Part, intire, there would be some Hope of recovering several Parts of the same Body, without a Mixture of others."[63] However, this hypothesis is contradicted by the existence of the physical motion of material particles, a motion devoid of any piety. Because of the perpetual "Circle" of particles of matter, "it may very well happen, that by taking this Compass, the same Part of Matter may have undergone several μετενσωματώσεις [transincarnations], may have inhabited more Bodies than the Soul of *Pythagoras*."[64] The result is an inflation of demand and a depression of divine supply: "Let us admit, if you please, for the sake of Example, that the first Posterity of *Adam*, or the Men of the first Ages should first reclaim their Bodies, and then, in Order, the People of every Age should require theirs: Scarce half Bodies will be remaining for the late Posterity of *Adam*, or the last Inhabitants of the Earth, all those Parts and Particles being torn from them which belong'd to the Bodies of their Ancestors."[65]

The translator and commentator of Grotius's treatise on the resurrection likewise tries to elude the difficulties of identity. Even when a body forever loses a part of itself to another body, it does not result that it would no longer be the same body. Ultimately, every body is in continual flux. "The continual transpiration of the particles that make up the body, which are also continually succeeded by other particles, change it no less than this accident [i.e. anthropophagy] of which we speak."[66] As Seneca demonstrated, time consumes our bodies with the same rapidity as a flame. "Nothing we see is stable and perpetual; even as I speak of this vicissitude, I make proof of it."[67] Under the pressure of anthropophagy, the move philosophy is forced to make is paradoxical: in order to conserve a problematical identity, the latter begins to be seen as precarious. The element that holds this improbable synthesis of moving particles together is a modern notion of time, in which the latter is experienced as speed.

Selective resurrection seems to be the answer of Humphrey Hody, a fellow of Wadham College, to the same difficulties of resurrection. The body will resurrect from the matter animated by God. Cannibalism is not a problem, though, as it only concerns flesh, which is not "integrant and necessary" to the identity of the body as bones, skins, and nerves are.[68] The learned John Tillotson, in a sermon preached in 1682 at Whitehall, dismisses the difficulty of cannibalism with a different argument. Not even the most consummate cannibals are able to ingest the entire substance of a corpse. The "more solid parts (skulls and bones) . . . it is not pretended that the cannibals ate them"; even if they do, the substance of a body, as proven by the experiments of Sanctorius, renews a few times every year. Therefore, the anthropophagi assimilate just one instance of a body and it will be no difficulty for God to retrieve a previous body for the victim of the cannibal at the time of theresurrection.[69]

In 1753, Louis Reinier, professor of philosophy at the Jesuit College in Breslau, published a translation of Athenagoras's discourse, accompanied by notes that extend for the entire length of the book, in a commentary that is as voluminous as the original text. The nature of this parallel text is in itself interesting, because it is an alloy of a very modern Enlightenment spirit and a conservative, religious tendency.

Reinier directly tackles the problem of cannibalism in a series of passages that show us he has made use of moderate naturalism, which he justifies in his polemics with modern philosophers such as Locke, La Mettrie, and Descartes. Willy-nilly, we are all cannibals. Nature maintains a kind of "traffic" between the two kingdoms of creation, the animal and vegetal, in which each appropriates what has become useless to the other. The grass growing on our ancestors' graves, the corpse juices that decompose and generate vegetation, as can be seen by anyone who has visited a battlefield—all these processes place substance in circulation. Plants feed at our expense, without us necessarily dying beforehand. Imperceptible transpiration is a process whereby we lose a part of ourselves: "Different species of atoms, which internal motion detaches from our bodies, take their flight." This humidity penetrates into plants through their roots and leaves, and is then assimilated, thereby finding its way back to our dinner table, in the form of food.

All this flux of material particles does not raise any difficulties as far as resurrection is concerned, believes Reinier, because the substances that pass from man to plant do not represent matter proper to man, essential to his identity. It is true that, after resurrection, the vessels of the resuscitated body must be filled with fluid, "but on the other hand it would be absurd to imagine that all the accessory matter that has passed through the human body would have to be rediscovered on Judgment Day, and that from this transient matter a sufficient amount could not be found to fill every body, without having any other to dispute it."[70]

Thus we all partake in an involuntary, general cannibalism. In Reinier's theory, the difficulties raised by anthropophagy are resolvable by means of a harmonious fit between the parts of the universe. Everything conspires so that the anthropophagus will not be able to disturb the natural order: the quantities of matter, which are sufficient for the divine hydraulics; the internal organs, which of themselves distinguish the particles they must absorb; the spirit and its material body, which understand each other in spite of the radical difference in essence. This idea of harmony is one intensely exploited by Enlightenment philosophers, and only a few skeptics such as Voltaire and Hume seem not to have had the patience to explore its wonderful possibilities. Reinier approvingly cites Pope and Maupertius, in connection with the problem of harmony. His sources are eclectic, because he is an enlightened Jesuit who tries to translate the ideas of a second-century theologian into the scientific language of the eighteenth century. From the pitiless being of the anthropophagus, what the German Jesuit ultimately retains is a notion of universal cannibalism as a natural process, which transcends any individuality. The cannibal dissolves into nature, whence only a miracle can resuscitate his scattered particles. But in his dissolution, he transfers something of his being to the modern subject.

The majority of Enlightenment philosophers are less confident than Reinier that the difficulties cannibalism raises for the theory of identity are resolvable. In the *Dictionnaire philosophique* (article on "Resurrection"), Voltaire argues that there are "arithmetical objections" (*objections arithmétiques*) to the dogma of resurrection. Man and other animals feed on the substance of their predecessors, because human bodies turn to dust and are scattered over the earth and into the air. Thus they are assimilated and become "legumes." There is not a single man who has not ingested a tiny piece of our forefathers: "This is why it is said that we are all anthropophagi. Nothing is more reasonable after a battle: not only do we kill our brothers, but after two or three years we shall eat them, after they have put down roots on the battlefield."[71]

The article "Resurrection" in the *Yverdon Encyclopaedia* is, according to the author, a rewrite of that in the *Encyclopédie*. In fact, it is much more than that. Ironic and inventive in the original version, it now propagates an almost complete skepticism regarding the reality of the resurrection. Bodies decompose and their matter is absorbed in other bodies, it circulates in animals, vegetables, and other matter, which spring up in endless variation in nature. Some parts of the body might be eaten and digested by a ferocious wild beast, others may end up in a plant grazed by a cow, and then eaten by a man, and this man might be eaten by a cannibal. How can we then conceive of the resurrection? There is a difficulty here, which disappears only if we see that substances circulate and that the parts of which a body is made at the age of ten are no longer the same as those of which it is made at the age of twenty. Today's parts dissipate and are replaced by others. In spite of all these variations, man remains the same. Likewise, a house is the same after two hundred years, although nothing remains of its original parts. Self-awareness—reminiscence, memory, intrinsic feeling—is sufficient in order to constitute the identity of a person. It matters little what has become of the original particles after death, on condition that the soul is conserved and recognizes itself as the same person. However, is the soul not attached to a kernel imperceptible to our eyes, an indestructible germ that awaits only a new matrix in order to live again? This supposition is not contradictory, but it is highly unlikely, argues the *Yverdon Encyclopaedia*. At the level of the substantial reality of the resurrection, the authors are declared skeptics: as regards the question "How does the resurrection come about?" a modest "I do not know" would be the only acceptable answer. Undoubtedly, the creative power can give life to matter once more, but we do not know how it does so. Perhaps the germs of all the dead men in the sea will find there a matrix convenient to a new birth. Perhaps a new Adam will become the source of many successive generations, or perhaps an act of the divine will shall cause all the men who have existed to come back to life. As for the form in which we shall be resurrected, the authors plead equal ignorance in that respect.

Fontenelle's *Letter to the Marquis of La Farre* does not deal in doubts but rather certainties. It is a satirical denunciation of the consequences of the idea of resurrection. La Farre was a libertine of Palais-Royal circles who one day asked Fontenelle what he thought of the resurrection of bodies. In reply, the latter recapitulated some of the difficulties of the resurrection. The Scriptures promise that our bodies will be resurrected, but this is not evident if we accept that God created all the matter in the universe once and for all. The matter of which our bodies are composed has also been used to form the bodies of our ancestors and will be used to form the bodies of those who will come after us.

Fontenelle's theories are based on radical materialism, for which the mass of substance is framed within strictly quantitative limits. His theory depends on a principle of the economy of matter, which immediately makes visible the circulation of particles through the succession of individual bodies. The quantity of matter created by God neither increases nor decreases, "the void has no right over it." It is divided into "elements," whose movement and combination form different individuals: "The junction of these elements forms a body."[72] They destroy one other and determine one another at every moment, without their material substance being affected by what the "vulgar and ignorant" perception names creation and destruction.

Against this metaphysical backdrop, God is confronted with a veritable problem, the *Letter* reveals, because it is not clear what he might be able to do in order for the countless men who have shared the same particles to be contemporary. All these men have had a body because they have borrowed fragments of other bodies and there is no source of new particles from which any eventual shortfall might be met.

Happily, there is an "expedient," Fontenelle reveals amusedly. If we are resurrected one day, then the things that are necessary to this life will then become useless, for the simple reason that our bodies will no longer be subject to the rule of necessity. If nothing of what is spatial will be of any further use to man, and if the resuscitated bodies no longer have their initial forms and functions, then "the order and harmony of the universe will be overthrown, everything will become a heap of matter, a shapeless mass, chaos and confusion, as it was on the first day of Creation."

In such a situation, God should manifest his creative power anew. From this plastic matter, he will be able to give form to infinitely many spiritual men. And if indeed the problem of remaking material bodies arises, then in order to accommodate the shortage of matter, God will be able to make smaller people. From the matter of someone like La

Farre, who was grossly overweight, four other smaller men might be made. Cannibalism is here universal and automatic. In the ironic theory of the resurrection put forward by Fontenelle, bodies cannibalize one another in the flux of physical movement. Against the backdrop of this anonymous dynamic, the attempt to describe the geometric place of a soul that might define itself as individual is doomed to failure.

THE ENEMY OF GOD

Because it would have been riskier to imagine the like on Earth, Cyrano de Bergerac's Moon is the place where a fundamentally anti-Christian ideology holds sway. The moon-dwellers have ideas regarding the immortality of the soul (a false doctrine according to them), and one of them launches into a systematic attack whose target is the theory of resurrection.[73] Let us suppose that you eat a Muslim—the moon-dweller tells his terrestrial visitor—and you convert him to your own substance. Once digested, the Muslim is transformed partly into flesh, partly into blood, and partly into sperm. On "embracing" a woman, with the seed having been "entirely extracted from the Muslim's corpse, you will bring a little Christian into the world." Cyrano's text seems to suggest that the little Christian is an abortion, thereby bringing into discussion another subject disputed by the theologians, namely the fate of unbaptized children or fetuses. However, what will happen at the Last Judgment? Will the Muslim have his body returned? If so, it means the little Christian will remain without a body, because he is nothing "in his totality other than a part of the Muslim." If not, then the Muslim will remain without his body. But what if God creates matter to supplement the lack? The Moon-dweller is obviously up to date with the theological subtleties of the terrestrials. In this case, he argues, another "difficulty" arises, namely the damned Muslim is resuscitated with a new body, thanks to God, instead of that which was "stolen" from him by the Christian. However, the body is bound to the soul, and together they form a "single subject." In this case, God's gift means that a body other than that of the Muslim will be punished in Hell. Therefore a new "subject," other than the original Muslim, will be damned, because it is no longer a question of the same "individual," and the punishment deserved by one body will befall another, which "has not lent its organs to commit any crime." Thus God punishes someone other than the one deserving of Hell.

And what would be even more ridiculous is that his body would have deserved both Heaven and Hell at the same time, because, inasmuch as it belonged to the Muslim, it must be damned, but as a Christian it must be saved. Therefore God could not place it in Paradise because it would be unjust to recompense with glory the damnation it ought to have merited as a Muslim, and nor can He cast it into Hell, because it would be unjust to recompense with eternal death the beatitude that it would have merited as a Christian. Consequently, if God wishes to be equitable, he must eternally damn and save the same man.

After this speech, it seems to the earthly visitor that the "Antichrist" has spoken. In these passages, the purpose of the cannibal is not only to muddle the theologians but also to stupefy God.

Simultaneous with libertinism and the philosophical radicalism of the Enlightenment, the cannibal becomes, from difficulty incarnate, the vehicle for a critique of the Christian religion. He can play the same role because he is already associated with the most scandalous atheism. A transgressor of the natural law enunciated by God, he is in essence a rebel against the Divinity. An implacable enemy of Heaven, he embodies a monstrous inversion of Christian principles. In the Middle Ages, he personifies the extremes of atheism and heresy. However, modern writers hijack this potential for a critique of religious fanaticism. First, they appeal to the figure of the anthropophagus in order to depict the cruelties of the wars of religion. In a pamphlet of 1646, *An Arrow against all Tyrants and Tyranny*, leveler Richard Overton dubs the intentions of the clergy as "lupine, cannibal and inhuman." In *A Modest Enquiry into the Mystery of Iniquity* (1664), Henry More argues "the modes of villainie are infinite. There seems nothing more detestable then that cruelty of *Canniballs* that eat mans flesh. But how far short would it fall thereof, if we should suppose that the Instruments and Adherents to this Antichristian power [i.e. Spain] did riot it with the Brains of men, and set upon the table the Dugs of women fried like Tripes; whom they first ravish, and then cut off their breasts with some parcel of those parts which modesty will hardly name?"[74]

To the advantage of atheism, the Enlightenment radicals recycle another difficulty of the Christian religion, one also associated with anthropophagy. It is a question of the cannibal implications of the dogma of transubstantiation. If the consecrated bread and wine are indeed the body and blood of Christ, does it not result that Christians are cannibals? This is an implication known to and discussed by medieval theology, and one which eighteenth-century philosophers will be keen to promote in the context of subversive arguments.[75]

In Radicati's *A Comical and True Account of the Modern Canibals's [sic.] Religion, by Osmin True Believer* (1734), a traveler whose ship is captured by pirates ends up a prisoner in a land named Taurasia, where he is pressured into converting to a strange religion. This involves a ceremony in which he wears white robes and visits a "mosque." There, he is asked things he does not understand and to which another answers in his stead. Water is poured on his head, whereby he becomes a "pagan," by means, it would appear, of the "occult quality" of the liquid in question.[76]

After conversion, he discovers a terrifying secret of the Taurasian religion. The second incarnation of the local divinity takes the form of a "wafer," which the worshippers believe to be the "real flesh and blood of the humanis'd Being."[77] Because they always eat large quantities of these wafers, the pagans have become the "most expert Butchers of Human flesh in the world."[78] Christians are thus "Modern Canibals." After examining their "Koran," the neophyte reaches the conclusion that vicious priests have corrupted the religion. Disgusted, he converts to Deism, in the manner of any good Enlightenment philosopher.

In the *Account*, the cannibal takes on a guise that he will assume in many of his subsequent appearances: the mask of satire. The cannibal as a figure who draws the amused gaze of the public is one of the enduring legacies of the Enlightenment diehards. Radicati exposes a grotesque version of the theory of circulating particles in the body of the cannibal. Thanks to digestion, he ascertains, these have been scattered throughout the world via the "conduits, by which Nature discharges herself of her superfluities."[79] In time, submitting to the "eternal course of Nature," these particles "joyn themselves to their first Principles, till they concur together to the formation of another compound Body."[80] In this way, "it is evident that not only the Waters, the Plants and all the Productions of the Earth are impregnated by these Divine Particles; but that even the Atoms, in process of time, shall all be Deify'd."[81] Such an absurd religion is the result of corruption introduced by priests, Radicati concludes.[82]

The idea that the mysteries of the Christian religion include cannibalism recurs in Hume's *Natural History of Religion*. A priest asks a Turkish prisoner in Europe, on the day after he has converted to Christianity and received the sacrament, "How many gods are there?" To which the Turk replies: "None at all. . . . You have told me all along that there is but one God: And yesterday I ate him."[83]

From the classical difficulties of resurrection and transubstantiation, the critics of Christianity turn to criticism of religion in general and of Christianity in particular. In *Jewish Letters* (1742), Boyer d'Argens attacks the institution of monasticism. He argues that the most Parisian *paterfamilias* behave as barbarously to their daughters as those tribes in

Peru that keep women captured in war, feed them well and make children with them, before eating them. The French, in their turn, once they have three or four daughters, marry off the eldest, while the others are doomed from birth to be sent to a kind of prison (obviously a convent), where they endure thousands of torments.[84]

The opening salvo in this war against the rituals of the Catholic Church had been fired decades before, in the *Description of Formosa* (1704), a forgery authored by a certain George Psalmanaazaar.[85] Here we are treated with extravagant descriptions of the "Formosan" priests who rip the hearts from twenty thousand children's chests and distribute to believers pieces of human flesh the size of an egg, boiled in human blood.[86]

In a text published anonymously in 1770, D'Holbach makes an indictment of religion in general. The founders of religions imagined terrible gods, to whom sacrifices were made. Human blood began to flow over the altars, and the most painful, barbarous, and revolting sacrifices were used in order to win the favor of these anthropophagous gods. Nations have ended up plucking children from their mother's breast in order to serve them as food to their God. D'Holbach argues that the sacrifices of the Bible show us that the God of the Christians is at least as cruel and inimical to the human kingdom as the gods of the Greeks, Phoenicians, and Mexicans.[87] D'Holbach was to repeat this charge in *The System of Nature* (1781). Theology is the true source of evils on Earth. Sacrifices have claimed humans, because an infinite Divinity can only be appeased by an infinite victim.[88]

In his epistolary novel *The Letters of Amabed* (1769), Voltaire also resorts to the comparison between Christianity and cannibalism. The novel is set in Goa, and the letters are sent by an Indian couple, who are arrested by the Inquisition under the accusation of heresy. The inquisitors are named *anthropophages* and their religion a "religion of bandits." In the *Dictionnaire philosophique* (article on "Atheism"), Voltaire argues that it is religious fanatics who are dangerous to society. Hobbes, who "passed for an atheist," lived a tranquil and innocent life while the religious fanatics of his day bathed England, Scotland, and Ireland in blood. "Spinoza was not only an atheist, but also preached atheism; . . . it was assuredly not he who chopped the de Witt brothers into pieces and ate them grilled."[89] In the *History of the American Indians*, James Adair reflects on the gruesome cruelty of the Indian women who torture prisoners of war. This is a result of their upbringing and customs, he argues. The same thing happens in Europe, for example in Lisbon, "where tender-hearted ladies are transformed by their bloody priests, into so many Medeas, through deluded religious principles; and sit and see with the highest joy, the martyrs of God, drawn along in diabolical triumph to the fiery stake, and suffering death with lingering torments."[90] In *Robinson Crusoe*, the Englishman learns from Man Friday that there are priests on the latter's island. Whence the conclusion: "There is *Priestcraft*, even among the most blinded ignorant Pagans in the World; and the Policy of making a secret Religion, in order to preserve the Veneration of the People to the Clergy, is not only to be found in the *Roman*, but perhaps among all Religions in the World, even among the most brutish and barbarous Savages."[91]

Setting out from a graphic description of the different kinds of cannibalism, the *Yverdon Encyclopaedia* (article on "Flesh") claims that the origin of these aberrant acts is "delirium," an extremely versatile term. Hence originate embarrassing customs, such as smashing the nose, piercing the ears or lips, elongating the earlobes, chopping pieces from the fingers, removing a testicle, compressing the body, making incisions, poking needles in the buttocks, shaving off the body hair, pulling out teeth, immolation, anthropophagy—the list continues in the same fashion for quarter of a page and includes the aberrant custom of writing moral tracts on benevolence and charity!

The opponents of the philosophers return the compliment. In *Philosophical Catechism* (1749), the abbé Flexier de Réval compares the new philosophy of impiety to a corrosive powder that bites into the living flesh, boring into bone as far as the marrow. Jacob-Nicolas Moreau, in an article for *Mercure de France*, published in 1757, on the "Cacouacs" attacks the philosophers: "A nation of savages, more ferocious and more redoubtable than ever the Caribs were has recently been discovered on the 48th parallel of the northern hemisphere."[92]

The philosophers also invoke the specter of anthropophagy in their critique of various religious practices. In *Recherches philosophiques sur les américains*, de Pauw perorates against circumcision and infibulation. The modern Jews "circumcise in a manner most disgusting and which alone would be capable of inspiring horror at their religious absurdities."[93] A mohel, who has the privilege of never cutting his nails and "who is infinitely respected because of this holy deformity" (*qu'on respecte infiniment à cause de cette sainte difformité*), excises the child's prepuce, while the latter screams the while "as though he were being murdered" (*qui crie comme si on l'égorgeoit*). Afterward, "the circumciser gives a number of grimaces, applies his tongue to the genitals of the neophyte, puts those parts in his mouth and begins to suck with all his might," in order to extract the blood. Sometimes he spits, or else he swallows the child's prepuce, "as the circumcisers of Madagascar do."[94]

The excesses of the savages and the anthropophagi are a mirror in which the Enlightenment discovers the excesses of religious faith. By means of these comparisons, official Christianity is reconstructed by the Enlightenment radicals as an artifact incompatible with the progress of civilization. The Christianity/cannibalism duality brings to light a historic development that increasingly appears as morally suspect.

A SUBJECT WORTHY OF AN ACADEMY

In a note to *Aline and Valcour*, Sade claims that the origin of anthropophagy is a question "impossible to resolve."[95] However, what is certain is that "the custom was general on our planet and is as old as the World," although the reason why a piece of human flesh reached another's dinner table is "absolutely indefinable." For Sade, the impossibility of discovering the first cause is a handicap proper to the science of History. Otherwise, philosophical analysis is perfectly capable, through a kind of imaginary regression, of discovering the reasons that "legitimated this custom." Here, his procedure is similar to that of Rousseau, who in *Discourse on the Origin of Inequality* argues that it is impossible to establish the historical origins of inequality, although we are able to establish at a philosophical level what has made it permanent. It would not be a subject unworthy of an academy, concludes Sade, if a competition were held with a prize "for the author who would reveal the incontestable origin of this custom."

Even without Sade's prize, the philosophers attempted to discover the origin of cannibal customs. Thus they unleashed a polemic that is not limited to the problem of anthropophagy. The question regarding the origin of cannibalism, understood as a cultural institution, is transformed, through a kind of reversal, into one about the origins of social institutions. This occurs because anthropophagy is regarded by the philosophers of natural law as an institution that has its origin at the beginnings of society. To shed light on its sources thereby clarifies the question of the origins of the first forms of association.

The theory according to which rituals have their origin in acts of cannibalism was frequently circulated in the eighteenth century. In a section entitled *Des Anthropophages* in the 1771 edition of *Recherches philosophiques sur les Américains*, de Pauw, whom Sade claimed had written the most on the problems of the origin of cannibalism without however resolving it, states that "some philosophers have believed that the custom of sacrificing human victims derives primitively from anthropophagy" (*quelques Philosophes ont cru que l'usage de sacrifier des victimes humaines dérivoit primitivement de l'Anthropophagie).*[96] He accepts that all nations have formerly made human sacrifices, but it is no longer possible to prove that all nations have been anthropophagous, because this barbaric state occurred before recorded history. Pluche is of the opinion that the "inhumanity" of cannibalism, resulting from pride and wrath, was universal before the flood.[97] Human sacrifice, writes Virey, has its origin in anthropophagy, which in its turn is a product of the violent passion for revenge rather than of hunger. Barbarity is inseparable from anthropophagy and almost all nations were once cannibal.[98] In *The New Science*, Vico compares the sacrificial rites of barbarous times with the anthropophagous sacrifices of America.[99]

The question of the origins of the ritual is important for the Enlightenment philosophers insofar as it is an element of the theory about the origins of society in general. We have seen that in the context of the explanations of natural law the existence and nature of society are clarified by setting out from a preassociative, even savage state. But society is not purely and simply the fact of a number of people being together. What is important for philosophers and jurists is what exactly binds these people, what keeps them together, the significant addition that makes the sum of their presence more than merely numerical. Speculative dissertations on the origin of language, popular in the eighteenth century (Rousseau and Monboddo wrote two of the best known such works), are in fact studies of the origin and nature of society in general. Language is necessary to communication, which has meaning only insofar as people form a group. This means that in order to discover the origin of language, it is necessary to discover the fount and purpose of society. And vice versa: only insofar as we understand how and why society came into being can we clarify what language was used for and what forms it took in primitive society.

The discussion about the origin of ritual is also in part explicable through such a need for a system. As long as religion and religious worship are reckoned necessary conditions for the existence of society, then elucidation of their origin becomes a part of the discourse on the nature of the social body. In its turn, this sheds light on the origins of religion in general and of worship in particular. Anthropophagy does not occur accidentally in this equation. If the man of the state of nature was a cannibal, then his first form of religious worship was bloody and idolatrous. This inference seems even more likely if we recall that in discussion of the state of nature the actions of natural man are imputed to his passions: for example, to the passion of fear. The formation of religion is explained, from Hobbes to Hume, as the genesis of superstition from primitive man's sentiment of terror.

But the authors of the eighteenth century also have more particular reasons for exploring the idea that cannibalism originated in religious worship. In a period in which the discourse on the origin of institutions is part of official narratives of legitimization, the idea that all nations have passed through such an ignoble state and that their first religious worship was anthropophagous has a definite subversive potential. If it is true, then it means that natural man was not innocent and that the history of the origins of the civilized nations must be viewed with circumspection.

Among the manifestations of religion that attract the attention of the philosophers, sacrifice has an especial significance. In the history of Christian worship, the repulsion toward certain types of sacrifice has considerable weight. The philosophers adopt this subject and place a question mark over the causes and justification of religious sacrifices. In the article "Anthropophages" in the *Dictionnaire philosophique,* Voltaire argues that religious fanaticism is capable of leading to anthropophagy and human sacrifice. This is evident from the sacred books of the Jews, where Moses tells the people that if they do not respect the ceremonies then mothers will end up eating their children. In the time of Ezekiel, it is probable that the Jews ate human flesh, as can be seen in the books of the prophet, which show that they will eat not only the horses of their enemies but also the riders. Voltaire comments: "And in fact, why should the Jews not have been anthropophagi? It would be the only thing lacking from the people of God to make them the most abominable on earth."[100]

The hypothesis of the cannibal origin of ritual is ancient. It is formulated in the second book of Porphyry's *De abstinentia,* which examines animal sacrifices and touches on the problem of cannibalism. His aim is to justify vegetarianism, and one of his arguments is that the sacrifice of animals, even when necessary, should not lead to the conclusion that we must eat the flesh of the victim. In order to demonstrate this fact, he draws a parallel with human sacrifice. After expositing a history of human sacrifice, which he claims is still practiced, Porphyry argues that this does not authorize the consumption of human flesh. On the basis of this special example, he goes on to announce a general conclusion, namely that the eating of flesh does not result from the necessity of animal sacrifice. Porphyry reveals that some animal sacrifices were human sacrifices at their origin. In time, the human was replaced by an animal victim. The conclusion of the Neo-Platonist philosopher is categorical: from this example we can see that not only are we not obligated to eat the flesh of sacrificed animals but we are forbidden to do so, just as there would, of course, have been an interdiction to eat the flesh of human sacrifice.

In the eighteenth century, this theory reappears against the backdrop of the preoccupation with the effects of superstitions. The article on "Anthropophages" by the abbé Edme Mallet in the *Encyclopédie* puts forward the idea that anthropophagy is at the origin of rituals involving human sacrifice. He presents a theory of the cultural history of humanity in which anthropophagy is "not in the least the vice of a country or nation, but that of an age. Before men were tamed by the birth of the arts and civilized by the imposition of laws, it seems that the majority of nations fed on human flesh. It is said that Orpheus was the first to convince men of the inhumanity of this custom and to succeed in abolishing it."[101]

The arguments of the philosophers of the Enlightenment will resurface again in the twentieth century's most influential theory of anthropophagy and the origin of ritual and society, that of Sigmund Freud. In *Totem and Taboo* (1913), he sets out from the idea according to which there are links between the mental processes of neurotics and those of savages. As for the latter, Freud seems to believe that anthropophagy is a natural occupation, as proved by his remark about the Australian aborigines: "The most backward and miserable of savages . . . these poor, naked cannibals."[102] The phenomenon that intrigues Freud the most is the similarity between adoration of the totem and obsessive neurosis. Savages and obsessive neurotics, he argues, display the same attitude to certain things. Freud is here in search of an explanation for a strange phenomenon, namely the prohibition on incest. It is precisely the common or rather universal prohibition of incest that is problematic. Savages, who otherwise lead a life lacking in many of the restrictions of civilized man, also respect the prohibition of incest, which shows that this interdiction is not imposed by civilization. Freud's hypothesis is that we are dealing with a universal cause, more precisely one that acts at an unconscious level.

In order to unravel this cause and to understand its effects, Freud appeals to a variation on the state of nature, more precisely what he names "Darwin's primal horde,"[103] the tribe gathered around the totem, the determining entity as regards the identity of primitive society. Freud cites a theory of Garcilasso de la Vega, according to which the totem originates in "the need felt by clans to distinguish themselves from one another by the use of names."[104] The analysis in *Totem and Taboo* sets out to explain the emergence of this distinction of name, as borne out by the choice of totem, and what role it plays. The primitive horde, as Freud understands it, very much resembles the patriarchal family of the classical political philosophers. It is a restricted Hobbesian group, in which a male wields arbitrary power over a few females and children: "All that we find there is a violent and jealous father who keeps all the females for himself and drives away his sons as they grow up."[105]

Had it remained at this stage, the primitive family would have disappeared against the backdrop of animality. However, Freud introduces a major discontinuity into the history of natural forms of government, a social contract that is concluded between the marginalized and isolated sons of the primitive tyrant: "One day the brothers who had been driven out came together, killed and devoured their father and so made an end of the patriarchal horde."[106] Cannibalism here appears as the culmination of a pact that draws mankind out of the state of animality. For Freud, anthropophagy is a necessary complement to archaic revenge:

> Cannibal savages as they were, it goes without saying that they devoured their victim as well as killing him. The violent primal father had doubtless been the feared and envied model of each one of the company of brothers: and in the act of devouring him they accomplished their identification with him, and each one of them acquired a portion of his strength. The totem meal, which is perhaps mankind's earliest festival, would thus be a repetition and a commemoration of this memorable and criminal deed, which was the beginning of so many things—of social organization, of moral restrictions and of religion.[107]

After the slaying of the father, the murderous brothers would have been overwhelmed by remorse, for which reason they would have attempted symbolically to invert the meaning of the events, forbidding the killing of the totem, which is a substitute for the deceased. Totemic religion, that is, the complex of beliefs that gives identity to primitive groups of humans, arises "from the filial sense of guilt, in an attempt to allay that feeling and to appease the father by deferred obedience to him. All later religions are seen to be attempts at solving the same problem."[108] The brothers would have attempted to reject the fruits of their crime, by renouncing the rights they had won over the women of the horde (who had now been "freed"), whence the prohibition of incest. Consequently, the incest taboo originates in a kind of political calculation. The brothers united against the father because they desired his women, but once the father had been eliminated and the women gained, it was the same desire that divides them. The alternative to renouncing the women is a Hobbesian state of nature, sustained by passion and a kind of natural equality, which can be overcome only by a transfer of primitive rights:

> The new organization would have collapsed in a struggle of all against all, for none of them was of such overmastering strength as to be able

to take on his father's part with success. Thus the brothers had no al-ternative, if they were to live together, but ... to institute the law against incest, by which they all alike renounced the women whom they desired and who had been their chief motive for despatching their father. In this way they rescued the organization which had made them strong—and which may have been based on homosexual feelings and acts, originating perhaps during the period of their expulsion from the horde.[109]

The primal family ruled by a patriarchal despot, the state of natural anarchy, the idea of the contractual foundation of society and the trans-fer of natural rights, the origin of rituals in bloody sacrifice accompa-nied by anthropophagy, the horde of primitive cannibals and sodomites: all these elements are part of scenarios that long fascinated classical phi-losophy and anthropology, but which find relatively few echoes in the scientific anthropology of the nineteenth century. Viewed from this angle, the theory of totemism is a remarkably orthodox revival of the protag-onists of the theater of natural law, which is hardly surprising given that philosophical reading was such an important formative element in Freud's career.

The schema of *Totem and Taboo* is nevertheless not merely a reitera-tion of classical arguments. While the cannibal is recuperated to the ad-vantage of a reconstruction of the history of society and fundamental social institutions, he is at the same time alienated. What distinguishes Freud's cannibal from that of Enlightenment anthropology is the fact that he is an abysmal figure, an actor in the psychology of the unconscious. A creation of nature and source of society, the Freudian anthropopha-gus is an eminently private tyrant, whose primitive tragedy is already consummated and whose residue is unconscious. Freud thus encloses the cannibal in exoticism and fundamental primitivism. The cannibal of the classical authors celebrates his feast in the ecstasy of victory or is crushed by the reign of necessity. Freud's cannibal is compacted by his own impulses, and in this implosion he is repositioned as a source of the history of the social consciousness.

CHAPTER SIX

A Question of Taste

Theodore de Bry, *Cannibalism among Brazilians*

AN IMPOSSIBLE DIET

How suitable for consumption is human flesh? This is not only a question with gastronomic implications. In the case in which human flesh proves to be a nourishing and healthy foodstuff, then anthropophagy cannot be rejected on the basis of speculative or experimental physiology. Graver still: if man can thrive on human flesh, then we can glimpse the possibility of anthropophagy being integrated into the circuit of those nutritive substances sanctioned by the law of nature. This is why philosophers are interested in establishing to what extent human flesh is a foodstuff compatible with the human constitution.

The formidable difficulty raised by this apparently simple question is as follows: while it is formally susceptible to confirmation by experiment, in reality it is one of the forbidden experiments, impossible to conduct due to moral considerations. The most notorious such forbidden experiment is that in which children are raised in isolation, in order to establish the nature of the primal language they will begin to speak.[1]

Epistemological and moral barriers have made the problem of the anthropophagous diet difficult to resolve. Virey argues that we do not know whether some authors are right when they claim that human is tastier than animal flesh to cannibals, but that this is unlikely. He supplies no proof of this claim but merely argues that "it is a dreadful topic that has been dwelled on overly much."[2] Certainly, Virey's predecessors seem to have found this topic inexhaustible.

The initial impression was that some unusual types of flesh, including human flesh, were unnatural foodstuffs and hence produced discomfort, nausea, and even illness. Marco Polo says a nation that eats raw flesh is coarse and stupid, to the point of impotence. In the *Essays*, Montaigne argues that, in the Indies, there are peoples "to whom our Diet and the Flesh we eat, were venomous and mortal."[3] In the eighteenth century, such accounts are disseminated by, among others, Adam Smith. In his lectures on jurisprudence, delivered in Glasgow in 1763, he observes that "diseases arising from indigestion and crudities are nowhere so frequent as among the savage nations, and we are surprised to find melancholy and hypocondriack disorders more prevalent amongst them than anywhere else."[4] In Jean-Baptiste Labat's book on western Ethiopia, we discover that the barbarians of those parts accustom their children to eat human flesh. They believe that the best flesh is that of women. It is no wonder that the wretches are infected with leprosy and syphilis. They eat infected bodies and drink corrupted blood.[5] Virey believes that those in southern climes cannot digest flesh very well, whereas those in northern regions can sometimes eat it raw. The Negroes eat putrefying flesh, which causes them skin diseases.[6] In the article on "Flesh" in the *Yverdon Encyclopaedia*, we discover that there are anthropophagi in America, but that the majority eats human flesh and drink blood only out of necessity or bravado. Some then vomit this food, which is one most incommodious to them.

Other scholars who had studied this problem closely arrived at diametrically opposing conclusions. In *Recherches philosophiques sur les américains*, de Pauw rejects the idea that eating human flesh is harmful. Some authors, he informs us, have claimed that the salt in human flesh and blood predisposes the anthropophagi to certain illnesses such as the "venereal plague" (*contagion vénérienne*). The theory that anthropophagy causes venereal diseases was advanced by Italian physician Fioravanti. He carried out experiments on dogs, which he fed with the flesh of other dogs for two months; the hapless beasts seem to have contracted a disease not dissimilar to "venereal sickness" (*mal Vénérien*). Bacon also claims that victualers sold salted human flesh to the French troops besieging Naples in 1494, the place where syphilis was first detected in Europe, proving that the disease originated from the abuse of eating people.[7]

Opposing this theory, de Pauw raises a series of objections, influenced by the spirit of empiricism. Bacon should have seen that, in Dominica, where the natives are not cannibals, there are more venereal diseases that anywhere else, "which absolutely destroys this hypothesis," because the hotbed of the malady ought to have been in the Caribbean rather than the Antilles.[8] As for the experiments with dogs, these are supposed to have been repeated by Astruc.[9] The latter, after feeding a dog on the flesh of other dogs for six months, concluded that the animal suffered neither disgust nor loss of hair, and nor any of the symptoms described by the Italian. It is possible, speculates de Pauw, that there was a "sensible difference" between the two experiments: Fioravanti may have used "foetid and putrefying" (*chairs fétides & putréfiées*) flesh, while Astruc used "fresh and healthy" (*sanglantes et saines*) flesh. The French physician's experiment proves, concludes de Pauw, that animals suffer no ill effects after devouring one another.[10]

Fragments of the human body were long an ingredient of magical pharmacopoeia. Theories as to the curative virtues of blood circulated until the industrial age. Women were brought to the abattoirs of Chicago in order to be served with a glass of fresh cow's blood, which was thought to cure anemia. Human blood was considered to be efficacious against convulsions. Powdered human skull was supposed to have an effect against outbursts of madness, while the fat of hanged men was used as an ingredient in various ointments. In Protestant areas of Germany, the blood of those beheaded on the scaffold was sold, and sometimes drunk at the scene by epileptics and other unfortunates, a custom last attested in Marburg in 1865. In 1843, near Hanover, a number of epileptics gathered around the scaffold with cups, but were driven away by a physician, on the grounds that blood would have no effect on their illness. An official of the local court felt sorry for the epileptics and provided them with a certificate from two professors of Göttingen University, which attested that drinking the blood might have a beneficial psychological effect.[11] The compassionate professors are, however, the exception. In the eighteenth and nineteenth century, advances in pharmaceutics and penal reform would eliminate such extreme remedies. It was also during this period that beliefs in vampires enter into decline. Dom Augustin Calmet's *Dissertations sur les Apparitions des Anges, des Démons & des Esprits, et sur les Revenans et Vampires* (1751) argues that men see vampires due to a chemical process, an influence of the effluvia that rise from the earth of cemeteries, which is imbibed with the blood of the dead and their volatile spirits.[12] These vapors excite the imagination of the overly credulous. Once eliminated by the natural sciences, the vampire will henceforth haunt only the literary imagination.

Modern science seals the fate of the debate concerning the baneful properties of human flesh. In the nineteenth century, the theory of pathogenic germs has a dual effect. First, as new sources of contamination are identified, it eliminates traditional sources of explanation for maladies: contagion by effluvia, vapors, and other mysterious particles are replaced by the hypothesis of infection. The decimation of populations of primitives and their lamentable state of health can henceforward be explained as effects of squalor. Filth and disgust were always part of the sentiments aroused by the presence of savages. Du Tertre describes an Indian drink made of saliva and ingredients masticated by old people "whose mouths stink like latrines."[13] However, the presence of squalor especially comes to the fore in the nineteenth century, against the background of Western man's growing awareness of hygiene. Malthus compiles a catalogue of the squalor of savage nations in *An Essay on the Principle of Population* (1803 edition). In Tierra del Fuego, the natives are crusted in filth and vermin; on the Northwest coast of America, an explorer found a house in which eight hundred persons slept and ate; in other parts, the people are "swarming with vermin, which they pick off and eat," while the stench of their cabins is worse than that of the den of any known animal; tribes in Siberia never clear away the putrid remains of fish or their children's excrements. The savages, observes Malthus, fall ill from "putrid food and the putrid exhalations" amid which they dwell.[14] Due to

pestilence, entire regions of America have been transformed into a waste-
land of skulls, ribs, spines, and other human remains.

The theory of the consequences of squalor, which replaces the debate
about poisoning produced by human flesh, signals an epistemological
shift. While the discussion of human flesh was part of a speculative
medicine that, in its turn, was related to the science of natural law, the
notion of squalor is an element of social science. In the eighteenth and
nineteenth centuries, squalor creates a universe of perceptions on which
the new sciences of political economy and sociology are constructed, as
well as the new ideologies of class struggle and social revolution. Against
this backdrop, the anthropophagus disappears in favor of the impoverished wretch, a figure who is discovered in all types of society and who
may thus become the subject of a universal science of inequality and
want. In order for this to occur, the question of aberrant diet will appear as a social problem and not as a key to decipher human nature.

DEFENDING VEGETARIANISM

In *De esu carnium* (*On the Eating of Flesh*), Plutarch relates how Diogenes ventured to eat a raw octopus, in order to avoid the inconvenience
of cooking it. "This philosopher," the disgusted Plutarch exclaims,
"risked his life struggling with a raw octopus—in order to brutalize our
lives!"[15] To eat or be eaten: these are the limits of an interval of possibility that has interested philosophers to the highest degree. In connection
with the meat-eating diet, they identify two major questions: one of
right (whether man has any right to the flesh of the creatures on which
he feeds) and one of fact (whether man is destined by his nature to consume flesh). The first leads to an analysis of the natural law that dictates
diet, while the second leads to speculative physiology. Anthropophagy
arrives to complicate the calculations of both these sciences.

The first important representatives of philosophical vegetarianism
were the Pythagoreans. The latter are described in Porphyry's *De vita
pythagorica*. One of the reasons why the sect abstained not only from
flesh but also beans (*Vicia faba*) seems to have been the fear of anthropophagous connotations. Pythagoras held that, at the beginning of the
cosmos, when chaos reigned, the germs that were scattered and sown in
the earth rotted together, resulting in a promiscuous mulch of animals
and plants. From this putrefaction were formed men and beans. His
proof is irrefutable, at least for the Pythagoreans. Peel a bean, expose it
to the warmth, and then return after a short time. You will smell the
odor of human semen. When it flowers, place it in a pot, and then come

back in ninety days: you will find either the head of a child or female sexual organs.[16]

Porphyry's great apology for vegetarianism can be found in *De abstinentia*, in which Stoic and Epicurean ideas in favor of flesh eating (*kreophagia*) are discussed. The latter argued that if the Pythagorean philosophy of the transmigration of souls were true, then this would be an argument not against but rather in favor of the killing of animals. Thus, we would liberate a soul from its animal prison more quickly. On the other hand, the precautions Pythagoras is supposed to have taken in order to save people from anthropophagy are absurd. The idea that there is no difference between eating pork or beef and eating one's fellows would sooner incite anthropophagy. If anthropophagy did not exist in that epoch, then why was such a precept necessary? Porphyry rejects this rationale of flesh eating, using arguments that are applicable, though not specific, to the case of the eating of human flesh: animals are part of the *logos*, and if our purpose is to resemble God, then we should preserve our innocence before all beings.

Plutarch's essay, a considerable portion of which Rousseau will insert in *Émile*, demonstrates that man is not carnivorous by nature and that the usual motives put forward in favor of the consumption of flesh are mere pretexts. Thus we eat flesh neither out of necessity nor out of defense. If the latter were the case, Plutarch argues, then we would have to eat lions and tigers rather than domestic animals. How costly is the meal for which a creature has lost its life? Plutarch urges us consider "which are the philosophers who serve the better to humanize us: those who bid us eat our children and friends and fathers and wives after their death, or Pythagoras and Empedocles who try to accustom us to act justly toward other creatures too?"[17]

Christianity brings both religious justification and growing popularity for restrictions on the eating of flesh, but these do not eliminate the ethical and utilitarian arguments of the philosophers. One of the commonest theories is that regarding the cruel nature of butchers and hunters. More's utopians argue that hunting is a vile and abject pleasure, unworthy of a free man. In Utopia, butchers are appointed only from the ranks of the bondmen.[18] For Monboddo, the "change of man from a frugivorous to a carnivorous animal" produced "a great change of character." Man was innocuous as long as he "fed upon the fruits of the earth," and thus "more disposed to fly from an attack than to make one." However, "as soon as he became a hunter . . . he grew fierce and bold, delighting in blood and slaughter."[19] The end result of this process was anthropophagy: "War soon succeeded to hunting; and the victors eating the vanquished . . . for, among such men, war is a kind of hunting."[20]

An extreme variant of vegetarianism appears in a French utopia, *Nouveau voyage de la Terre Australe, par Jacques Sadeur* (1676) by Gabriel de Foigny. In the book, strange hermaphrodite creatures from Australia discourse, presenting doctrines fundamentally opposed to European ideas. In theoretical questions such as natural liberty or suicide, the inhabitants of the Austral regions hold opinions that are suspiciously radical. In some passages, absolute vegetarianism is advocated. The Australians hate animals to such an extent that they try to eliminate them completely. Every day, they take stupendous measures to exterminate them, destroying entire islands and leveling mountains a league high, any places where the animals might find shelter. Nor are fishes any more popular with the Australians. They eat no flesh at all and cannot understand why the Europeans do so. The reasons for their vegetarianism are set out in a list containing five points: (1) flesh is too cruel a food for mankind; (2) the flesh of animals is so similar to that of man that those who eat the former might easily end up eating the latter; (3) flesh is deleterious to the digestion; (4) we become like the brutes on whose flesh we feed; (5) animals are base.[21]

The most important discussion of diet, from the perspective of political philosophy, was that regarding the possibility that natural man may have been vegetarian. Since, in the theories of natural law, man in the state of nature lives under the dictatorship of natural laws, it is important to clarify whether this law prescribes or forbids cruelty toward other creatures and, not least, toward other humans. As a vegetarian, man in this state no longer appears as a dangerous transgressor of natural law or a being irreconcilable with the presence of society.

This is a possibility glimpsed as early as antiquity. Diodorus Siculus speculates that the first humans fed on uncultivated fruit and roots.[22] Modern philosophers grasp the potential of this theory and integrate it into speculations on natural man. In the *First Treatise of Government*, Locke argues that Adam was a vegetarian. It was not until Noah that God granted permission to use animals for food. Locke sees this permission as limited, however. The alternative would have been to recognize a right granted by God to the first patriarchs to use living creatures as they pleased. This would be unacceptable, because it would imply the idea of an absolute power to dispose of living things and would inculcate cruel inclinations: "Sir Robert [Filmer] should have carried his monarchical power one step higher, and satisfied the world, that princes might eat their subjects too, since God gave as full power to Noah and his heirs, chap. ix. 2. *to eat every living thing that moveth.*"[23]

The question of flesh eating in the state of nature is of central importance to Rousseau. In the *Discourse on the Origins of Inequality*, he tries to establish that natural man is a good and peaceful creature, who is far from living in a Hobbesian universe. If it were a passion for flesh and the absence of any norms that made the anthropophagus, then this man would be an evil creature, whom a political superior has every right to dominate. As Rousseau wishes to prove the exact opposite, namely that man is good by nature and the political order is an act of usurpation, he must clearly confront the question of primitive diet. His solution is radical: natural man is a vegetarian. Of course, the main objection would be that there are numerous savage peoples who are carnivorous and even cannibals. The classic example is that of the Caribs. Rousseau avoids this difficulty on the basis of an extremely partial appeal to the authority of travel literature. In a note to the *Discourse*, he claims that anatomical observations prove that the human species is "frugivorous" not carnivorous. Prey is the only reason for struggle between carnivorous animals, Rousseau writes, in a passage influenced by Buffon's *Natural History*; those animals that do not consume flesh enjoy continual peace.[24] For Rousseau, the vegetarianism of the natural man proves that life was easy in the state of nature and that there were few reasons for man to abandon this state, an idea which is then taken up by Mercier, in *L'Homme sauvage* (1784), which presents an idyllic image of blissful Indians. Their primitive meals are modest and comprise only "tasty herbage, coconuts, succulent roots and occasionally game."[25]

In *Essay on the Origin of Languages*, Rousseau puts forward another proof of natural man's vegetarianism. It is not possible to consume raw flesh, he believes; even savages fry it over a fire. However, fire already presupposes a social grouping. Fire puts animals to flight, but it also gathers around it an organized human group, not the solitary in the state of nature.[26]

In *Émile*, we find a fresh dissertation on nourishment. Although the subject of the work is the education of civilized man, the question of alimentation in the state of nature is decisive, because Rousseau believes that the child whose ideal education he is planning must, at least in certain respects, be like unto natural man. There is no better physician than one's own appetite, he claims. In the primitive state, the most agreeable foods were the healthiest, and the first food that nature offers us is milk, which, according to Rousseau, is a substance vegetal rather than animal in nature. Such a theory was not unique at the time: it is inspired by John Arbuthnot's essay on the nature of foodstuffs.[27] After vegetal milk, the first foodstuffs that natural man consumes are "fruit, vegetables, and finally a few grilled viands, without seasoning or salt: these were the feasts of the first men." Such primitive tastes should be reserved for the child as long as possible.[28] That the taste for flesh is not inborn is proven, Rousseau believes, by children's "indifference" to meat. It is known that they prefer "vegetal nourishment, such as milk products, pastries, fruits, etc. It is important above all not to denature this primitive taste, and not at all to turn children into meat-eaters."[29] Such nourishment is good for the "character." But why should a child that has been stuffed with milk and pastries become a better citizen? Rousseau propounds a thesis that he probably met in La Mettrie's *L'Homme machine*, according to which meat-eaters have a dose of ferocity. According to *Émile*, the biggest meat-eaters (*les grands mangeurs de viande*) are generally cruel to their fellow men: "This observation is [valid] for all times and places: English barbarity is well known. . . . All savages are cruel . . . this cruelty comes from their food. They go to war as though to the hunt, and they treat humans like bears . . . the biggest miscreants are inveterate drinkers of blood."[30] Another source might be Montaigne's *Essays*, where we discover that children have an inclination toward cruelty that adults cannot unfortunately suppress. "These are the true Seeds and Roots of Cruelty, Tyranny and Treason."[31]

Speculating on the human constitution, Monboddo believes that, although his teeth seem to place him somewhere between the herbivores and the carnivores, man must have been frugivorous by nature. One proof might be Bougainville's account of the Falkland Islands, where all the animals approached him and were friendly. "If man had been naturally an animal of prey," the Scottish philosopher muses, "their instincts would have directed them to avoid him." Hence it results that, in his "original state," man was a vegetarian, and "he only becomes an animal of prey by acquired habit."[32]

At the close of the eighteenth century, the implication of anthropophagy no longer numbers among the arguments in favor of vegetarianism, which begin to be supported above all on the basis of the ascertainment that creatures killed for their flesh possess a sensibility similar, at least in physiological terms, to that of man. For Bentham, animals' capacity to feel pain is what confers on them privileges similar to those of man and excludes them by right from the alimentary circuit. Tolerance toward cruelty, which was an important ingredient of modern man's cookery, begins to decline. The agonies of the flesh suddenly become visible on the everyday table. Addison marks this change in emotional register, when he relates, in *The Tatler*, a meal at which the host declares, "I am sure you will like the pig, for it was whipped to death . . . I must confess," Addison writes, "I heard him with horror, and could not eat of an animal that had died so tragical a death."[33]

The fact that Helvétius gave up the ghost after gobbling a capon at the table of Frederick the Great would suggest that not all Enlightenment philosophers were predisposed to vegetarianism. Some even argued that a meatless diet was unhealthy, a "mortification" proposed by their adversaries, the religious fanatics. Brissot de Warville believes that, in nature, every creature has the right to eat another if it is hungry, and that those who believe otherwise are enthusiasts. But what marginalizes the arguments regarding natural vegetarianism is not so much the gastronomic preferences of the philosophers as much as realization of the fact that the appetite for human flesh is a profound passion.

AN EXTREME TASTE

The first texts to mention a special taste for flesh as a reason for anthropophagy are medieval. Marco Polo mentions a kingdom in which the inhabitants are passionate for human flesh, which they eat with the greatest pleasure. In contrast to other peoples with strange alimentary customs, who seem to end up eating human flesh by virtue of a confused notion of cookery, the latter seem very selective. They refuse to eat the flesh of those have died of illness. In a short time, a theory of taste that explains the cannibal habits of some peoples will appear. De Léry argues that the Indians of Brazil do not consume human flesh only out of hunger or revenge, but also "for its taste." According to these Indians, human flesh is incredibly good. They eat everything, including the ears, but not the brain, which they will not touch. Some savages eat the children of their captives. The Indians offer human flesh to their European allies, and if the latter refuse to eat it, they become suspicious of their loyalty. Some Europeans also seem to have been convinced of the quality of human flesh, for de Léry mentions that a few men of Normandy, who led the life of "atheists" among the Indian women, boasted that they had killed and eaten captives.[34]

De Poincy's book about the Caribbean Islands offers further details. There are anthropophagi in the region who are greedy for human flesh. The Floridians believe that such flesh is "extremely delicate, from whatsoever of the Body it be taken, but they affirm, that the sole of the foot is the most delicious bit." This part of the body is usually served to the chief. Some savages of New Spain eat even their compatriots. In Java, there are some that love such abominable nourishment so much that they kill their parents and "toss the pieces of their flesh one to another like balls." The most "inhuman and detestable" are the Amures, a people of Brazil, who "eat in effect their own Children, member after member, and sometimes opening the wombs of great belly'd women, they take out the fruit thereof, which they immediately devour." They crave the flesh of their own species so badly that they sometimes hunt people as they would hunt beasts.[35]

If anthropophagy is a question of taste, what results is a need to classify the quality of the different kinds of human meat. The cannibal thereby becomes the arbiter of a bizarre species of taste. The purpose of these dissertations on the gastronomical qualities of the various kinds of human flesh is often political. De Poincy claims that the Carib warriors have tasted many different races, and they believe that the French are the most "delicate," while the Spanish are harder to digest, a diagnosis also confirmed by du Tertre, who adds that some Caribs died after eating a missionary. Since then, they have given up eating Christians; they merely kill them and leave them there. Beasts too have selective tastes when it comes to human flesh, Alexandre-Olivier Exquemelin reveals. The crocodiles of America never touch white men unless they are accompanied by a black man.[36] Monboddo believes that once some animals, such as the hippopotamus, have tasted human flesh, they "are fonder of it than any other."[37]

Swift's *A Modest Proposal* gives voice to the idea that children's flesh is so delicious that it might be served at "merry meetings, particularly at weddings and christenings." One of the other advantages of institutionalized anthropophagy would be progress in the culinary art: "A well-grown, fat, yearly child . . . roasted whole, will make a considerable figure at a Lord Mayor's feast," whereas pork is in "no way comparable, in taste or magnificence." In the article "Anthropophages" in the *Dictionnaire Philosophique*, Voltaire illustrates the excesses of fanaticism by the example of a woman chandler in Dublin, who, during the time of Cromwell, sold "excellent candles made of English fat."[38] Confronted with a customer dissatisfied with the lesser quality of his most recent purchase, the vendor was forced to explain that she had run out of Englishmen.[39]

The theory of taste is also developed in the *Yverdon Encyclopaedia*, in the article on "Flesh." In North America, the savages find the flesh of the French and English poor, as it is too salty, while the Indians of Paraguay tried to eat a missionary precisely because he was a European with salty flesh. Such passages are not credible, argues the compiler of the encyclopedia, who does not doubt that the Indians wished to eat a Jesuit, but believes that they had motives far more serious than those cited by Charlevoix and Muratori. The purpose of such clarifications is to condemn European expansionism. The Iroquois like the flesh of the neck; the Caribs that of the feet. They do not eat children or women, while the Spanish dogs of war eat the Indian children thrown to them. It is sad that the history of this wretched planet has been "ravaged by such occurrences." If our posterity does not resemble us, then it will believe that this world was inhabited by demons, he concludes.

The eccentric taste for human flesh marks the difference between civilization and primitivism. This is why the civilization of the savages is sometimes presented as an education of culinary practices. Defoe, in Robinson Crusoe, also puts forward the theory of addiction to human flesh. Robinson's first reaction when faced with the remains of a cannibal feast, is one of horror and repulsion at the "Degeneracy of humane Nature; which tho' I had heard of often, yet I never had so near a View of before." He then vomits "with an uncommon Violence."[40] On discovering that Friday still craves human flesh and "was still a Cannibal in his Nature," he hatches a plan to "bring [him] off from his horrid Way of feeding, and from the Relish of a Canibal's Stomach."[41] Surprisingly, Friday is so delighted with English cooking that he gladly gives up human flesh.

The terms of the relation between the tastes of civilized man and those of the savage are overturned in Robert Boyle's observations on the eating of shellfish (1665). One of the advantages of voyages is that they prevent us from believing that the customs of others are worse than our own merely because they are different. We ascribe to the barbarous Indians the eating of raw flesh. However, why is this custom any worse than eating raw fish as we do when we eat shellfish? And our way of eating seems even more barbarous than theirs, points out Boyle, because they at least kill animals before eating them, while we devour them alive and kill them not with our teeth or hands but in our stomachs, where they begin to be digested before dying.

> Among the Savagest Barbarians we count the Cannabals [sic.], and as for those among them that kill men to eat them, their inhumane cruelty cannot be too much detested; but to count them so barbarous merely upon the score of feeding on man's flesh and bloud, is to forget that woman's milk, by which we feed our sucking Children, is, according to the received Opinion, but blanched Bloud; and that Mummy is one of the usual Medicines commended and given by our Physicians for falls and bruises, and in other cases too. And if we plead that we use not Mummy for food, but Physick, the *Indians* may easily answer, that by our way of using man's flesh we do oftentimes but protract sickness and pain, whereas they by theirs maintain their health and vigour. . . . But lastly, as the highest degree of Brutishness, our Travellers mention the practice of the Soldanians at the *Cape of Good hope*, who not onely eat raw meat, but, if they be hungry, eat the guts and all of their Cattle, with the Dung in them.[42]

However, Boyle knows several of his compatriots ("and perhaps some fair Ladies too") who, in order "to prevent the Scurvy and the Gout, drink their own or Boy's Urine: not that the women themselves do oftentimes take *Parmacitty* inwardly, though the Latin name (*Sperma Ceti*) sufficiently declare what excretion of a Whale it is (though perhaps mistakenly) believed to be."[43] Under the name *Album Graecum*, dog feces are "commonly given to Patients of all sorts and qualities against sore Throats," while in Holland it is usual "to mingle Sheep's dung with their Cheeses, only to give them a colour and a relish."[44] How are we any better than the savages when "we devour Oysters whole, guts, excrements, and all; nay, when not for Physick, but only for Delicacies, and our Courtiers and Ladies are themselves wont to make sawce for the bodies of Lobsters of that green stuff, which is indeed their Dung"?[45] We laugh at others' customs only because we have not been educated in the same fashion.

The theory of taste signals one of the most important transformations in the debate about cannibalism. Within its framework, the consumption of human flesh is explained not as a product of necessity or of the primary passions, but as a question of education, custom, preference, and in the last instance, "taste." Thus it connects with what was, during the eighteenth century, the great ascension of "aesthetics." This term initially denotes the science of human sensory perception and only afterward comes to be understood as the study of the more elevated human pleasures. The truth revealed by aesthetics is one of limited validity, a certainty that is born at the surface of contact between the individual and the surrounding world. Considerations of "taste," a concept that designates a capacity for choice relatively independent of external criteria and based on immediate sensations, are therefore inseparable from the new attention toward the specific circumstances of the subject. The replacement of the explanations of natural philosophy with those extracted from the theory of subjective sensations made it possible to reinterpret anthropophagy from the perspective of the aesthetic categories.

In hell's cannibal kitchen, the philosophers will henceforth discover only the caprices of subjectivism. An entire science of human nature and the body politic is abandoned after the discovery of extreme tastes. This move is what enables the irruption of the theories of moral relativism.

The theory according to which morals and notions of the good are relative has always been known to philosophers. One of the first mentions of cannibalism as an example of this relativity can be found in a text by Mo Tsu, a Chinese philosopher of the fifth century BC. In antiquity, there was a tribe named K'ai-shu, where the firstborn was dismembered and devoured immediately after birth, in order to bring luck to his younger siblings. If the husband died, the wife was abandoned in a deserted place. Officials looked on such practices as government regulations, while the ordinary people regarded them as normal. Although they were neither good nor just, they were treated as such thanks to the force of custom.[46] In antiquity, the best-known passage treating the relativity of customs can be found in Herodotus: the comparison of Greek and Indian funeral rites. Darius summons some Greeks and asks them how much he would have to offer them in order to make them eat their dead parents. The Greeks reply that there is nothing in the world that would make them do such a thing. Darius then summons those Indians, also called Calliatae, who eat their parents, and asks them how much money he would have to give them in order to cremate their parents. The latter are aghast and cry out that the king should not utter a thing so appalling. Herodotus suggests that this occurrence proves to us that some things are questions of custom, and that Pindar was right to claim that "custom is king of all" (*nomos pantôn basileus*).[47]

In the modern age, moral relativism is the primary lens through which the custom of cannibalism is viewed. For a large part of modern moral philosophy, the good and evil associated with some customs are no more than an effect of viewpoint. The question that the relativist ethicist poses is not whether an act is good or evil in itself, but to what extent it is the result of norms accepted in a given society, a normal result of education. This theory is enunciated in the context of the new sensationalist theories of knowledge and education in the seventeenth and eighteenth centuries. From Locke to the French materialists, the philosophers compete to demonstrate that human behavior results, in principle, from the sum of empirical influences.

This theory of the powers of education and experience finds its expression, in the literature of the eighteenth century, in a literary genre that sets the varieties of national custom in opposition, in order to illustrate the relativity of moral ideas and, in consequence, to criticize the moral and political principles of a given society. As a rule, these texts are structured either as dialogues between a European and an outsider, or as tales or letters whose presumptive authors are foreigners who describe the strangeness of continental morals. One of the most famous examples of this genre is Montesquieu's *Persian Letters* (1721).

The interest in the relativity of morals and in the critique of European morality explains why the philosophers of the Enlightenment were attracted to the exotic figure of the cannibal as an illustration of the power of education and influence of environment. In this period, the idea that the customs of savages are the product of the education they receive was a commonplace. Montesquieu, in the *Essay on Natural Laws*, argues that anthropophagy is learned rather than inborn. The abbé Pluche argues that the anatomy of the stomach proves that man can eat anything that is "nourishing," in contrast to animals, which must limit themselves to a certain type of food. Given that it is thus, why then should man not become anthropophagous? The dominion of man, he recognizes, is universal, like his power, "and he does not degenerate into barbarity except when the despite of his conscience transforms him into a monster." Therefore, it is a kind of pathology of the conscience that compels man to eat a food that is otherwise not rejected by his constitution. Man arrives here by an excess of reason: "This reason does not err except when it wishes to come first or when it wishes to go alone [in other words, without relying on the Revealed Word]. Thus it haps that the Indian philosopher respects the blood of a fly, while the Brazilian philosopher drinks that of his neighbor." For Pluche, this "reason" does not furnish the "first rule" as regards morals. This plastic force is rather habit, education. "If we had been born among the cannibals of Terra-Ferma or among the anthropophagi of Brazil, prolonged habit and the accessory idea of a complete victory would have made us discover an appearance of right or pleasure that can produce in other nations nothing other than the most terrible pangs of nausea, a shuddering of the heart, the reason and their entire being."[48]

It is by no means accidental that the cannibal is one of the main protagonists of this genre of philosophical analysis. Anthropophagous, atheist, and polygamous, the Indian cannibal is equal, by definition, to the quintessence of crimes against nature. A tradition that in Christian Europe goes back, via Aquinas and Augustine, to ancient sources, argues that man, as a rational being, has a natural and inborn knowledge of moral norms. The cannibal, however, more than any other figure, is a living demonstration that belief in God and respect for the natural law are not ideas that are present by nature in the spirit of every man.

In the eighteenth century, the most formidable critic of innate ideas was John Locke. In the first book of the *Essay concerning the Human Understanding*, he attacks the main arguments used to demonstrate that there are ideas implanted by nature in the human mind. As a rule, his arguments are read as being directed against an epistemology of Cartesian inspiration, but the list of theses against which he objects show us that what he has in view are above all the arguments of natural law regarding the inborn character of moral principles. Thus he discusses the consecrated argument about the meaning of universal consent. Even if this consent existed, he argues, it would not prove anything about the origin of the ideas in question. And this consent presupposed by the defenders of innate ideas does not even exist, "because there are [no universal principles] to which all mankind give an universal assent."[49] The case of "children, idiots, savages, and the grossly illiterate" is decisive, because the latter are "the least corrupted by custom or borrowed opinions." For "what general maxims are to be found" among them, "what universal principles of knowledge?"[50] While, at the level of speculative knowledge, there are no universally accepted ideas, the situation in the sphere of "practical" principles is even more dramatic. Here, the diversity of customs clearly demonstrates, Locke believes, that there are no innate ideas, something which is evident even "to any who have been but moderately conversant in the history of mankind, and looked abroad beyond the smoke of their own chimneys."[51] In chapter 3 of the *Essay*, Locke enumerates a series of atrocious customs to prove that man by his nature has no idea of the good: nations that kill their children "if a pretended astrologer declares them to have unhappy stars," that lay out their sick on the earth before they are dead, or allow their canonized saints "to lead lives which one cannot without modesty relate."[52] Among the extreme customs mentioned in this passage we discover anthropophagy. Garcilasso de la Vega has described "a people in Peru, which were wont to fat and eat the children they got on their female captives," while de Léry, as Locke tells us, relates that "they have not so much as the name for God, no acknowledgement of any God, no religion, no worship."[53]

This theory of cannibalism as a proof of the falsehood of the theory of innate ideas occurs before Locke's *Essay*. That there is no inborn rule of morality is also evident to the marquis d'Argens, likewise based on a consideration of the Indians. In *La Philosophie du bon-sens* (1687), he mentions the Caribs and "numerous peoples of Peru," who fatten and eat their own children, and the Druzes of the Lebanon, who marry their own daughters.[54] That we have no innate idea of God is proved by the atheist peoples of the Mariana Islands.[55] D'Argens criticizes the theory of innate ideas, as formulated by Descartes, in the name of a system that is inspired by the atomism of Gassendi, for whom the soul is material and ultimately mortal.

Once innate ideas have been eliminated, the empiricist philosophy of the Enlightenment will reduce morality to a sum of opinions. Anthropophagy will now be interpreted through the same lens. The *History of the Filibuster Adventurers* contains a digression on the differences between the customs of the Caribs and the Europeans. They each have their own justification and "the customs of the Indians should not seem to us any stranger [than our own]."[56] In *Remarques sur la politesse des sauvages de l'Amérique Septentrionale*, Benjamin Franklin believes that we call the North American Indians savages because their mores differ from ours and because we regard ours as the "perfection of politeness."

They, on the other hand, "have precisely the same opinion about theirs."[57] Debating with himself the problem of cannibals on his island, and endeavoring to discover what exactly "God himself judges in this particular Case," Robinson Crusoe realizes that anthropophagy is not a crime from the perspective of the savages: "They do not know it to be an Offence, and then commit it in Defiance of divine Justice. . . . They think it no more a Crime to kill a Captive taken in War, than we do to kill an Ox; nor to eat humane Flesh, then we do to eat Mutton."[58] Neither conscience nor reason reveals to the savages the criminal nature of their customs. This does not mean that for Crusoe the act is pardonable in its nature, because it nevertheless contravenes the divine law. However, "these People were not Murderers in the Sense that I had before condemned them in my Thoughts; any more than those Christians were Murderers, who often put to Death the Prisoners taken in Battle."[59]

In the eighteenth century, setting out from the critique of innate ideas formulated by Locke, the philosophers formulate what is today the dominant perspective in matters of moral attitude: there are no universal morals or innate "practical" ideas, and within their own framework all ideas are susceptible of justification. Far from being merely a difficulty for the new science of ethics, the cannibal was in this period even the vehicle for the progress of the theory of moral relativism.

The origin of this typically modern perspective is to be found in the speculations of the classical philosophers. The latter were the earliest to formulate the examples that a philosopher such as Locke would repeat within the context of the critique of innate ideas. The fullest ancient theory as regards the relative nature of the prohibition on eating human flesh is contained in the writings of Sextus Empiricus. The initial preoccupation of this skeptic thinker does not regard the thing itself, but rather the form of judgment we associate with it. In relation to any subject, it is possible to issue differing, even diametrically opposed judgments. His preferred method is to enumerate these opposing arguments and thereby demonstrate that each theoretical position has a counterposition with the same degree of probability and plausibility. Possession of a firm truth is therefore not recommended and ultimately impossible. What the skeptic hopes to achieve by this technique is a liberation from the tyranny of opinions and dogmas. Between two opinions of equal likelihood, he prefers to suspend judgment, in favor of an attitude that the ancient texts name *ataraxia*, which might be translated "impassiveness."

The problem that Sextus discusses in book 11 of *Adversus dogmaticos*, titled *Adversus ethicos*, is the relevance of the theoretical distinction between good and evil. The definitions of good advanced by the philosophers do nothing more than to demonstrate the impossibility of knowing the good by means of definitions. If the nature of the good is not known in advance, then how can the properties of this good be known, wonders Sextus.[60]

If there is a thing good or bad by nature, reasons Sextus, then this thing must be thus for everyone, beyond any conflict of opinion. What would occur would be something similar to the case of the qualities of a natural thing: fire is hot in general, not hot for some and cold for others.[61] However, Sextus is sure that nothing is good or bad in such a way that would be common to all and therefore nothing is good or bad by its nature.[62] The demonstration of the fact that evil and good do not have a nature of their own rests on skepticism, on an analysis of exceptional experiences, of aberrations from the common norm.

Some of these examples of aberrations are those proposed by Stoic doctrines. Zeno justifies incest, a practice later associated with cannibals. The examples that interest us here are those regarding the legitimacy of anthropophagy for the Greek Stoics. Chrysippus, in *On What Is Fitting*, is supposed to have argued that when our parents die we must use the simplest method of burial, in accordance with the idea that the body is of as little import to us as nails or hair and does not require our further attention. If flesh is useful as food, then people should make use of it, including their own amputated limbs, such as a leg, for example. In *On Justice*, Chrysippus is similarly said to have argued that we should not bury or discard our amputated limbs, but rather eat them so that they will give being to our other parts.[63]

Such is the piety of the Stoic toward those who depart this world, according to Sextus. They believe that it is right not only to eat the dead but also the flesh of our own flesh, should this happen to be amputated. However, in contradistinction to modern texts, where the cannibal is a figure of relativism, in *Against the Ethicists*, the theory of anthropophagy is an example of dogmatic doctrine that must be dissolved in the acid of skeptical criticism. The Stoics, he argues, recommend this idea assuming that the young either will or will not put it into practice. In the second case, the doctrine is redundant, since its practice is impossible. The situation could be likened to that of a painting in a city where everyone was blind. More problematic still is the first option. Sextus Empiricus argues that it is certain that the Stoics recommend these things not with a view to them being put into practice, because the laws would forbid it. One possible exception might be the case in which we should choose to live like the Laestrygonians or Cyclopes.[64] The passage in question is curt, but it is probable that Sextus Empiricus is referring to the laws of nature in general and not to the norms established by convention. A community in which men ate one another would be impossible. If this is the meaning of the passage, then it contains one of the earliest examples of the logical argument regarding the impossibility of a republic of cannibals.

The aim of Sextus Empiricus's argument is only partly related to that of modern relativism. Both the ancient and the modern skeptic reject the idea of the absolute nature of good and evil, or at least the thesis that this nature might be knowable. However, the similarities end there. Whereas modern relativism attempts to justify a new, preferably libertine morality, Sextus Empiricus negates the idea that the entire science of morals is of any use in life. The modern relativist is often a social critic, while Sextus Empiricus seems to be more inclined to justify abidance by the established customs. Last, and most important, relativism sets out to legitimize the variety of opinions. Each moral point of view has a certain justification. The ancient skeptic demands a distancing of opinion (and of science) in general, in favor of the suspension of judgment that brings impassiveness: it would be impossible for anyone to live happily if he conceived certain things as good or bad by their nature.[65]

Having fallen into neglect, the theories of ancient skepticism became current once more with the translation, in the late fifteenth century, of the works of Sextus Empiricus. Another channel by which ancient philosophy's arguments on the relativity of opinions found their way into European intellectual circles was the rediscovery of Stoicism in the sixteenth century. In this period, the major text on the relativity of morals was Montaigne's *Essays*. In chapter 22 of the First Book ("Of Custom, and that We Should not Easily Change a Law Received"), he presents a list of highly eccentric practices in order to prove that "the Laws of Conscience, which we pretend to be derived from Nature, proceed from Custom."[66] Some sell their barren women; others circumcise them. Some priests put out their eyes in order better to receive oracles. In some places, "in eating they wipe their Fingers upon their Thighs, Genitories, and the Soles of their Feet."[67] Some cut neither their nails nor their hair. In some places, the women piss standing and the men crouching. And so on, for a number of pages. Nor is cannibalism absent, in conjunction with infanticide, promiscuity, and poverty: "In one Place Men feed upon human Flesh, in another 'tis reputed a charitable Office for a Man to kill his Father at a certain Age; and elsewhere, the Fathers dispose of their Children whilst yet in their Mothers Wombs, some to be preserved and carefully brought up, and others they proscribe either to be thrown off, or made away . . . in another Place, [the women] are common, without Offence . . . [elsewhere] Riches were in such Contempt, that the poorest and most wretched Citizen would not have deigned to stoop to take up a Purse of Crowns."[68]

Nor is Montaigne's argument wholly comparable to the modern argument which holds that education can explain everything. The passages in the *Essays* about the diversity of customs are complex, and the power of custom and education is but one of the themes they employ. At a deeper level, Montaigne wishes to highlight not merely the power of education but above all the incapacity and weakness of human reason, which is ever ready to stray at the slightest temptation. The variety of customs is a sign of this weakness. For Montaigne and other authors, things are complicated because they believe, at the same time, in the formative power of the climate and in the idea that some perceptions and inclinations can be transmitted hereditarily via the father's seed.

The purpose of Montaigne's list of bizarre customs is to correct rather than relativize judgment: "Human Understanding is marvellously enlightened by daily Conversation with Men, for we are otherwise of ourselves so stupid as to have our Sight limited to the Length of our own Noses."[69] For Montaigne, the philosopher is a citizen of the universal city of the Stoics, while the man of common opinion is closed behind his narrow bars, and then evils that befall him take on an exaggerated importance for him. When the village vines are nipped with frost, the parish priest concludes that "the Indignation of God is gone out against all the human Race, and that the Cannibals have already got the Pip."[70] "But whoever shall represent to his Fancy, as in a Picture, that great Image of our Mother Nature, pourtrayed in her full Majesty and Lustre, whoever in her Face shall read so general and so constraint a Variety . . . that Man alone is able to value Things according to their true estimate and Grandeur."[71] From the perspective of universal law, there is an acceptable justification of Cannibalism, namely, that put forward by the ancient "Stoical Sect." Chrysippus and Zeno "were of Opinion, that there was no Hurt in making Use of our dead Carcasses, in what Kind soever, for our Necessity, and in feeding upon them too; as our Ancestors, who being besieg'd by Caesar in the City of Alexia, resolv'd to sustain the Famine of the Siege with the Bodies of their old Men, Women, and other Persons, who were incapable of bearing Arms."[72]

These arguments of the classical and early-modern philosophers were what enable the ascent of contemporary theories about the relativity of morals. In the nineteenth century, with the triumph of juridical positivism, this entire history will lose its importance under the influence of a theory that begins to present itself as purely analytical. For John Austin, in *The Province of Jurisprudence Determined* (1832), it is so clear that there is no natural moral law that he believes this is a conclusion that requires no demonstration. The moral sentiments of different ages "have differed to infinity. . . . This proposition is so notoriously true, and to every instructed mind the facts upon which it rests are so familiar, that I should hardly treat my hearers with due respect if I attempted to establish it by proof."[73] Austin's position on the relativity of moral principles is not original. However, it is something else that lends his system of jurisprudence a suspect glory. In the classical view, the ideas of the relativity or universality of morals are enunciated in the context of a discourse on the variety of nations, beyond which lies the universal city of the Stoics and the laws that govern it. Austin abandons such references because—is it not so?—we already know that morality is relative. This means not only the abandonment of the glittering style of philosophical geography in favor of one that is flat, that of positive ethics, but above all the invention of a morality that no longer attains the status of a universal science, because it wishes only to be an art of circumstances.

CHAPTER SEVEN

The Anthropophagus in the City

Francisco Goya, *Saturn Devouring One of His Sons*

ABERRANT FAMILIES

RATHER THAN SOLITARY INDIVIDUALS, a traveler through the state of nature described by the philosophers would have encountered primitive families, dominated, each, by a despotic father. Although the natural condition is one in which humans live unassociated in any state, it is not, for a majority of classical and modern authors, a solitary condition. As Lord Bolingbroke stated, there was never a time when individuals led isolated lives, because "we are born to assist, and be assisted by one another."[1] Even Hobbes, often considered to be the most extreme supporter of individualism in the state of nature, admitted, in his polemic with Bishop Bramhall: "It is very likely to be true, that since the Creation there very likely never was a time when Mankind was totally without Society."[2] Thus those persons who are marginal in relation to the political order because they are incapable of an independent existence—women, children, and slaves—become fellows with the man of nature. The latter is seen simultaneously as parent and master, and his power is regarded as natural, because it is anterior to any form of political association properly speaking.

The second direction whence the family penetrates into classical theories is from the analysis of the nature of the body politic. Aristotle's definition, according to which the *polis* is an association of families, is the best known among those hypotheses that make the family a cell of the social body.[3] In *Utopia*, Thomas More argues that a commonwealth "is as it were one family or household."[4] In the *Dictionnaire philosophique*, Voltaire says that "a country is a composite of numerous families."[5] Both conceptions, that of the natural family and of the civilized family as a constitutive element of the republic, are ultimately similar. In both cases we are dealing with a similar move, whereby analysis breaks down the state into its raw materials: uncivilized individuals and their dependents, in the case of the state of nature, and the heads of free but associated families, in the case of the civil order.

Without necessarily being a political entity, the family is a touchstone for some of the major categories of the science of the state. Whether it is a matter of the natural or the civil family, the authority of the father is the object of special attention. The principal problem that demands clarification is that of the relations between this power and political power. If the *polis* should be understood, in terms of its origins or nature, as an association of families, then it means that the power of the father somehow enters into the composition of political power, at least as a stage that demands to be left behind. On the other hand, the state seems to furnish a convenient model for the analysis of the family, which some authors such as Filmer see as a kind of primitive monarchy.[6] Patriarchal power and regal power: these are the two terms that political philosophy's discourse on the family is called on to elucidate.

This task is by no means simple due to the fact that an intermediate notion interposes itself between these two terms: despotic power. The family to which the classical sources refer is the extended family, the family of the owner of land and slaves. Otherwise, the genealogy of common terms clarifies the extent to which these topics are related. The term *despot* originally signifies "master of slaves," and in Greek society such a slave master was also the lord of the house, who enjoyed political representation in the *polis*.

Beginning in the sixteenth century, two things occur. Whereas up to then the family had been seen as more of an infrapolitical unit, and despotic power was sooner regarded as an aberration, from this moment patriarchalist authors begin to draw absolutist conclusions from the classical theory of the family, establishing that the natural authority of the father is identical to that of the sovereign. More precisely, the sovereign is presented as a kind of father (or as the inheritor of the powers of the biblical patriarchs), and his kingdom as a family over which he wields his authority. Patriarchalism therefore tends to erase the differences that the classical philosophers had postulated between monarch and father/despot. Sometimes the vision put forward is a patrimonial one: the monarch owns his kingdom as his private property, and the citizens are reduced to the level of his slaves or servants.[7]

One theory about the despotic sources of political power and about natural families occurs in the work of Jean Bodin. In the *Six Bookes of a Commonweale* (1576), he defines "commonwealth" as a "lawfull gouernment of many familie, and of that which unto them in common belongeth."[8] In discussing the difference between state and family, Bodin argues that the good governance of the family is the true model for government of the commonwealth. He is one of the first writers to attempt to legitimize the absolute power of the father over the family and to present this idea as a reinstatement of a venerable arrangement. The title of one his chapters is revealing: "Of the power of a Father, and whether it be meet for the Father to haue power of life and death ouer his children, as had the auntient Romans." Bodin insists on this power of life and death because in the epoch in question this was a current definition of political power: the power to dispose of the lives of subjects. Just as the king is the supreme judge in his kingdom, so too is the father in his family. Bodin relies on a reading of the ancient sources in order to convince us that the Roman laws recognized a father's power of life and death over his children and in order thereby to discover the roots of political authority. He knows that this power was no longer recognized by Roman jurisprudence after Ulpian and Paul,[9] but he argues that it should be reinstated. For, in a well-governed republic, parents must be restored the power of life and death over their children that the laws of God and of nature have granted them. His aim is to formulate a theory of sovereignty in which the latter is seen as absolute and perpetual power over the citizens and subjects of a commonwealth.

However, in the age of discovery, the philosophers find aberrant families in the state of nature, in which power over spouses, children, and servants takes forms hard to explain or reconcile with classical notions. The legal right of the father described by Roman jurists suddenly seems to entail a cruel and irrational right to dispose of the lives of those who depend on the master of the family. The most enduring image transmitted to the public by Garcilasso de la Vega's *History* is that of the fusion and perversion of the institutions of family and slavery. He describes how the Indians of the Andes transform their captives into concubines, with whom they then conceive children. They raise these children until the age of thirteen, feeding them well, in order to fatten them. They then kill them and eat them. They do the same to the mothers when they are no longer capable of bearing children. In his book on the Caribbean, de Poincy writes that what is "superlatively strange" is that these barbarians bestow their "Daughters for Wives on those enemies." When they eventually kill them, "the Wife herself eats first, if it be possible, of the flesh of her Husband; and if it happen that she hath any Children by him, they are serv'd in the like manner, kill'd, rosted, and eaten; somtimes as soon as they come into the World."[10] In *Relation historique de l'Ethiopie occidentale* (1732), Labat in his turn argues that some savages are organized in families. They devour suckling babes; sometimes, the mothers eat their own children. They split open the womb of pregnant women, remove the fetus and eat it, because they reckon it to be a delicate morsel.[11] In *Of the Law of Nature and Nations*, Pufendorf writes that near the Black Sea there used to live a tribe in which the fathers and mothers ate with relish the flesh of their own children; the Mesagetes kill their own parents and eat them. In the *Short Skeptical Treatise*, La Mothe le Vayer argues that there are nations where one does not find filial respect for parents, such as the case of those Indians who kill their parents and devour them.[12] Adam Smith describes how poverty in China is so dire that "marriage is encouraged . . . not by the profitableness of children, but by the liberty of destroying them. In all great towns several are every night exposed in the street, or drowned like puppies in water."[13] It would seem that there are even people who earn a living from this "horrid office."

Besides cruelty, another problem raised by savage families is the variety of conjugal relations, which may be reconstructed as a violation of natural law. The primitives and barbarians live either in absolute promiscuity—in which case the absence of the family becomes a problem in relation to the classical science of society—or else practice extreme customs. Pufendorf reveals that some tribes allow adultery, especially with foreigners; in old Bretagne, a woman had numerous men, in Parthia the opposite. Rochefort describes how in America there are savages to whom the institution of marriage is unknown and who couple at random, like wild animals.[14]

The case of anthropophagous families is discussed by Locke in the *First Treatise of Government*, which is dedicated to refuting the patriarchalist theses of Filmer.[15] According to the latter, kings have an absolute power which has its origins in the authority that Adam, as the first patriarch, received from God and which he wielded over his family in his capacity as father. Filmer believes that all kings inherit their power from the first father: "Adam was the father, king and lord over his family. A son, a subject and a servant or a slave, were one and the same thing at first."[16] Locke is, of course, in disagreement, and one of his reasons is that he believes Filmer's arguments demand we accept an unacceptable idea of the family, a family in which anthropophagy is a legitimate institution, as is the case with those nations described by travelers.

According to Locke, fatherly authority claims the father has an "absolute, arbitrary, unlimited, and unlimitable power over the lives, liberties, and estates of his children and subjects." Were there such a power, we would have to accept that the prince or the father "may take or alienate [his subjects'] estates, sell, castrate, or use their persons as he pleases."[17] This type of argument is augmented in chapter 6 ("Of Adam's Title to Sovereignty by Fatherhood"). Here, Locke directly accuses Filmer's theory of implying an acceptance of anthropophagy. He argues that there is a contrast between what we see in nature and what Filmer's theory teaches us. While animals care for their young and sometimes even sacrifice their lives for them, Filmer's parents are crueler than the most savage wild beast, because they can exercise the right to do evil to their own children. An example of "this absolute fatherly power in its height and perfection" is furnished by history, claims Locke: in Peru, people "begot children on purpose to fatten and eat them." Because the "story is so remarkable," Locke reproduces a lengthy quotation from Garcilasso de la Vega, probably taken from the French translation of 1633. In the paragraph that follows, Locke argues that the "busy mind of man can carry him to a brutality below the level of beasts, when he quits his reason" and gives himself up to "fancy and passion." He is then "ready for every extravagant project." What folly begins is then consecrated by custom. Whoever surveys the nations of the world "will have but little reverence for the practices which are in use and credit amongst men." Were precedent sufficient to establish a rule in this case, Filmer might also find in the Bible children sacrificed by their parents, even "amongst the people of God themselves," although this divinity was wrathful to see the land polluted with innocent blood. Filmer argues that it was usual for the parents of antiquity to "sell and castrate their children." Locke answers that it was a still greater power by which they "begat them for their tables, to fat and eat them." With such arguments, he goes on, we may justify absolutely anything, including adultery, incest, and sodomy—a list of outrages that is commonly associated with communities of savages. In the *Second Treatise of Government*, Locke argues that, on the contrary, parents are obligated before their children and that this is, in fact, the law of nature.[18]

If later discussion of the natural family no longer engages the major concepts of political theory, it is because the very concept of the family has begun to change. A change in social and juridical sensibility causes the Roman idea of the father's right of life and death over his children to be regarded as archaic and cruel. Heineccius, for example, asserts "it is plain, that the end of this society does not require the power of life and death over children." Consequently, the "ancient rigid power" of Roman law was abusive. Perhaps only in the state of nature might such a right occur, where families are very large and the men wield power "not as fathers, but as sovereigns."[19] He does not mention families of anthropophagi, but he does allude to ancient customs such as child exposure, punishments and mutilations, and sale into slavery.

However, the most important change occurs at the level of the theories about the nature of the family. Although Bodin exerted an important influence on Hobbes, the English philosopher works with a highly atypical conception of fatherly power.[20] In chapter 9 of *De cive*, entitled "De Jure Parentum in Liberos, et de Regno Patrimonali" (Of the Right of Parents over Children and of Patrimonial Authority), he adopts a part of the suppositions of the patriarchalist school, especially the thesis according to which "children are subject to fathers no less than slaves to masters and citizens to the state."[21] However, he argues that this is not a purely natural power. According to Hobbes, it is by no means evident that in the state of nature power over children belongs to the father. Power over children in this period belongs to the being in whose power they find themselves, and on whom their fate depends. And this being is the mother. Hobbes does not insist on the possibility of a mother wielding a tyrannical power over her children, because he is sooner interested in moving beyond this moment of the natural state toward the situation in which the two sexes make a kind of pact to regulate the power relations between them. He speculates that the power of the masculine over the feminine sex is too small to ensure man's domination over woman without resorting to war. Custom is also too fragile a support, because there are plenty of examples in which women have been superior, such as the case of the Amazons. Last, in the state of nature, the woman is the one who is able to know and point out who is the father of the child. After these clarifications, the family can no longer fulfill in Hobbes theory the unproblematic role of natural form of government that it has had in other theories. In *De cive*, it is an artificial unit, a "civil person."[22]

For Hobbes, natural law is not the key to a reading of the power relations that sustain the familial contract. An evident objection is whether there are not somehow acts that are criminal in their nature regardless of the stipulations of civil law. In the first chapter of *De cive*, Hobbes claims knowledge of this objection, on which occasion he mentions parricide. His solution is purely conceptual: the term "son, in the natural state, cannot be understood to be him who finds himself, as soon as he is born, in the power and under the authority of the one to whom he owes his conservation: that is, to his father, to his mother, or to the one who ensures his subsistence, as has been demonstrated in Chapter IX."[23] What this obscure passage is telling us, together with the chapter mentioned, is that Hobbes does not conclude that the relationship of blood has any kind of priority over the exigencies of natural law and, above all, those of the civil pact that regulates the duties of children. For him, "son" is a juridical notion.

Hobbes's theory marks the moment at which a new, contractual rather than natural, family is inserted into the analysis of the body politic. This idea of the family as based on a contract between spouses has a long tradition in the West.[24] It was promoted by the church, and we also find it at the level of popular practices. However, in the eighteenth century, it almost entirely displaces the idea of the natural character of the family. Under these circumstances, in the theories of the jurists and the philosophers, the cannibal of nature can survive in tribes or as an isolated individual, but henceforward he will no longer have a family.

EXTREME SLAVERY

The history of the discussion about nature and the legitimacy of slavery confronts us with a paradoxical situation. In antiquity, when slavery was a consecrated institution, speculative theories about it were few, and their significance within the system of political science was limited. In the medieval and early modern periods, when slavery becomes a rarity in the West, philosophy discovers it as an essential concept of the analysis of political power.

For the ancients, slavery is above all a category of the economy of the household.[25] As part of the extended family, the slave is therefore merely a figure in the discourse about domesticity. The depth of his insertion in the social body also explains the grounds whereby he becomes a special subject in the context of ancient civil jurisprudence, as private property or as a deviant from the established order. In none of these occurrences is slavery a general notion, worthy of philosophical attention, but rather an individual reality, knowledge of which relates to the practical arts of the economist or jurist. Philosophical and political contestation of slavery is extremely rare and limited. As a rule, we are dealing with theories that justify slavery, the best known of which is that of Aristotle, who argues in the *Politics* that slavery is natural in origin.[26]

After the fall of the Roman Empire, the institution of slavery becomes a minor reality in the societies of the civilized West. It had almost never been central in the ancient world, in spite of the impression that the discourse of nineteenth-century historians might give. The decline of slavery is, however, almost absolute in the Middle Ages, when it is marginalized in favor of other forms of exploitation. The influence of the church, which propagates a doctrine of equality, is an important factor in this evolution.

While slavery is discredited at the level of social practices, at the level of philosophical abstractions it becomes an intensely disputed subject. This odd situation is due to the influence of the classical texts. At the same time as the rediscovery of Roman law and the philosophy of Aristotle, the two fundamental authorities of the scholastic period, ancient justifications of slavery are also rediscovered, particularly Aristotle's theory in the *Politics*, according to which any war against those who do not accept to be governed is a just war.[27] In their turn, the ancient arguments inspire a reconsideration of the biblical and patristic passages in which slavery appears as a legitimate institution. Scholastic and modern philosophers must now confront an archaic concept, which, however, has the capacity to affect the order of Christian societies.

The main reason why the philosophers unleash the debate on slavery is to clarify the nature of political authority itself. That the master of slaves has domestic power is a well-known fact. The problem is whether his power is similar to political power. Is the sovereign a despot? Can a despot be a good Christian? These questions do not, of course, arise in a vacuum. The new centralized regality of the late Middle Ages and early modern period claims inheritance of the imperial Roman mantle and begins to support the progress of Roman law against local traditions or canonical law. Likewise, insofar as antiquity is called on to supply an excellent model of state, this is, as a rule, also the Roman Principate and, more rarely, the Roman Republic, and both these states practiced slavery.

The recycling of the intellectual inheritance of antiquity is highly selective, however. Scholastic and modern philosophers are not very interested in the thesis of natural slavery, and many of them even argue against this theory. The idea of slavery as an institution supported by the authority of Roman law is almost completely abandoned at the dawn of the modern age, after having been circulated almost exclusively in political and juridical circles. There are two directions from which modern authors consider that an argument in favor of despotism might be constructed. On the one hand, there is the thesis of absolute power as being divine in origin. This is the famous "divine right of kings," which is legitimized by theological arguments drawn from the Old Testament.[28] Although it seems a medieval ideology, this idea is sooner subversive in relation to feudal customs, which established a kind of reciprocity between vassal and superior. On the other hand, in the philosophical texts of the philosophers and theologians we are dealing with a thesis that mobilizes considerable philosophic interest on the part of theologians, jurists, and philosophers until well into the eighteenth century. It is the question of the theory of slavery as a consequence of just war. Divine mandate and the right to dispose of prisoners: these justifications will be put to the test by a new political geography.

In the Middle Ages, the Europeans discover the huge presence of Asiatic despotism. This was known to the ancient Greeks, in its Persian incarnation, but the Roman Empire caused the perception of eastern despotism to become blurred. When the great Arab, Mongol, and above all, Ottoman empires reach the borders of European Christendom, the philosophers are required to investigate the nature of a form of government that does not seem to be directed by the classical principles of political association, which are sooner participatory and interested in safeguarding public utility. Oriental despotism appears as a consequence of pure political power, free of moral justifications and threatening to subjugate the Western world.[29]

To the extent that the rest of the globe is discovered, the Europeans ascertain the omnipresence of despotism and slavery, in its most abject forms. Accounts of China and Japan, or the African and Indian kingdoms, cause Europeans to become aware of the fact that some monarchs are not merely kings, but have an absolute power over their

subjects that seems to be confused with a right of property limited only
by the imagination of its possessor. Of the anthropophagi of Ethiopia,
Thévet claims that they love their king so much that if he loses a part
of his body, they mutilate the same part, as they are unable to countenance the impertinence of remaining whole and thus offending their
king.[30]

Perceptions of despotism are far from generating only negative ideas.
In fact, the question of despotism is an occasion for philosophers and
jurists to explore alternative forms and sources of political power useful
for a social and philosophic agenda. But some of the newly discovered
forms of slavery seem so extreme that they raise fundamental questions.
What is remarkable in connection with these forms is the fact that the
power of the slave master seems to exceed every limit. In the ancient
world, the slave was frequently treated as a mere object, and ferocious
punishments were dictated against him. This does not mean that there
were no reservations, however. In 319, Constantine issued an edict laying down what owners of slaves were not allowed to do. In essence,
they could not make excessive use of their rights: for example, they
could not punish a slave using punishments reserved for the state, that
is, to have them torn apart by beasts or burn their bodies.[31] Nothing of
the harshness of the ancients prepares the philosophers for the dehu-
manization of the slave in savage and despotic societies.

In *Les Moeurs des sauvages Américains*, Lafitau describes the tortures
and torments that the Indians' prisoners of war must endure, tortures
that culminate in the cannibalization of the victim, whom he consistently refers to as a "slave" (*esclave*). After the intended victim fathers a
child, he too is eaten, a barbarism that Lafitau declares "without equal,
beyond which there is nothing more evil and which is the summit of the
brutality of these cannibals."[32] Charlevoix describes how the Indians of
Illinois massacred all their enemies in battle, and then ate the limbs of
the slain at their victory feast. A woman is tortured horribly, chopped
into pieces and her flesh given to the slaves to eat.[33] In *Essay on the
Principle of Population* (1803), Malthus claims that the object of war
between the Indian tribes is not conquest but rather the total destruction of the adversary, a destruction that it sometimes pushed as far as
cannibalism: "Among the Abnakis, when a body of their warriors enters an enemy's territory, it is generally divided into different parties, of
thirty or forty; and the chief says to each, 'To you is given such a hamlet
to eat, to you such a village.'" Likewise, "the chief of the Nootka Sound
savages, in the southern island of New Zealand, is reported to be "so
addicted to this horrid banquet" of human flesh that "in cold blood, he
kills a slave every moon to gratify his unnatural appetite."[34]

The possibility that the philosophers discover in the extreme slavery of the savages and Orientals is that the power of life and death over slaves, a power already allowed by Roman law, implies a crime against nature. This conclusion has considerable implications. It throws into question not only the theory of despotic power, as it was handed down from antiquity but also current notions of sovereign power in general.

In the medieval and modern periods, the theory of slavery is discussed, as a rule, in the context of the theory of the just war.[35] This innovation in relation to ancient doctrines has the advantage of not working with a type of slave who is part of the domestic economy, but with one who is the protagonist of an eminently political power relation. War is the supreme right and attribute of the sovereign, who wields over his enemies a legitimate right of life and death.

Mentioned by Greek authors, the theory of the just war is then developed by the Church Fathers, particularly by Augustine. In the scholastic and early modern period, this idea begins to interfere with the most diverse topics. Some of the reasons for this phenomenon are social. Europe of the sixteenth and seventeenth centuries has numerous opportunities for conquest. On the other hand, during the Reformation, writers inclined to pacifism bring the legitimacy of war into question with a renewed intensity. However, the main reason for the new attention philosophers devote to the just war and the right to enslave is sooner purely philosophical.

On the one hand, a new historical sensibility has been mobilized. Any conquest, as long as it is no longer a current event, derives its legitimacy in terms of a history. In the sixteenth and seventeenth centuries, the theory of the just war is applied with great attention to historical narratives in order to establish or contest their validity. Why this occurs is hard to specify exactly. It is probable that this is a matter of the heightened skepticism regarding historical chronicles. The great sources of historical certitude—antiquity and religious stories—are critically scrutinized by commentators who attempt to extract a rational nucleus from historical materials.

On the other hand, and probably more important, the theory of the just war is used as a means of conceptual analysis that is believed to penetrate to the essence of the body politic. Before Grotius, the theory of the just war was somehow accessory to a general science of the body politic. In the debate about the right to wage war (*jus ad bellum*), the medieval casuists emphasized that there must be three necessary ingredients: just cause, legitimate (public) authority, and a noble aim. To a great extent, the pre-Grotius theories are calibrated to elucidate these conditions. This is why they acquire the aspect of a discussion of cases.

Descriptive concepts of the body politic are here presupposed as givens. However, with Grotius there appears a systematic reconstruction of the relation of political subordination, in which the theory of the just war plays a well-defined and essential role.

The importance of this innovation is considerable. The modern theory of the just war is capable of recuperating the historic narrative and revealing its rational kernel. On the other hand, and probably more interestingly for authors after Grotius, the relation of subordination subsequent upon just war is assimilated to "tacit consent." The utility of this reformulation is clear: the science of the body politic will be able to emancipate itself from the idea that authority is a natural or supernatural given. In the place of the traditional vision, the modern philosophers will justify a relation between sovereign and subject that is secular in content and juridical in form. Last, one aspect that generates mixed reactions concerns the extent of the political power that the right to conquer legitimizes. As Grotius sees it, the right to conquer does not give grounds to anything other than a relation of absolute domination.

Hobbes also promotes this very strict doctrine in *De cive*. The slave is a prisoner of war who has been spared and to whom a modicum of physical freedom is granted, in exchange for absolute obedience. There is also a type of slave who is not held in chains, in which case it is not the right of the strongest that dominates between him and his master. It is not contrary to natural law for this servant to flee or to kill his master. However, slavery based on convention generates a similar despotic power. There is no kind of evil the master does to his slave that is not based on the latter's consent, given at the moment he accepts the terms of slavery.

Hobbes does not seem to be interested in exploring whether there are acts a despot might commit against the slave that might constitute transgressions of natural law. This would be difficult, as long as the English philosopher treats slavery as an institution based on convention. The only limit that he enunciates is the interdiction for the master to transgress "divine laws," but he does not tell us what these laws mean in relation to the slave. He does not state openly that the power of the despot can legitimately go as far as eating his slave, but he is neither far from that conclusion. At the close of the same chapter on slavery, Hobbes inserts a paragraph in which he argues "the right over animals lacking in reason is acquired in the same way as that over men, that is, through natural power and force."[36] The two situations are similar, and it is not accidental that Hobbes continues with the derivation of a right to consumption: "In the state of nature, because of the war of all against all, anyone may subjugate and even kill men, when this thing seems to his advantage; this will all the more so be the case with animals."[37] This means, Hobbes goes on, that each may, at his own discretion, bring into his service those animals that might be domesticated or be useful, while waging ceaseless war against all others as being harmful, hunt them and kill them. This domination against animals "has its origin in the law of nature and not in positive divine law" (*originem habet a jure naturae, non a jure divino positivo*). If no similar law had existed before promulgation of the Scriptures, no one would have justly been able to butcher animals for food. And the condition of men would certainly have been very harsh as long as they could not devour beasts. As long as it corresponds to divine law that animals may kill a man, the same law dictates that a man may slaughter an animal.

However, travelers' stories begin to reveal the unacceptable implications of this theory of the despot's or conqueror's absolute power. Suddenly, anthropophagy is no longer merely a logical possibility, but even a directly ascertainable fact of this kind of power. More seriously, in the extreme slavery of the savages there can be detected the signs of a reversal of terms: anthropophagy is no longer one right among others, which the despot might have over the slave or prisoner, but even its fundamental purpose. In travelers' accounts, the savages' prisoners of war seem purposely intended for consumption.

In his book on the Caribbean, de Poincy devotes an entire chapter to the treatment the natives mete out to their prisoners of war. We shall dispense with details, because de Poincy's introduction says it all: "We are now going to dip our Pen in Blood, and to draw a Picture which must raise horrour in the beholder; in this there must appear nothing but Inhumanity, Barbarism, and Rage; We shall find rational Creatures cruelly devouring those of the same *species* with them, and filling themselves with their Flesh and Blood, after they had cast off Humane Nature, and put on that of the most bloody and furious Beasts."[38] Garcilasso de la Vega describes some Indians who are so greedy for human flesh that they do not even wait for their enemy to die before they throw themselves upon his wounds to suck his spurting blood.[39] Afterwards, they chop the dying man into pieces and eat him all up, licking their fingers. Others tie their prisoners to trees, and then hack strips off them, eating them alive, swallowing the morsels without chewing. They reckon such flesh sacred, and the women and children smear themselves with human blood.[40]

Labat's *Relation historique de l'Éthiopie occidentale* describes an African tribe that eats the dead on the battlefield. If they find blood in the corpses, they drink it; if it is clotted, they daub themselves with it. They hold a "terrifying Sabbath" (*sabat effroyable*), so that not even the most

ferocious wild beasts dare approach. The manner in which they slay a
prisoner is inhuman: five men hold him down, a sixth hacks his joints
loose, they then pull him apart with all their strength, dismembering
him, after which each bears off his share of the flesh. They break the
bones of the dead and suck out the marrow.[41] Raynal also reveals that
the fate of prisoners of war has varied depending on the different epochs of reason. "Civilized [*policées*] nations ransom them, exchange
them, or return them when peace is restored; the semibarbarous nations
enslave them, the common savages massacre them without torturing
them, but the most savage of men "torture them, strangle them and eat
them. This is their execrable law of nations."[42]

Confronted with these grave implications of the theory of slavery
and just war, the philosophers attempt to revise a part of the premises
of the classical theories. One of the first to take this path was Jean
Bodin. Those who take prisoner those who have waged an unjust war
have the right to slay them, but not the right to enslave them based on
the fact that they have spared their lives. As for the argument which
holds that slavery could not have existed for so long had it been an
institution against nature, Bodin argues that free will exists, but men
sometimes choose what is evil, that is, what is against nature and
divine law.

> We know right well that there can be no more cruell or detestable a
> thing than to sacrifice men, and yet there are almost no people which
> haue not vsed so to doe, who all for many ages couered the same with
> the vaile of pietie and religion: as yet vnto this our age they of Peru
> and Brasiles doe, and certaine other people vpon the riuer of Plat. . . .
> With like pietie and deuotion the Thracians also vsed to kill their fa-
> thers and mothers, growne weake with age, and so afterwards did eat
> them, to the end they should not languish with sicknes, nor being dead
> become meat for wormes; as they aunswered the Persian king. . . . we
> must not measure the law of nature by mens actions, bee they neuer
> so old and inueterat: neither thereof conclude, that the seruile estate
> of slaues is of right naturall.[43]

Natural law does not justify absolutely any kind of abuse of authority,
and the aberration of anthropophagy, which, according to Bodin, is impossible to legitimize, reveals to us the limits of the right of slavery.

In *Two Treatises of Government*, Locke argues, setting out from Grotius, that slavery is the result of just war. Those who have transgressed
natural law and given another justified grounds for war are in the power
of the victor, who may decide whether to take their life or to enslave
them. The latter are subject to the master's dominion and absolute

authority as ones who have "forfeited their lives, and with it their liberties."[44] However Locke had previously argued that a man does not have power over his own life, whence it is to be seen that slavery cannot be based on consent.[45] Once consensus has been excluded, there still remains the possibility of slavery being natural. Locke is categorical: the power to dispose of another's life as one pleases is not to be found in the natural state. What then shall we understand from the idea according to which authority over the slaves captured in a lawful war is nonetheless one that is despotic? Locke eludes the difficulty, at least for the time being, arguing that this power is nothing more than the state of continual war.[46] Slavery is thus a temporary institution, a kind of suspended death. It is not at this level that we shall find the limitations of the right of slavery in Locke. They are detectable, on the one hand, in the idea that princes are also subject to the law of God and of nature, an idea common since the Middle Ages, which implies for Locke and many others that they must not be cruel. On the other hand, the chapter "Of Conquest" puts forward a set of conditions that circumscribe the right of slavery. Now, slavery appears as a juridical, individualized punishment, rather than a general right of the conqueror over a territory and its inhabitants. Locke argues that the conqueror has no kind of despotic power over the children of those conquered, or any permanent right of property over all the things in that country, and that the conquered people are not slaves.

The despot finds himself before his subjects not in a political relation but in the state of nature, where everything is allowed and there is no common judge.[47] For Locke, the state of nature is in fact preferable to the despotic relation, because the arbitrary will of the magistrate leaves men in "a far worse condition than in the state of nature," a state of despotism where they live under the threat of a collective power to which they have given themselves up, only for it now "to make a prey of them when he pleases."[48]

Montesquieu discusses the right of slavery in the De l'esprit des lois in connection with the doctrines of Roman law and natural law.[49] He demonstrates that slavery was legitimated by war, by the enslavement of insolvent debtors, or by the extreme need that impels a father who cannot feed his children to sell them as slaves. Montesquieu argues that these reasons put forward by the jurisconsultes are not at all rational. The right of war authorizes us only to place our enemy in a position in which he can no longer harm us. It is false to presuppose that we can enslave him because we have spared his life, because natural law does not authorize us to kill in cold blood subsequent to the heat of battle. Such an absolute right of life and death, Montesquieu argues, would be equivalent with that claimed by those cannibals who eat their prisoners.

Rousseau also employs the argument of anthropophagy in *The Social Contract* to denounce the theory of slavery in Grotius and Hobbes. The first appearance of this critique is in the chapter "The First Societies," which shows us that what Rousseau has in view is a critique of all the conceptions that place political domination on natural foundations rather than the consensus of those governed. Grotius and Hobbes, Rousseau argues, upheld that by virtue of a right of slavery the human kingdom has come under the rule of a limited number of men. Were this so, it would mean that the human race is "divided into herds of cattle, each with a master who preserves it only in order to devour its members."[50] This theory is said to have first been put forward by Aristotle and then Caligula.

The implication of anthropophagy intervenes for a second time in the chapter "Slavery" in the *Social Contract*. Here, the argument concerns the more restricted question of the utility of absolute domination. One of the philosophers' arguments about absolutism is that which establishes its legitimacy from its supposed utility. Absolute power would be justified because it guarantees civil peace. In a passage where the influence of Locke is palpable, Rousseau argues that the price of such a peace is unacceptable: "It will be said that a despot gives his subjects the assurance of civil tranquility. . . . What do the people gain if their very condition of civil tranquillity is one of their hardships? There is peace in dungeons, but is that enough to make dungeons desirable? The Greeks lived in peace in the cave of the Cyclops awaiting their turn to be devoured."[51]

What must be one of the last occurrences of this critique of extreme slavery is to be found in a letter that Friedrich Heinrich Jacobi wrote to Jean-François de La Harpe in 1790. Aristotle's theory of natural slavery and the idea according to which slavery is justified by the inequality of the rational faculties lead—according to Jacobi—to the absurd consequence whereby the intellectual superiority of a man justifies fattening and eating his intellectual inferior.[52]

These critiques of the theory of slavery and of war in the state of nature possess at first sight an air of unreality in the eighteenth century, when colonial slavery finds ever fewer defenders among the philosophers and when those prepared to legitimate it usually put forward cultural, religious, and economic arguments rather than theses drawn from the jurists of natural law or Aristotle.[53] From this perspective, the practical impact of such speculations inimical to despotic law was limited. Their importance, however, is assured on the theoretical level: through the critique of despotic power they were one of the forces that distanced the political thinking of the Enlightenment from its classical roots, as well as from the obligatory references of early modernity.

INVERTED REGALITY

Up until the Enlightenment, the analysis of regality is the principal form and immediate aim of political science. Of course, what classical political philosophy wishes to elucidate, in a fundamental manner, is the nature of the body politic and of political power. In order to achieve this aim, the form it assumes is that of classification, comparison, and analysis of political regimes. We have already designated this theoretical formula as "the classical analysis of political regimes." But this model is useful only to describe the fundamental architecture of classical political theories. From a more practical perspective, however, this science sooner appears to be represented only by one of its components, namely the analysis of monarchy.

This occurs because in the classical schema of political regimes, only monarchy constantly mobilizes the attention of the philosophers. Of course, there are also analyses and legitimizations of aristocracy, democracy, and the "republic" (which as a rule is seen as a mixed regime). However, these are more specific to radical authors. For the majority of medieval and modern writers, on the other hand, monarchy is the political regime par excellence, the best in ideal terms and the most suitable in practical terms. This does not come about only because monarchy seems, in one form or another, to have been dominant in the Western world up until the emergence of republics and modern democracies. Greek writers also place monarchy in a privileged position, although the political unit in which they lived was the aristocracy or oligarchy. There are two probable explanations for this anomaly. Even to those outside it, monarchy seems to be a dominant form of government. Thus, for Greek writers, the Persian or Egyptian monarchy was, from strategic and cultural motives, an interesting subject. However, the deeper reason why the majority of writers favored the monarchy might have had to do with considerations of system. Monarchy is the regime in which one alone rules, and this is why it seems the simplest, most elementary, and most natural form of government. Moreover, the oneness of the sovereign seems to reflect the oneness of the Divinity that governs the Cosmos. Monarchy is therefore the image of divine system of governance. This theory of the correspondence between king and God is oriental in origin, and penetrated the Western world via the writers of the Hellenistic period, after which it became a major ingredient in the political theories of Christendom.

This discourse on regality assumes many forms, all of which nevertheless have in common an insistence on the virtues and vices of the monarch. Because monarchy is a regime in which it is the will of one person that rules, it means that on the inclinations of the ruler's character depend public happiness and the good order of the state. This is why one of the preeminent models of the discourse on monarchy is the so-called "mirror of princes."[54]

The images reflected in these learned mirrors are not always those of virtuous and rational regality, however. What the analysis of regality describes as a rule is a pair of figures: the good and the bad monarch. This is not merely the result of a wish to moralize. By their nature, the tyrant and the monarch are two aspects of the same form of governance: the rule of one person, as opposed to the rule of the few (aristocracy/oligarchy) or the rule of the many (democracy). Of course, the king is distinct from the tyrant according to the second criterion of classification in the classical table of political regimes: the kind of governance (good/evil, legal/illegal etc.). However, the fact that regality and tyranny dwell, as it were, on the same floor of the edifice of political categories make them intelligible in relation to one another. Tyranny is a reversed regality, a monstrous inversion of good monarchy. Both inconstancy and the tendency toward corruption of human affairs cause monarchy to be animated by an inner tension that predisposes it to tyranny. Tyranny is monarchy's shadow, over which the latter must leap. This ambivalence inspires a major part of classical and early modern thought. In the Greek city-states and in republican Rome, "king" is often synonymous with "tyrant." Later too, in the *Discourse of Voluntary Servitude*, for example, La Boetie refers to kings as oppressors. The analysis of tyranny is therefore an essential part of classical political science.[55]

The most influential model of the discourse on tyranny is that of the tyrant/wild beast. He first appears in a passage ascribed to Thales, preserved by Diogenes Laertius, where it is argued that the tyrant is the most ferocious of wild beasts. However, the canonical formulation is that in book 8 of Plato's *Republic*, where we encounter, in the context of an analysis of the transformation of political regimes, a degenerative process that begins with the transformation or more precisely the degradation of the soul of the citizens. The transformation of the democratic state into a tyrannical state has an anthropologic correspondent, namely the transformation of democratic man into a lover of tyranny. In the democratic state, thanks to the liberty that reigns there, the souls of the citizens are more and more attracted to forbidden pleasures. This is especially valid for young people, whose appetites are held in check by no authority. In time, this leads to a state in which the soul degenerates, because in its structure the higher, rational faculties no longer fulfill their natural function of controlling the lower passions.

The democratic city-state is a society in which the appetites that originate in the lower strata of the soul rise to the surface unhindered. Appetite for wealth, as well as lack of respect toward authority, dominates in a democracy, and Plato qualifies these passions as characteristic of infantile personalities. How can this decadence of the soul be pushed any further? The answer is to be found in one of the refinements of Plato's theory of the soul. In the *Republic*, the soul is presented as an entity made up of three principal elements.[56] The first is a rational element, whose dominant inclination is love of the good and justice. In a consummate soul, it expresses itself as a love of wisdom and order, and controls the activity of the other components of the soul. The second element is one that is passionate and affective, inclined toward honors. The dominance of this element produces an aristocratic temperament. Lastly, the lowest element is that which is inclined toward material pleasures and desires. The oligarch and the democrat are variations of the telluric character. The democrat's passions impel him toward a situation in which he no longer takes account of any law or custom, being used to having no master. This is the moment at which another stratum of the soul, the deepest, awakens and expresses itself as an irrational passion for forbidden food and extreme pleasures.

At that moment, individuals inspired by anarchic desires associate with one another, some of them even coming from beyond the city in order to find their fellows.[57] They will dare to commit any kind of act in order to sate their appetites. If the rest of the city is not sufficiently powerful to hold them in check, they will find themselves a leader, who will necessarily be the most degenerate amongst them and whom they will assist to seize power. From private person, the tyrant thereby becomes a public figure. He is the "most evil" type of man, whose waking life is no different from his nightmarish dream state.[58] This is the subject that supports the transition of anthropophagy from the status of private accident to that of political calamity. Plato marks the distinction between the two types of tyranny, private and public, arguing that the second is "even more wretched" (*athliôteros*).[59] The public tyrant is surrounded only by enemies, with whom he is in a state of permanent war.[60] He is like a woman, a prisoner in his own house, living in fear of going outside. The tyrant, the man who rules others without being able to govern himself, is in fact a slave of his own power. Moreover, he is a composite being, a cross between man and beast:

> Is it not likewise the case that the leader of the people who has gained control of a docile mob does not shrink from shedding kindred blood? With the usual unjust accusations he drags a citizen through the courts and has him killed, and thus erasing a human life, with impious tongue and lips he tastes the citizens' blood, exiles some and slays others, hinting that he will cancel debts and redistribute land. Does not fate decree that such a man should be slain by his enemies, or be turned from man to wolf, becoming a tyrant?[61]

The transformation of the tyrant into a monster is similar, argues Plato, to that described in a history about those who taste human entrails mixed with the minced flesh of sacrificial victims and thereby become wolves. Tyranny, a constellation of transgressions that includes parricide, incest, cruelty, and cannibalism, is a species of *miasma*.[62]

Plato's tyrant places the degradation of the individual and political disorder in relation with one another. He is the detestable agent at the center of the collapse of the *polis* into criminal anarchy, a process in which citizens and politicians, each in their own way, become prey to extreme passions. The cannibal-tyrant becomes an accidental fact of nature, an accident of civilization.

Plato's theory of the tyrant as an anthropophagous monster remained, until the eighteenth century, an important subject in the discourse on the abuse of power. In *De officiis*, Cicero argues that the species of tyranny should be eliminated from human society. The paragraph is one of the first to justify tyrannicide: just as a gangrenous limb must be amputated in order not to infect the rest of the body, so the tyrant, the human incarnation of bestiality and savageness, must also be eliminated.[63] In the *Six Books of a Commonweale,* Jean Bodin compares the true king to the tyrant, a figure who tramples underfoot the laws of nature and of God. While the first taxes his subjects as little as possible and takes nothing from them except in case of public necessity, the tyrant "drinketh his subiects blood, gnaweth their bones, and out of them also sucketh even the marrow, so by all meanes seeking to weaken them."[64] *Vindiciae contra tyrannos* (1579), one of the most important expositions of the Protestant theory of resistance against despotic authority, argues that those who instead of obeying the law obey the tyrant-king prefer to be governed by a wild beast rather than a man. In the seventeenth century, Marchmont Needham names the tyrant a *carnivorum animal* in the *Case of the Commonwealth.* Algernon Sydney tries to extend this perspective on tyranny to an analysis of monarchy in general. According to him, there are only two cases in which regal government is allowed: when one person has more virtue than the entire nation together, or when the nation is so brutalized that it is absolutely incapable of rational science or governing itself. Aristotle names these "servos naturae." It is said that some nations of Asia and Africa are like this. But these men, from the political point of view, differ but little from wild beasts.[65]

Locke uses the same representation of tyranny in the *Second Treatise of Government*. An absolute sovereign would place his subjects' lives in danger, and men would have no reason to emerge from the state of nature if, having avoided "what mischiefs may be done to them by polecats or foxes," they "think it safety to be devoured by lions."[66] In another passage, he writes: "Who would not think it an admirable peace betwix the mighty and the mean, when the lamb, without resistance, yielded his throat to be torn by the imperious wolf? Polyphemus's den gives us a perfect pattern of such a peace, and such a government, wherein Ulysses and his companions had nothing to do, but quietly suffer themselves to be devoured."[67]

It is in the same period that Gianvicenzo Gravina repeats almost to the letter the Platonic analysis of tyranny. In the *Spirit of Roman Laws*, a work known to the French encyclopedists, he argues that some kings turn into bloodthirsty tyrants, as we are shown by the fable that describes those who feed on human flesh at the altar of Jupiter of Lycia and become wolves. In contrast to the tyrant, who is prey to the anarchy of the passions, the excellent king knows how to rule his own soul.[68] *Cato's Letters*, a series of texts that promote a form of aristocratic republicanism, reveals that "an arbitrary prince is only the most exalted and successful beast of prey in his own dominions, and all the many officers under him are but so many subordinate beasts of prey, who hunt and rob and devour his people for him and themselves; and he and his officers do but constitute a long link of armed tigers terrible to behold, who leap furiously upon every man and every thing that tempts their eye or their appetite."[69] It is highly likely, admits Raynal, that anthropophagy is nothing criminal in itself, and nothing to outrage morals. However, how could its consequences not be perilous? "When you authorize man to eat human flesh, if his palate will find it savory, it remains only to make effluvia of blood pleasant to the tyrant's smell. Imagine then these two phenomena common over the surface of the world, and then rest your gaze on the human race, if you can bear the spectacle."[70] During the French Revolution, Marie Antoinette is described in a pamphlet as resembling those carnivorous and venomous beasts, to slay which is deserving of reward. Another rag claims she has drunk blood from the skulls of Frenchmen, purchased for gold.[71]

To these theories of Platonic inspiration focused on individual figures of tyrants can be added a theory applied to a collective person. In *De ira*, Seneca presents a Hobbesian perspective on contemporary morals:

> Among those whom you see in civil garb, there is no peace: one is led to destroy the other for small recompense. None gains except by the loss of another; they hate the wealthy, they despise the poor: they are oppressed by their superiors, and oppress their inferiors . . . for petty pleasure and spoils they desire the perdition of all. Their life is no different from that in a school for gladiators, living and fighting together are the same. It is an assembly of wild beasts: except that animals are placid among themselves and refrain from biting their own kind, while these men glut themselves on mutual laceration. Only in this do they differ from animals: while animals grow tame to those who feed them, humans' frenzy is fuelled by those who feed them.[72]

If the Romans were right that kings are beasts of prey, then what kind of animal is the Roman people, wonders Hobbes in *De cive*. However, it is not until the age of the masses and the popular regimes that the context in which the figure of the anthropophagous tyrant will be abandoned in favor of collective representations of savagery. French royalist Mallet du Pan says of revolutionary propaganda: "A diabolical tactic . . . worthy of the monsters that invented it . . . fifty thousand savage beasts, foaming with fury and howling like cannibals, throw themselves with the utmost rapidity upon soldiers whose courage has been excited by no passion."[73] In the eighteenth century, the anthropophagus will begin to be visible not only in the midst of the criminal anarchy of the crowd, but also in connection with the systematic conceptions of the new social sciences.

THE PATHOLOGY OF POPULATION AND
ECONOMIC POVERTY

Among the major collective figures of the theory of the body politic, the populace is the most modern and complex. "Mob," "mass," and "plebeians" are, at their origins, immediate perceptions of the crowd. Concepts of "people" and "nation" presuppose more complex reasoning, such as that regarding the social hierarchies necessary to a body politic or its historical origins. However, the populace is a highly elaborate construct, whose outlines reveal themselves at the terminus of technical reasoning. How many people live in a territory, what is the dynamic of their number, to which resources does a given crowd correspond, what relation does this populace have with the power and prosperity of the state, or with commerce: these are all questions whose answer can only be extracted using formal methods from well-organized series of empirical data. The two conditions for the possibility of a political theory of the population are accumulation of systematic information regarding a large number of people and mathematization of the social sciences, both of which are achieved during the emergence of the modern, bureaucratic state. In the eighteenth century, population excess or deficiency is seen as a source of power or, on the contrary, the ruin of the state. Dissertations on population become a major genre of political discourse.

This science of population is not strictly arithmetical. The individuals that comprise a population are not mere units whose addition produces a significant sum. The quantities with which the science of population works are sooner moral quantities: labor, pass-times, objects of consumption, the characters of individuals, their reproductive habits. Even the riches of a territory are not exactly a passive quantity, because they depend, in their turn, on man's capacity to extract them from nature and endow them with value. This is why the theories of population are inseparable from an analysis of moral agents. The traits of individuals determine their number in given conditions and allow interpretation of these values against the background of a theory of the body politic. And vice versa: the size of the population explains the moral profile of individuals, through the restrictions or opportunities it introduces.

In the system of the moral arithmetic that is the classical science of population, the intervention of an immoral entity is a source of problems and possibilities. Because the presence of the cannibal results in the material absence of other men, the anthropophagus plays the role of a negative operator in the political arithmetic of population. The cannibal short-circuits the path between resources and population. In principle, these slowly move together in the space of analysis, with the relations of causality between them taking on not necessarily direct forms. If the population itself is seen as a resource for the cannibal, the efficiency of the latter can immediately be ascertained. This is why his voraciousness imposes him as a term opposed to the presence of population. This opposition takes three main forms.

First, it appears as a strictly speculative argument that has in view the impossibility of a society of perfect cannibals. As long as these cannibals eat each other, it results that, at the extreme, the point will necessarily be reached at which only a single individual remains. Anthropophagy and population are therefore essentially incompatible. That an entire nation has devoured itself, as we discover is supposed to have happened with the "Savanese," is not at all true, argues the *Yverdon Encyclopaedia*, because it is impossible for there to be a state of civil war of all against all. Such a society would immediately be destroyed. The aim of this scenario of the self-destruction of a society seems, as a rule, to be to demonstrate the limits of egoism and absolute anomie and, consequently, the impossibility of a completely evil state of nature. James Adair, in *The History of the American Indians*, argues that the presence of a population excludes the existence of cannibalism and human sacrifice in the New World. Either the accounts of Acosta and other travelers about towers of skulls and great sacrificial ceremonies are lies or else Peru and Mexico should have been depopulated before they arrived there.

A second form of the opposition between anthropophagy and population is that of the scenarios of population decline that are at times developed in the context of the opposition to the threat of despotism.[74] If it is true that the Caribbean Indians ate, over twelve years, tens of thousands of people whom they kidnapped from the island of Puerto Rico, then undoubtedly we should view these islanders as enemies, claims the article "Flesh" in the *Yverdon Encyclopaedia*. Anthropophagy is therefore one of the numerous guises of vice, along with idleness, alcoholism, and atheism, which erode the foundations of the social order. Or it becomes a weapon for the destruction of a community: Edmund Spenser suggests, in *A View of the Present State of Ireland* (1596), that since the English should not bother to pacify the barbarous race of the Irish as the latter descend from Scythians, then they should be subjected to scorched earth policies, so that they "would quicklye consume themselves, and devoure one another."[75]

Last, anthropophagy and population reach a kind of accommodation. In this formula, anthropophagy is merely opposed to the healthy, civilized presence of civilization. It is a commonplace in literature about savages that the latter live either in isolation or in small groups. The insufficient population of America and other continents was one of the arguments used to justify the occupation of these territories by the Europeans.

However, from the eighteenth century, the negative valences of anthropophagy will become active in the context of a theory of another pathological form of population: relative or absolute excess. From pure negativity, anthropophagy now ironically ends up being a remedy for a disease of the body politic. In Jonathan Swift's pamphlet *A Modest Proposal to the Public for Preventing the Children of Poor People in Ireland from being a Burden to their Parents or Country, and for making them Beneficial to the Public* (1729), the problem addressed is the relative overpopulation of the poor, a constant topic for the reformers of the time.[76] Not every Irish family can support their children, argues Swift. And until the offspring reach an age when they can provide for themselves by thieving or can be sold, they will be a drain on the public purse. A "very knowing American" of Swift's acquaintance assures him that "a young healthy child well nursed is at a year old most delicious, nourishing and wholesome food, whether stewed, roasted, baked, or boiled" and he does not doubt that "it will equally serve in a *fricassee* or a *ragoust*."

Inspired by Garcilasso de la Vega, Swift proposes that of the one hundred and twenty thousand poor children born annually, twenty thousand should be set aside for "breed."[77] As for the others, they may "be offered in sale to the persons of quality and fortune through the kingdom; always advising the mother to let them suck plentifully in the last month, so as to render them plump and fat for a good table. A child will make two dishes at an entertainment for friends; and when the family dines alone, the fore or hind quarter will make a reasonable dish." The project has an economic rationality of its own. The business would be profitable for parents, and the skin could be turned into "admirable gloves for ladies, and summer boots for fine gentlemen." As for Dublin, the town would stand to gain by the opening of butcher's shops selling the meat of babies, although the author recommends "buying the children alive."

The advantages of the scheme would be manifold. A solution to the problem of poor children would be merely the first of these. After this would come in turn avoidance of abortion and a reduction in domestic violence, because husbands would have a joint interest in the fate of the fruit of their partners' wombs. Marriages would also thereby be encouraged, and the population of Ireland would prosper. Finally, the number of papists would be reduced. The only potential disadvantage would be for the population to decrease too greatly.

Swift's pamphlet is both national and political at the same time.[78] It unmasks English abuses, as well as rural exploitation: the great landowners are invited to consume this food "as they have already devoured most of the parents" and thus "seem to have the best title to the children."

Voltaire's *L'Homme aux quarante écus* (1768) is an acid critique of physiocratic theories. His target is a very well known work of the period, published in London a year previously, entitled *L'Ordre naturel et essentiel des sociétés politiques*, by Pierre-Paul Le Mercier de la Rivière. Voltaire's idea, one that makes his text memorable, is to imagine, in the manner of modern statistics, a kind of average man, a Jacques Bonhomme, whose income is equal to the statistical average, respectively forty *écus*. The purpose of this idealization is to test what would happen in the hypothesis in which the physiocrats came to power in France and applied their theories. What would happen if the population grew too large, our man wonders. Le Géomètre answers with a succession of precise scenarios: either income would be reduced, or the economy would have to be doubled, or half the nation would have to be sent overseas to America, or else "half the nation would eat the other half."[79]

Voltaire's argument, concerning cannibalism as a consequence of excessive numbers of people in a given surface area, is not new. It is known in the Middle Ages, and in the eighteenth century it was repeated by Raynal and Diderot, among others. However, what remains a mere inference until the Enlightenment and not always applicable precisely to the human realm now becomes an element in a science of population, which in its turn is connected to the major themes of natural law and political economy. Up until the eighteenth century, the relation of opposition between cannibalism and population is reversible. The cannibal can be the agent of depopulation, but the population (its excess or deficit) can also be a cause of cannibalism. In the late eighteenth century, this relation begins to be thrown into imbalance. From this moment, in the context of the theories of population, anthropophagy becomes dependent on variations in the number of people.

In the *Philosophical Dictionary*, Voltaire argues that anthropophagy has its origin in a state of penury that was simultaneously a deficit of population. In the times when there were no civilized nations, he speculates, the same thing happened to man as now happens to elephants, lions, and tigers, whose numbers have declined very much. "At the time when a land was sparsely populated with men, they had little craft, they were hunters. The custom of feeding on what they had slain made them treat their enemies like their stags and their boars. It is superstition that makes men immolate human victims; it is necessity that makes them eat them."[80]

In the *Social Contract*, Rousseau argues that there is a connection between climate, alimentation, and population. In hot countries, the soil is fertile, while in the north it is poorer and requires more labor. Moreover, the same number of people eats less in hot countries than in cold countries, and their food contains less and less flesh. Finally, the food of hot countries is more substantial and succulent. It results that hot countries can feed more inhabitants, which will always produce a surplus to the advantage of despotism. This explains why regimes are despotic in the south, moderate in temperate zones, and barbarous in the north. However, the type of regime and population are not directly determined by the action of climate on characters, as in versions anterior to this theory, but proportional to surplus, which in its turn determines the kind of regime and the number of inhabitants. According to Rousseau, in hot zones the size of the surplus supports a larger and therefore more repressive government; at the same time, it causes the same number of inhabitants to occupy a larger surface area. States therefore become bigger, but less populated, which again enhances the force of government in relation to subjects. "The least populous countries are thus the most fitted to tyranny; wild beasts reign only in deserts."[81]

Virey in his turn argues that the ease of life in the state of nature would have produced an increase in population. Thus people spread to all the climactic zones, including to those where it was necessary to resort to hunting and fishing in order to survive. In these circumstances, man became a ferocious carnivore.[82]

The major text on the theory of population is *Essay on the Principle of Population* by Malthus.[83] According to Malthus, population, when it is not limited, grows in geometric proportion while the means of subsistence grow only in arithmetical proportion. This is the natural tendency in the evolution of the two quantities, considered in themselves. However, Malthus believes there are forces (poverty and vice) that check this growth in population, which are activated, in their majority, by this very dynamic. In the last instance, hunger is the power that reduces population, having temporarily emerged from its natural limits, in accordance with the possibilities of a territory. Hunger seems to be the ultimate and most terrible resort of nature. The power of population is so superior to the power of the land to produce subsistence that death in one guise or another must always haunt the human race. The vices of mankind are active and able agents of depopulation. They are harbingers of the great army of destruction; often they themselves complete the horrible task.

In the first edition of the *Essay* in 1798, Malthus does not mention anthropophagy in the context of the discourse about hunger and vice. It is not until the edition of 1803 that he will discover cannibalism as one of these terrible vices in the life of primitive societies. Reproducing the passage from Raynal about the insular origin of anthropophagy, he argues that the problem raised by the French author is a universal one, valid for every country and continent, because in respect of "superabundance of population" the whole earth is an island: "The Abbé does not seem to be aware that a savage tribe in America surrounded by enemies, or a civilized and populous nation, hemmed in by others in the same state, is, in many respects, circumstanced like the islander."[84]

What happens at the end of the eighteenth century with arguments such as those in Malthus's *Essay* is not only a simplification of the relations between cannibalism and the theory of population. In this period, the idea of the deficit or excess of the population in the state of nature begins to be less and less relevant compared to the problem of political order, because in the context of the politics and institutions of the modern state, populations becomes a malleable object of social engineering. Thus the theory of population begins to see anthropophagy merely as a possible evolution in special conditions, such as those in some primitive societies. Cannibalism viewed as a consequence of overpopulation will therefore remain a hypothesis relevant only in the field of historical anthropology. But even for this science, it no longer appears as an eminent incarnation of vice, but rather as a secondary element in the causal chain of poverty.

For the political economy of the eighteenth and nineteenth centuries, the dynamic of population is ultimately interesting precisely because it explains poverty—or is explained by it. Malthus, for example, criticizes Kames's theory according to which American tribes have not progressed to agriculture because they have not multiplied sufficiently in order to resort to animal husbandry or cultivation. On the contrary, these tribes have not multiplied because they have remained at the stage of hunters and have therefore been exposed to hunger. However, between poverty and anthropophagy the relations are by no means simple. One of the most counterintuitive aspects of the history of theories about anthropophagy is the difficulty of formulating the hypothesis of hunger as a cause of cannibalism understood as a social institution.

The link between hunger and cannibalism is not at all direct. At first sight, it would seem that hunger ought to be the privileged explanation of anthropophagy. But things stand very differently: for many authors, hunger is in fact one of the causes least worthy of consideration. Among the four possible reasons for cannibalism enumerated by Sade in *Aline and Valcour* (superstition, disordered appetite, revenge, and depraved refinement), hunger is conspicuous in its absence. Even for those authors who mention it, hunger occurs only as an element in a constellation of motives. Lack of food does not automatically produce cannibalism because numerous other things can occur up to that point. The number of those who compete for a morsel of food can fall dramatically due to war, infanticide, or other customs. Before eating the flesh of his neighbor, man can resort to a host of other foods, some of them highly improbable. It is as if the entire universe suddenly becomes comestible. Travelers of the seventeenth to nineteenth centuries are disgusted to discover a bestial gastronomy. Discussing the most primitive nations, Malthus reveals that they are in a state of chronic hunger and continually wander in search of food. Dwarves, skeletal and deformed, the primitives are ready to gobble up anything. They climb trees to catch flying squirrels, they nibble maggots from tree trunks, they cook ants. The American

Indians eat spiders, lizards, and a kind of greasy soil; they preserve the bones of snakes and fish, which they grind up and eat; some Indians eat tree bark, and their own shoe leather. In Africa, the women are more wrinkled than Europeans at the age of sixty; veritable walking skeletons, with a child or two on their backs, they pick and eat grass.[85]

For classical and early modern authors, hunger explains only accidental cannibalism. Lack of food is at the origin of the cannibal temptation, but this lack is conceived by premodern writers as an exceptional event, which affects either individuals (i.e., the shipwrecked) or an isolated community (the favorite example being the siege). This is the more remarkable given that hunger is, up until the eighteenth century, a normal presence in the experience of European man.[86] However, hunger has its cycles. Abbé Galiani, in his work on the grain trade, refers to those provinces "whose wealth is in the earth and whose fate is in the heavens." Rather than being a product of an economic system, hunger results from an intersection of natural rhythms and human activities.

In the sixteenth century, Cardano is the first to explain the anthropophagy of the savages of the New World based on an economic argument.[87] The Indians end up eating human flesh, he argues, because the land is poor in America and because the animals they can hunt are few. The Enlightenment is the period in which hunger ceases to be a simple cause and becomes an element that demands to be explained in its turn. Explanation is necessary because the starvation of a population is viewed rather as a result of an economy of poverty and less as a consequence of a chain of causes exterior to society.

This is the moment in which the Europeans discover the great reality of economic poverty. In the texts of ancient authors, poverty is a marginal element in the comparative analysis of nations. The distinction between barbarians and Greeks is not one of wealth. Up until the eighteenth century, the perception of Byzantine, Chinese, Ethiopian, Turkish, or Indian wealth does not seem to be coupled to an economically differential diagnosis. The discovery in the seventeenth century of impoverished regions in northern Europe is the occasion for the first theories of systematic poverty and its consequences. In Isaac de la Peyrere's *Description of Iceland* (1644) we discover that poverty produces promiscuity: "The girls, who are very beautiful in this island, are very poorly dressed, [they sleep with German merchants] for bread, biscuits or other objects of very little worth. Even the fathers present their daughters to the foreigners."[88] However, this poverty is not fundamentally bad. De la Peyrere's Icelanders dwell in huts like the rustics in Virgil's *Bucolics*, without physicians or medicaments, and can live to the age of one hundred. For Shefferius, in the *History of Lapland* (1674), the Laplanders are so poor that the king of Sweden considered that it would be too costly to make a public declaration of war on them. He preferred to treat them as wild beasts and to promise government over them to the private individual who conquered them.[89] In Robert Molesworth's *An Account of Denmark* (1694), we discover a theory of destitution. He argues that despotism produces poverty, while freedom brings prosperity. The Danes have fallen into a situation more pitiful than that of the Negro slaves of Barbados because they have gone from an elective regality to one that is absolute and arbitrary. Their poverty impels them to eat cheap foods such as salted fish, for which reason attacks of apoplexy are very frequent, making it hard to walk the streets of Copenhagen without coming across a sufferer rolling on the ground, foaming at the mouth, surrounded by gaping onlookers.[90] Nonetheless, in none of these authors is extreme poverty associated with cannibalism. Only in the context of the comparison between the European and the savage economy can such a conclusion be formulated, because between the two a difference of nature will be discovered in the following century.

The *Yverdon Encyclopaedia* (article "Flesh") argues that what is to blame for cannibalism is hunting, which keeps the Indians in poverty. Hunter and prey are equally savage. For de Pauw, it is a product of the "harsh necessity" of savage life. The same theory occurs in Voltaire's *Essay on Morals*. Revenge and hunger are to blame for the anthropophagy of American tribes. Hunger, in its turn, is a product of the chronic shortage of food, a consequence of climate and poor soil. The aridity of the environment cause both hunger and a deficit of population. Contrary to Robertson, who had claimed that anthropophagy has its origin in the passion of revenge, Malthus argues that it must originate in extreme necessity, but then it is supposed to continue for other reasons. "It seems to be a worse compliment to human nature and to the savage state to attribute this horrid repast to malignant passions, without the goad of necessity, rather than the great law of self-preservation."[91]

What explains anthropophagy for these authors is the system of the savage economy, which fatally leads to poverty and generalized hunger. In the *Wealth of Nations*, Adam Smith observes that vice and hunger are consequences of a simple economy, where the division of labor, private property, and the accumulation of wealth are unknown. This is an economy different to that of contemporary Europe, but as long as natural law retains the state of nature and its savage inhabitants as a first moment in the formation and evolution of society, this economic order must necessarily be inscribed in a history of types of economic organization. In the eighteenth and nineteenth centuries, this takes the form of a theory of successive social stages, in which primitivism based on hunting is followed by barbarism, characterized by animal husbandry, by the agrarian stage, and finally by commerce. The importance of this schema will enter decline in the late nineteenth century, but not before leaving behind it an enduring image of cannibalism as a product of the circumstances of an economy of poverty.

PRIMITIVE COMMUNISM

Let us imagine a society where all are equal and free, where there are no punishable offences and no state authority, where private property is unheard of and each has sufficient according to his needs, where there is no money, where people are healthy and robust and live to over a hundred, where there is no need to work, where the most diverse pleasures are enjoyed, where the women are at the disposition of whomsoever feels the urge, and from whence religion has been banished.

A communist utopia? Perhaps, if we place ourselves within the horizons of nineteenth-century socialist expectations. However, up until the eighteenth century, a reader would sooner have recognized the features of a cannibal society in the above description. How did it come about that a set of characteristics specific to anthropophagous tribes was transferred to a political ideal?

Socialism, or communism, takes shape as a modern political ideology in the early nineteenth century. (In this period, the two terms refer to the same doctrine, therefore we here employ them without taking into account the differences of emphasis that appeared especially in the second half of the twentieth century.) It was a complex process that can be concisely described, for the purposes of our discussion, as one in which the older doctrines of radical egalitarianism were reinterpreted in the context of the institutions of the modern state.

These doctrines of radical egalitarianism have a considerable history. Up until the seventeenth century, they are religious in inspiration, reveries of a Golden Age that was supposed to have existed in the past and whose reinstatement was imminent. The peasant communism of the Middle Ages was such a vision, in which the godless oppressors would be exterminated, and the true believers would rule an earth transformed into paradise. During the Civil War, the English sect of the Levelers revived the pious ideals of equality.[92] In the same domain of religious sources for extreme egalitarianism, we must also recall the monastic experience. The monastery is an early model of a society without private property, and condemnation of wealth and riches is a constant topic for the theologians, especially the Franciscans.[93]

In the seventeenth and eighteenth centuries, the most important source for ideals of an egalitarian society is, however, secular: the encounter with societies outside Europe. In this period, the West discovers, with considerable astonishment, a host of peoples for whom political authority is entirely lacking. In the face of such a lack, the reactions of the learned can be reduced to two positions. On the one hand, some reckon that the lack of government signifies mere savagery or barbarism. Visions of a negative state of nature, proper to savages, fall into this category. However, no fewer are those who find that the absence of authority and political institutions, at least in their traditional forms, has positive aspects. What fascinates the most is the almost absolute freedom of the savages. Without any governmental apparatus, these people live, in the opinion of those who observe them, in a state of liberty and equality that has no equivalent in Europe. Numerous texts contrast the savages' way of life with its European counterpart, and find that the latter is inferior in comparison. An entire subversive literature now springs up, exalting the virtues of the savage. And it seems the latter has plenty of virtues. He is free and dignified; he is strong. Superiors and the inequality of private property are unknown to him. He does not believe in superstitions (especially Christian ones). He lives a life of plenty. Of course, the list of the savage's supposed gifts varies depending on the degree of enthusiasm on the part of the author and upon the latter's specific aims. Thus not all authors discover that the savage lives a life of abundance. However, even among those who admit that he is impoverished, there are plenty of thinkers who believe that his poverty is virtuous. Such poverty is a result of the fact that the savage limits himself to the satisfaction of his vital needs, which is remarkable in itself given this was something far from assured for a great many Europeans of the time.

As far as I know, what historians of ideas of extreme egalitarianism have not yet observed is that not every primitive society corresponds precisely to this set of characteristics: liberty, equality, and absence of government and property. Many regions of primitivism, including Africa, were not even considered from the perspective of the egalitarian ideal. As a rule, the incarnation of extreme egalitarianism and liberty is the society of anthropophagous savages in America and, occasionally, that of the primitives of the Pacific islands. Whether good or bad, the protocommunist savage is a cannibal.

The oldest visual depiction of American cannibals, which dates from 1505, shows a savage gnawing a human arm, while other body parts are roasted over a fire. The text that accompanies this image associates anthropophagy, anarchy, anomie, promiscuity, incest, and communism: "No one also has anything, but all things are in common. And the men have as wives those who please them, be they mothers, sisters, or friends, therein make they no distinction. They also fight with each other. They also eat each other even those who are slain, and hang the flesh of them in the smoke. They become a hundred and fifty years old. And have no government."[94] With rare exceptions, such as Fourier, a pathological optimist, who believed that once a collectivist order was established the polar icecaps would melt and the oceans turn into lemonade, longevity is the only merit in the schema that the later propagandists of the system of public property overlook.

The characteristics of cannibal society are rarely treated separately from one another. As a rule, such a society is described in terms of an almost unvarying set of traits. Liberty and equality are merely the most obvious of these. The anthropophagi are eminently eligible for life outside the state because they are closest to the animal way of life. Their condition is one of natural freedom, in which there are no superiors or authority. In cannibal society, each conducts himself according to his own appetites, without fear of any superior law.

At the same time, the anthropophagi are almost invariably described as living in a state of communal ownership. They ignore private property and everything they have is for the common use. Jean Struys claims to have met such communists *avant la lettre*: "They possess nothing of their own and what they steal from strangers they bring, in good faith, to the common goods, over which all have the same right."[95] The reason why primitives in general and cannibals in particular are regarded as not possessing any private property is dual. Savage communism is attested by travelers, who do not recognize property in its European forms in the society of the primitives. But it is more likely that this idea of the communism of the primitives was a learned reconstruction, the result of a deductive process. In natural law, private property has, in essence, two major forms: property based on the right of first occupancy and property "by convention," in other words, property as established on the basis of positive laws. However, even the oldest of these forms, that based on occupancy, requires a form of legal guarantee, otherwise it is unstable. The logical conclusion is that in the state of nature, that is, in a state characterized by the absence of any higher legal authority, private property cannot exist or is reduced to perfectly elementary forms, such as the right to own one's own labor. From the viewpoint of the theory of natural law, therefore, an absolutely primitive society is necessarily one without private property.

Such a society should be seen as diametrically opposed to property-based European society, as results from the story that Montaigne relates in *On Cannibals*: the chief of a tribe of savages is asked, after a visit to

Rouen, what he found most remarkable there. He answers that nothing astonished him more than "that there were amongst us, Men full and cramm'd with all manner of Conveniencies, whilst in the mean Time, their Halves were begging at their Doors, lean, and half-starv'd with Hunger and Poverty." The Indian finds it strange that the latter "did not take the others by the Throats, or set Fire to their Houses."[96] The theory of the class struggle did not have to wait until the emergence of the proletariat in order to find its theoretical voice. Even the idea of a revolution of the oppressed is also present in the literature about the savages. In the *History of the Two Indies*, Raynal holds that only the liberty of America is authentic. In his view, the killing of the European masters is comparable to emancipation from tyranny: "All men speak of liberty, but only the savages possess it. It is not only the entire nation, but it is also the individual who is truly free. The sentiment of independence is at work in all his thoughts and actions. . . . He cannot but hate his master and kill him."[97]

A striking aspect of this common property is the communal possession of wives. This too necessarily follows from the essence of primitive society, as it is known to natural law. While it is true that, up until the eighteenth century, the family is viewed as the oldest and most natural form of association, it is no less true that some philosophers question whether the family may have existed at some primitive stage, when men lived a brutish life, as separate individuals or in bands, and women were shared commonly. Again, travel literature furnishes evidence of the communal possession of women. On his first voyage to America, Columbus discovers an island of "Amazons," who live separately from the men, limiting themselves to furtive, nocturnal visits.

Another aspect of communism and absolute equality is the lack of any interest in work. While work, in one form or another, is a curse of European man, from which he is unable to escape, the savages seem to live in a kind of indifference and torpor. Some writers even believe that the savages live in a paradise of natural abundance, where work is virtually unnecessary.

The most bizarre aspect of this savage communism is that which views human flesh as the property of the entire group. This is an idea that appears not only in connection with the American anthropophagi, and therefore its origins must be sought elsewhere than in travel literature. Shipwrecked sailors are also mentioned as having the custom of dividing flesh up equally; and it is believed that wolves share their prey equally. The cannibals of America are frequently presented as sharing flesh out in equal portions.

Last, atheism should not be omitted from this portrait of communism. For sixteenth-century man, the atheist was a figure so monstrous that he was impossible even to imagine. As for the idea of a society of atheists, this was seen as a kind of logical contradiction. Laws presuppose religion, and the absence of religion results in an absence of laws and therefore of society. This is why, in the seventeenth century, the Jesuits' suggestion that the Chinese might be such a nation of atheists whips up a storm. Bayle's speculation, according to which a society of virtuous atheists is imaginable, is similarly received. But before the Chinese and the atheist libertines, the Europeans discover, particularly in America, nations that seem to have no form of religious worship and correspond to the speculations of the philosophers regarding a bestial mode of life. For a time, these savages maintain the idea that they are superstitious or idolatrous, or that they practice a natural religion. However, numerous authors end up grasping that an integral savage cannot be anything other than an atheist. The savage sometimes ends up as the leading figure in the antireligious struggle: free of superstition, the anthropophagi are presented as persecuting and even eating the missionaries who come to Christianize them.

Of the characteristics that will later define modern revolutionary ideologies and groups, the only one that is not associated with cannibal communities is that of conspiracy. It is a commonplace in the literature about savages that they are cunning and secretive. But we do not find anything equivalent to the theory of secrecy and conspiracy that is formulated in connection with revolutionary political ideals, beginning in the radical Masonic lodges of the period immediately preceding the French Revolution. In the nineteenth century, this theory becomes an essential component of revolutionary tactics. However, even if it also has speculative sources, conspiracy is, to a large extent, a response to the pragmatic necessities of modern political struggle. It is not part of the substance of communist utopia, and this is why it plays only a marginal role in the history of the deeper origins of the communist ideology.

Equal, free, wholly communist, and atheist: these are the cannibals, as known to the European public of the seventeenth and eighteenth centuries. How is it that such traits then came to be used to describe an ideal of civilized society? Is there any genetic link between the literature about cannibals and the first plans for a communist society?

The answer is straightforward if we bear in mind that the image of the cannibal is not necessarily one that is direct and unmediated, but rather one that is artificial, projected by the complex optics of the theory of natural law. The state of nature or, if we prefer, primitive democracy is a state whose characteristics are derived speculatively or by appeal to the classical authorities. Of course, it is also important that there are descriptions of the savages and cannibals to confirm the philosophical theses. However, the literature on cannibals in its turn circulates images, ideas, arguments, and values of modern and classical natural law.

In the history of political philosophy, the anthropophagus was rarely associated with the institution of private property. Neither his absolute egoism nor his total capacity for domination and private consumption destined him for the role of apologist for individualism and individual property. Only a few passages in the Cynics and Stoics might seem to legitimize cannibalism on the grounds of strictly individual rights.

Between the Cynic school of philosophy and the first modern representations of cannibals there is a certain connection. Named after the fact that they led a life outside social norms, like dogs, the Cynics were the favorite example of the rustic philosopher. In the Middle Ages, beyond the bounds of Europe there lived cynocephali, dog-headed anthropophagous creatures, and in the time of Columbus, the cannibals, their human-faced relatives, were discovered living in the Caribbean. We have already seen that a part of the modern literature on cannibals recycles ancient images of nations of anthropophagi. In the modern age, descriptions of cannibal society multiply and become more detailed and linked to the major themes of political and moral theory. This abundance will then be exploited by some authors to the advantage of radical ideas.

The missing link between literature about cannibals and the first dissertations in support of political communism is a group of texts in which some aspects of savage society are justified, particularly liberty, equality, and communal property, while political institutions, authority, inequality, and private property are condemned. The practice of anthropophagy is not always mentioned, probably for tactical reasons, although it is a notorious aspect of the societies under discussion.

One of the first works of this type is a book by baron de Lahontan. First published in 1702 and then republished by Nicholas Gaudeville in 1705, in an even more radical version, it provoked scandal from the very outset.[98] Conceived as a dialogue between a Huron and a European, it eulogizes primitive society and criticizes European society. The savage-philosopher constantly urges his interlocutor over the ocean to become a fellow Huron. He argues that the Europeans would live more happily if they gave up the distinction between "mine" and "yours." All the clichés of the primitive society are present here, except one. Neither the Indian nor his partner in dialogue mention that which no cultivated reader of the period could ignore: namely that the Hurons were cannibals.

Before Lahontan, Rochefort argues that the cannibals of the Caribbean, in contrast to the Asiatics of Java, "who cannot converse even
with their own brother without brandishing a dagger" (*qui ne parlent
pas mêmes à leurs freres sans luer Poignard à la main*), live in harmony,
and hold all their goods in common. Their houses have no locks or
doors, but, in contrast to the Spartans, with whom Rochefort constantly
compares them, they have no notion of theft, and if something is missing from their hut, they conclude, "A Christian has passed this way!"
(*un Chrétien est venu icy*). They eat together in communal houses, and
their food is very tasty. They are polygamous, and each man has as
many wives as he merits. The Caribs live freely, without ambitions, de-
spising gold, like the ancient Spartans. They are content with what nature provides them. They are "incomparably more well-fed and well
disposed than us [*incomparablement plus gras & plus dispos que nous
ne sommes*]."[99]

In *Supplément au Voyage de Bougainville*, Diderot presents us the
paradisiacal life of the inhabitants of the Pacific islands. They live in accordance with the principles of nature, which Europeans seem to ignore.
The womenfolk give themselves to any man. The men obey no man,
because they have no government or written laws. They know no inequality of wealth or rank. An old man of Tahiti confounds the Europeans when they try to demonstrate that their society is superior. Nor does
Diderot pay any attention to the cannibalism of the natives, although
there are numerous accounts from the period in which he is writing that
mention the anthropophagy of the South Sea islanders.

By his influence and ingeniousness, Rousseau is, however, the extreme
example of the theories that exalt the institutions of cannibal society
while passing over anthropophagy in silence or denying it. The philosophers of natural law were speaking of savage man when they were in
fact describing civil man, he believes. None of them has come to describe the state of nature correctly, because they have done nothing more
than to "transpose the ideas they have found in society upon the state
of nature."[100] The supposed passions of natural man are nothing other
than those of civil man: pride, desire, need, cupidity, oppression.

What Rousseau proposes is "to begin by setting all the facts to one
side, because they in no way concern" the question of the state of nature.[101] In place of these facts, he substitutes what he seems to believe is a
much more solid approach from the methodological point of view: "hypothetical and conditional reasoning" (*raisonnemens hypothétiques &
conditionnels*). This reasoning leads Rousseau to the idea that natural
man was a good, healthy, and pacific being. He is as robust as the Spartans, he thinks little, sleeps much, lives to a venerable age, has such

sharp senses that he sees with his naked eye what Europeans can only see by means of a telescope, and "drinks European liquor like water."[102] Ultimately, he is concerned only with self-preservation.

From the treatises of natural law we know that this legitimate sentiment of self-preservation is the departure point whence an entire casuistry of extreme acts, including anthropophagy, is constructed. Rousseau's plan, in the *Discourse on the Origins of Inequality*, is to demonstrate that, on the contrary, it is the civilized peoples who are most depraved. Civilization, not the state of nature, is based on murder: countless people have died in wars, in shipwrecks, and by consuming counterfeit liquor, or "monstrous mixtures of foodstuffs."[103] Nature "makes us pay dearly for the scorn with which we treat her lessons."[104] Civil order means murders, poisonings, highway robbery, and abortions; even the punishment of crimes contributes to this decadence, because it doubles the loss suffered by the human species. Rousseau transfers the Hobbesian state of nature into the heart of political society. Civilized men have brutal and depraved tastes, tastes unknown to savages and animals.[105]

The problem is that the facts are resistant to such kinds of speculation. The next step is thus their selective negation. Of all the existing nations, the savages of the Caribbean (the cannibals, in other words) have strayed the least from the state of nature, asserts Rousseau. However, such model citizens of nature could not be anthropophagi: our author claims that modern travelers have shown that the inhabitants of many Caribbean islands die if they eat flesh.

Rousseau thus constructs an ideal of society that is inspired from descriptions of the state of nature. His problem, and that of the majority of those who exalt natural man, is that the most natural state—at least within the limits of the theory of natural law—seems to be that of the anthropophagous Caribs. His solution, like that of others, is therefore to deny or ignore that they are cannibals and to refer only to their equality, liberty, and natural socialism.

In the case of Radicati, anthropophagy appears in the context of an argument in favor of equality and liberty, but their relation is one that is external. The story of the modern cannibals in *Recueil des pièces curieuses sur les matières les plus intéressantes* is narrated by "Zelim the Muslim," "translated from the Arabic," and printed in Rome by "Nicolas Machiavel." It is accompanied by a number of other radical pieces, such as a *History of the Persecuted Priesthood* and *Moral and Political Discourses*. In the latter, Radicati is one of the first in the history of political ideas to propose a perfectly secular and communist government. After expositing the classic schema of political regimes, he argues that democracy is "the oldest and most convenient to the natural condition and freedom of mankind."[106] The democracy to which he refers is quite different to the democracy of the ancients, as it is a regime based on the "general consensus" of the centrally administered of the populace, where the people are equal in "nobility, power and wealth" and where the sovereign authority vigorously propagates a secular ideology. One essential ingredient of this regime is not mere equality of wealth but the elimination of private property:

> All goods must belong to the Republic, and she, like a good mother of the people, shall share them to each according to his needs. In this way, none shall be obliged to beg and none shall have any surplus. According to these maxims, it is possible to establish and conserve a popular government. However, if they are not respected, and if the words *meum & tuum* shall be allowed to be reintroduced into society, its ruin is inevitable. This is why we should never tolerate the expressions: "my goods," "my mother," "my children," "my brothers and sisters," because they are incompatible with the nature of a democratic government.[107]

For Radicati, as well as for other radicals, the elimination of private property is more fundamental than that of the ownership of things.

Radicati's volume thus represents a mixture of traditional terms—not always organically interconnected—and modern ideas. Between the covers of the book are found together the subjects of anthropophagy, atheism (or at least anti-Christianity), equality, the absence of private property, and communism of the sexes. Cannibalism is not lacking from this recipe. Besides the story of "Zelim," Radicati also includes a plagiarism of Swift's *A Modest Proposal*, in which the idea of regulating the population by consuming the babies of the poor is put forward.

In the seventeenth and eighteenth centuries, to travel literature, radical pamphlets, and philosophic speculation can be added the literature about pirates, as one of the sources of ideas about extreme egalitarianism. At the beginning of the modern period, before it is eliminated in the early nineteenth century, piracy becomes an important institution, which sometimes even gains official sanction. It is no mere coincidence that the main area of pirate activity is the Caribbean. Pirate societies present some of the characteristics frequently associated with cannibal Indians: crimes against the law of nations, cruelty, atheism, sodomy, drunkenness, and gambling. However, the most striking trait of such societies is their egalitarianism. Some pirates, it would seem, formed egalitarian associations, which were free in their own way, and in which property was shared or regarded as communal. In *History of the Filibuster Adventurers*, Exquemelin relates that the latter reckoned themselves a maritime brotherhood. He describes the elaborate rituals for sharing booty and expenses. They seem also to have known a form of sexual communism named *matelotage*, in which women were drawn by lots between two pirates, with whom they slept "alternately."[108] A group of pirates established a colony in Madagascar around the year 1690, named Libertalia, where property was communal and the government democratic.[109]

It is not impossible that some of the sources of communist ideas may have been local and pragmatic rather than literary. The most frequently cited example is that of the village communes of serfs, which many Russian radicals (Herzen, Bakunin, and others) hold to have been egalitarian and communist. The reality of the Russian village seems to have been different, but it is clear that utopian communist ideas used to circulate in Russian folklore, also influencing the practices of some Orthodox religious sects. Until the late nineteenth century, there were even expeditions to find these mythic regions of Belovode, Nutland, and Kitezh.[110] But whether such speculations are an exclusive product of the Russian spirit is a question that is far from having been settled. The first printed attestation of such legends dates from 1807, and the lands described are usually situated "beyond the sea," which suggests that the accounts of them might be an echo of the travel literature of egalitarian societies in America.

This constellation of texts about the communist anarchy of the savages constitutes a great reservoir of images and arguments that will later be employed in the doctrines of modern communism. This ideological transfer will be facilitated by the existence of those texts in which savage society is proposed as an ideal superior to European society. However, the decisive step is taken only after the appearance of projects for the fundamental reform of Western political society, in accordance with the natural legislation that the anthropophagi have made visible.

In 1780, an anonymous work entitled *Recherches philosophiques sur le droit de propriété dans la nature* was printed, probably in Paris. It belonged to the young Brissot de Warville and is a discussion of cannibalism against the backdrop of natural law, a purely speculative treatment, almost wholly lacking in learned references, in which the author tries to deduce an entire theory of property by setting out from the physics of moving particles. All beings must feed in order to exist, and hence our philosopher deduces that each living being has a right of property over that which is necessary for its survival. In a section entitled "Over what can the right to property be exerted?" (*Sur quoi le droit de propriété peut-il être exercé?*) we learn that this coincides with an immediate right of disposal. Anything can become the object of this natural law, including man himself: "Yes, man, animals, every body in nature has a right over all others. They have rights over one another. Man has a right over a bull, the bull over the grass, and the grass [Brissot believes that plants have senses, like animals] over man." This reciprocity of rights causes natural harmony to dissolve in a universal struggle for existence: "A struggle for property that seems to tend towards the destruction of nature, but which brings life, renews it, destroying its forms."[111] This argument is perhaps inspired by Buffon, who argues, in *Histoire naturelle, générale et particulière,* that violent death is legitimate and necessary in the order of nature and that animals devour one another according to a natural law, which alone can limit the number of the species.[112]

This "truth," as Brissot discerns, raises a number of important questions, which, he believes, have not been satisfactorily answered up to now. "Must men feed only on vegetables? May they feed on the flesh of animals? Do they have the right to feed on their fellows? Do animals and vegetables have the same rights over us? How far does ownership over beings extend?"[113]

It would seem that it extends a very long way. "I have only one word to say in answer to these questions, and that word is dictated by nature herself: *Beings have the right to feed in any way that is proper to satisfy their needs.*"[114] Brissot admits that this principle would have "terrifying" consequences, but why should the truth unsettle us, especially when it succeeds in overthrowing "prejudices"?

Experience itself supplies us with the most powerful argument in favor of the idea that animals of the same species have the right to eat one another. Some argue that there is a kind of "invincible repugnance against tearing apart things of the same species and eating them."[115] This is demonstrably false, Brissot claims. Many animals, such as the wolves of the forest, eat one another; rats eat their young; insects and fish likewise. In the event that anyone is still skeptical, and after a whole string of such proofs, Brissot declares himself ready to accompany the doubter "to the anthropophagi. There, as a spectator of the feasts of human flesh, where gayness presides, I would ask him where this supposed repugnance towards the flesh of one's fellows was to be found . . . finally, I would take him to the Caribs, who feel no disgust in devouring the still palpitating limbs of their own children, whom they have fatted."[116]

Were the education of the savages what has erased their disgust for such nourishment, then what good would innate principles be? And why is it important for us to have them if they are so easily done away with? For Brissot, the usual relations are inverted: there is no natural sense that excludes anthropophagy, but rather one in its favor. Nature is a reservoir of desires repressed by culture, which reveals the aberrant extent of civil life: "Perhaps the savage anthropophagi, who are not at all spoiled by our social institutions, do nothing more than to follow the impulse of nature."[117]

The universe whose law Brissot attempts to decipher is one inspired by mechanical physics, a place where moral distinctions disappear in favor of the exigencies of motion, causing the hierarchies of the chain of being to become irrelevant. What import do the divisions of the species have, the philosopher exclaims: they are nothing but definitions, "chimerical divisions" (divisions chimériques) that have no existence in nature. All bodies belong to the same nature. Within this space, there has been established the capacity of some beings to dispose of others, a capacity that Brissot dubs the "right of property."

Of this "right," Brissot then argues that it is not "exclusive" but "universal": "There is no exclusive property in nature. This word has been erased from its code."[118] In other words, the only form of property that is found in nature is a kind of communism of force, in which each creature seizes what it can. This is the sacred property that should be respected by all, Brissot believes. "Hunger, this is its title. Depraved citizens, reveal another, more powerful!"[119]

In spite of the radicalism of his position, it should not escape our attention that Brissot is working within the horizons of the dominant theories of natural law, whose concepts he merely attempts to hijack. The idea that hunger or absolute need in general give an immediate right of disposal which, in the realm of necessity, is higher than that of property is one that is common in natural law, from Thomas Aquinas to the eighteenth century. However, Brissot believes that this entitlement is one that makes all others invalid. According to him, social property has been disguised as natural property, a transformation of which he accuses the "blind defenders" of private property. He refers to the derivation of civil property from one form or another of natural property, a move that is again very common in natural law. Brissot identifies two theories of the origin and legitimacy of property: one that makes property a right resulting from conquest, and another that derives it based on "first occupancy." Curiously enough, what is missing here is the idea—one otherwise current in natural law—of property based on consent. Brissot's target is Hobbes and a group of jurists, whom he does not name but whom we may guess includes Grotius and Pufendorf.

His argument unfolds on two levels. The first is the exaltation of natural property, which is, as we have discovered, alone legitimate. Who else is the natural proprietor par excellence if not the savage? If we wish to see man as truly great [*vraiment grand*], truly a proprietor, then behold the savage born in the depths of Canada. The Canadian is, according to Brissot, the perfectly free man, who enjoys perfect ownership over the riches of nature: woods, animals, and other suchlike. As regards ownership of women, Brissot presupposes that this is amiable, because here need means "love."

On the other hand, Brissot vehemently criticizes the institution of private property, which he claims is "frivolous and useless." It presupposes a contradiction: the natural law of property is universal, but private property is individual, therefore particular. It is clear that the two are opposed. The only legitimate foundation of property is need, which for Brissot seems completely to exclude property in political societies, the property of the wealthy financier, who has built proud palaces on the ruins of public wealth, of the avid prelate, of the idle bourgeois. The sin of the latter is that they have more than they require for the satisfaction of the most elementary needs. And to Brissot need appears as a kind of immediate and irresistible pulsation rather than something stable and calm. Criticizing the idea of the right of first occupancy, he argues that the right of stable possession does not result from any eventual need: if someone no longer needs a place, why then should he continue to occupy it? It is because of the need of the one to destroy the entitlement that the other might have had over a piece of land.

Why then should property only take a legitimate form in nature? Because, explains Brissot, although each has a right to all in the state of nature, natural man has only one criterion: utility. Utility would thus be a kind of barrier that nature erects in the path of usurpation of the right of property. Things seem to stand slightly differently, admits Brissot, when two men, in nature, lay claim to the same right over the same thing. In this case, he argues, he who has the greater need has the right to property; if the need is equal, then he who is more powerful shall prevail, a situation that Brissot describes in a strictly objective manner, like the collision of two billiard balls.

A society in which people become balls manipulated by base needs and who collide destructively with one another is not exactly the blessed city of the philosophers. Brissot argues that we should nonetheless not lose sight of the fact that the discussion has been about property in natural law. "It would be dangerous to apply it to our societies. One can forgive Father Jean who ate the thigh of an English suicide. He was in the Siberian wastes, almost dead of hunger. However, woe betide him who in our society might acquire a taste for human flesh! The laws would severely punish him."[120]

But it is not clear why things should be thus, as long as the same laws and the same society have been condemned as unjust, and the rich man has been called a "thief." Man in society is "a slave," who, when he is hungry, ends up "humbly" begging charity, apparently without knowing that ownership of beings is universal. Brissot ultimately admits that this right of natural property, which he has just discovered, is relevant to civilized societies and should serve as a criterion for judicial reform. The courts should not punish those who have stolen out of hunger so harshly. They have done nothing but fulfill the wishes of nature. Brissot writes that he would be happy if the lives of those innocents were saved, apparently ignoring the fact that such offences were no longer capital in the majority of civilized jurisdictions. Such a work of humanity would merit "centuries of immortality" (*siècles d'immortalité*), he asserts in the closing paragraph of the work, whether ironically or in an access of modest it is hard to say hard to say. Whichever it might have been, death was closer than Brissot suspected. During the French Revolution, he was one of the leaders of the Girondists, in which capacity he promoted revolutionary war as a crusade for liberty in Europe. After the French army suffered a series of defeats, the Girondists were deposed, and in 1793, Brissot was guillotined, devoured by the revolution among whose parents he numbered.

Recherches philosophiques sur le droit de propriété dans la nature is not a work that is, as a rule, remembered in discussions about the origins of the communist doctrine. However, its importance may have been considerable, not only for the ideas it contains, but also because it is a piece in the history of the establishment of revolutionary egalitarianism before 1789. Brissot was one of those who frequented Palais Royal circles and was a friend of Restif de la Bretonne, who was the first to employ the term *communism*, in 1782, referring to a project for the abolition of private property. Restif was also a friend of Mercier, the writer whose *L'an 2240, rêve s'il en fut jamais* (*The Year 2240, A Dream Such as Never Has Been*) included proposals for radical reform. Restif corresponded with a certain Joseph-Alexandre-Hupay de Fuvea, a provincial writer, who, in a letter, was the first to describe himself as an *auteur communiste*. Hupay was also the author of a project for a secular communist society, entitled *Project for a Philosophical Community* (1779). The sources that inspire Hupay are Rousseau, Mably, and accounts of the Indians.[121] Finally, it was also Restif who was the link binding these authors to the revolutionary printing press of Nicolas Boneville and, through the latter, to Sylvan Maréchal and Gracchus Babeuf, who were to be at the center of the Conspiracy of Equals, the first attempt to instate an order of extreme and secular egalitarianism in a modern state.

ECSTATIC CONSUMPTION

The communist ideology seems to be characterized by the special attention it accords the problem of poverty. It is a form of egalitarianism, and this egalitarianism's reason to be seems to derive from the existence of poverty. This, in any case, is the interpretation that the apostles of modern communism have sanctioned and which has become current coin.

However, if communism had been nothing more than a project to resolve the problem of poverty, it would have remained, in all likelihood, one of the thousands of such schemes that have been concocted in the last two or three hundred years. That this did not happen is an indication of the fact that the communist doctrine had at its heart something other than the concept of poverty. At its origins, it was rather a doctrine of abundance. This seems strange, if we think that the experience of communist societies is synonymous with mass poverty. However, before the instatement of the "popular" regimes, and even before the formation of the socialist and communist parties and their participation in the political struggle, thus before the bitter test of reality, the prime mover of the communist imagination was abundance.

The abundance that communistic authors glimpse should not be understood as "sufficiency." In the context of the seventeenth and eighteenth centuries, even this was radical. In conditions in which poverty and wretchedness were dominant realities, a proposal for a society in which each achieved sufficiency was a utopia with subversive overtones. However, the abundance of the radical egalitarian projects should not be confused with a mere satisfaction of vital needs and, eventually, a little extra thrown in. It is in every respect an extraordinary abundance. Before all else, communism is, at its origins, the systematization and legitimization of a society in which other than ordinary desires can be gratified, in manners other than those consecrated. For those who invent it, the communist order is one of ecstatic consumption.

What the radical authors find attractive in the natural society of the cannibals is, as we have seen, liberty, equality, fraternity, and prosperity. Liberty is an attribute that seems out of place in a discussion of communism, which has made possible some of the most repressive states that have ever existed in history. The liberty to which these authors refer is not, however, the civil liberty of the modern liberal and democratic tradition, but one that is natural and communal, a liberty of the tribe or "republic," by virtue of which the regimentation of individuals is not only possible but also desirable. But the liberty of the cannibals goes beyond even the liberty of the Spartans. It is one of beings who are free by nature, which makes it all the more revolutionary in comparison with any political liberty. It gives immediate and inalienable entitlement to everything.

This natural liberty is what brings within the horizons of the appetite objects that are new, impossible, or improbable for civil man. Here, in the opinion of the radical authors, is the root of the savage cannibals' superiority over the man of the city. The cannibal can desire that which the other cannot conceive or cannot accept to desire. Moreover, his desires are legitimate thanks to the law of nature, while the desires of civilized man are awakened against a backdrop of culpability.

Human flesh is one such object of prohibited consumption, probably even the forbidden object par excellence. This interdiction, under whose sign they rest, has produced a delectable fascination in numerous texts about cannibals. The savages' feasts of human flesh are viewed in an ambivalent manner by the writers of the Enlightenment. On the one hand, they mark out the primitivism of the Indians, but on the other hand they are proof of a natural liberty that is more comprehensive than civil liberty. It is the same liberty that the treatises of natural law and casuistry argued was legitimate and took precedence, in certain conditions, over political liberty. In the name of this natural liberty, the savage satisfies an appetite that political man can only entertain in secret.

In order to understand the nature of equality in primitive communism, we should avoid seeing it under the species of civilized equality, proper to a contemporary liberal society. The world of the authors of the seventeenth and eighteenth centuries was one that was fundamentally hierarchical, in which equality inhabited only restricted ecological niches. The suggestion of a society of equals was, in these circumstances, more than radical: it verged on blasphemy. The equality of the revolutionaries is one that is fundamentally irreverent. For them, hierarchies are not only unknown or ignored, as in the age of mass democracy. They exist and demand to be overcome in a demonstrative manner, verging on Carnival, the main occasion on which the hierarchies of traditionally society are overturned or derided. Lack of respect and violent and coarse language are not merely fireworks to which the communist propagandists make recourse in the heat of political battle, but rather aspects of such a rhetorical demolition of inequality. The unpolished Indians are the ideal spokesmen of a doctrine that sets out to trample underfoot the entire symbolism of reverence. In the *Philosopher-Soldier*, a work published anonymously by Naigeon and dedicated to a critique of Malebranche's theory of religion, the critic demands that his interlocutor "should not be shocked by the crude terms that I sometimes let slip when I speak of your religion. I play the role of a free, indifferent person . . . the role of a savage whose spirit is unaffected by superstition."[122] During the French Revolution, a new genre of agitating journalism will hone the jargon of the primitives to perfection. In *Père Duchesne*, Hebert does not miss a single occasion to slip in a *foutre* or *bougre*. The titles of the revolutionary pamphlets are also suggestive in this respect.[123]

The atheism of the modern communist also has its precedents in the literature about cannibals. In the nineteenth century, Lammennais is one of the first to suggest that Christianity was a kind of socialism, and in the twentieth century, "liberation theology" also promoted similar ideas. However, the majority of the communist doctrinaires propagated violent atheism, which is incomprehensible as mere nonbelief. The satisfactions of blasphemy are a more likely explanation for their frenzy. In Soviet Russia, there was a movement named "priest-eating" (*popoedstvo*), which agitated for the idea of the elimination of the priesthood without delay. Some of their posters depicted peasants feeding on the intestines of a dismembered Christ.[124]

Liberty and equality interpreted in a subversive key: this is the reason for the legitimization of nudity, another theme that connects the literature about the savages to that of revolution and egalitarianism. The origins of the attractions of nudism in the radical political discourse of the nineteenth century are complex, and classical art is in part responsible. However, nudity as a political and moral value also has other sources. During the Reformation there appeared a sect named the Adamites, who promoted nudity based on the idea that our protoparents were naked, according to the Scriptures. In the seventeenth and eighteenth centuries, however, the major protagonist of nudism is undoubtedly the savage. In his book on the Caribs, Rochefort tells us how the savages go naked; if someone hides his privy parts, they mock him. In the face of European objections, they reply that this is how we all came into the world.[125] A 1640 travel relation from Madagascar presents a people, happy albeit somewhat slothful, who go naked as they seem not bothered by original sin; their diet is simple as they have no need to spice their food, and drink only water, a feat unheard in Europe.[126] In *Letter on the Nudity of the Savages, to the Marquis of* ***, probably written by Fontenelle, we discover that *pudeur* is merely the effect of upbringing and habit. Why should the Caribs blush, the author wonders, when they go naked in the state of nature? Ultimately, almost all the peoples of history and on other continents have gone naked or dressed in their own fashion, such as the Hottentots, who smear themselves in dung. The savages and Cynic philosophers likewise teach us that we should not be embarrassed to perpetuate the species and hide the organs intended for this noble purpose. It is true that the socialist parties of the nineteenth and twentieth centuries were sooner conservative from the moral point of view, an inevitable consequence of the industrialization of the communist movement and the attraction of the working class into the parties of the proletariat. However, the idea of nudism continued to survive at the margins of official socialism. In the 1920s, there was a movement in Soviet Russia named "Down with Shame!" for which the original garb of Adam was the democratic uniform par excellence, and which held nudist demonstrations in Moscow and Kharkov.[127]

A nineteenth-century socialist, Pierre Leroux, imagined an even more bizarre form of communitarianism. According to his theory of "circulus," everything that traverses our stomach acquires a fertilizing quality. Instead of making fun of socialistic ideas, Leroux warns, we should better donate to the State our excreta (*notre fumier*). This would be a sort of social tax that will be put to good use, in order to double agricultural output.[128]

The fraternity of the radical egalitarian authors of the eighteenth century is similarly one that cannot be superimposed on the common ideas of social solidarity. Classical, particularly Aristotelian political philosophy speaks of *philia* (friendship, love) as the fundamental affective link in any well-ordered city. The consequences of this are notable at the level of property: between friends, all things should be shared, warns Aristotle. However, reciprocal affection in republics of savages is fascinating because it takes hyperbolic and licentious forms, such as homosexuality and the communism of women. As soon as he steps on the soil of the New World, Vespucci notices that every Indian takes as many women as he fancies.[129] The total availability of women is what most inflames the imagination of the protocommunist authors. In *Le Pornographe: Idées d'un honnête homme pour un projet de réglement des prostituées* [*The Pornographer: Ideas of an Honest Man for a Project to Regulate Prostitutes*] (1769), Restif de la Bretonne, one of the best known "pornographers" of his day, proposes a centralized system of brothels, with fixed tariffs, for the satisfaction of citizens' appetites, which would also offer girls under the age of fourteen. Restif discovers the model of public women in ancient history (Spartan women, he claims, were shared) and in the experience of the "free savages," whose women are supposed to follow "natural instincts."[130] Later, after the 1917 Revolution, some Bolsheviks would seriously consider abolishing the family.

The absence of private property is, indisputably, one of the pillars of communist doctrine. However, the idea has rather mysterious origins, which many pages of more or less ideologically regimented history have failed to elucidate satisfactorily. Today, private property is seen as one of the two terms of a polar relation, with public property situated at the opposite extreme. To attempt to discover such a duality in the context of radical discussion of property in the sixteenth to eighteenth centuries is, however, to commit an anachronism. What the authors of that period set in opposition to private property was not public property, for the simple motive that the latter, at least in the forms in which it was elaborated during the nineteenth and twentieth centuries, did not yet exist. The common property to which these writers refer was one inspired by the theses of natural law and translates as a right to appropriation, based on necessity, from an otherwise common fund—here "common" means, as a rule, "common to all men." In this sense, for example, it is possible to say that the open sea is "common."

This communist of the state of nature is therefore not a juridical institution to be superimposed on the state property of a later period. On the contrary, it is a pre- and even antijuridical institution. Savage communism is not merely content to ignore private property, but rather represents its complete inversion. This is why private property is, as a rule, theorized as theft. It is no coincidence that Proudhon will, in the nineteenth century, link theft and property. His theory has antecedents in the dissertations about savages written in the preceding centuries. That the savages live in a state of nature, where private property is unheard of, is well known. However, the law of nature, as we have already seen, is one that empowers the savages to pass over the distinction that civil man sets up between *mine* and *yours*. The original communism is therefore one of generalized theft, where each grabs what he can. It is exactly in this way that cannibal societies are described and it is exactly in this way that the revolutionaries will urge the mob to act. From Warville to Lenin, theft is seen as a component of natural freedom usurped by the civilized order. The savages are not, of course, the only source of this strange idea of property. In antiquity, the Spartans are described as legitimizing theft in certain conditions, a fact that did not escape the attention of the Enlightenment radicals. Banditry and piracy are two activities associated with a form of popular justice. However, neither of these sources describes, to the same extent as the literature about cannibals, a society in which private property is impossible because each helps himself to whatever he can lay his hands on.

At the origins of the communist doctrine, there can be found a concept of man in nature and about natural society. By virtue of natural law, whose restoration is demanded, the subject of the communist discourse is one of extreme desires. In the utopia of primitive communism, he lives surrounded by women and forbidden pleasures; he blasphemes to his heart's content and lays his hands on whatever object he likes.

This idea of a society of equals is then adopted by the first modern communist and socialist writers, who were thereby more faithful to their doctrinal sources than many historians might think, ready as they are to see only a symptom of individual delirium in the eccentricities of these authors. When Fourier argues that a women in his phalansteries should give herself to fifteen thousand men during her lifetime and leave each with "pleasant memories," and that children should be sent to clean up feces, because this is in keeping with their "passions"; when Proudhon argues that the origin of private property is theft; when Marx and Engels speculate on the abolition of private property and the family; and when Lasalle speaks of the "right to idleness," we are dealing with subjects that originate in a radical literature where the cannibal played the leading part. The cannibal, more than figures such as the worker, the peasant, the monk, or the pirate, is the founder of modern communism. This is perhaps what Lenin knew when he wrote, in a letter of March 19, 1922, marked "Top Secret" and addressed to the members of the Politburo, urging them to take decisive measures to install the new order: "Now, and only now, when they have started to eat human flesh in the regions where there is famine, and when hundreds if not thousands of bodies lie on the roads, is the moment in which we can (which means we must) confiscate the goods of the Church with the most savage and merciless energy, not hesitating to crush any resistance ... so that we can lay our hands on a fund of a few hundred millions of gold roubles."

CHAPTER EIGHT

The Agent of Absolute Cruelty

Theodore de Bry, *Mutilation of Natives by the Spanish*

THE DOWNFALL OF MORAL GEOGRAPHY

IN AN ANONYMOUSLY PUBLISHED UTOPIA of 1795, the hero, who finds himself abandoned on an island, observes smoke in the distance. "The first thought that occurred was, that it proceeded from the fire of some Indians, and perhaps Cannibals."[1] For this reason, he quickens his pace to arrive amongst these other men. This passage shows us that the figure of the anthropophagus is on the way to losing his negative valences. At the beginning of the century, in *Robinson Crusoe*, the hero runs in the opposite direction as soon as he suspects the presence of cannibals on his island, a suspicion aroused by the print of a bare foot in the sand. Crusoe flees "terrify'd to the last Degree," looking behind him at every two or three steps, and barricades himself in his "castle" for three days: "For never frighted Hare fled to Cover, or Fox to Earth, with more Terror of Mind than I to this Retreat."[2]

Having up until then been one of the main actors in the drama of natural law, the cannibal, reflecting the new theoretic sensibility of the beginning of the nineteenth century, is relegated to the status of eccentric figure. The causes of this decline are not clear. Can it have been the exhaustion of the theories of natural law that eliminated the cannibal from the ranks of persons influential in the human sciences? Such an explanation is not entirely satisfactory. While it is true that the theories of natural law collapse, at least in their classical forms, this is due in a not at all negligible degree precisely to the discrediting or marginalization of some of their elements. In this history of decline, the cannibal makes his presence felt once more, in quite a paradoxical fashion. He is brought into learned discussion because doubts begin to arise as to his existence. This heralds not only the cannibal's exit from the stage, but also the decline of the sciences in which he participated.

A pure skepticism regarding the existence of anthropophagi was hard to sustain in the face of the impressive accumulation of firsthand accounts, but it was not nonexistent. In *A Voyage to Guinea, Brazil and the West Indies* (1735), John Atkins, "against the authority of grave authors," repeatedly denies that "there be any such Men [as Cannibals] on the face of the Earth."[3] Most of the skeptics admit that anthropophagy exists, but argue that it is exceptional. Virey notes that Atkins and Dampier have contested the existence of cannibals. He is not so certain, because there are "uncontestable proofs in favor of their existence," but he admits that their number has been "excessively exaggerated."[4] In the article "Flesh" in the *Yverdon Encyclopaedia*, we read that there are three kinds of American cannibal, but they are very rare, and their

anthropophagy is accidental, not essential. There are those who kill captives in order to eat them, and those who eat those who die of sickness
or wounds. But their number is very small—there are no more than
"three known tribes where the custom of interring parents in the entrails
of their posterity has really been established" (*peut-être connu trois peu-
plades où la mode d'enterrer les parents dans les entrailles de leur posté-
rité fût réellement établie*). In addition, there can be found "those who
eat only the appendages of the human body, such as the Topinambours
and Tapuiges, who devour only the tunic and part of the umbilical cord
of the newborn babies, or the Peruvians, who sprinkle with human blood
their sacred bread."[5]

The anthropophagy of the Caribs, the cannibal nation par excellence,
also begins to vanish from learned accounts. In his first voyage to America, Columbus doubted the locals' accounts of a fierce tribe named
"Caniba" that ate humans. These might be the men of the Chinese Great
Khan, Columbus believes, who the other Indians believed ate their comrades. In his diary, he repeatedly writes that the Indians lie and deceive.
It is not until he encounters a group of hostile Indians that he admits
that he has seen cannibals, or at least their neighbors. In the seventeenth
and eighteenth centuries, the number of skeptics increases. Du Tertre
claims that the usual diet of the Caribs does not include human flesh.[6]
In the *Universal Dictionary* (Trevoux), there is no article on cannibals.
There is a short article on anthropophagy, and an even shorter one
about anthropophagi, as well as a mention of the dispute between the
Greeks and the anthropophagous Indians in Herodotus, in the article on
"Sepulture." The most surprising omission comes in the article on the
"Caribs." Almost half the text discusses the origin of the name, while in
the rest we discover facts about this people that are far from sensational. In spite of the fact that the bibliographic references refer to works
in which cannibalism is abundantly illustrated, and although it results
from the article on anthropophagy that American man-eaters have "sur-
passed all others in their ferocity," the author manages to pass over the
incidence of cannibalism among the Caribs in total silence. Perhaps the
reference to the preachers who have already made the Gospels known
to the eaters of human flesh explains this suspect silence. A similar omission occurs in the first book of Père Labat, *Voyages to the Isles of America* (1724), where the description of the Caribs contains no reference to
anthropophagy. This is not because the worthy priest had any qualms
about mentioning cannibalism. It is more likely that we are dealing with
a calculated omission. Labat claims that it is an error to believe that the
Caribbean Indians form anthropophagous societies, as so many authors
have tried to convince us. He further claims that he has proofs regarding

the contrary that are as clear as the light of day. He attempts to discredit the learned accounts of Indians' cannibalism. They marry their captives, but they rear the children born of these unions without any thought of killing them. The worst thing that they believe they can do to their captives is to sell them to the Europeans. Cases of the dismemberment of prisoners are explicable as a desire to preserve trophies of victory.

Some authors, especially Protestant writers, deny the existence of cannibalism among the Indians on political and religious grounds. In *The History of the American Indians*, Adair claims that Spanish missionaries' accounts of cannibalism in the New World are fabrications. The Spanish hated the Mexicans and the Peruvians, they slew them to steal their gold, and that is why they described them as abominable cannibal idolaters who offered up human sacrifices and ate their unnatural victims. Montesquieu manages to omit cannibalism in the Indies from his discussion of the right of slavery, although the sources he cites (including Garcilasso de la Vega) offer numerous examples of this practice. For Montesquieu, as for Raynal, religion was the pretext of the crimes in the Indies, and the Spanish superficially and implausibly justified slavery on grounds of differences in civilization, subjugating the Indians because they smoked tobacco or did not trim their beards *à l'espagnole.*

At the close of the Enlightenment, it is not only the figure of the individual cannibal that vanishes from the philosophic landscape. In its turn, the cannibal nation, as a collective personage, is on the way to losing its theoretical significance. Buffon explains why this concept is no longer current in the new social philosophy. He argues that the authors who spoke of the customs of savage nations did not observe that what they regarded as the customs of an entire society were in reality nothing more than "actions proper to a few individuals, often determined by circumstances or caprice."[7] Some nations, he tells us, eat their enemies; others mutilate or burn them. Some are in a state of perpetual war; others seek to live in peace. In some tribes, the fathers are killed at a certain age; in others, the parents eat their children. These accounts, related with "such complaisance" by travelers, can be reduced, according to Buffon, to tales of particular facts and signify nothing more than that a certain savage ate his enemy, that another burned or mutilated him, and that yet another killed or ate his child. This might occur in many tribes of savages, for wherever there is no order, established society (*société habituelle*), law, or master, we are not so much dealing with a nation as much as with a "tumultuous assembly of barbarous and independent men."

The regions annexed by the extreme imagination become more civilized in the eighteenth and nineteenth centuries. In the scholarly literature, this causes a narrowing of the potential space for cannibalism.

John Ogilby's *Atlas* (1670) presents Africa as a collection of well-organized kingdoms, not as an assembly of savage tribes. The illustrations show ordered settlements, with officials of various ranks, well-built houses, and cultivated fields. The most spectacular example is America, however. While America was in the sixteenth and seventeenth centuries the continent of primitivism par excellence, in the time of Tocqueville and Hegel it becomes the "land of the future." The elimination of the cannibal from the map of the world is signaled by the *Yverdon Encyclopaedia* (in the article "Flesh"), which notes that Europeans have almost entirely exterminated the nations that ate human flesh. The progress of civilized manners also signals a change in cookery. In *Robinson Crusoe*, the shipwrecked Englishman asks Man Friday whether he will eat people once he has returned to his own country. The conversion of the cannibal seems definitive: "No, No, Friday tell them to live good, tell them to pray God, tell them to eat Corn-bread, Cattle-flesh, Milk, no eat Man again."[8]

From the point of view of the consequences for moral theory, more important than the civilization or extermination of the anthropophagi was the growing disbelief in classical travel literature. A dose of skepticism regarding the veracity and relevance of travelers' accounts was probably a natural component of reactions to the genre. In the *History of the Conquest of Mexico*, Solis says that the religion and customs of the Indians was a mixture of all that is most abominable in the idolatry of other parts of the world but that to repeat such atrocities is "tedious": it is "instruction that is very little necessary, which produces no pleasure and is not useful."[9] Rochefort argues that the Carib savages never marry and reproach the Europeans for their passion for travel. They therefore "have the honor of resembling Socrates" (*ils ont l'honneur de ressembler à Socrate*), who never left Athens.[10]

In the eighteenth century this skepticism begins to be cultivated more consciously, and accounts of savage customs begin to be censured for their exuberance. In *The New Science*, Vico argues that there are three "universal and eternal" customs, practiced by all nations: religion, marriage, and burial of the dead. As the travel literature does not seem to bear out his schema, Vico argues that it circulates untruths: "Let not our first principle be accused of falsehood by the modern travelers who narrate that the peoples of Brazil, South Africa, and other nations of the New World live in society without any knowledge of God, as Antoine Arnauld believes to be the case also of the inhabitants of the islands called the Antilles. . . . These are travelers' tales, to promote the sale of their books."[11] In reference to doubtful accounts of the Mariana Islands, Raynal is adamant that no authority could convince us to believe such an absurdity. Lafitau in his turn claims that many ancient and modern accounts of nations with extraordinary customs are mere fables. In *The Intelligencer* (1728), Thomas Sheridan denounces the storytellers who tell of such unbelievable things, a passion that above all predominates among travelers.[12]

In the *Discourse on the Origins of Inequality*, Rousseau puts forward a systematic critique of travel literature. "In the two or three centuries since the inhabitants of Europe have been flooding into other parts of the world, endlessly publishing new collections of voyages and travel, I am persuaded that we have come to know no other men except Europeans." Under the "pompous name of the study of man," these authors have produced nothing more than a study of the men of their own nation. "Individuals travel here and there in vain; it seems that philosophy does not travel." Rousseau finds the cause in the nature of those who compile such travel accounts, at least the accounts that concern faraway lands: "There are hardly more than four sorts of men who make long-distance voyages: sailors, merchants, soldiers and missionaries. Now it can hardly be expected that the first three classes should yield good observers, and as for the fourth. . . . Besides to preach the Gospel usefully, it is only necessary to have zeal and God supplies the rest; but to study man it is necessary to have talents that God is not obliged to give to anyone, and which are not always possessed by the saints."[13]

Thus there is a lack of any travel literature written with philosophical intention or ability. It might be objected that such a literature not only exists but Rousseau even approvingly quotes from it. Indeed, his position in the *Discourse* is that only some parts of travel literature are suspect— of course, those which are most inconvenient to the author. We learn that China has been well observed by the Jesuits, and that everything seems to have been said about Persia. Of the nations of the West Indies we know nothing, he believes, because they have been visited by Europeans who were more interested in filling their purses than their heads. The whole world is full of nations of which we know nothing more than their name, and yet we presume to judge the human race, he exclaims. Suggestively, the most important voyage that a new Montesquieu, Buffon, Condillac, or d'Alembert of geography might make is to the Caribbean, Florida, or other savage lands, a voyage that should be undertaken with the utmost care.

This skepticism toward travel literature leads Rousseau to an innovation in political theory. In *The Social Contract* (1762), the geographic references disappear almost entirely. The emphasis on comparative analysis moves into the region of history. This absence is all the more remarkable given that, according to Rousseau's own confession, *The Social*

Contract is a "treatise." In other words it discusses the same subjects and follows the same conventions as the great treatises of natural law by the likes of Grotius, Locke, and Pufendorf, whom we have seen relied heavily on information gleaned from travel literature.

In *Émile*, Rousseau continues his attack on geography. The study of the diversity of nations is not necessary, because man is the same in all his states [*états*]. He is animated by the same passions: if you know one, you know them all, at least as far as man in the civil state is concerned. It is an error for children to learn geography, which has the disadvantage of substituting obscure symbols for concrete realities. In a section entitled *On Journeys*, Rousseau states that all books cause us to neglect the "book of the world."

Similar arguments are also repeated by Virey. What are the causes of anthropophagy? he wonders. Some have claimed hunger, others an especial taste for human flesh. "What horrible absurdities!" We should not believe such "atrocious scenes" in travel literature, Virey asserts, because they are the product of the superstitions of travelers who want to arouse interest in their writings. Missionaries, in their turn, have served up the same "spectacles of horror" in order to highlight their own merits.[14]

In the eighteenth century, the cannibal vanishes from the traditional ecological niches he formerly occupied in the scientific disciplines. As early as 1580, Reginald Scot doubted that witches practiced anthropophagy. It is "untrue, incredible, and impossible" that witches "boile infants . . . untill their flesh be made potable." They are not "kin to the Anthropophagi and Cannibals," Scot claims, and there is no "honest man in England nor in France, will affirme that he hath seene any of these persons."[15] From the late seventeenth century, when demonism enters irrevocable decline, this kind of skepticism becomes current coin. The cannibal will then also vanish from the less-questionable specialist areas of theology. The difficulties of resurrection supposed by cannibalism and accepted by radicals will become irrelevant for later authors. The main reason for this shift of emphasis is probably the evolution toward a theory of the resurrection of the spiritual body combined with a marginalization of the idea of the resurrection of the flesh. Whatever the reasons might have been, it is certain that anthropophagy no longer troubles the theologians' sleep. In his treatise on *The Death of the Righteous, or, the Way of Holy Dying*, Jean de la Placette writes that an infinite number of persons accept the objections regarding the resurrection. What exactly these objections are we are not told. The list of arguments in favor of resurrection show that La Placette is familiar with the classical literature, but for reasons that are not clear he prefers to pass over the subversive travail of the cannibal in silence. The English theologians of the same period debate at length the fate of the dead; however, they seem to be equally unconcerned with the difficulties of the resurrection of a body that reverts to its primary elements. One divine claims that the body of the righteous will be preserved in the grave "by the all-powerful Providence as in a cabinet of rest and sweetest sleep."[16] Another divine, Edward Calamy, insisted that the bodies of the godly, though turned to dust, are nevertheless united with Christ, in a grave "sanctified, sweetened and perfumed."[17] Matthew Fowler and William Bates concurred: the body enjoys a "joyful rest" in a "bed of Peace."[18] The reason of this relative neglect seems to have been the reluctance of the English theologians to fully accept a sharp, Platonic, distinction between body and soul. John Dobson stated bluntly, in a sermon from 1670, that the separation between the two is "against the nature of the soul."[19] The English theologians chose rather to employ a Thomistic approach, and consider the soul and the body as one entity, the soul being for the body what form is for substance.[20]

Perhaps the most obvious development is that which omits the anthropophagus from the famous tableau of the lifeboat of shipwreck survivors. Pufendorf's *Rights of Man and the Citizen* (1673) mentions the lifeboat in the context of cases of necessity that suspend legal, primarily positive obligations. The right that justifies the actions discussed in this section is, of course, the right to one's own self. How far can this right be extended and what are the consequences of its postulation? Pufendorf begins by setting to one side the inessentials, superappended to the schema of natural law, in order to reach a deeper level of rights and obligations. The right to dispose of ourselves is not one that is discretionary. We do not have the right to destroy or to place our body in peril based on pure whim, but we have the right to amputate a limb attacked by an incurable disease, in order to prevent the rest of the body from perishing. Having thus established a right to dismemberment, Pufendorf goes on to analyze the situation in the lifeboat, albeit omitting any reference to cannibalism. This omission is rather surprising, since the list of cases cited in continuation resembles that in his major treatise, where anthropophagy is nevertheless mentioned, alongside the case of the shipwreck survivors who dispute ownership of a plank, the case of the fleeing man obliged to kill an innocent, and that of the two men in danger, where one hastens the death of the other. In the lifeboat, the conflict of fundamental rights is immediately highlighted: we are dealing with a raft that is too small for everyone.[21] Ignoring the question of extreme hunger, he argues that in this case, those in the lifeboat should draw lots to determine who should be cast into the sea. If any of them refuses to draw lots, then the others have the right to throw him overboard.

In the three massive tomes of *Dictionary of Cases of Conscience* (1730), Jean Pontas mentions the lifeboat once, in the article on *Shipwrecks*. This time the craft is laden with "merchants," who no longer debate who should be thrown overboard or eaten, but merely whose wares should be jettisoned and how he should be compensated on reaching port. Pontas's extravagant enumeration of cases and situations, sometimes highly improbable, does not include anthropophagy. There is a single article ("Scandal," case 11) concerning the consumption of forbidden flesh. A clergyman is captured by Algerians and in prison made to eat "salted flesh," which the infidels intentionally serve the priest during a fast, in contempt of the Christian religion. The other Christian captives are "scandalized" as the priest eats. Pontas's answer: the priest is a sinner. According to the opinion of Thomas Aquinas, he ought rather to risk his life than eat the flesh and thereby risk scandalizing the others.[22]

The casuistry of natural law is gradually purified of the cannibal's presence, not only on the high seas but also on dry land. In the discussion of the right to burial in *The New Science* (1744), Giambattista Vico suggests the existence of an improbable creature, a degenerate vegetarian that swarms among corpses:

> Finally [to realize] what a great principle of humanity burial is, imagine a feral state in which human bodies remain unburied on the surface of the earth as food for crows and dogs. Certainly this bestial custom will be accompanied by uncultivated fields and uninhabited cities. Men will go about like swine eating the acorns found amidst the putrefaction of the dead. And so with good reason burials were characterized by the sublime phrase "compacts of the human race" [*foedera generis humanis*], and with less grandeur were described by Tacitus as 'fellowships of humanity [*humanitatis commercia*].[23]

One of the arguments that consigns the eater of human flesh to ethical insignificance is that which makes him an isolated accident, a product of normal physiology not imputable to moral will. Thus the anthropophagus is deprived of the connotations of moral monster, of physiological aberration, or of possessor of rights as primitive as they are incompatible with civilized life. He is transformed into the result of common environmental factors. A growing number of authors begin to argue that anthropophagy is merely a product of extreme hunger. However, far from being a natural idea, as it seems to us, this speculation appears at the end of a complex reasoning process, whose aim is restrictive. By eliminating alternative explanations, the theory in which the cannibal-monster is a necessary ingredient, as a subversive image of subversion of the moral order, is thereby suspended.

This transformation takes place within the space of the new science of political economy. In the *Two Treatises of Government*, Locke explains the existence of an essential difference of wealth between primitive and civilized societies, a difference resulting from labor, in the first place the labor that improves the productivity of the soil. Locke observes that there is a paradoxical situation in the New World: although the Indians have a great amount of land at their disposal, they are always very poor. In his words, "a king of a large and fruitful territory there, feeds, lodges, and is clad worse than a day-labourer in England."[24]

For Cornelius de Pauw, hunger and not exceptional physiology produces cannibalism. Some naturalists have advanced a "ridiculous" theory of cannibalism, which is supposed to be the product of a different anatomy of the stomach. The true principle of cannibalism is the harsh necessity of savage life. This had already been announced by the abbé Mallet, author of the article "Anthropophagy" in the *Encyclopédie* (1751): "Some physicians have ridiculously imagined that they have discovered the principle of anthropophagy in the bitter, bilious humor which is found in the membranes of the ventricle and which produces by irritation the terrible voracity remarked in various maladies."[25] The article "Flesh" in the *Yverdon Encyclopaedia* fuses de Pauw's text with that of the *Encyclopédie*, similarly reaching the conclusion that the physiological explanation of cannibalism as a product of an acrid humor (*une humeur pleine d'acrimonie*) in the membrane of the stomach (*dans la membrane de l'éstomac*) is so ridiculous that it is not worthy of mention (*cette explication est si près du ridicule ou de l'absurde, qu'elle ne mérite aucun examen*). The progress of skepticism is clear if we compare these articles with that on anthropophagy in the 1740 edition of the popular *Universal Dictionary* (Trevoux). There, physicians are reported to have found the principle of anthropophagy in a black and bitter humor, which lodges in the tunics of the ventricle and excites voracity; they are supposed to have given many examples of such inhuman hunger.

This ordinary hunger is no longer an experience that directly connects the spectator to the anarchic universe of crimes against nature. In *Theory of Moral Sentiments* (1759), Adam Smith argues that we can sympathize with the distress of excessive hunger "when we read the description of it in the journal of a siege, or of a sea voyage," imagining ourselves "in the situation of the sufferers." But the degree to which we sympathize is, according to Smith, limited because "we do not grow hungry by reading the description." Smith thereby thrusts excessive hunger into the penumbra of moral knowledge, and it is no coincidence that this occurs in the late eighteenth century, when hunger ceases to be a common social experience in the West.

THE DISMEMBERMENT OF NATURAL LAW

The history of the alienation of anthropophagy as a figure of natural law commences with Hobbes's formulation of a theory of the state of nature, whose consequences are almost universally regarded as universal, in the seventeenth and eighteenth centuries. In *Leviathan*, the state of nature is a situation where there is no sovereign authority to impose order. This natural condition of mankind is one of primitivism and universal strife: "In such condition, there is no place for Industry; because the fruit thereof is uncertain: and consequently no culture of the earth; no navigation, nor use of the commodities that may be imported by sea; no commodious building; no instruments of moving, and removing such things as require much force; no knowledge of the face of the Earth; no account of time; no arts; no letters; no society; and which is worst of all, continuall feare, and danger of violent death; and the life of man, solitary, poore, nasty, brutish, and short."[26]

Thus in the state of nature reigns natural anarchy, savage and bloody, where natural law is perfectly compatible with brutality. The deeds that a man commits in the state of nature are justified by this law. Where there is no civil law, there is no crime or even sin, on condition that the intention be just.

The most subversive idea that Hobbes introduces is that of natural liberty. That necessity gives an absolute right to anything is a well-known theoretical proposition, discussed and even accepted up to a certain limit. In the natural state, man was seen as subject to the empire of necessity, and in this respect the natural right that each would have to commit any act necessary to his survival is one that is ultimate and inevitable. However, Hobbes argues that the freedom of natural man implies an absolute right to anything. Necessity, which is at the origin of the acts of natural man, does not exclude liberty. The water that flows downstream is "free" to follow its course, but at the same time it flows by virtue of necessity. For man, liberty is merely the absence of any external obstacles in the path of his will. This species of liberty, taken as a simple capacity to move an animate body, may coexist with the severest necessity. Hobbes repeats the Stoic example of the man who throws his goods into the sea during a storm, in order to demonstrate that a man may be both free and constrained to commit an act at the same time. There are two kinds of constraint in connection with which Hobbes speaks of liberty. One is political constraint, wielded by a sovereign over a subject, a kind of constraint that brings into view the domain of civil liberty. On the other hand, and more important for our discussion, there is also natural constraint. In the state of nature, where "amongst masterlesse men, there is perpetuall war" men enjoy another kind of liberty, which is "full and absolute."[27] In *De cive*, he compares necessity to a falling stone and argues that this excuses every act: the first foundation of natural law is therefore that each man protects his own life and limbs as far as he is able.

Hobbes thus elaborates a theory within the limits of which man is invested by nature with a supreme right to commit any kind of act, and this not merely by virtue of necessity, but as part of his liberty. For him, man is a species of beast of prey, and the (relative) peace that characterizes the civil order is obtained only at the price of a supreme power that should inspire fear.

Anthropophagy here appears as a natural consequence of natural law. In chapter 14 of *Leviathan*, Hobbes describes the state of nature in a way that would suggest he is thinking of cannibalism: "In such a condition, every man has a right to every thing; even to one another's body." From the point of view of natural law, this does not seem to pose any problem, because "nothing can be unjust [in the state of nature]. The notions of right and wrong, justice and injustice have there no place."[28] The possibility of anthropophagy is also implicit in the exposition of the doctrine of necessity. If the sovereign orders someone to abstain from "food, air, medicine, or any other thing, without which he cannot live; yet hath that man the liberty to disobey."[29] In *A Dialogue between a Philosopher and a Student of the Common Laws of England*, Hobbes repeats the idea according to which the state of nature implies anthropophagy: "Without Law, every thing is in such sort every Man's, as he may take, possess, and enjoy without wrong to any Man, every thing, Lands, Beasts, Fruits, and even the bodies of other Men, if his Reason tell him he cannot otherwise live securely."[30] It is true that this point of view is put forward by the personage of the lawyer, but the philosopher replies to him: "All this is very Rational."

Although anthropophagy is a rigorous consequence of his theory about the state of nature, and although the literature about the savage Americans he had read constantly presented them as anthropophagi, Hobbes nevertheless avoids declaring man in the natural state a cannibal. The reasons for this omission are not at all clear, and it is possible that anthropophagy may have had a status similar to that of atheism in Hobbes's philosophy. Whether or not he was an atheist, whether his Christianity was as orthodox as he claimed, and whether Hobbes was an adherent of one or another form of heresy are questions that are still being debated. For in matters of religion his true opinions are difficult if not impossible to distinguish behind the formulae dictated by prudence.

The same prudence might have determined him to avoid describing natural man as a justified anthropophagus, in order to exempt him from showing that anthropophagy, far from being a crime against nature, is legitimate from the viewpoint of general natural law—something that would have constituted an incendiary conclusion and complicated the already problematic reception of his writings. From the point of view of political philosophy, Hobbes is interested, during the period between *De cive* and *Leviathan*, in imposing his method inspired by the mechanical science of nature and by mathematics rather than conducting polemics on the subject of the history of the natural state. Likewise, it is possible that the relative absence of cannibalism from his reconstruction may be explicable by the fact that his attention is focused on the excessive cruelty of civil man. Ultimately, his celebrated formulation "man is a wolf to man" (*homo homini lupus*) does not describe natural anthropophagy, but rather the state of war that leads to the absence of supranational sovereignty. Whatever his reasons, Hobbes did not mislead his critics. Immediately after its publication, *Leviathan* was violently attacked, first of all for its religious opinions.[31] In time, however, Hobbes became a subversive author, thanks to his ideas of the natural passions of man and the state of nature as the war of all against all.

For the philosophers of natural law, Hobbes's theory raises a series of complications. On the one hand, it is certain that the method of Hobbes's philosophy was extremely influential, even for authors who reject the conclusions of the English philosopher. On the other hand, however, the consequences rigorously derived by Hobbes from the notion of the right of the natural individual are almost uniformly regarded as erroneous, scandalous, and unacceptable. In this context, the question of anthropophagy implies the most serious of difficulties. To admit that man in the state of nature is a cannibal and that this quality is sanctioned by natural law means to renounce the classical idea according to which anthropophagy is a crime against nature. Such a renunciation, in its turn, leads to the need for a universal legitimization of cannibalism in the state of nature, a theoretic progression that most authors are far from willing to accept. This is why theoreticians of natural law post-Hobbes are required to elaborate a theory of the state of nature and of natural man that will avoid the implication of anthropophagy.

This theoretical shift unfolds at many levels. One is the critique of ideas about the nature of slavery in the state of war. In the chapter "Of Conquest" in the *Second Treatise of Government*, Locke investigates the kind of power that a master wields over a slave. Although Locke was familiar with travel literature, which describes a despotic and cruel domination in the extreme, in the passages on the "purely despotical" power of the victor in a just war, Locke neglects to mention that the kind of power he admits is "absolute" would be one that implied anthropophagy. This omission is even stranger given that Locke had repeatedly shown that absolute power brings about a state of war between men, and the one who exercises such a power becomes like a wild beast.[32] At a given moment, Locke writes, probably in reference to Hobbes, "he that thinks absolute power purifies men's blood, and corrects the baseness of human nature, need read but the history of this, or any other age, to be convinced of the contrary."[33] However, this is exactly the history that Locke uses so selectively in his polemic, in order to preserve the fiction of an absolute power of master over slave that nevertheless does not degenerate into anthropophagy.

In all probability, Locke's omission is intentional. We have already seen that, in the *First Treatise of Government*, he criticizes Filmer's conception of absolute power, arguing that it legitimizes cannibalism as practiced by families of anthropophagous Indians. The problem is that this critique is quite probably gleaned from the writings of Filmer himself and then turned against him. It is Filmer who, in passages it is hard to believe Locke did not observe, criticizes Hobbes's theory of the state of nature, arguing that it would imply anthropophagy.

In a book published in 1652 (and republished posthumously in 1679–80, when Filmer's works were printed in the second edition that Locke studied when working on the *Two Treatises*), entitled *Observations Concerning the Originall of Government*, Filmer inserts a passage about "Mr Hobs 'Leviathan.'" Here, he argues that divine benevolence causes the Hobbesian state of nature, which includes cannibalism, to be impossible:

> It is not to be thought that God would create man in a condition worse than any beasts, as if he made men to no other end by nature but to destroy one another. A right for the father to destroy his children or eat them, and for the children to do the like by their parents, is worse than cannibals. This horrid condition of mere nature when Mr Hobbes was charged with, his refuge was to answer "that no son can be understood in the state of nature" [*De cive* chapter 1, section 10]—which is all one with denying his own principle. For if men be not free-born, it is not possible for him to assign and prove any other time for them to claim a right of nature to liberty, if not at their birth.[34]

Filmer further connects Hobbes's theory of the state of nature with anthropophagy, by means of categories of population. If there is a state of nature as Hobbes claims, then "I do not see why such a condition must be called a state of war of all men against all men." Hobbes's theory would presuppose overpopulation, although this is not evident in *Leviathan* or *De cive*: "Indeed if such a multitude of men should be created as the earth could not well nourish, there might be cause for men to destroy one another rather than perish for want of food."[35] What allows Filmer to affirm the implausibility of the Hobbesian idea of the state of nature is also an attribute of divine benevolence. God has had the foresight to create sufficient room on the earth and sufficient resources for all, "so that there is no absolute necessity of war in the state of pure nature."[36] At the level of secondary causes, therefore, the immensity of the physical world defies multiplication with connatural finality.

The critiques of Locke and Filmer herald what in the eighteenth century will become almost universal skepticism regarding the validity of the Hobbesian theory of the state of nature. The evisceration of this theory is at the center of the process whereby the edifice of natural law is dismantled. By the late eighteenth century, the state of nature becomes a suspect concept, if not one that is somehow ridiculous and incoherent. This is a gradual process, in which the difficulties presupposed by the existence of cannibalism play an important role. However, the anthropophagus does not draw his destructive powers from a void. If he remains a disturbing presence, it is because modern theories of the state of nature do not succeed or do not wish to integrate anthropophagy into the background of natural law.

In the Age of Enlightenment, the identification between primitives and man in the natural state, which had been established by philosophers and travelers, is called into question. In the *Treatise of Human Nature*, Hume argues that a traveler who claimed to have met men with exactly the same character as those in Plato's *Republic* or Hobbes's *Leviathan* would be greeted with the same justified incredulity as the traveler who claimed to have found a "climate in the fiftieth degree of northern latitude, where all fruits ripen and come to perfection in the winter, and decay in the summer."[37] In *Of the Origin and Progress of Language*, Monboddo writes that a state of nature as Hobbes understands it, as perpetual war, "neither does exist, nor ever did exist, in any species of animals."[38] Discussing the right of slavery, Heineccius argues that the master has a right of life and death over someone in "perfect servitude," a notion whereby he understands that slavery results from a just war. However, he does not treat the possibility that such a master might violate the law of nature. What limits the master's power to dispose of his slave, according to Heineccius, are the provisions of civil law. For the German jurist, the state of nature is no longer one in which all kinds of aberration demand an explanation and justification. This state, he argues, was not as bad as Hobbes and Pufendorf thought. They did not place enough emphasis on the fact that here too men have obligations to one another. The evils that they commit in the state of nature do not result from the nature of that situation, but from the "evil of mankind," which inevitably also makes itself felt in the civil state.[39]

Skepticism regarding the fruitfulness of the notion of natural man is propagated in the eighteenth century by authors such as Francis Hutcheson. In a lecture given in 1730 on the social nature of man, he attacks Locke's critique of innate ideas. Since the latter put forward this theory, the Scottish philosopher argues, many honorable writers have wholly avoided any investigation regarding the existence of natural ideas and judgments, or regarding the senses whereby different types of things are perceived. Locke's theory would be relevant only with reference to certain ideas, but not as far as the existence of natural faculties is concerned, specifically a moral sense. The critics of innate ideas ought to take into consideration a developed moral subject in order to question the naturalness of this subject's perception. But instead of doing so, they study immature beings. They would do better to investigate judgments, perceptions, and appearances as revealed by nature, rather than disputing what can or cannot be observed in an animalcule that will later develop into a man, or in those wretches born in some barren corner of the world, who lead a harsh and brutal existence devoid of the conditions necessary for life.[40]

In the *Essay on Morals*, Voltaire criticizes the theory of the state of nature that supposes man to have lived a harsh and solitary life. Such speculations are worthless, he argues, because they are based on faulty reasoning. If man now lives in society, we have no reason to believe that he once existed in a state where he was solitary. "Man, in general, has always been what he is . . . we were not made to live in the manner of a bear" (*L'homme, en général, a toujours été ce qu'il est . . . nous n'étions donc point faits pour vivre à la manière des ours*). Cases of wild children lost in the woods (*enfants égarés dan les bois*) prove nothing. There are also stray sheep, but that does not prove that sheep are not meant to live in flocks.[41]

In the lectures on jurisprudence delivered in Glasgow in 1763, Adam Smith says, in reference to homicide, that there is, as far as he knows, only one case in which it is justified to take the life of an innocent man in order to save our own. This is "the instance commonly given by authors, which is when two men after a shipwreck get upon the same plank, and it appears evident that they can not be both saved by it."[42] However, Smith's memory is undoubtedly very selective. He had a good knowledge of the authors of natural law, as proven by his references to

Pufendorf, among others. However, these authors also enumerate other cases. Smith chooses to pass over their examples, probably because he does not wish to confront the problem of cannibalism. This coyness is also apparent in *The Wealth of Nations* (1776). Discussing the extreme poverty that afflicts primitive nations of hunters and fishers, Adam Smith claims that they are frequently forced to kill or abandon their children, their old folk, and their sick, leaving them to "perish with hunger, or to be devoured by wild beasts." Neither here nor in the following example does Smith mention the possibility that excessive hunger might lead to cannibalism. In China, the explosion in population has led to absolute poverty for the lower classes. In Canton, people are "eager to fish up the nastiest garbage thrown overboard from any European ship. Any carrion, the carcass of a dead dog or cat, for example, though half putrid and stinking, is as welcome to them as the most wholesome food to the people of other countries."[43]

In *Essay on the Origin of Languages*, Rousseau presents a vision of the state of nature that, while not explicitly excluding anthropophagy, causes it to become irrelevant. According to him, the first barbarians were hunters and meat-eaters rather than eaters of cereals or bread, a type of nourishment that began to be consumed only after the establishment of property. The vocation of hunter is favorable to anthropophagy, a custom which for Rousseau seems to be an obscure truth of progress in the political order. The first hunters, he writes, became ferocious and began to hunt humans. "War and conquests are nothing more than man hunts. After conquering them, there is nothing left to do but eat them: this is what their successors learnt to do."[44] This hint at anthropophagy is not, however, relevant to the analysis of the state of nature, but exclusively to the civil order. The activity of hunting, Rousseau argues, is not favorable to population growth. Hence it results that very sparse population characterizes the state of nature. It is true that a man "abandoned alone on the face of the earth, must have been a ferocious animal. He was ready to do to others all the evil he feared from them."[45] He attacks in order to defend himself. However, such attacks were scarce in the state of nature, because men lived in isolation, due to their limited needs and primitive way of life, with each content with what nature offered him. Encounters were therefore rare. Everywhere there was a state of war, but peace reigned on the earth.

According to Rousseau, it is an error that the state of nature was conceived as a war of all against all. Hobbes did not observe, our author believes, "the same cause that impedes savages from using their reason, as our *juristconsultes* would have it, impedes them at the same time from abusing their faculties."[46] Natural man is capable of unacceptable outrages. This is the struggle for food in the mists of primitive time, as Rousseau imagines it:

> When he ate, savage man was at peace with all nature and friend with all his peers. Is he not now in the situation of disputing his meal? He never comes to blows without comparing the difficulty of conquering with that of finding food elsewhere, and as pride is not mixed up in the struggle, it will end after a few punches. The victor eats, the vanquished seeks his luck elsewhere and is wholly pacified.[47]

Had the modern philosophers tackled the problem of the existence of anthropophagy in the state of nature, they would have been faced with an extremely difficult dilemma. Is the anthropophagy of the natural man legitimate under the species of natural law? This question is radically different in relation to the classical question of whether man circumstantially fallen into the state of ultimate necessity has the right to become a cannibal. Rejection of the legitimacy of anthropophagy in the state of nature presupposes a natural man who is, at least potentially, a criminal in relation to natural law, a construct that poses evident problems. However, acceptance of anthropophagy is, in its turn, a problematic tactic, and available only for radical writers such as Voltaire or Sade. This is why modern philosophies of natural law prefer to work with a notion of the state of nature that denies the incidence of anthropophagy among men in the natural state or else makes it irrelevant.

But this evacuation of the cannibal from the sphere of the state of nature, far from stabilizing the theory of natural rights, heralds its decomposition. It thus occurs that the anthropophagus is, for a long intellectual tradition, one of the articulations of a theory of natural law, a conceptual figure who causes the existence of a natural legislation to become visible. With the disappearance of the cannibal, and after the other characters in the theater of nature have exhausted their theoretical fruitfulness, the idea of reconstructing the law in purely utilitarian and political terms may emerge. This process comes to a close in the early nineteenth century, when natural law, as a model of the philosophy of law, is replaced by the positive science of law.

This process makes its debut on the Continent. In the Germany of the 1830s, the historical school of law thrusts the writers of the previous century into anonymity. Of course, this transformation does not have a strictly theoretical scope. In the nineteenth century, the formula of the modern bureaucratic and national state reaches maturity. Legislation more and more appears as an activity guided by pragmatic criteria, a situation in which the jurists eliminate or marginalize in their treatises the level of natural legitimatization, in favor of a set of positive arguments.

That the law is the will of the sovereign is an idea that circulates in the scholastic period, but the question of the legitimacy of this will is now no longer posed in terms of respect for divine law. What is important is also the nature of the sovereignty implied by this new understanding of the law. Increasingly, it is depersonalized, against the backdrop of what has become the "political system." The law is now understood as a sum of artifices of the ruling class. Natural law disappears on the Continent, under the pressure of the political bureaucracies of new states, legitimized by pragmatism or nationalism.

In Anglo-Saxon countries, this process is slower, but equally as sure. An important moment in the depreciation of natural law is John Austin's book *The Province of Jurisprudence Determined*. Published in 1832, it will become influential in Britain and America after 1860, being one of the founding statements of modern juridical positivism. For Austin, the matter of jurisprudence is no more than "law, simply and strictly so called: or law set by political superiors to political inferiors." As for the so-called "law of nature," Austin claims that we are dealing with an "ambiguous expression."[48] Each law is merely a kind of commandment. There are, indeed, divine commandments, which make up the law of God, but jurisprudence cannot, however, occupy itself with these. According to Austin, "the distinction of positive law into *natural* and *positive*, with the various distinctions which rest upon that main one, are utterly unintelligible."[49]

The problem he correctly identifies is the question of whether a genus of moral sense or instinct exists. A tradition going back to Plato and Aristotle identifies a certain naturalness of moral judgment, whence norms derive their obligation. Austin puts forward a different criterion for the derivation of legal norms, namely public utility. However, public utility is a social criterion, a result of the existence of a civil order. It is therefore necessary to demonstrate that the norms do not and cannot have any deeper foundation, visible in the natural state prior to political association.

In order to demonstrate this, Austin repeats, in a ridiculous key, the thought experiment of the man abandoned in the state of nature. Let us consider, he writes, a child who has grown to maturity alone in the wilderness, without the help of society.

> I imagine that the savage, as he wanders in search of prey, meets, of the first time in his life, with a man. The man is a hunter, and is carrying a deer which he has killed. The savage pounces upon it. The hunter holds it fast. And in order that he may remove this obstacle to the satisfaction of his gnawing hunger, the savage seizes a stone, and

knocks the hunter on the head. Now, according to the hypothesis in question, the savage is affected with *remorse* at the thought of what he has done. . . . Shortly after the incident which I have now imagined, he meets with a second hunter whom he also knocks on the head. But, in this instance, he is not the aggressor. He is attacked, beaten, wounded, without the shadow of provocation: and, to prevent a deadly blow which is aimed at his own head, he kills the wanton assailant.[50]

According to the hypothesis of the naturalness of moral sentiments, the savage ought to feel a remorse in the first case that could not have originated in any social convention; in the second case, he should not feel the same, because his act has been legitimized by an obvious principle (obvious to an intellect capable of apprehending natural law) of self-preservation. The problem, Austin believes, is that there is no evidence that such natural sentiments exist. The hypothesis of the wild child therefore does not assist us in discovering a natural substance of morality.

Possibly. However, there is another problem, which Austin is not prepared to apprehend. In the account of the natural man, he avoids considering him as an anthropophagus. Indeed, the primitive and the hunter fight over a piece of animal flesh. Even after killing the hunter, the savage does not seem to crave anything more. Cannibalism regarded as a simple possibility would have led us to two kinds of consideration. On the one hand, if the savage had refrained from the anthropophagous act, then we would have had a natural prohibition. Austin would then have had to explain something probably inexplicable within the framework of this theory, which seeks precisely to substitute the exclusively artificial character of laws for this thesis. On the other hand, if the savage had been an anthropophagus, then this would have introduced supplementary elements into an otherwise simple equation: the right to feed or the right to self-defense. Anthropophagy seems to be the kind of act which by its cruelty implies, together with its mere presence, the need for moral censure. Or contrariwise, a justification based on absolute, urgent, and natural necessity.

Austin completes this demonstration by attacking the notion of natural law as formulated by Ulpian. It is true that some laws have instincts as their cause, argues the English philosopher, above all those that refer to relations between men and women or parents and children. However, the law should not be confounded with instinct. The instincts are not laws and they do not form the object of jurisprudence. But why might they not furnish preliminary matter, as in Hobbes? Austin has no time for such subtleties. He asserts merely that "natural law is what nature taught to every animal" (*jus quod natura omnia animalia docuit*) is "a conceit peculiar to Ulpian, and that this most foolish conceit, though inserted in Justinian's compilations, has no perceptible influence on the detail of the Roman law."[51]

After Ulpian it is the turn of Grotius and Montesquieu. Austin rejects these authors' doctrine of natural law on the grounds that it is unclear. In connection with the definition, in *The Spirit of the Laws*, of laws as necessary relations, determined by the nature of things, Austin comments: "What, I would also crave, is the nature of things? . . . The terms of the definition are incomparably more obscure than the term which it affects to expound."[52]

The "nature of things" and "relations" are abundantly discussed in the treatises of the philosophers of natural law, but Austin feels no need to give an account of them. This is because his selective reading of the arguments of jurisprudence censored any theoretical articulation that would have allowed natural law to be brought into the field of his attention as an absolute foundation of law and morality. The absence of the cannibal is one of the conditions that make juridical positivism possible.

CONCLUSION: STATE AND NATURAL HISTORY

The gradual disappearance of the anthropophagus from the territories of philosophy does not leave behind it brighter skies for the moral imagination. On the contrary. In the sixteenth century, a species of moral degradation more profound than that of the cannibal begins to be acutely felt.

The condemnation of the human passions was the first, limited domain in which this kind of argument was brought to bear. The association between avarice and anthropophagy has a venerable tradition. In *De beneficiis*, Seneca describes the legacy hunter awaiting his moment at the bedside of the dying man: "As birds of prey that feed on carrion watch over animals wasted by disease and about to fall, such a man hangs over the deathbed, and wheels around the corpse."[53] In More's *Utopia*, the sheep become anthropophagous: the "sheep that were wont to be so meek and tame and so small eaters, now, as I hear say, be become so great devourers and so wild, that they eat up and swallow down the very men themselves."[54] For Jean de Léry, the French usurers are crueler than the American cannibals. They suck blood and marrow, and they eat widows and orphans alive; it were better if they killed them with a single blow rather than torturing them so much. With the institutionalization of economic egoism, anthropophagy becomes a useful term of comparison in condemning the capitalist system. Such is the case in Moses Hess, one of the radical German authors who influenced Marx. In his tract *On the Essence of Money* (1843), Hess describes money metaphorically as the coagulated blood and sweat of those who sell their inalienable property. Laborers exchange their vital activity for capital and thus cannibalistically feed on their own fat. Money is an alienated form of human flesh and blood, which thus renders us all cannibals, beasts of prey, vampires. Hegelian jargon is here placed in the service of a denunciation of the social order. Besides its general intention, Hess's text has a particular target: the Jews. In Christian Europe, he argues, there lives a nation that feeds on this financial blood. Life lived in the form of money is brutal and cannibalistic, and in the natural history of the social animal, it is the Jews who have the historical mission of bringing out the beast of prey in man. Hess believes that the Jews have now accomplished this historical task: the ancient Jewish respect for blood has thus revealed itself in the mystery of the predatory beast.[55]

The duel is among the modern customs that have been unfavorably compared with the savagery of cannibals. In *An Essay on the Nature and Immutability of Truth in Opposition to Sophistry and Scepticism* (1773), James Beattie argues that a history that placed modern customs such as dueling, gambling, and adultery in their true light "would exhibit specimens of brutish barbarity and sottish infatuation, such as might vie with any that ever appeared in Kamschatka, California, or the land of Hottentots."[56] In the *Letter to d'Alembert*, Rousseau condemns the style of duel named *au premier sang* during the epoch as follows: "To the first blood, great God! And would you drink the blood, ferocious beast? Would you drink it?" (*Au premier sang, grand Dieu! Et qu'en veux-tu faire de ce sang, bête féroce? Le veux-tu boire?*)

The comparison between religious fanaticism and cannibalism was made as early as the Middle Ages. In Orderic Vitalis's history, which recounts the events of the first crusade, we learn that when the Christian army was faced with starvation, the soldiers were forced to devour unclean, strange, unpleasant, and even forbidden things indiscriminately. The account reveals that some of them even ate the flesh of the Turks. Neither the chronicler nor the nobles present at the scene seem to have seen any fundamental problem (although the latter are said to have been ashamed and horrified), because not one of the cannibals was punished. Vitalis's denies that the crusaders' cannibalism was based on the grounds that they voluntarily suffered hunger in the name of God. He admits that they acted illegally but were compelled to do so by necessity.[57]

During the age of the wars of religion, cannibalism becomes a label for the depravity and cruelty aroused by fanaticism. Jean de Léry, a Protestant whose book was published in Geneva not long after the Saint Bartholomew's night massacre, claims that in the bloody tragedy in France, the fat of those slain was auctioned publicly and the liver, heart, and other body parts were eaten by the killers. This execrable slaughter exceeds all those of the American anthropophagi, de Léry believes, because the latter kill only their enemies, whereas in France relatives, neighbors, and fellow countrymen are murdered.[58]

The radical philosophers of the eighteenth century will repeat these arguments in order to denounce the consequences of organized religion in general and Catholicism in particular. In the *Natural History of Religion*, David Hume writes that the human sacrifices of the Carthaginians, Mexicans, and other barbarous nations did not exceed the bloodshed committed by the Inquisition in Rome and Madrid. Those sacrifices were probably not as dangerous to society, Hume speculates, because the victims were chosen by lot or "by some exterior signs" and thus did not affect the rest of society, while the Inquisitors particularly direct their fury against those who possess "virtue, knowledge, love of liberty." These qualities are expelled from society, leaving it to the mercy of "shameful ignorance, corruption, and bondage."[59]

From criticism of customs and fanaticism, the philosophers arrive at a general critique of modern civilization, in which the anthropophagus is employed in the position of social critic. In *Sketches of the History of Man*, Lord Kames reconstructs the entire history of mankind as a succession of abuse and cruelty. "No savages are more cruel than the Greeks and Trojans were, as described by Homer," he believes. Likewise, "a scene representing a woman murdered by her children, would be hissed by every modern audience; and yet that horrid scene was represented with applause in the Electra of Sophocles." The Jews and Romans were also cruel: the latter treated their children "like cattle, to be the father's property."[60] Lafitau, in *Moeurs des sauvages amériquains*, asserts that other peoples have been as cruel. The Romans, for example, held gladiatorial games. The evil of modern Europeans astonishes the primitives, who, according to Lafitau, however barbarous they might be, treat their fellow countrymen better than the Europeans. "With good reason, they view the barbarity of duels as something more barbarous and more ferocious."[61] Individualism is also subjected to an early critique through the eyes of the natural savage. For Europeans, the death of someone belonging to the same nation seems to be of no interest to anyone: this is an example of irresponsibility that amazes the Indians. In the *Essay on Morals*, Voltaire argues that if savages are those who live in poverty, in small families, speaking an unintelligible language, ignorant and ready to kill one another as soon as the drum is beaten in the village, then in Europe such savages are everywhere. The tribes of Canada and the Kaffirs, concludes Voltaire, "are infinitely superior" to us, because they at least are free, while our nations are not.[62]

It is the civilized nations that are cruel and depraved, writes Rousseau in the *Discourse on the Origins of Inequality*. In a sequel to the *Discourse on Arts and Sciences*, he had argued that such nations might, paradoxically, play a moderating role toward the people they have corrupted. Let us leave the arts to sweeten the ferocity of civilized people and thereby "offer food for these tigers, so that they will not devour our children."[63] In the *Final Response*, another text that continues the polemic in this *Discourse*, he admits that in Africa and America there are many vicious tribes, but that a number of examples of virtue are also to be found, whereas among the civilized nations there are none. The civilized nations are also unfavorably compared to savages in the *Essay on the Origin of Languages*. With progress in the arts, law, and commerce, a stage in the history of mankind commences in which nations are formed, followed 'like the waves of the sea . . . by men gathered in a few places . . . in order to devour one another and make a terrible desert of the rest of the world, a worthy monument to social union and the utility of the arts."[64]

Against the background of this critique of modern civilization, the philosophers descry a figure that begins to eclipse all others: the state. The formation of the modern state is the event that dominates the political history of seventeenth- and eighteenth-century Europe. The emergence of a new, bureaucratic agent of sovereignty arouses profound anxieties. The attitudes of the philosophers toward this process were various, while some of them, in particular French and German Enlightenment thinkers, hailed some of its aspects. However, we must avoid reading the history of ideas from the perspective of a present for which the mere fact of the state's existence is solid, impenetrable to historical skepticism. There is no question here of estimating whether and to what extent some of the policies of the modern state were legitimized by the philosophers, but rather of capturing their reaction to the seismic shift that gradually led to a new, unusual, and irresistible presence in human existence. From the perspective of anyone who examines the philosophy of history in the Age of Enlightenment, the emergence of the state traumatically rewrites the data of fundamental problems tied to political power.

This process is one in which the classical notions of the state are profoundly affected and altered. In classical political science, the state is an association whose purpose is the good life. There is, of course, a pathological sovereignty, just as there are authors, such as Machiavelli, who cast the significance of this supposition into doubt. However, what is certain is that the classical state presupposes an essence of good and justice. As Augustine argues in *The City of God*, not even thieves are lacking in respect for a kind of justice among themselves. This is why the suggestion that there might be a kind of state whose subjects and sovereigns are all criminals against nature and whose purpose is contrary to the good is profoundly problematic within the horizons of classical philosophy.

Such a kind of state nonetheless begins to be discovered by travelers. Marco Polo writes of a place in Asia where there are public butchers of human flesh. However, this state is that of connatural beings, of cynocephalous monsters. Garcilasso de la Vega argues that such a state existed in the Andes before the civilizing works of the Incas. The most striking aspect of his work *History of the Inca Kings* concerns the presentation of cannibalism as a social institution and not merely an individual aberration. De la Vega's anthropophages are not primarily degenerates, monsters, or mere participants in orgiastic rituals. For him, cannibalism is integrated into the social order. Of course, this is an order at the dark limits of disorder and barbarity. The cannibals of the Andes live in poverty, under the rule of petty tyrants and spend their life in a continual exercise of murder and theft. The women and men go naked or dressed only in animal skins. They are atheists or idolaters and practice sodomy. However, this is not the state of nature found in isolated individuals or small groups, but a political state, proper to a republic of horror, in which there are "butcher's shops for human flesh, where sausages are prepared, in order for nothing to be wasted."[65] The cruelty of the cannibals of the Andes is even more shocking than that of wild beasts or natural man because it is socially organized. Moreover, it does not appear to be a response to an extreme situation, for example, hunger or the exigency of a devil-worshipping religion. It sooner appears to be an institutionalization of consuming hunger in defiance of reason. Against the precepts of the classical political philosophers, the anthropophagous state of the Andes is one founded on the most unlikely and anarchic passions.

The republic described by Marco Polo and De Garcilasso are extreme types, situated at the margins of civil order, because they are associations of barbarians. However, in the Age of Enlightenment, the philosophers explore the possibility that anthropophagy might coexist with an otherwise civilized order. In the travel accounts and the philosophic commentaries of the geographers, there are mentions of authentic states that accept cannibalism. In the book of Struys's journeys we read of an anthropophagous people in Asia, which sends ambassadors to a neighboring kingdom, to offer military assistance. The hosts, knowing how little these creatures abide by their undertakings, refuse the offer.[66] On this occasion, we also learn something of the inhabitants of the cannibal land. Their trade can be read on their faces, it seems, for their countenance is described as "terrifying, their attitude haughty, their bearing terrible." In the *Encyclopédie*, the article on "Ansico" mentions an African kingdom where the inhabitants are anthropophagi and where "there are public butcher's shops selling human flesh, in which limbs can be seen hanging up" (*ils ont des boucheries publiques, où l'on voit pendre des membres des hommes*). "They butcher two hundred people a day to serve them at the table of the *great Macoco*, which is the name of their monarch" (*on tue deux cents hommes par jour pour être servis à la table du* grand Macoco; *c'est le nom de leur monarque*). However, the author of the article argues that such accounts are hard to believe. "For we must suspect all travelers and historians of slightly inflating matters" (*il faut soupçonner en général tout voyageur et tout historien ordinaire d'enfler un peu les choses*), at least if we do not want to end up believing the most absurd fables. More credulous in man's capacities, Sade describes in *Aline and Valcour: A Philosophical Novel* an African kingdom, Butua, where anthropophagy is commonplace. Sarmiento, a Portuguese lodged at the court of King Ben Miacoro, makes an apology for cannibalism, and then says grace before a table of human flesh. Our reserve is merely the fruit of habit, he tells the traveler, a mere absurdity. There is no moral good; we merely have appetites formed by nature, to which our actions are indifferent. Good and evil should be considered only depending on the customs of the country in which we find ourselves. In Butua, there is no difference between eating a man or an ox, and this is in accordance with the intentions of nature, which operates by destroying its works.[67] From Sarmiento's eulogy, we deduce that it is this African kingdom, more than European states, which has been founded on the law of nature. Hierarchy and not equality is the basis of the state, continues the Portuguese philosopher, and the mightiest is always right.

The vision of a republic where the civil law accommodates cannibalism signals that the modern state, in distinction to the body politic of classical moral philosophy, is not in principle incompatible with crimes against nature. Thereby a movement is initiated whereby modern sovereignty results from primitive forms of excessive power and which is described not so much as a science of natural law as much as one that is positive, of the body politic.

Meditating on the possibility that cannibals have invaded his island, Robinson Crusoe ponders the military superiority he enjoys thanks to the firearms that would allow him to kill groups of savages. However, a moral difficulty causes him to avoid provoking the savages: if he killed a dozen today, another dozen tomorrow, and so on *ad infinitum*, then he "should be no less a Murderer than they were in being Man-eaters, and perhaps much more so."[68] What is interesting here, together with the imagination's momentary inversion of the moral relations between anthropophagy and civilization, is the fact that Crusoe's superiority seems assured. Inspired by the information of geography and the history of colonization, the philosophers of the eighteenth century described and explained the imbalance in the power relations between the savages and the civilized world as being the merit of superior organization. In the historical schema put forward by Adam Smith in his lectures on jurisprudence of 1763 and then recycled in the *Wealth of Nations* (1776), savage nations cannot wage large-scale war because they live in small tribes. This form of cohabitation is determined by their diet. Hunting, he argues, cannot support large numbers of people. This economic causality determines differences of military organization. A savage nation, continues Smith, cannot undertake a large military expedition, because the men would not be able to take sufficient provisions with them (they have no carts), and what they gather from hunting is not enough to support large numbers. A scalping party rarely numbers more than a dozen men. "A nation of hunters can never be formidable to the civilized nations in their neighbourhood," Smith believes. A nation of shepherds can be, however. By the growth that conquest of new territories makes possible in the pastoral state, huge armies can be raised, as history has shown in the case of the Tartars.[69]

For Smith, the savages suffer from economic incompetence and defective military structures, as well as a deficit of population. Abbé Raynal discovers that the population growth possible under good government is not available to the savages. The dynamic of population differs depending on the type of nation we have in view. For civilized nations, population growth is to be desired. For savage nations, population growth is baneful, because they barely ensure their own subsistence and excessive population will devastate the places they inhabit.[70]

Weak and few in number, savage societies will be swept from the historical stage by a new type of organization. The philosophers describe this historical process as one in which there appears, over and above the classic outrages to natural law, a new, qualitatively different threat. In the *Politics*, Aristotle had observed that the evil man is the most abominable of beasts, because his intelligence offers him greater means to do ill. Hobbes points to civil war as an occasion for depravity which exceeds that aroused by the passions in the state of nature. In the eighteenth century, the analysis gradually shifts from the territory of the passions to that of institutions. In his satire of 1756, Edmund Burke does not mention anthropophagy, but he is probably the first to put forward the idea that political government is, by its very nature, criminal: "The slaughter of mankind, on what you will call a small calculation, amounts to upwards of seventy times the number of souls this day on the globe. . . . Political society is justly chargeable with much the greatest part of this destruction of the species."[71] In *Principles of Natural Law*, Burlamaqui compares crimes against the law of nature with those against the law of nations and argues that the sovereign who disobeys the latter is at least as guilty as the individual who disobeys natural law, because his evil actions have more baneful consequences. In *The Social System* (1773), D'Holbach also contributes to this line of argument, applying the concept of the state of nature to relations between states. This is not in itself a novelty. As early as *De cive* (1642), Hobbes had argued that sovereigns find themselves in a state of nature in relation to one another, because they are not under the rule of any common power. However, D'Holbach transfers the elements specific to the primitive state on that of the modern state. He argues that civilized nations still conserve vestiges of the savage state. Their leaders, like true savages, live in the state of nature, in perpetual war and unjust quarrels, although there is nothing more contrary to reason. They sacrifice their subjects lightly, which proves that the majority of them are "Caribs or true cannibals." However, the latter rule only over "disorganized and undisciplined hordes," while the former have armies of slaves at their command, which have learned the art of methodically devastating and slaughtering entire nations.

Sovereignty and war were always closely associated in the tradition of political thought. Against the protests of Plato in the *Laws*, which argues that peace and not war must be the scope of a constitution, against all the writers of the seventeenth and eighteenth centuries, war was viewed from Bodin and Machiavelli until the late eighteenth century as the capital preoccupation of political man. But the modern state brings with it a new competence in matters of war, which absolutely surpasses anything the classical authors could have imagined. While for the latter the key to military supremacy is to be found in the personal qualities of the subjects or sovereign, modern authors realize that the essence of the modern state is to manifest itself as an accumulation of power that has its own ruthless and efficient logic, based on the exploitation of resources unknown or inaccessible to the classical republics. With Francis Bacon, there emerges a systematic theory of the role of modern science in augmenting the military power of a state.

Paradoxically, it is precisely the augmentation of a state's civilization that is now discovered to be a source of danger. In *Sketches of the History of Man*, Lord Kames argues that progress in the art of war, in particular in artillery, renders fortifications useless. The only defense still available to the sovereigns of weaker states is to unite in a confederation whenever one of them is attacked by a stronger force. Rousseau deals with the problem of modern warfare in the *Discourse on Political Economy*, published in the *Encyclopédie*. The invention of artillery and fortifications forced European sovereigns to procure professional troops. The consequence is an augmentation of poverty. Rousseau suggests that even here we are dealing with a historical process whose logic is inevitable and whose consequences are grim. He sees regular armies as dangerous institutions whose rapid expansion threatens the imminent depopulation of Europe and the ultimate ruin of the continent's nations. This is a world in which pacifism is ultimately impossible. The pacifist Quakers would long ago have been devoured, writes Voltaire in the *Essay on Morals*, had they not been protected by their bellicose neighbors.

In his short work *Perpetual Peace: A Philosophical Sketch* (1795), Kant points toward the nature of the modern state as being productive of wars. The aggressive stance of states that maintain standing armies leads to instability, and the loans contracted by the authorities lead to the formation of a fund that can finance military adventures on an unimaginable scale. The state is the enemy of peace exactly as the enemy of peace is man in the universal war of the state of nature. Men associated in national states and isolated men in the state of nature may be judged according to exactly the same criteria, "for they are a standing offence to one another by the very fact that they are neighbours." From the same comparison, Kant does not derive the moral superiority of the state over the solitude of natural man. He argues that we are used to viewing with contempt the "the way in which savages cling to their lawless freedom." Instead of abandoning this state of war, each nation seeks greatness in the liberation from any "legal constraints," and the "glory of its ruler consists in his power to order thousands of people to immolate themselves for a cause which does not truly concern them." Here, Kant believes, there can be seen "the main difference between the savage nations of Europe and those of America is that while some American tribes have been entirely eaten up by their enemies, the Europeans know how to make better use of those they have defeated than merely by making a meal of them. They would rather use them to increase the number of their own subjects, thereby augmenting their stock of instruments for conducting even more extensive wars."[72]

In the Kantian analysis, the power of the modern Christian sovereign grows according to an ascendant and implacable logic, which leads to a devastating denouement of universal signification. This is the moment at which the cannibal disappears as a subject of the science of moral order, because he has been eclipsed by the State, the new agent of absolute cruelty.

NOTES

Introduction

1. Denis Diderot, *Opuscules philosophiques et littéraires, la plupart posthumes ou inédites* (Paris, 1796), pp. 193–94. "B: Que deviennent-ils en se multipliant sur en espace qui n'a pas plus d'une lieue de diamètre?" For the context of speculations on the dynamics of population, see Anita Fage, *Les doctrines de population des Encyclopédistes*, in *Population* (French Edition), 6e Année, no. 4 (Oct.–Dec. 1951).

2. "A: Ils s'exterminent et se mangent; et de là peut-être une première époque très-ancienne et très-naturelle de l'anthropophagie, insulaire d'origine."

3. "Tant d'usages d'une cruauté nécessaire et bizarre, dont la cause s'est perdue dans la nuit des temps, et met les philosophes à la torture."

Chapter 1 A Hobbesian Life Raft

1. In the closing paragraph of chapter 42, *Of Power Ecclesiasticall*. For Hobbes's idea of science, see David Boonin-Vail, *Thomas Hobbes and the Science of Moral Virtue* (Cambridge University Press, 1992); prudence and language are discussed in Donald W. Hanson, "Science, Prudence, and Folly in Hobbes's Political Theory," *Political Theory*, vol. 21, no. 4 (Nov. 1993); see also Pierre J. Payer, "Prudence and the Principles of Natural Law: A Medieval Development," *Speculum*, vol. 54, no. 1 (Jan. 1979). On political science vs. political order, see Robert R. Albritton, "Hobbes on Political Science and Political Order," *Canadian Journal of Political Science/Revue canadienne de science politique*, vol. 9, no. 3 (Sep. 1976).

2. See Quentin Skinner, *Reason and Rhetoric in the Philosophy of Hobbes* (Cambridge University Press, 1996); and David Johnson, *The Rhetoric of Leviathan: Thomas Hobbes and the Politics of Political Transformation* (Princeton University Press, 1986).

3. See, inter alia, Edmund Leites, ed., *Conscience and Casuistry in Early Modern Europe* (Cambridge University Press, 1988); and Edward Vallance, "The Kingdom's Case: The Use of Casuistry as a Political Language 1640–1692," *Albion: A Quarterly Journal Concerned with British Studies*, vol. 34, no. 4 (winter 2002). A general history of casuistry is Albert Jonsen and Stephen Toulmin, *The Abuse of Casuistry: A History of Moral Reasoning* (University of California Press, 1990).

4. On the beginnings of the great modern "censorship" of the imagination, see Ioan Petru Culianu, *Eros and Magic in the Renaissance* (University of Chicago Press, 1987). The use of images was a central part of the "art of memory" studied by Frances Yates, in *The Art of Memory* (London, 1966); see also Jonathan D. Spence, *The Memory Palace of Matteo Ricci* (London, 1985); Paolo Rossi, *Clavis universalis* (Paris, 1993); and Mary Carruthers, *The Craft of Thought: Meditation, Rhetoric, and the Making of Images, 400–1200* (Cambridge University Press, 2000).

5. Cf. Ann Blair, *The Theater of Nature: Jean Bodin and Renaissance Science* (Princeton University Press, 1997), p. 153.

6. On curiosities, see Neil Kenny, *The Uses of Curiosity in Early Modern France and Germany* (Oxford University Press, 2004); and P. Fontes da Costa, "The Culture of Curiosity at the Royal Society in the First Half of the Eighteenth Century," *Notes and Records of the Royal Society of London*, vol. 56, no. 2 (May 2002).

7. *The Petty Papers*, edited from the Bowood Papers by the Marquis of Landsdowne (London, 1997), p. 172.

8. Jean-Pierre Camus, *L'Amphithéâtre sanglant* (Paris, 2001), pp. 179–80.

9. David Hume, *Philosophical Works*, vol. 4 (Edinburgh, 1827), p. 445.

10. *A Plurality of Worlds*, trans. Glanvill (London, 1702), p. 8.

11. On machinery in the baroque theater see José Antonio Maravall, *Culture of the Baroque: Analysis of a Historical Structure* (Manchester, 1986), pp. 231–40; for observations on the relation between one's gain being another's loss see ibid. pp. 166–67.

12. *Oeuvres complètes* (Paris, 1824), vol. 2, p. 253. "La scène est un tableau des passions dont le germe est en notre coeur."

13. *Metaphysics*, 982b, "dia gar to thaumazein hoi anthrôpoi kai nun kai to prôton êrxanto philosophein."

14. *Le spectacle de la nature ou entretiens sur les particularités de l'histoire naturelle* (Paris, 1752), vol. 1, p. 3. On curiosity and its new epistemological status, see Hans Blumenberg, *The Legitimacy of the Modern Age* (MIT Press, 1985).

15. *Le spectacle de la nature*, vol. 3, p. 477.

16. On the organization of punishment, see Richard J. Evans, *Rituals of Retribution: Capital Punishment in Germany, 1600–1987* (Oxford University Press, 1996).

17. A sermon preached by Robert Bolton in 1621. Quoted in *Cambridge History of Political Thought: 1450–1700*, ed. J. H. Burns (Cambridge University Press, 1991), pp. 350–51.

18. Hugo Grotius, *Of the Rights of War and Peace* (London, 1715), vol. 1, p. 182. The same passage from Grotius is also repeated by Pufendorf, in *The Law of Nature and Nations* (*Le Droit de la Nature et des Gens, Système Général des Principes les plus importans de la Morale, de la Jurisprudence, et de la Politique*, trans. Jean Barbeyrac, 5th ed. [Amsterdam, 1734]).

19. *An Essay on the Principle of Population; or, A View of its Past and Present Effects*, 6th ed. (London, 1826), vol. 1, pp. 68–69.

20. The incident is related by Cornelius de Pauw, in *Récherches philosophiques sur les grecques* (Berlin, 1788), vol. 2, pp. 414–20. He is probably referring to a case in 1782, when a band of two hundred Gypsies were accused of having cooked and eaten a few dozen Hungarian peasants. After torture, during which some confessed to the crime, forty-one were hanged. An inquiry ordered by the emperor later revealed that the supposed victims of the Gypsies' appetite were still alive.

21. Herodotus, *Istorii*, ed. and trans. Adelina Piatkowski and Felicia Ştef, 4 vols., bilingual ed. (Bucharest: Teora, 1998–99), I, p. 216.

22. Ibid., IV, pp. 64–65.

23. *La Chanson d'Antiochie*, quoted in Danielle Régnier-Bohler, *Croisades et Pélerinages. Récits, croniques et voyages en Terre Sainte* (Paris, 1997), pp. 150–51. See also Jeffrey Jerome Cohen, "On Saracen Enjoyment: Some Fantasies of Race in Late Medieval France and England," *Journal of Medieval & Early Modern Studies*, vol. 31, no. 1 (winter 2001).

24. *The Travels of Marco Polo the Venetian*, trans. Marsden, ed. Thomas Wright (London, 1854), pp. 366–67. "Those who inhabit the mountains live in a beastly manner; they eat human flesh, and indiscriminately all other sorts of flesh, clean and unclean."

25. Jean de Léry, *Histoire d'un voyage faict en la terre du Brésil, autrement dite Amérique* (Geneva, 1580), pp. 212–13.

26. *Histoire générale d'Espagne, du. P. Jean de Mariana* (Paris, 1725), vol. 5, p. 137.

27. *Conseils pour former une Bibliothèque peu nombreuse, mais choisie* (Berlin, 1746), p. 24.

28. "[L]e plus heureux traité de l'éducation naturelle." J. J. Rousseau, *Oeuvres complètes. Émile* (Paris, 1834), vol. 1, p. 258. "Quel est donc ce merveilleux livre? Est-ce Aristotle? est-ce Pline? est-ce Buffon? Non; c'est Robinson Crusoé."

29. Denis Diderot, *Oeuvres Complètes* (Paris, 1876), vol. 14, pp. 28–29. "Ils sont en général tristes, rêveurs et paresseux, mais d'une bonne constitution, vivant communément un siècle. Ils vont nus; leur teint est olivâtre. Ils n'emmaillottent point leurs enfants, qui, dès l'âge de quatre mois, marchent à quatre pattes, et en prennent l'habitude, au point de courir de cette façon, quands ils sont plus âgés, aussi vite qu'un Européen avec ses deux jambs. Ils ont plusiers femmes qui ne sont point jalouses les unes des autres. . . . Elles accouchent sans peine. . . . Ils mangent leurs prisonniers rôtis, et en envoient des morceux à leurs amis. . . . Quand un d'entre eux meurt, on tue son nègre qu'il aille le servir dans l'autre monde." See also Paul Honigsheim, "The American Indian in the Philosophy of the English and French Enlightenment," *Osiris*, vol. 10 (1952).

30. *Retorica* [*Rhetoric*], ed. Maria-Cristina Andrieş and Ştefan-Sebastian Maftei, bilingual ed. (Bucharest: Editura IRI, 2004), 1360a30: "enteuthen gar labein estin tous tôn ethnôn nomous."

31. Francis Bacon, *The New Organon*, trans. Michael Silverhome (Cambridge University Press, 2000), p. 69.

32. *The Tatler*, no. 254, Thursday, November 23, 1710. *The Tatler; corrected from the Originals*, ed. A. Chalmers (London, 1817), vol. 5, p. 199. On Locke's interest in travel literature, see Nicholas Dew, "Reading Travels in the Culture

of Curiosity: Thévenot's Collection of Voyages," *Journal of Early Modern History*, vol. 10, no. 1–2 (2006).

33. *De ira*, II, 15–16, in *Opera Philosophica*, ed. Emil Ferdinand Vogel (Leipzig: Nauck, 1830).

34. *Recherches philosophiques sur les Américains, ou Mémoirs intéressantes pour servir à l'Histoire de l'Espèce humaine* (London, 1771), vol. 1, pp. 116–17. "Les Tunguses suspendent leurs morts aux arbres; les Illinois de l'Amérique les suspendent de même, parce qu'ils sont trop paresseux pour les brûler, & que la terre, souvent gelée à vingt, à trente pieds de profondeur, ne se laisse point ouvrir . . . La Religion chrétienne, quoiqu'originaire d'un pays où l'on embaumoit grossiérement les cadavres, n'a contribué en rien à la révolution générale de cette partie de nos moeurs."

35. Ulpian, *Institutiones* (Oxford, 1880), lib. 1, tit. ii. "Ius naturale est, quod natura omnia animalia docuit, nam ius istud non humani generis proprium est, sed omnium animalium quae in caelo, quae in terra, quae in mari nascuntur, hinc descendit maris atque feminae coniugatio quam nos matrimonium appellamus; hinc liberorum procreatio et educatio. Videmus etenim cetera quoque animalia istius iuris peritia censeri."

36. *De republica*, 3,22, in *Librorum de republica quantum superest in palimpsesto. Bibliothecae Vaticanae praecipue repertum ordinavit et prolegomenis scholiis que illustratum*, ed. A. M. Rome: Consilium Prop. Fidei., 1846. "Recta ratio, naturae congruens condiffusa in omnes. . . . Nec erit alia lex Romae, alia Athenis; alia nunc, alia posthac sed et omnes gentes, et omni tempore una lex et sempiterna et immutabilis continebit."

37. *Essais de Montaigne*, ed. Charles Louandre (Paris, 1854), vol. 2, p. 507. "C'est seule enseigne vraysemblable par laquelle ils puissant argumenter aulcunes loix naturelles, que l'université de l'approbation: car ce que nature nous auriot veritablement ordonné, nous l'ensuyvrions sans doubte d'un commun consentement."

38. Ibid., pp. 508–9. "Il n'est rien si horrible à imaginer que de manger son père."

39. Ibid., p. 513. "La plus saine philosophie souffre de licences esloingnees de l'usage commun, et excessifves."

40. Ibid., p. 508. "Il est croyable qu'il y a des loix naturelles, commes il se veoid ez aultres creatures; mais en nous elles sont perdues."

41. *The Law of Nature and Nations; The Second Edition, carefully Corrected, and Compared with Mr. Barbeyrac's French Translation* (Oxford, 1710), pp. 101–2. On the Thomistic background of some of these arguments, see E. A. Goerner, "On Thomistic Natural Law: The Bad Man's View of Thomistic Natural Right," *Political Theory*, vol. 7, no.1 (Feb. 1979).

42. Locke, *Political Essays*, ed. Raymond Geuss, Quentin Skinner, Mark Goldie (Cambridge University Press, 1997), p. 113. See also Herman Lebovics, "The Uses of America in Locke's Second Treatise of Government," *Journal of the History of Ideas*, vol. 47, no. 4 (Oct.–Dec. 1986). On the epistemological status of the theory of the state of nature in Locke, see the discussion in Richard Ashcraft, "Locke's State of Nature: Historical Fact or Moral Fiction?" *American Political Science Review*, vol. 62, no. 3 (Sep. 1968).

43. Locke, *Political Essays*, p. 115.

44. Ibid., p. 98.

45. *Sketches of the History of Man* (Edinburgh, 1774), vol. 2, pp. 250–51.

46. J. J. Burlamaqui, *Principes du droit naturel et politique* (Geneva and Copenhagen, 1764), vol. 1, pp. 221–23. "Mais ces mêmes Sauvages . . . ont entr-eux un Droit & des Régles; le bonne-foi est estimé là comme ailleurs, & un Coeur reconnoissant ne reçoit pas moins d'éloges parmi eux qu parmi nous."

47. Locke, *Political Essays*, p. 128.

48. Lactantius, *The Divine Institutes*, V, 16, in *Opera*, ed. O. Fridolinus Fritzsche. Leipzig: Tauschniz, 1842, Vol. 10, p. 259.

49. See Philodemus, *On the Stoics*.

50. 1110a 25–27.

51. "hoc ipso luet maximas poenas, etiam si cetera supplicia quae putantur – Etenim si nemo est, quin emori malit, quam converti in aliquam figuram bestiae, quamvis hominis mentem sit habiturus; quanto est miserius in hominis figura animo esse efferato?"

52 Johann Gottlieb Heineccius, *A Methodical System of Universal Law, or the Laws of Nature Deduced from Certain Principles and Applied to Proper Cases* (London, 1763), vol. 1, p. 116.

53. *Of the Law of Nature and Nations; The Second Edition, carefully Corrected, and Compared with Mr. Barbeyrac's French Translation* (Oxford, 1710), p. 162.

54. See the text in *Les déclarations des droits de l'homme (Du débat 1789–1793 au Préambule de 1946)*, ed. Lucien Jaume (Paris, 1989), pp. 169–70.

55. For the factual aspects of the case, we have followed A. W. Brian Simpson, *Cannibalism and the Common Law: The Story of the Last Voyage of the "Mignonette" and the Strange Legal Proceedings to Which It Gave Rise* (Chicago, 1984). A general history of the case of shipwrecked sailors is Neil Hanson, *The Custom of the Sea* (New York, 1989).

56. See Mónica Brito Vieira, "Mare Liberum vs. Mare Clausum: Grotius, Freitas, and Selden's Debate on Dominion over the Seas," *Journal of the History of Ideas*, vol. 64, no. 3 (Jul. 2003).

57. This is a doctrine that already occurs in Roman law; see Justinian's *Digest*, 1.8.2, in *Imperatoris Iustiniani Institutionum libri quattuor*, ed. John Baron Moyle (Oxford: Clarendon, 1883), vol. 1, p. 92.

58. Modern positive law has not, as a rule, codified anthropophagy as an offence, since deliberate cannibalism, unmotivated by extreme necessity, has usually been treated as an aggravating circumstance in cases of murder. However, there are exceptions, where anthropophagy is directly mentioned by legislatures, such as Australian legislation, which was extended over the primitive peoples of Papua New Guinea in 1902, in which case we are obviously dealing with an attempt to reform primitives rather than with a typical penal code. See Thomas M. Ernst, "Onabaslu Cannibalism and the Moral Agents of Misfortune," in Goldman (ed.), *The Anthropology of Cannibalism* (Westport, 1999). In Europe, cannibalism does not seem to have been treated as a separate category by legislators. An exception from this rule would be the decision of the Soviet

authorities, during the Leningrad siege, to impose the death penalty for cannibalism (see Richard Overy, *Russia's War* [London, 1998], p. 107).

59. *The Life and Strange Surprizing Adventures of Robinson Crusoe of York, Mariner*, 3d ed. (London, 1719), p. 132.

60. *De Officiis*, trans. Walter Miller (Harvard University Press, 1913), III, p. 107.

61. See, inter alia, Lorraine Daston, *Classical Probability in the Enlightenment* (Princeton University Press, 1995).

62. *Les Voyages de Jean Struys en Moscovie, en Tartarie, en Perse, aux Indes & au plusiers autres Païs étrangers* (Lyon, 1682), pp. 323–24. "Il est vrai que la Loi ordonne d'aimer son prochain, & qu'elle défend l'homicide: mais est-il rien qui nous soit plus proche que nous-memes?"

63. Ibid. "Faux raisonemment, faux principes, répondit un de ceux à qui il parloit, la défense de tuer personne est si expresse dans la Loi, que nulle raison ne nous en dispense. Ces paroles—Tu ne tuerais point!—sont formelles et ne souffrent nulle exception . . . sachez que si vous continuez dans un si pernicieux dessein vous devenez l'ennemi de Dieu."

64. *Histoire de la Nouvelle-France* (Paris, 1617), p. 59. "Ce qui fut executé . . . la chair . . . fut departie également entr'eux tous, chose si horrible à reciter que la plume m'en tombe des mains." Lescarbot's work predates that of Nicolaus Tulpius, *Observationes medicorum* (Amsterdam, 1641), which A. W. Simpson, in *Cannibalism and the Common Law* (University of Chicago Press, 1984), p. 122, claims to be the first mention of cannibalism in a lifeboat of shipwreck survivors.

65. S. Pufendorf, *Les devoirs de l'homme et citoyen, tels qu'ils lui sont prescrits par la loi nauturelle*, trans. J. Barbeyrac (Paris, 1822), vol. 1, p. 229. "Ainsi celui à qui appartient la chaloupe, n'en doit point être chassé, et n'est pas point obligé de tirer au sort."

66. Ibid., pp. 231–32. "En ce cas-là, le droit du premier occupant exclut toute prétention des autres, à qui la planche n'appartenait pas plus qu'à celui qui s'en est saisi."

67. Ibid., p. 233. "Il faut supposer que ce soit un grand chemin; car si l'enfant ou le boiteux était sur son fonds, il aurait par-là un droit particulier qui empêcherait que celui qui est poursuivi ne pût préférer sa propre conservation au soin de celle d'autrui." On Barbeyrac's theory of conscience, see Tim Hochstrasser, "Conscience and Reason: The Natural Law Theory of Jean Barbeyrac," *Historical Journal*, vol. 36, no. 2 (Jun. 1993).

68 See Istvan Hont and Michael Ignatieff, eds., *Wealth and Virtue: The Shaping of Political Economy in the Scottish Enlightenment* (Cambridge University Press, 1983).

69. There is a massive literature on Locke's conception of property; see inter alia Karl Olivecrona, "Appropriation in the State of Nature: Locke on the Origin of Property," *Journal of the History of Ideas*, vol. 35, no. 2 (Apr.–Jun. 1974).

70. Jean Henry Samuel Formey, *Principes du droit de la nature et des gens. Extrait du grand ouvrage latin de M. de Wolff* (Amsterdam, 1758), p. 334.

71. *Questions de droit naturel: Sur le Traité du droit de la Nature de M. le Baron de Wolff* (Bern, 1762). On Vattel, see Francis Stephen Ruddy, *International Law in the Enlightenment: The Background of Emmerich de Vattel in Le Droit des Gens* (New York, 1975).

72. *Questions de droit naturel*, p. 208.

73. See Barbara Godwin, *Justice by Lottery* (University of Chicago Press, 1992).

74. Jean Janszoon Struys, *Journeys of Jean Struys* (Lyon, 1682), pp. 327–28. "leur proposa de tirer au sort, que nul de la Troupe n'en fait exemt & il leur dit que celui sur qui le Ciel le feroit tomber, seroit jugé digne de sa mort."

75. *Histoire et Description Générale de la Nouvelle France* (Paris, 1744), vol. 1, pp. 34–35. "Dans ce désespoir quelqu'un s'avisa de dire qu'un seul pouvoit sauver la vie à tous les autres aux dépens de la sienne, & une si étrange proposition, non-seulement ne fut pas rejettée avec horreur, mais fut extrêmement applaudie. On étoit presque convenu de tirer au sort pour sçavoir quelle seroit la victime, qu'on immoleroit au salut des autres, lorsqu'un Soldat . . . déclara qu'il vouloit bien avancer sa mort, qu'il croyoit inévitable, pour reculer de quelques jours celle de ses Compagnons. Il fut pris au mot, & on l'égorgea sur le champ, sans qu'il fit la moindre résistance. Il ne fut pas perdu une goute de son sang, tous en bûrent avec avidité, le corps fut mis en piéces, & chacun en eut sa part."

76. Herodotus, III, 25. "epei de es tên psammon apikonto, deinon ergon autôn tines erĝasanto: ek dekados gar hena spheôn autôn apoklêrôsantes katephagon."

77. Pufendorf, *Le Droit de la Nature et des Gens*, vol. 1, p. 324 ff. Pufendorf goes on to invoke other possibilities: a raft that is too small, sailors who throw one another overboard, shared goods, etc.

78. Johann Gottlieb Heineccius, *A Methodical System of Universal Law*, vol. 1, p. 117.

79. See Wolff, *Principes du droit de la nature et des gens* (Amsterdam, 1758), vol. 2, pp. 333–40.

80. Vattel, *Questions de droit naturel*, p. 210. On permissive natural law, see Brian Tierney, "Permissive Natural Law and Property: Gratian to Kant," *Journal of the History of Ideas*, vol. 62, no. 3 (Jul. 2001).

81. Vattel, *Questions de droit naturel*, p. 212.

82. Ibid., pp. 215–16.

83. Ibid., p. 322.

84. Ibid., pp. 353–54, 340.

85. Ibid., pp. 329–32.

86. Ibid., pp. 331–32. On Pascal and casuistic arguments, see David F. Bell, "Pascal: Casuistry, Probability, Uncertainty," *Journal of Medieval and Early Modern Studies*, vol. 28, no. 1 (winter 1998).

CHAPTER 2 THE TORTURES AND FATE OF THE BODY

1. See Trevor J. Saunders, *Plato's Penal Code: Tradition, Controversy, and Reform in Greek Penology* (Oxford University Press, 1994).

2. See, inter alia, J. H. Burns, "*Jus Gladii and Jurisdictio*: Jacques Almain and John Locke," *Historical Journal*, vol. 26, no. 2 (Jun. 1983). On the Roman origins of *Jus gladii*, see Peter Garnsey, "The Criminal Jurisdiction of Governors," *Journal of Roman Studies*, vol. 58, parts 1 and 2 (1968).

3. *Two Treatises of Government* (London, 1824), II, 1, 3.

4. See the account of this episode in R. Po-Chia Hsia, *The Myth of Ritual Murder: Jews and Magic in Reformation Germany* (Yale University Press, 1998), pp. 73–82. A history of conceptions of due process and individual rights is Kenneth Pennington, *The Prince and the Law, 1200–1600: Sovereignty and Rights in the Western Legal Tradition* (University of California Press, 1993); see also Michael Frassetto, ed., *Christian Attitudes toward the Jews in the Middle Ages* (London, 2007).

5. *Les Voyages de Jean Struys en Muscovie, en Tartarie, en Perse & en plusieurs autres Pays étrangers* (Lyon, 1682), vol. 2, pp. 323–24.

6. Abby M. Schrader, "Containing the Spectacle of Punishment: The Russian Autocracy and the Abolition of the Knout, 1817–1845," *Slavic Review*, vol. 56, no. 4 (winter 1997).

7. A theoretical overview is Eli Sagan, *Citizens and Cannibals: The French Revolution, the Struggle for Modernity, and the Origins of Ideological Terror* (Lanham, MD, 2001). Nineteenth-century accounts of crowd violence are discussed in Alain Corbin, *The Village of Cannibals: Rage and Murder in France, 1870* (Harvard University Press, 1992).

8. "Of Cruelty," *Montaigne's Essays*, trans. Charles Cotton (London, 1743), vol. 2, pp. 110–11.

9. Lescarbot, *Histoire de la Nouvelle France* (Paris, 1617), p. 624. "Ce people brutal non content de ce qui s'étoit passé ouvrit encore le ventre du mort, & jetta ses entrailles dans le lac: lui arracha le Coeur qu'ilz couperent en morceux & le baillerent à manger à un sien frere aussi prisonnier & autres ses compagnons."

10. Cf. Richard A. Bauman, *Crime and Punishment in Ancient Rome* (London, 1996), p. 7. See also Daniel Baraz, "Seneca, Ethics, and the Body: The Treatment of Cruelty in Medieval Thought," *Journal of the History of Ideas*, vol. 59, no. 2 (Apr. 1998).

11. See, for instance, Nicholas Terpstra, "Piety and Punishment: The Lay *Conforteria* and Civic Justice in Sixteenth-Century Bologna," *Sixteenth Century Journal*, vol. 22, no. 4 (winter 1991).

12. Samuel Pufendorf, *Le Droit de la Nature et des Gens* (Amsterdam, 1734), vol. 2, pp. 454–55.

13. *Sketches of the History of Man* (Edinburgh, 1774), vol. 1, p. 250.

14. *Traité des délits et des peines*, (Philadelphia, 1765), p. 40. See also Marcello Maestro, "A Pioneer for the Abolition of Capital Punishment: Cesare Beccaria," *Journal of the History of Ideas*, vol. 34, no. 3 (Jul.–Sep., 1973).

15. Crucé, *The New Cyneas* (Philadelphia, 1909), p. 42.

16. *Œuvres de François Mothe le Vayer* (Dresden, 1756), vol. 2, part 1, p. 89. This topic, of abandoning prisoners in a state of nature as a form of punishment, also appears in literature, following the adventures of Robinson Crusoe or Jules Verne's *Mysterious Island*.

17. See, inter alia, Randall McGowen, "Civilizing Punishment: The End of the Public Execution in England," *Journal of British Studies*, vol. 33, no. 3 (Jul. 1994).

18. See, inter alia, Stephen Kern, *A Cultural History of Causality: Science, Murder Novels, and Systems of Thought* (Princeton University Press, 2004).

19. Michel Foucault, *Les anormaux. Cours au Collège de France 1974–1975* (Paris, 1999), p. 85.

20. Locke, *Two Treatises of Government* (London, 1824), II, 11. See also Cicero, *De republica*, 2, 47, in *Librorum de republica quantum superest in palimpsesto. Bibliothecae Vaticanae praecipue repertum ordinavit et prolegomenis scholiis que illustratum*, ed. A. M. Rome: Consilium Prop. Fidei., 1846: "No animal more terrible, more repugnant [than the tyrant], to gods and to man, can be imagined. Although human in appearance, by the evil of his character he is worse than the most destructive wild beasts. Who can name someone who obeys no law, who accepts no human bond with his fellow citizens or even the entire human race a 'man'?" (*neque tetrius, neque foedius, nec dis hominisque invisius animal ullum cogitari potest: qui quamquam figura est hominis, morum tamen immanitate vastissimas vincit belluas. Quis enim hunc hominem rite dixerit, qui sibi cum suis civibus, qui denique cum omni hominum genere nullam iuris communionem, nullam societatem velit?*) In *De ira*, Seneca compares a murderer to a venomous serpent.

21. *Three Early Modern Utopias*, ed. Susan Bruce (Oxford University Press, 1999), pp. 89–90.

22. *De civitate dei*, 1, 13. *City of God*, trans. Henry Scowcroft Bettenson (Harmondsworth, 2003), p. 21.

23. Ibid., p. 22.

24. Diogenes Laertius, 2, 11. *Lives of Eminent Philosophers*, trans. R. D. Hicks (Harvard University Press, 1925), vol. 1, p. 141.

25. *Tusculanarum disputationum, libri quinque*, ed. Raphaël Kühner (Jena, 1829), 1, 43. "Istis quaeso, inquit, ista horribilia minitare purpuratis tuis. Theodori quidem nihil interest, humine an sublime purescat." The same occurrence is also recounted by Seneca in *De tranquillitate animi*, 14, 3–4, in *Opera Philosophica*, ed. Emil Ferdinand Vogel (Leipzig: Nauck, 1830), pp. 175 ff.

26. See Arthur Darby Nock, "Cremation and Burial in the Roman Empire," *Harvard Theological Review*, vol. 25, no. 4 (Oct. 1932), pp. 321–59.

27. *Digesta*, 11.7.43, in *Imperatoris Iustiniani Institutionum libri quattuor*, ed. John Baron Moyle (Oxford: Clarendon, 1883), vol. 1, p. 92. "Nam propter publicam utilitatem, ne insepulta cadavera iacerent, strictam rationem insuper habemus, quae nonnumquam in ambiguis religionum quaestionibus omitti solent: nam summam esse rationem, quae pro religione facit."

28. Seneca, *De beneficiis*, 5, 20, in *Opera Philosophica*, ed. Emil Ferdinand Vogel (Leipzig: Nauck, 1830). "Patrem *alicuius* in solitudine *exanimem* inveni, corpus eius sepelivi. Nec ipsi profui (quid enim illius intererat, quo genere dilaberetur?) nec filio: quid enim per hoc commodi accessit illi? Dicam quid consecutus sit: officio solemni et necessario per me functus est. Praesiti patri eius, quod ipse praestare voluisset, nec non et debuisset. Hoc tamen ita beneficium est, si non misericordiae et humanitati dedi, ut quodlibet cadaver absconderem: sed si

corpus agnovi, si filio tunc hoc praestare me cogitavi. At si terram ignoto mortuo inieci nullum habeo huius officii debitorem, in publicum humanus."

29. Lactantius, *Divinae institutiones*, 6, 12, in *Opera*, ed. O. Fridolinus Fritzsche. Leipzig: Tauschniz, 1842, Vol. 11, p. 29.

30. *De cura pro mortuis*, 9.

31. *Of the Rights of War and Peace* (London, 1715), vol. 2, p. 422.

32. *Discours sur l'origine et fondemens de l'inégalité parmi les hommes* (Dresden, 1755), p. 50. "Un animal ne passe point sans inquiétude auprès d'un animal mort de son Espéce."

33. *Tusculanarum disputationum, libri quinque*, ed. Raphaël Kühner (Jena, 1829), 1, 45. "In Hyrcania plebs publicos alit canes; optimates, domesticos. nobile autem genus canum illud scimus esse: sed pro sua quisque facultate parat, a quibus lanietur; eamque optimam illi esse censent sepulturam. permulta alia colligit Chrysippus, ut est in omni historia curiosus: ita tetra sunt quaedam, ut ea fugiat et reformidet oratio."

34. *Istorii [Histories]*, ed. and trans. Adelina Piatkowski and Felicia Ştef, 4 vols, bilingual ed. (Bucharest, 1998–99), IV, 26. "Pais de patri touto poieei, kata per Hellênes ta genesia."

35. Cannibalism in funerary rites was documented in the basin of the Amazon until recently. See Beth A. Conklin, "'Thus Are Our Bodies, Thus Was Our Custom': Mortuary Cannibalism in an Amazonian Society," *American Ethnologist*, vol. 22, no. 1 (Feb. 1995), pp. 75–101.

36. *Political Writings* (Cambridge University Press, 1991), p. 210.

37. Samuel Pufendorf, *Le Droit de la Nature et des Gens* (Amsterdam, 1734), vol. 1, p. 215.

38. *La description geographique des provinces et villages les plus fameuses de l'Inde Orientale* (Paris, 1556), p. 102.

39. *Moeurs des sauvages amériquains, comparées aux moeurs des premiers temps* (Paris, 1724), vol. 2, p. 405. "Quelques Nations de l'Amerique Meridionale, qui ont encore cette coûtume de manger les corps de leurs parents, n'en usent ainsi que par piété; piété mal entenduë à la verité, mais piété colorée néanmoins par quelque ombre de raison; car ils croyent leur donner une sépulture bien plus honorable, que s'ils les abandonnoient en proye aux vers & à la pourriture."

40. *États et empires de la Lune*, in *Libertins du XVIIIe siècle*, ed. Jacques Prévot (Paris, 1998), pp. 977–79.

41. *Recherches philosophiques sur les américains, ou Mémoires intéressants pour servir à l'Histoire de l'Espece Humaine* (London, 1771), vol. 1, p. 179. "La façon de décomposer les éléments bruts & matériels d'un être qu'on a dépouillé de son organisation intime & de sa sensibilité, est sans doute une action indifférente par elle-même . . . il n'importe si les vers, les Cannibales ou les Iroquois rongent un cadavre."

42. *Recherches philosophiques sur le droit de propriété considéré dans la nature pour servir de premier chapitre à la Théorie des loix de M. Linguet, par un jeune philosophe* (Paris, 1780), pp. 76–77. "Je paroîtrai étrange; mais combien plus devons—nous le paroître aux yeux des sauvages, quand ils nous voient enterrer les cadavres sanglans de nos ennemis, au lieu de les manger! . . . Ces

sauvages croient avoir autant de droit sur les cadavres de leurs ennemis, que les corbeaux ou les vers. . . . Eh! Pourquoi ne s'en nourriroient-ils pas? Quelle est la raison pour laquelle nous mangeons les animaux? C'est qu'ils sont remplis de molécules organiques qui s'assimilent parfaitement aux parties de notre corps, servent à notre nutrition, à l'accroissement, à la propagation de l'espece. Or, un loup trouvera dans un loup, l'homme dans l'homme, ces molécules organiques qui seules peuvent entretenir l'économie animale."

43. "Je parus un peu scandalisé; elle s'excusa en disant qu'il valait mieux manger son enemi mort que de le laisser dévorer aux bêtes, & que les vainqueurs méritaient d'avoir la préférence."

44. ". . . à la cuisine des corbeaux & des vers. C'est là qu'est l'horreur, c'est là qu'est le crime; qu'importe, quand on est tué, d'être mangé par un Soldat, ou par un corbeau & un chien?"

45. "Les Nations qu'on nomme policées ont eu raison de ne pas mettre leurs ennemis vaincus à la broche; car s'il était permis de manger ses voisins, on mangerait bientôt ses compatriotes; ce qui serait un grand inconvénient pour les vertus socials."

46. *Essays and Treatises on Several Subjects* (London, 1788), vol. 2, p. 500.

47. *Histoire naturelle du genre humain, ou Recherches sur ses principaux fondemens physiques et moraux; précédées d'un Discours sur la nature des êtres organiques et sur l'ensemble de leur physiologie. On y a joint une Dissertation sur le sauvage de l'Aveyron* (Paris, an IX [1801]), vol. 1, p. 57.

48. *La mort dans la littérature et la pensée françaises au siècle des lumières* (Lyon, 1978), p. 32.

49. Jean Henry Samuel Formey, *Principes du droit de la nature et des gens. Extrait du grand ouvrage latin de M. De Wolff* (Amsterdam, 1758), pp. 32–33, and 355.

50. Ibid., p. 354.

51. Ibid., p. 357.

52. Herodotus, *Istorii*, ed. and trans. Adelina Piatkowski and Felicia Ştef, 4 vols., bilingual ed. (Bucharest: Teora, 1998–99), III, 99.

53. Lafitau, *Moeurs des sauvages ameriquains, comparées aux moeurs des premiers temps* (Paris, 1724), vol. 2, p. 433. "L'avidité insatiable des Conquerans du Pérou & du Mexique, leur fit ainsi prophaner toutes les anciennes sepultures des Indiens, dans l'esperance d'y trouver les richesses immenses. . . . Les Indiens en étoient au déséspoir; & malgré la douleur extrême dont ils étoient accablés en voyant ces prophanations, ils ne pouvoient s'empêcher, disent les Auteurs de ces temps-là, de prier humblement ces impies prophanateurs de discerner les richesses dont ils étoient si avides, d'avec les cendres de leurs Ancêtres, qui ne pouvoient leur être utiles à rien: qu'à la bonne heure ils emportassent l'or & les bijoux dont leurs sepulchres étoient pleins, mais qu'ils laissassent les corps morts dans la lieu de leur repos, afin de ne pas rendre leur réünion avec leur ame au temps de la Resurrection future." A modern discussion of the ethical implications of the ideas on the integrity of the deceased is in Dorothy Nelkin; Andrews Lori, "Do the Dead Have Interests? Policy Issues for Research After Life," *American Journal of Law and Medicine*, vol. 24, no. 2/3 (1998).

54. On *Detestande feritatis*, see E. A. Brown, "Death and the Human Body in the Later Middle Ages: The Legislation of Boniface VIII on the Division of the Corpse," *Viator*, no. 12 (1981), pp. 221–70; and Bagliani A. Paravicini, "Démembrement et intégrité du corps au XIIIe siècle," *Terrain*, vol. 18 (1999), pp. 26–32. For the Jewish origins of the custom of reburial of the bones, see Simcha Paul Raphael, *Jewish Views of the Afterlife* Lanham, Md, 1994). See also Jeffrey M. Turnbower, *Rescue for the Dead: The Posthumous Salvation of Non-Christians in Early Christianity* (Oxford University Press, 2001).

55. On dissection, see Ruth Richardson, *Death, Dissection and the Destitute* (London, 1987), pp. 52, 54, and 221.

56. See Martin Fido, *Bodysnatchers: A History of Resurrectionists, 1742–1832* (London, 1988), p. 9.

57. On the history of dissection, see Andreea Carlino, *Books of the Body: Anatomical Ritual and Renaissance Learning* (Chicago University Press, 1999).

58. Similar legends circulated until the end of the twentieth century in some parts of Africa. According to the myths, there were vampires employed by the whites to suck the blood of the blacks. Red fire engines and ambulances, a new and suspect appearance in these regions, were associated with these practices. It is possible that these stories originated during the campaigns to collect blood during the world wars, when some Africans assumed that the blood was drunk by Europeans. See Luise White, "Cars out of Place: Vampires, Technology, and Labour in East and Central Africa," in Frederick Cooper and Ann Laura Stoller (eds.), *Tensions of Empire: Colonial Cultures in a Bourgeois World* (Berkeley, 1997).

59. On the history of the anatomical model in moral philosophy, see chapter 9 of Louis van Delft's *Littérature et anthropologie: Nature humaine et charactère a l'âge classique* (Paris, 1993).

60. Wolff, in Formey, *Principes du droit de la nature et des gens*, summarized, p. 362. A modern analysis of the ethics of using body parts is Michael Y. Barilan, "Bodyworlds and the Ethics of Using Human Remains: A Preliminary Discussion," *Bioethics*, vol. 20, no. 5 (Sep. 2006).

61. *Encyclopédie, ou dictionnaire raisonné des sciences, des arts et des métiers* (Neufchastel, 1765), vol. 12: "a donné au cabinet du roi une paire de pantoufles faites avec de la peau humaine, préparée selon ce procédé, qui n'a point détruit les poils de cette peau."

62. Ibid., p. 220. ". . . d'une consistence ferme, assez lisse sur la face extérieure, quoique les sillons qui environnent les mamellons en forme de losanges irréguliers, y paroissent plus profondément gravés que dans le naturel; la surface intérieure est inegale, &, pour ainsi dire, laineuse, parce qu'il y reste presque nécessairement des feuillets de la membrane adipeuse."

63. See Karl H. Dannenfeldt, "Egyptian Mumia: The Sixteenth Century Experience and Debate," *Sixteenth Century Journal*, vol. 16 , no. 2 (summer 1985).

64. "On assure que toutes les momies qui se vendent dans les boutiques des marchands, soit qu'elles viennent de Venise ou de Lyon, soit qu'elles viennent même directement du Levant par Alexandrie, sont factices, & qu'elles sont l'ouvrage de certains juifs qui, sachant le cas que font les Européens des vraies

momies d'Egypte, les contrefont en desséchant des squeletes dans un four, après les avoir enduits d'une poudre de myrrhe, d'aloès caballin, de poix noire, & d'autres drogues de vil prix & mal-saines (Article Momie)."

65. "le vrai moyen de tirer des substances osseuses un nourriture innocente." De Pauw, *Recherches philosophiques sur les Américains, ou Histoires intéressants pour servir à Histoire de l'Espece Humaine* (Berlin, 1777), vol. 1, pp. 194–95.

CHAPTER 3 CREATURES OF EVIL

1. III, 2, 2.

2. *Oeuvres* (Paris, 1829), vol. 15, p. 13. "Cet état de brutes où le genre humain a été longtemp dut rendre l'espèce très rare dans tous les climats."

3. Aristotle, *The Politics and the Constitution*, ed. Stephen Everson (Cambridge University Press, 1996), 1253a25. "Ho de mê dunamenos koinônein ê mêden deomenos di'autarkeian outhen meros poleôs, hôste ê thêrion ê theos."

4. [Lord Monboddo], *Of the Origin and Progress of Language*, 2d ed. (Edinburgh, 1774), vol. 1, pp. 384–85.

5. *The History of America* (London, 1780), vol. 2, pp. 161–62.

6. Ibid. pp. 163–67. On the cultural context of Indian death scenes, see Erik R. Seeman, "Reading Indians' Deathbed Scenes: Ethnohistorical and Representational Approaches," *Journal of American History*, vol. 88, no. 1 (Jun. 2001). An anthropological approach is found in Richard J. Chacon and David H. Dye, eds., *The Taking and Displaying of Body Parts as Trophies by Amerindians* (New York, 2007).

7. *Histoire philosophique et politique des établissemens et du commerce des Européens dans les deux Indes*, new ed. (Paris, 1820), vol. 8, p. 53. "Les uns lui sillonnent la chair avec des tisons ardens; d'autres la tranchent en lambreux; d'autres lui arrachent les ongles; d'autres lui coupent les doigts, les rôtissent, et les dévorent à ses yeux."

8. *The History of Barbados* (London, 1666), pp. 327–28. "One among them came and burnt [the prisoner's] sides with a flaming brand; another cut good deep pieces out of him, and would have made them bigger, had it not been for the bones, in several parts of the body: Then they cast into his smarting wounds that sharp kind of Spice which the Caribbians call Pyman . . . the young men take the body, and having wash'd it cut it in pieces, and then boyl some part, and broil some upon wooden Frames, made for that purpose, like Gridirons: When this delectable Dish is ready, and season'd according to their palates, they divide it into so many parts as there are persons present, and joyfully devour it, thinking that the World cannot afford any other repast equally delicious: The Women lick the very sticks on which the fat of the Aronague dropp'd; which proceeds not so much from the deliciousness they find in that kind of sustenance, and that fat, as from the excessive pleasure they conceive in being reveng'd in that manner of their chiefest enemies. . . . they gather that fat to be afterwards distributed among the chiefest of them, who carefully keep it in little Gourds, to pour some few drops thereof into their Sauces at their solemn

Entertainments, so to perpetuate, as much as lies in their power, the motive of their Revenge."

9. *L'Art de perfectionner l'homme* (Paris, 1809), vol. 2, p. 436. "Ils [subissent] à leurs prisonniers de guerre tous les tourmens qu'ils peuvent inventer."

10. *Histoire et Description Générale de la Nouvelle France* (Paris, 1744), vol. 3, pp. 242–48.

11. Joseph-François Lafitau, *Moeurs des sauvages amériquains comparées aux moeurs des premiers temps* (Paris, 1724), vol, vol. 2, p. 277. "On commence par les extrémités des pied & des mains, en montant peu à peu vers le tronc: l'un lui arrache un ongle, l'autre décharne un doigt avec les dents, ou avec un méchant couteau; un troisiéme prend ce doigt décharné, le met dans le foyer de sa pipe bien allumée, le fume en guise de tabac, ou le fait fumer à l'Esclave lui-même."

12. Ibid., p. 278. "Souvent ils lui font une espece de chemise avec l'écorce de bouleau à laquelle ils mettent le feu."

13. Ibid., p. 279. "après avoir cerné la peau de la tête, arraché cette peau de dessus la crane, versé sur ce crane découvert une pluye de feu, de cendres rouges, ou d'eau boüillante."

14. Du Tertre, *Histoire générale des Antilles habitées par les françois* (Paris, 1667), vol. 2, p. 406.

15. James Adair, *The History of the American Indians; particularly Those Nations adjoining to the Mississippi, East and West Florida, Georgia, South and North Carolina, and Virginia: containing an Account of their Origin, Language, Manners, Religious and Civil Customs, Laws, Forms of Government, Punishments, Conduct in War and Domestic Life, and Habits, Diet, Agriculture, Manufactures, Diseases and Method of Cure, and other Particulars* (London, 1775), pp. 390–91.

16. Robertson, *History of America*, pp. 161–62.

17. Raynal, *Histoire philosophique et politique*, pp. 53–54. "Ils s'étudient à prolonger son supplice Durant des jours entiers, et quelquefois une semaine. Au milieu de ces tourmens le héros chante d'une manière barbare, mais héroïque. . . . Le patient meurt sans que le feu ni le fer aient pu lui arracher une larme, un soupir."

18. Joseph-François Lafitau, *Moeurs des sauvages amériquains comparées aux moeurs des premiers temps* (Paris, 1724), vol. 2, p. 284.

19. *Histoire et Description Générale de la Nouvelle France* (Paris, 1744), vol. 3, p. 383. "Mon Frere, prends courage, tu vas être brûlé, & il répond froidement: cela est bien, je te remercie."

20. *The Theory of Moral Sentiments; or, An Essay towards an Analysis of the Principles by which Men naturally judge concerning the Conduct and Character, first of their Neighbours, and afterwards of themselves*, 10th ed. (London, 1804), vol. 2, pp. 29–30.

21. *An Essay on the History of Civil Society*, 6th ed. (London, 1793), p. 152.

22. [Louis de Poincy], *The History of the Caribby-islands, viz. Barbados, St Christophers, St Vincents, Martinico, Dominico, Barbouthos, Monserrat,*

Mevis, Antego &c in all XXVIII: in two books. The first containing the natural; the second the moral history of those islands, rendered into English by John Davies (London, 1666), p. 152.

23. Adair, *History of the American Indians*, p. 390.

24. Montaigne, *Essays*, trans. Charles Cotton (London, 1743), vol. 1, pp. 236–37.

25. *Histoire générale d'Espagne, du Jean de Mariana* (Paris, 1725), vol. 1, p. 18.

26. Henry Home Kames, *Sketches of the History of Man* (Edinburgh, 1774), vol. 1, p. 26.

27. Adam Ferguson, *Essays on the Intellectual Powers, Moral Sentiment, Happiness and National Felicity* (Paris, 1805), p. 34; the same idea is to be found in *Essay on the History of Civil Society*.

28. "L'air froid resserre les extrémités des fibres extérieures de notre corps; cela augmente leur ressort, et favorise le retour du sang des extrémités vers le coeur: il diminue la longeur de ces mêmes fibres; il augmente donc encore par là leur force." *De l'Esprit des Lois* (Paris, 1834), vol. 1, p. 419.

29. "Il faut écorcher un Moscovite pour lui donner du sentiment." Ibid., p. 423.

30. "Les Indiens sont naturellement sans courage . . . Mais comment accorder cela avec leurs actions atroces, leurs coutumes, leurs pénitences barbares." Ibid., p. 425.

31. William Robertson, *History of America*, 3d ed. (London, 1780), vol. 2, p. 163.

32. On Sparta in the European political imagination, see Elizabeth Rawson, *The Spartan Tradition in European Thought* (Oxford University Press, 1969).

33. *The Theory of Moral Sentiments*, 10th ed. (London, 1804), vol. 2, p. 27.

34. "Ces Canadiens étaient des Spartiates en comparison de nos rustres qui végètent dans nos villages." *La Philosophie de l'Histoire* (Autrecht, 1765), cap. 7 "Des Sauvages," pp. 29, 30.

35. Joseph-François Lafitau, *Moeurs des sauvages amériquains comparées aux moeurs des premiers temps* (Paris, 1724), vol. 2, p. 280. "J'ai vû moi-même un enfant de 5 à 6 ans, dont le corps avoit été brûlé par un accident funeste d'eau boüillante répanduë sur lui, qui toutes les fois qu'on le pançoit, chantoit sa chanson de mort avec un courage incroyable."

36. *Histoire universelle de Diodore de Sicile*, trans. Abbé Terrasson (Paris, 1737), vol. 1, pp. 364–65. "Quand même on les fait succomber sous les tourmens les plus extraordinaires, ils demeurent tranquilles, en regardant les playes qu'on leur fait, & inclinant seulement la tête à chaque coup qu'on leur donne."

37. *Essays*, trans. Charles Cotton (London, 1743), p. 287.

38. Richard J. Evans, *Rituals of Retribution: Capital Punishment in Germany, 1600–1987* (Oxford University Press, 1996), p. 259.

39. See, for example, Deslandes, *Reflections sur la mort des grands hommes qui sont morts en plaisantant* (Rochefort, 1755). On *ars moriendi*, see, inter alia, Richard Wunderli and Gerald Broce, "The Final Moment before Death in Early Modern England," *Sixteenth Century Journal*, vol. 20, no. 2 (summer

1989); and David E. Stannard, "Death and Dying in Puritan New England," *American Historical Review*, vol. 78, no. 5 (Dec. 1973).

40. *Essays*, trans. Charles Cotton (London, 1743), p. 287.

41. Ibid.

42. Ibid.

43. Ibid., p. 298.

44. Ibid.

45. *Histoire philosophique et politique*, vol. 8, p. 54. "Fanatiques de toutes les religions vaines et fausses, vantez encore la constance de vos martyrs! Le sauvage de la nature efface tous vos miracles."

46. Jean de la Placette, *Essais de morale*, 2d ed. (Amsterdam, 1716), vol. 3, pp. 267–68.

47. Lafitau, *Moeurs des sauvages ameriquains*, p. 280. "Ce heroïsme est réel, & il est l'effet d'un courage grand & noble. Ce que nous avons admiré dans les Martyrs de la primitive Eglise, & qui étoit en eux l'effet de la grace & d'un miracle, est nature en ceux-ci."

48. Henry More, *An Account of Virtue* (London, 1690), pp. 261–62.

49. Virey, *Histoire naturelle du genre humain, ou Recherches sur ses principaux fondemens physiques et moraux; précédées d'un Discours sur la nature des êtres organiques et sur l'ensemble de leur physiologie. On y a joint une Dissertation sur le sauvage de l'Aveyron* (Paris, an IX [1801]), vol. 2, pp. 42–43.

50. ". . . stratagême des Faquirs & des Bramines." *Récherches philosophiques sur les Américains* (London, 1771), vol. 2, p. 184. This rather improbable idea about tobacco as a powerful drug is of considerable age in Europe. Rodrigo de Jerez, a member of Columbus's party and the first man to smoke tobacco in Europe, was thrown into prison by the Inquisition, on grounds of witchcraft. In a papal bull of 1642, Urban VII forbade the smoking of tobacco in St. Peter's Cathedral, on pain of excommunication. Among the evils attributed to tobacco was also that it impeded reproduction; see *Drugs and Narcotics in History*, ed. Roy Porter and Mikulas Teich (Cambridge University Press, 1995). As for the anaesthetizing of the condemned, it seems that in Europe, there was a custom to serve them copious amounts of drink on their last journey; it is said that the Chinese administered opium.

51. *Politics*, 1338b, 15–25. "Polla d'esti tôn ethnôn ha pros to kteinein kai pros tên anthrôpophagian eucherôs echei . . . ha lêistrika men estin, andreias d'ou meteilêphasin."

52. *The Philosophical Works of David Hume* (Edinburgh, 1854), vol. 2, p. 259.

53. Adam Ferguson, *An Essay on the History of Civil Society*, 6th ed. (London, 1843), part 2, section 2, "Of Rude Nations, prior to the Establishment of Property," p. 152.

54. [Louis de Poincy], *History of Barbados* (London, 1666), p. 326.

55. James Adair, *History of the American Indians* (London, 1775), p. 391.

56. *Candide, ou l'Optimisme* (Paris, 1759), pp. 110–11. "Messieurs, dit Cacambo, vous comptez donc manger aujourd'hui un Jésuite; c'est très bien fait; rien n'est plus juste que de traiter ainsi ses ennemis. En effet, le droit naturel

nous enseigne á tuer nôtre prochain, et c'est ainsi qu'on en agit dans toute la Terre. Si nous n'usons pas du droit de le manger, c'est que nous avons d'ailleurs de quoi faire bonne chère; mais vous n'avez pas les mêmes ressources que nous; certainement il vaut mieux manger ses ennemis, que d'abandonner aux corbeaux et aux corneilles le fruit de sa victoire. Mais, Messieurs, vous ne voudriez pas manger vos amis. Vous croyez aller metre un Jésuite en broche, et c'est vôtre déffenseur, c'est l'enemi de vos ennemis que vous allez rôtir."

57. For example, the Cyclopes, in Homer's *Odyssey*. Diodorus Siculus (*Histoire Universelle*, Paris, 1737, vol. 1, p. 346) mentions Ethiopians with animal claws who lead a bestial existence and can only speak in high-pitched squeaks. Other titles on the history of ideas of monsters and hybrids: Alice Domurat Dreger, *Hermaphrodites and the Medical Invention of Sex* (Harvard UP, 2000); Bettina Bildhauer and Robert Mills, eds., *The Monstrous Middle Ages* (Toronto, 2003); and Debrahiggs Strickland, *Saracens, Demons, and Jews: Making Monsters in Medieval Art* (Princeton University Press, 2003).

58. See James Romm, *Dog Heads and Noble Savages: Cynicism before the Cynics*, in R. Bracht Branham and Marie Odile Goulet-Cazé (eds.), *The Cynics: The Cynic Movement in Antiquity and its Legacy* (Berkeley, 1996).

59. Cf. Frank Lestrignant, *Cannibals: The Discovery and the Representation of the Cannibal from Columbus to Jules Verne* (Berkeley, 1997), pp. 15–16.

60. Voltaire, *Essai sur les Moeurs et l'esprit des nations* (Stuttgart, 1829), vol. 1, pp. 13–14. "Il n'est pas improbable que dans les pays chauds des singes aient subjugué des filles. Hérodote, au livre II, dit que pendant son voyage en Égypte, il y eut une femme qui s'accoupla publiquement avec un boue . . . il est à présumer que des espèces monstrueuses ont pu naître de ces amours abominables. Mais si elles ont existé, elles n'ont pu influer sur le genre humain; et semblables aux mulets qui n'engendrent point, elles n'ont pu dénaturer les autres races." See also Allan Charles Kors, "Monsters and the Problem of Naturalism in French Thought," *Eighteenth-Century Life*, vol. 21, no. 2 (May 1997).

61. See David Morgan, *The Mongols*, 2d ed. (Oxford, 2007), p. 154.

62. Ambroise Paré, *Deux livres de chirurgie* (Paris, 1573), p. 365. "Monstres sont choses qui apparoisset contre le cours de nature."

63. "Si mulier partum ediderit formae insolitae, vetet autem lex hominem occidere; nascitur quaestio an partus sit homo. Quaeritur ergo, quid sit homo. Nemo dubitat, quin judicabit civitas, idque nulla habita ratione definitionis Aristotelicae, quod homo sit animal rationale." Hobbes, *De Cive*, 17, 12, in *Opera Philosophica quae Latine scripsit Omnia*, ed. William Molesworth, vol. 2 (London: John Bohn, 1839), pp. 157 ff. If a woman has given birth to offspring of strange shape, but the law forbids manslaughter; the question arises whether the offspring is human. Therefore, it is to be asked, What is a human? No one doubts that the state shall decide, and in this without taking any account of the Aristotelian definition, that man is a rational animal.

64. Georges Viagrello, *A History of Rape: Sexual Violence in France from the 16th to the 20th century* (Cambridge University Press, 2001), pp. 178, 188.

65. Joseph Acosta, *Histoire naturelle et morale des Indes, tant Orientales qu'Occidentales* (Paris, 1598), p. 214. On the new geography of Americas, see

Kar W. Butzer, "From Columbus to Acosta: Science, Geography, and the New World," *Annals of the Association of American Geographers*, vol. 82, no. 3 (*The Americas before and after 1492: Current Geographical Research*) (Sep. 1992).

66. Henry More, *An Explanation of the Grand Mystery of Godliness* (London, 1660), pp. 86–87.

67. De Pauw, *Récherches philosophiques sur les américains* (London, 1771), vol. 1, p. 178. "Les Péruviens, apparemment policés depuis plus long-temps que les Mexicains, n'égorgeoient plus des créatures humaines pour le service des autels: ils se contentoient de tirer de la veine frontale, & des narines des enfants, une certaine portion de sang, qu'on répandoit sur de la farine dont on pétrissoit des gâteux, que tous les sujets de l'Empire étoient obligés de manger à une grande solemnité annuelle. Il paroît que cela prouve assez que les Péruviens avoient été de vrais Anthropophages; mais que leurs moeurs & leurs habitudes s'étoient adoucies."

68. *The Life and Strange Surprizing Adventures of Robinson Crusoe of York, Mariner*, 3d ed. (London, 1719), p. 183.

69. On Bekker, see Andrew Fix, "Angels, Devils, and Evil Spirits in Seventeenth-Century Thought: Balthasar Bekkerand the Collegiants," *Journal of the History of Ideas*, vol. 50, no. 4 (Oct.–Dec. 1989); and Robin Attfield, "Balthasar Bekker and the Decline of the Witch-Craze: The Old Demonology and the New Philosophy," *Annals of Science*, vol. 42, no. 4 (Jul. 85).

70. See *Histoire de l'Academie Royale des Sciences et Belles Lettres: Année MDCCLIV* (Berlin, 1756), p. 112.

71. J. J. Burlamaqui, *Principes du droit naturel et politique* (Geneva and Copenhagen, 1744), vol. 1, p. 224.

72. See Ivan Hannaford, *Race: The History of an Idea in the West* (Baltimore, 1996), p. 209. On the history of conceptions regarding monsters, including civil and ecclesiastical jurisprudence on the subject, see Ernest Martin, *Histoire des monstres depuis l'Aniquité jusqu' à notres jours* (Paris, 1880).

73. *Émile* (Amsterdam, 1764), vol. 1, p. 1. "Il mutile son chien . . . il défigure tout: il aime la difformité, les monstres; il ne veut rien, tel que l'a fait la nature, pas même l'homme . . . il le faut contourner à sa mode, comme un arbre de son jardin."

74. See H. W. Janson, *Apes and Ape Lore in the Middle Ages and Renaissance* (London, 1952). The book that aroused the greatest interest in the orangutan was Edward Tyson's *Ourang-Outang* (1699). See also Richard Nash, *Wild Enlightenment: The Borders of Human Identity in the Eighteenth Century* (University of Virginia Press, 2003).

75. *Essay of the Intellect*, 3.11.16.

76. *Discours sur l'origine & les fondements de l'inégalité parmi les hommes* (Amsterdam, 1755), pp. 222–30. See also Francis Moran, "Of Pongos and Men: Orangs-outang in Rousseau's 'Discourse on Equality,'" *Review of Politics*, vol. 57, no. 4 (fall 1995).

77. *Of the Origin and Progress of Language*, 2d ed. (Edinburgh, 1774), vol. 1, p. 262.

78. Ibid., p. 268.

79. Ibid., p. 224.

80. Ibid., p. *223.*

81. See Maximillian Novak, "The Wild Man Comes to Tea," in E. Dudley and M. E. Novak (eds.), *The Wild Man Within* (Pittsburgh, 1972), p. 184. Also Robert Mankin, "Montesquieu and the Spirit of Childhood," *MLN*, vol. 117, no. 4, French Issue (Sep. 2002).

82. See Nancy Yousef, "Savage or Solitary? The Wild Child and Rousseau's Man of Nature," *Journal of the History of Ideas*, vol. 62, no. 2 (Apr. 2001). Before Rousseau, Condillac has commented, in *Traité des sensations*, on the case of the Lithuanian bear-child. On child-rearing and ideas about savages, see J. C. Stewart-Robertson, "The Well-Principled Savage, Or the Child of the Scottish Enlightenment," *Journal of the History of Ideas*, vol. 42, no. 3 (Jul.–Sep. 1981); and Julia Douthwaite, "Homo ferus: Between Monster and Model," *Eighteenth-Century Life*, vol. 21, no. 2 (May 1997).

83. The child was discovered in 1731; see Julia Douthwaite, "Rewriting the Savage: The Extraordinary Fictions of the 'Wild Girl of Champagne,'" *Eighteenth-Century Studies*, vol. 28, no. 2 (winter 1994–95).

84. *Histoire d'une jeune fille sauvage, trouvée dans les Bois à l'âge de dix ans* (Paris, 1754), pp. 19, 24, 30.

85. J. J. Burlamaqui, *Principes du droit naturel et politique,* vol. 1, pp. 57. ". . . ce seroit sans contredit le plus miserable de tous les animaux. On ne verroit en lui que foiblesse, ignorance & barbarie . . . & il seroit toujours exposé à périr, ou de faim, ou de froid, ou par les dents de quelque bête féroce."

86. *Relation abrégée d'un voyage fait dans l'intérieur de l'Amérique méridionale, par M. De La Condamine* (Paris, 1778), pp. 50–52.

87. See Jan Bondeson, "Animal Trials," in *The Feejee Mermaid and Other Essays in Natural and Unnatural History* (Cornell University Press 1999).

88. I am grateful to Alistair Ian Blyth for this reference.

89. *Le spectacle de la nature ou entretiens sur les particularités de l'histoire naturelle* (Paris, 1752), vol. 3, pp. 494–96.

90. *Robinson Crusoe*, p. 354.

91. *Histoires prodigieuses extraictes de plusiers auteurs* (Paris, 1598), pp. 190–91.

92. See Bill Bryson, *The Monster of God: The Man-Eating Predator in the Jungles of History and the Mind* (Pimlico: London, 2005).

93. *Witchcraft in Europe, 400–1700: A Documentary History*, ed. Alan Charles Kors and Edward Peters (Philadelphia, 2000), p. 293.

94. See Michel Foucault, *Histoire de la folie à l'âge classique* (Paris, 1960).

95. *Republic*, 571c–d, in *Opera*, ed. John Burnet, vol. 4 (Oxford: Clarendon Press, 1978): "to de thêriôdes te kai agrion, ê sitôn ê methês plêsthen, skirtâi te kai apôsamenon ton hupnon zêtêi ienai kai apopimplanai ta hautou êthê; oisth' hoti panta en tôi toioutôi tolmâi poiein, hôs apo pasês lelumenon te kai apêllagmenon aischunês kai phronêseôs. mêtri te gar epicheirein meignusthai, hôs oietai, ouden oknei, allôi te hotôioun anthrôpôn kai theôn kai thêriôn, miaiphonein te hotioun, brômatos te apechesthai mêdenos."

96. *De ira*, III, 20, in in *Opera Philosophica*, ed. Emil Ferdinand Vogel (Leipzig: Nauck, 1830).

97. "Apud regem omnis coena iucunda est." *De ira*, III, 15.

98. *De ira*, III, 15. "Sed hoc interim colligo posse etiam ex ingentibus malis nascentem iram abscondi et ad verba contraria sibi cogi."

99. *De clementia*, 14, in *Opera Philosophica*, ed. Emil Ferdinand Vogel (Leipzig: Nauck, 1830), pp. 253 ff. "Crudelitas minime humanum malum est, indignum tam miti animo. Ferina ista rabies est, sanguine guadere ac vulneribus; et abiecto homine, in silvestre animal transire. 15. Quid enim interest, oro te, Alexander, leoni Lysimachum obiicias, an ipse laceres dentibus tuis? Tuum illud os est, tua illa feritas. . . . Hoc est, quare vel maxime abominanda sit saevitia, quod excedit fines, primum solitos, deinde humanos. . . . Tunc ille dirus animi morbus ad insaniam pervenit ultimam, quum crudelitas versa est in voluptatem, et iam occidere hominem iuvat."

100. Charles de Rochefort, *Histoire Naturelle et Morale des Iles Antilles de l'Amérique* (Rotterdam, 1658), pp. 400, 405–6.

101. *Histoire générale des Antilles habitées par les François* (Paris, 1667), vol. 2, p. 406.

102. *The History of America*, 3d ed. (London, 1780), vol. 2, p. 149.

103. Ibid., pp. 149–50.

104. Ibid., p. 150.

105. Ibid., p. 151.

106. vol. 1, pp. 101–2.

107. *Moeurs des sauvages ameriquains, comparées aux moeurs des premier temps* (Paris, 1724), vol. 2, p. 406. "Dans l'Amérique Méridionale quelques Peuples décharnent les corps de leurs Guerriers, & les parens mangent leurs chairs, ainsi que je viens de le dire; & après les avoir consumées, ils conservent pendent quelque temps leurs cadavres avec respect dans leurs Cabanes, & ils portent ces squelettes dans les combats en guise d'Etandard, pour ranimer leur courage par cette vûë, & inspirer de la terreur à leurs ennemis."

108. *The History of Barbados* (London, 1666), p. 332.

109. *Histoire Philosophique et Politique des Establissemens & du Commerce des Européens dans les deux Indes* (Amsterdam, 1772), vol. 3, p. 336. "ont été tués avec certaines formalités. Il semble que la vengeance seule assaisonne un aliment que l'humanité répousse. . . . Ils gardent les os des bras comme des jambes pour en faire des flûtes, & les dents qu'ils attachent au cou en forme de collier. . . . Il est beau pour eux d'avoir été défigurés dans les combats."

110. *An Enquiry Concerning the Principles of Morals* (London, 1751), p. 151.

111. Herodotus, *Istorii*, ed. and trans. Adelina Piatkowski and Felicia Ştef, 4 vols., bilingual ed. (Bucharest: Teora, 1998–99), III, 11.

112. *Sketches of the History of Man* (Edinburgh, 1774), vol. 1, p. 34.

113. *Système social, ou principes naturelles de la morale et de la politique avec un examen de l'influence du gouvernement sur les moeurs* (London, 1773), vol. 3, pp. 67–69.

114. *Oeuvres* (Éditions de la Pléiade, Paris 1991), vol. 1, p. 241. Sade himself was accused during the French Revolution of having been a cannibal—a rumor circulated likely by his rival Restif ; see the Preface of Michel Delon to vol. I of Sade's *Œuvres*.

115. *Histoire philosophique et politique des établissemens & du commerce des Européens dans les deux Indes* (The Hague, 1774), vol. 3, pp. 32–33. "cette débauche honteuse qui choque la nature & pervertit l'instinct animal. On a voulu attribuer cette dépravation à la foiblesse physique, qui cependant devroit plutôt en éloigner qu'y entraîner Il faut en chercher la cause dans la chaleur du climat dans le mépris pour un sexe foible; dans l'insipidité du plaisir entre les bras d'une femme harrassée de fatigues; dans l'inconstance du goût; dans la bizarrerie qui pousse en tout à des jouissances moins communes; dans une recherche de volupté, plus facile à concevoir qu'honnête à expliquer."

116. Lescarbot, *Histoire de la Nouvelle France* (1617), pp. 828–30. "Les filles du Bresil ont licence de se prostituer si-tot qu'elles sont capables. . . . On pourroit penser que la nudité de ces peuples les rendroit plus paillars, mais c'est au contraire."

117. Virey, *Histoire naturelle du genre humain, ou Recherches sur ses principaux fondemens physiques et moraux; précédées d'un Discours sur la nature des êtres organiques et sur l'ensemble de leur physiologie. On y a joint une Dissertation sur le sauvage de l'Aveyron* (Paris, an IX [1801]), vol. 1, p. 241.

118. Sade, *Oeuvres*: "Dans cinq jattes de porcelaine blanche, étaient disposés douze ou quinze étrons de la plus belle forme et de la plus grande fraîcheur."

119. Ibid. "Je le sais: je suis un monstre, vomi par la nature pour coopérer avec elle aux destructions qu'elle exige."

120. Ibid. "Les répugnances sont des absurdités: elles ne naissent que du défaut d'habitude ; toutes les viandes sont faites pour sustenter l'homme, toutes nous sont offertes à cet effet par la nature, et il n'est pas plus extraordinaire de manger un homme qu'un poulet."

121. Ibid. "Ayant tué des hommes à la chasse avec les premiers, ayant bu et menti avec les seconds, ayant beaucoup foutu avec les troisièmes, je mangeai des hommes avec ceux-ci. J'ai conservé ces goûts: tous les débris de cadavres que vous voyez ici, ne sont que les restes des créatures que je dévore."

122. Sade is also aware of Montesquieu's theory of despotism; on the latter see Roger Boesche, "Fearing Monarchs and Merchants: Montesquieu's Two Theories of Despotism," *Western Political Quarterly*, vol. 43, no. 4 (Dec. 1990).

123. Sade, *Oeuvres*: "Je ne me couche jamais sans avoir déchargé dix fois. Il est vrai que l'extrême quantité de chair humaine dont je me nourris, contribue beaucoup à l'augmentation et à l'épaisseur de la matière séminale. Quiconque essayera de ce régime, triplera bien sûrement ses facultés libidineuses."

124. Ibid. "Il vous suffise de savoir qu'une fois qu'on en a goûté, il n'est plus possible de manger autre chose."

CHAPTER 4 THE CONQUEST OF THE SAVAGES

1. On the reactions of Indians to the written text, see Patricia Seed, "Failing to Marvel: Atahualpa's Encounter with the Word," *Latin American Research Review*, vol. 26, no. 1 (1991), pp. 7–32.

2. The practice of reading proclamations is studied in Patricia Seed, "Taking Possession and Reading Texts: Establishing the Authority of Overseas Empires,"

William & Mary Quarterly, 3rd Ser., vol. 49, no. 2 (Apr. 1992), pp. 183–209. From 1512, after the Laws of Burgos, the language of the proclamation became standardized in the form that was known as the *Requeriemiento*, but the potential for abuse remained. In the words of a contemporary scholar: "[The *Requeriemiento*] was read to trees and empty huts. Captains muttered its theological phrases into their beards on the edge of sleeping Indian settlements, or even a league away before starting the formal attack. Ship captains would sometimes have the document read from the deck as they approached an island" (Lewis Hanke, *The Spanish Struggle for Justice in the Conquest of America* [Philadelphia, 1949], pp. 43–44). The *Requeriemiento* was enforced until 1573, when it was replaced by another set of regulations. On the concept of "discovery," see Wilcomb E. Washburn, "The Meaning of 'Discovery' in the Fifteenth and Sixteenth Centuries," *American Historical Review*, vol. 68, no. 1 (Oct. 1962), pp. 1–21. The establishment of the Spanish authority in the Indies is discussed by C. H. Haring, "The Genesis of Royal Government in the Spanish Indies," *Hispanic American Historical Review*, vol. 7, no. 2 (May 1927), pp. 141–91. A general overview of the spread of Christianity in America is Mark A. Noll, *A History of Christianity in the United States and Canada* (Grand Rapids, MI, 1992).

3. On the missionary activities before the colonization of America, see James D. Ryan, "Missionary Saints of the High Middle Ages: Martyrdom, Popular Veneration, and Canonization," *Catholic Historical Review*, vol. 90, no. 1 (Jan. 2004). On the history of conversions, see *Conversions: Old Worlds and New*, ed. Kenneth Mills and Anthony Grafton (Woodbridge, UK, 2003).

4. Cf. R. Po-Chia Hsia, *The Myth of Ritual Murder* (Yale University Press, 1988), p. 114.

5. Gilles of Rome [Aegidius Romanus], *On Ecclesiastical Power* (Woodridge, UK,1986), chapter 11.

6. See Walter Ullmann, *Medieval Papalism: The Political Theories of Medieval Canonists* (London, 1949).

7. This intervention resulted in the papal bull *Romanus Pontifex* (1455), which accepted the Portuguese claim to the Canaries. See Frances Gardiner Davenport, ed., *European Treaties Bearing on the History of the United States and its Dependencies to 1648* (Washington, DC, 1917), pp. 20–26. A recent collection of papal documents on the evangelization of the New World is *America pontificia primi saeculi evangelizationis 1493–1592. Documenta pontificia ex registris et minutis praesertim in Archivo Secreto Vaticano existentibus collegit, edidit Josef Metzler mandatu Pontificii Comitatus de Scientiis Historicis* (Vatican City, 1991).

8. On the interpretation of *Inter caetera*, see Glen Carman, "On the Pope's Original Intent: Las Casas Reads the Papal Bulls of 1493," *Colonial Latin American Review*, vol. 7, no. 2 (Dec. 1998).

9. Cf. Hayden White, "The Forms of Wilderness: Archaeology of an Idea," in Edward Dudley and Maximillian Novak (eds.), *The Wild Man Within: An Image in Western Thought from the Renaissance to Romanticism* (Pittsburgh, 1972), p. 18.

10. Lewis Hanke, *The Spanish Struggle for Justice in the Conquest of America* (Boston, 1965), p. 111.

11. Charles de Rochefort, *Histoire Naturelle et Morale des Iles Antilles de l'Amérique* (Rotterdam, 1658), p. 413.

12. Garcilasso de la Vega, *L'Histoire des Yncas, Roys de Perou* (Amsterdam, 1704), vol. 1, pp. 48–49.

13. Joseph Acosta, *Histoire naturelle et morale des Indes, tant Orientales qu'Occidentales* (Paris, 1598), p. 211.

14. See Patrick Riley, *General Will before Rousseau: The Transformation of the Divine into the Civic* (Princeton University Press, 1986).

15. *Traité de la grâce générale* (1715), vol. 1, p. 90.

16. *Écrits sur le systeme de la grâce générale* (1715), vol. 1, p. 52. On the Augustinian background of the debates centered on the situation of the Indians, see Peter Goddard, "Augustine and the Amerindian in Seventeenth-century New France," *Church History*, vol. 67, no. 4 (Dec. 1998).

17. *The History of Barbados* (London, 1666), pp. 272–89.

18. Alexandre-Olivier Exquemelin, *Histoire des avanturiers filibustiers* (Paris, 1699), vol. 2, p. 311. "Pour revenir à ceux qui n'ont point de Religion, quand on leur parle de Dieu, & de les convertir, ils disent que si Dieu est tout-puissant, il n'a que faire d'eux."

19. *An Essay Concerning Human Understanding*, I, 4, 8.

20. *Essai sur les moeurs et l'esprit des Nations* (Stuttgart, 1829), Introduction, section 5 "De la religion des premiers hommes."

21. See Las Casas, *Apologetica Historia de las Indias* (Madrid, 1909), cap. 123, 127, and 163.

22. de la Vega, *L'Histoire des Yncas*, vol. 1, pp. 145–46. On the reaction of the Spanish to the religion of the Incas, see Kenneth Mills, *Idolatry and Its Enemies: Colonial Andean Religion and Extirpation, 1640–1750* (Princeton University Press, 1997).

23. On Lafitau, see Michel de Certeau and James Hovde, "Writing vs. Time: History and Anthropology in the Works of Lafitau," *Yale French Studies*, no. 59, *Rethinking History: Time, Myth, and Writing* (1980), pp. 37–64.

24. For details see Lee Eldridge Huddleston, *Origins of the American Indians: European Concepts, 1492–1729* (University of Texas Press, 1967); and Robert Williams Jr., *The American Indian in Western Legal Thought* (Oxford University Press, 1990).

25. It occasioned a polemic with Jean de Laet; for details of the theories on the origin of American Indians, see Joan-Paul Rubiés, "Hugo Grotius's Dissertation on the Origin of the American Peoples and the Use of Comparative Methods," *Journal of the History of Ideas*, vol. 52, no. 2 (Apr.–Jun. 1991).

26. J. J. Burlamaqui, *Principes du droit naturel et politique* (Geneva and Copenhagen, 1744), vol. 1, p. 17

27. *The Life and Strange Surpizing Adventures of Robinson Crusoe*, 3d ed. (London, 1719), pp. 258, 259

28. Ibid., p. 286. The Puritans developed an argument in favor of colonization based on the freedom to preach the Gospel; for details see Peter Harrison,

"'Fill the Earth and Subdue it': Biblical Warrants for Colonization in Seventeenth-Century England," *Journal of Religious History*, vol. 29, no. 1 (Feb. 2005), p. 3–24.

29. Muratori, *Relation of the Missions of Paraguay, wrote Originally in Italian* (London, 1759), p. 26.

30. Ibid., p. 41.

31. *A Discourse of Inequality*, trans. Maurice Cranston (Harmondsworth, 1984), pp. 169–70.

32. On Montesinos and the controversy he ignited, see Patricia Seed, "'Are These Not Also Men?' The Indians' Humanity and Capacity for Spanish Civilisation," *Journal of Latin American Studies*, vol. 25, no. 3 (Oct. 1993), pp. 629–52.

33. On Vitoria's doctrine of intervention, see James Muldoon, "Francisco De Vitoria and Humanitarian Intervention," *Journal of Military Ethics*, vol. 5, no. 2 (Jun. 2006).

34. Lewis Hanke, *Aristotle and the American Indians: A Study in Race Prejudice in the Modern World* (Chicago, 1959), p. 16.

35. Juan Gines de Sepulveda, *Democrates Segundo, o de las justas causas de la guerra contra los indios* (Madrid, 1984), p. 33. On the theory of the "natural slaves" see Robert E. Quirk, "Some Notes on a Controversial Controversy: Juan Ginés de Supúlveda and Natural Servitude," *Hispanic American Historical Review*, vol. 34, no. 3 (Aug. 1954), pp. 357–64; see also Malcolm K. Read, "From Feudalism to Capitalism: Ideologies of Slavery in the Spanish American Empire," *Hispanic Research Journal*, vol. 4, no. 2 (Jun. 2003).

36. Gines de Sepulveda, *Democrates Segundo*, p. 38.

37. Ibid., p. 104.

38. Fray Bernardino Minayo, quoted in Lewis Hanke, *Estudios sobre Bartolomeo de Las Casas* (Caracas, 1968), pp. 76–77.

39. *De procuranda indorum salute* (Madrid, 1984), p. 66.

40. Ibid., pp. 292, 302, and 168.

41. Francisco de Vitoria, *Political Writings*, ed. Anthony Padgen and Jeremy Lawrance, trans. Jeremy Lawrance (Cambridge University Press, 1991), p. 225.

42. Ibid., p. 9.

43. Ibid., pp. 16–17.

44. Ibid., p. 37.

45. Ibid., p. 250.

46. Ibid., pp. 331–32.

47. For an overview of French attitudes toward Spain, see Paul Ilie, "Exomorphism: Cultural Bias, and the French Image of Spain from the War of Succession to the Age of Voltaire," *Eighteenth-Century Studies*, vol. 9, no. 3 (spring 1976). The denunciation of the treatment of Indians in anti-Spanish and anti-Catholic literature is part of what was later called the "Black Legend" of Spanish cruelty and fanaticism; for details, see William S. Maltby, *The Black Legend in England* (Duke University Press, 1971); and Maria de Guzman, *Spain's Long Shadow: The Black Legend, Off-Whiteness, and Anglo-American Empire* (University of Minnesota Press, 2005)

48. Richard Baxter, *A Holy Commonwealth* (Cambridge University Press, 1994), pp. 103–4.

49. On authority and property for nonbelievers, see Ockham, *A Short Discourse on Tyrannical Government* (Cambridge University Press, 1992), book 3. On papal power in relation to non-Christian nations, see book 5, chapter 14.

50. *Mare Liberum/De la liberté des mers* (Paris, 1990), pp. 669–71.

51. *Le Droit de la Nature et des Gens, Système Général des Principes le plus importants de la morale, de la jurisprudence, et de la politique. Traduit du latin par Jean Barbeyrac*, 5th ed. (Amsterdam, 1734), vol. 1, p. 388.

52. Ibid., vol. 2, p. 556.

53. *A Methodical System of Universal Law, or the Laws of Nature Deduced from Certain Principles and Applied to Proper Cases* (London, 1763), vol. 2, pp. 189, 192.

54. *Robinson Crusoe*, p. 199. On cannibalism, property, and natural law in *Robinson Crusoe*, see "*Terra nullius*, cannibalism and the natural law of appropriation," in Wolfram Schmidgen, *Eighteenth-Century Fiction and the Law of Property* (Cambridge University Press, 2002).

55. *Robinson Crusoe*, p. 202.

56. Ibid.

57. Ibid., p. 203.

58. Ibid., p. 204.

59. *Histoire naturelle et morale des Iles Antilles*, p. 267.

60. *Voyage du Père Labat aux Iles de l'Amerique* (The Hague, 1724), vol. 2, p. 108. "C'était une action toute éxtraordinnaire chez ces peuples: c'était la rage qui leur faisait commétre ces excès; parce qu'ils ne peuvaient se venger pleinement de l'injustice que les Européens leur faisoient de les chasser de leurs terres, qu'en leur faisant périr, quand ils les prenoient, avec des cruautez qui ne leur sont pas ordinaires, ni natureles."

61. *Le Nouveau Cynée: The New Cyneas* (Philadelphia, 1909), p. 126.

62. Ibid., p. 130.

63. *The History of Barbados, St. Christopher, Mevis, St. Vincent's, Antego, Martinico, Monserrat, and the rest of the Carriby-Islands* (London, 1666), p. 329.

64. *History of the Filibuster Adventurers*, vol. 2, (Paris, 1686), pp. 310–11.

65. *Montaigne's Essays*, trans. Charles Cotton, 6th ed. (London, 1743), vol. 1, p. 234. The positive treatment of the natives of America is foreshadowed in a text by Antonio de Guevara, a Spanish preacher, where a savage "peasant of the Danube" extols the virtues of living in a better society than his civilised (that is, Spanish) contemporaries; this piece contributed to the formation of the myth of the "good savage" and his author was read by Montaigne. See Carlo Ginzburg, "Making Things Strange: The Prehistory of a Literary Device," *Representations*, vol. 56, *Special Issue: The New Erudition* (autumn 1996).

66. *Montaigne's Essays*, p. 228.

67. Ibid., p. 229.

68. Ibid., p. 230.

69. Ibid., p. 233.

70. *Histoire naturelle et morale des Iles Antilles,* pp. 383–85, 403.

71. *Histoire générale des Antiles* (Paris, 1667), vol. 2, p. 357.

72. *Émile, ou l'Education* (Amsterdam, 1744), p. 16. "Les Caraïbes sont de la moité plus heureux que nous."

73. G. T. Raynal, *Histoire philosophique et politique des établissemens et du commerce des Européens dans les deux Indes* (Paris, 1820), vol. 5, p. 24. "Au Brésil, les têtes des ennemis massacrés dans le combat ou immolés après l'action, étaient conservées très-précieusement. On les montrait avec ostentation, comme des monumens de valeur et de victoire. Les héros de ces nations féroces portaient leurs exploits gravés sur leurs membres par des incisions qui les honoraient: plus ils étoient défigurés, et plus leur gloire était grande. . . . mais que pouvaient des sauvages contre les armes et la discipline de l'Europe?"

CHAPTER 5 THE PREDICAMENTS OF IDENTITY

1. References are to the text of *The Acts of the Christian Martyrs* (Oxford University Press, 1972).

2. A number of disputes on the issue of the Jewish theory of resurrection are previously recorded in Judaism and probably originate in the period before the destruction of the Temple. "Since the dead are but dust, how can dust revive ?" asks one text. Later, the philosopher Eunamaos of Gadara attempted to refute Rabbi Meir's belief in the resurrection. See A. Marmorstein, "The Doctrine of the Resurrection of the Dead in Rabbinical Theology," *American Journal of Theology,* vol. 19, no. 4 (Oct. 1915), pp. 577–91; also H. Birkeland, "The Belief in the Resurrection of the Dead in the Old Testament," *Studia Theologica* 3 (1950): 60–78.

3. See *The Martyrdom of St. Ignatius* and St. Irineus of Lyon, *Adversus haereses.* Occasionally, similar ideas occur in the Jewish texts of martyrdom, such as the story of a mother and her seven sons. Despite the dismembering and the frying of organs in cauldrons, the martyrs affirm their belief in the resurrection of the body. Cf. Shmuel Shepkaru, "From after Death to Afterlife: Martyrdom and Its Recompense," *AJS Review,* vol. 24, no. 1 (1999), pp. 1–44.

4. The origins of the dogma of the resurrection are pre-Christian, especially Jewish and Persian; see Alfred Bertholet, "The Pre-Christian Belief in the Resurrection of the Body," *American Journal of Theology,* vol. 20, no. 1 (Jan. 1916), pp.1–30. A different viewpoint is in Hugh Jackson, "The Resurrection Belief of the Earliest Church: A Response to the Failure of Prophecy?" *Journal of Religion,* vol. 55, no. 4 (Oct. 1975), pp. 415–25. See also William O. Walker, Jr., "Christian Origins and Resurrection Belief," *Journal of Religion,* vol. 52 (January 1972): 51–52. The case of the resurrected body of Jesus was regarded, of course, as sui generis; see Shirley Jackson Case, "The Resurrection Faith of the First Disciples," *American Journal of Theology,* vol. 13, no. 2 (Apr. 1909), pp. 169–92. See also Robert M. Grant, "The Resurrection of the Body," *Journal of Religion,* vol. 28, no. 2 (Apr. 1948), pp. 120–30; and Jaap Mansfeld, "Resurrection Added: The Interpretatio Christiana of a Stoic Doctrine," *Vigiliae Christianae,* vol. 37, no. 3 (Sep. 1983), pp. 218–33.

5. Fear toward the impossibility of resurrection of the body seems to have existed in the Jewish circles too, especially regarding the fate of the *insepulti* (corpses denied burial for being eaten by wolves or drowned) and *ahori* (abortions). There is a story about a group of Jewish children captured by the Romans who first thought of drowning themselves, but renounced it for fear of not being resurrected. On the other hand, the decomposition of the flesh had often an expiatory role in Jewish theology and burial customs. See Eric M. Meyers, "The Theological Implications of an Ancient Jewish Burial Custom," *Jewish Quarterly Review*, n.s., vol. 62, no. 2 (Oct. 1971), pp. 95–119.

6. See N. Clayton Croy, "Hellenistic Philosophies and the Preaching of the Resurrection (Acts 17:18, 32)," *Novum Testamentum*, vol. 39, fasc. 1. (Jan. 1997), pp. 21–39. Richard A. Horsley, "'How Can Some of You Say That There Is No Resurrection of the Dead?' Spiritual Elitism in Corinth," *Novum Testamentum*, vol. 20, fasc. 3. (Jul., 1978), pp. 203–31, makes the point that the reaction of the Corinthians to Paul's sermon is motivated by a Gnostic obsession with the liberation from the body. For a different interpretation, which stresses Gnostic and Pauline convergence on the topic of resurrection, see Elaine H. Pagels, "'The Mystery of the Resurrection': A Gnostic Reading of 1 Corinthians 15," *Journal of Biblical Literature*, vol. 93, no. 2 (Jun. 1974), pp. 276–88.

7. On the disputes on attribution of this text to Athenagoras, see the articles of Bernard Pouderon, "L'authenticité du traité sur la résurrection attribué à l'apologiste Athénagore," *Vigiliae Christianae*, vol. 40, no. 3 (Sep. 1986), pp. 226–44, and "'La chair et le sang': Encore sur l'authenticité du traité d'Athénagore," *Vigiliae Christianae*, vol. 44, no. 1 (Mar. 1990), pp. 1–5.

8. Cf. Caroline Walker Bynum, *The Resurrection of the Body in Western Christianity, 200–1336* (New York, 1995), p. 26. Gnosticism was likely a threat to the Jewish rabbis who, during the same period, battled criticism of the dogma of the resurrection coming from individuals such as the apostate Elisha ben-Abuja, who is known to have carried with him Gnostic writings.

9. See Malcolm Peel, *The Epistle to Rheginos: A Valentinian Letter on the Resurrection (Westminster Press,* 1969). This text, however, is probably from the fourth century AD, meaning it is posterior to the earliest treatises on resurrection of the Church Fathers.

10. Minucius Felix, *Octavius*, trans. Sir David Dalyrmple (Lord Hailes) (Cambridge, 1854), 11, 4f.

11. *De civitate dei, City of God*, trans. Henry Scowcroft Bettenson (Harmondsworth, 2003), XXII, 12.

12. *Discours d'Athenagore sur la resurrection des morts* (Breslau, 1753), pp. 31–32.

13. Tatianus Assyrius, *Oratio ad Graecos: Corpus Apologetarum Christianorum Saeculi Secundi*, ed. Johann Karl Theodore Otto, vol. 6 (Jena: Friedrich Mauke, 1851), 6.

14. A practical difficulty not unknown in the modern age: on June 27, 2007, *The Times* of London reports that the Islamic imams of Baghdad issued a *fatwa* declaring the carp caught in the river as "unclean" and unfit for human consumption due to the numerous human bodies polluting the water.

15. See Donald G. Kyla, *Spectacles of Death in Ancient Rome* (London, 1998), pp. 186 and 190.

16. Athenagoras, Pouderon, *L'authenticité du traité sur la resurrection*, 60–61.

17. Aristotle, *Generation of Animals*, 725a, 12–15. See also Yii-Jan Singh, "Semen, Philosophy, and Paul," *Journal of Philosophy and Scripture*, vol. 4, no. 2 (spring 2007).

18. On the feeding of the fetus in the womb, see Edward Engelbrecht, "God's Milk: An Orthodox Confession of the Eucharist," *Journal of Early Christian Studies*, vol. 7, no. 4 (winter 1999), pp. 509–26.

19. *On the Resurrection of the Flesh*, 32. On the treatise of Tertullian, see Robert Sider, "Structure and Design in the 'De resurrectione mortuorum' of Tertullian," *Vigiliae Christianae*, vol. 23, no. 3 (Sep. 1969), pp. 177–96.

20. Athenagoras, Pouderon, *L'authenticité du traité sur la résurrection*, pp. 60–61.

21. Ibid., p. 53.

22. *Traité de la verité de la religion chrétienne* (Utrecht, 1692), p. 122. "Mais comment ne pourroit-il pas faire dans ce grand Univers, dont il est le maître absolu, ce que nous voyons faire aux Chymistes dans leur fourneaux, & dans les instrumens de leur art, où aprés avoir comme détruit une chose en la dissolvant, ils la reproduisent en réünissant ses partes?" On Grotius's views on the resurrection of Christ, see William Lane Craig, *The Historical Argument for the Resurrection of Christ during the Deist Controversy*, vol. 23 (Lewiston, NY, 1985).

23. *Traité de la verité de la religion chretienne*, p. 122. "Tout ce raisonnement . . . parôit assez foible."

24. Ibid. "Il suppose un miracle dans le cours ordinaire des choses."

25. Ibid., p. 123. "On peut assurer que l'expérience détruit cette supposition, & que ceux d'entre les Amériquains qui font repas de la chair de leurs ennemis vaincus, en sont aussi parfaitement nourris que de quelque autre aliment que ce soit."

26. *A Discourse concerning the Being and Attributes of God, the Obligations of Natural Religion, and the Truth and Certainty of the Christian Revelation, in Answer to Mr Hobbes, Spinoza, the Author of the Oracles of Reason, and Other Deniers of Natural and Revealed Religion, being Sixteen Sermons preached in the Cathedral-Church of St Paul, in the Years 1704–5, at the Lecture founded by the Hon. Robert Boyle, Esq.* (Glasgow, 1823), pp. 325–26.

27. Ibid., p. 326.

28. Ibid., p. 326.

29. Ibid.

30. Ibid., p. 327.

31. Ibid.

32. Ibid.

33. *Selected Philosophical Papers of Robert Boyle* (Indianapolis, 1991), p. 204. On Boyle's theory of particles, see Marie Boas, *The Establishment of the Mechanical Philosophy*, *Osiris*, vol. 10 (1952), pp. 412–541. On the theological context of Boyle's theories, see Jan W. Wojcik, *Robert Boyle and the Limits of Reason* (Cambridge University Press, 1997). Sanctorino Sanctorius speculated about the "insensible perspiration" of the human body in order to account for

the difference of mass between the food ingurgitated and excretions; he devised a "weighting chair" to study the difference; see Lucia Dacome, "Living with the Chair: Private Excreta, Collective Health, and Medical Authority in the Eighteenth Century," *History of Science*, vol. 39, no. 4 (Dec. 2001).

34. The analogy between the composition and analysis of flesh and that of metals goes back to Justin Martyr.

35. *Selected Philosophical Papers of Robert Boyle*, p. 203.

36. Ibid.

37. Ibid., p. 204.

38. On the theories of moral probability, see Ikka Kantola, *Probability and Moral Uncertainty in Late Medieval and Early Modern Times* (Helsinki, 1994).

39. *The Enchiridion on Faith, Hope, and Love*, trans. Thomas S. Hibbs (Washington DC, 1996), pp. 105 ff.

40. *Treatise of Principles*, in *On First Principles*, trans. G. W. Butterworth (New York, 1966), II, 10.

41. Mansi IX. 516 D. Chadwick, in "Origen, Celsus, and the Resurrection of the Body," claims that it was not so much Origenes, but the Origenists of the Byzantine sixth century who developed this doctrine.

42. Origen ap. Methodius, in *On First Principles*, trans. G. W. Butterworth (New York, 1966), 1.20.4. See also Henry Chadwick, "Origen, Celsus, and the Resurrection of the Body," *The Harvard Theological Review*, vol. 41, no. 2 (Apr. 1948), pp. 83–102.

43. See Chadwick, "Origen, Celsus, and the Resurrection of the Body." Chadwick claims that it is probable that Augustine had in mind these objections of Porphyry when he devised his arguments against the implications of cannibalism in *De civitate Dei*.

44. For the history of ideas of omnipotence see T. Rudavsky, ed., *Divine Omniscience and Omnipotence in Medieval Philosophy* (Dordrecht and Boston, 1985); M. T. Fumagalli and Beonio-Brocchieri, eds., *Sopra la volta del mondo: onnipotenza a potenza assoluta di dio tra medioevo e età moderna* (Bergamo, 1986); and Francis Oakley, *Omnipotence, Covenant, and Order: An Excursion in the History of Ideas from Abelard to Leibniz* (Cornell University Press 1984).

45. See Ralph Lerner, "Maimonides' 'Treatise on Resurrection,'" *History of Religions*, vol. 23, no. 2 (Nov. 1983), pp. 140–55.

46. See M. Friedländer, "Life and Works of Saadia," *Jewish Quarterly Review*, vol. 5, no. 2 (Jan. 1893), pp. 177–99. Saadia Gaon does mention the patristic difficulty of resurrection: "But suppose a lion were to eat a man, the lion would drown and a fish would eat him up, and then the fish would be caught and a man would eat him, and then the man would be burned and turned to ashes. Whence would the Creator restore the first man? Would He do it from the lion, from the fish, from the first man, from the fire or from the ashes?" See Saadia Gaon, *The Book of Beliefs and Opinions* (Yale University Press, 1989), VII, 7.

47. *Apud* Chadwick, "Origen, Celsus, and the Resurrection of the Body."

48. Sextus Empiricus, *Adv. Math.*, 9.178–79.

49. *Encyclopédie ou Dictionnaire raisonné des sciences, des arts et des métiers* (Neufchastel, 1765), vol. 14, p. 197. "D'ailleurs on a vu des exemples

d'hommes qui en mangeoient d'autres, comme les Cannibales & les autres sauvages des Indes occidentales le pratiquent encore à l'égard de leurs prisonniers."

50. Ibid. "Mais le réponse de M. Leibniz paroît être plus solide."

51. Ibid. "On peut répondre à cela sur les principes de M. Locke, que l'identité personelle d'un être raisonable consiste dans le sentiment intérieur, dans la puissance de se considérer soi-même comme la même chose en différens tems & lieux." On Locke's own theory of identity, see John W. Yolton, "Locke's Man," *Journal of the History of Ideas*, vol. 62, no. 4 (Oct. 2001).

52. See F. R. S. Chambers, *Cyclopaedia, or, an Universal Dictionary of Arts and Sciences*, 5th ed. (London, 1743).

53. Henry More, *An Explanation of the Grand Mystery of Godliness* (London, 1660), pp. 221–29.

54. Thomas Browne, *Religio medici* (London, 1643), section IV, XXXVII.

55. *A Treatise concerning the State of Departed Souls, Before, and At, and After the Resurrection*, trans. from Latin by Mr. Dennis, 2d ed., corrected (London, 1739), p. 236. Burnet's *Treatise*, together with that of Hody, will be sources of another debate on resurrection, in a series of newly discovered letters exchanged by four Jewish thinkers in 1773; see David Malkiel, "The Rimini Papers: A Resurrection Controversy in Eighteen-Century Italy," *Journal of Jewish Thought and Philosophy*, vol. 11, no. 2 (2002). For the English debates on the resurrection of the bodies in connection with the theories of personal identity and individuation, see Udo Thiel, "Personal Identity" and "Individuation," in M. Ayers and D. Garber (eds.), *Cambridge History of Seventeenth-Century Philosophy* (Cambridge University Press, 1998); and Dennis M. Welch, "Defoe's 'A True Relation,' Personal Identity and the Locke-Stillingfleet Controversy," *Studies in Philology*, vol. 100 (2003).

56. *A Treatise concerning the State of Departed Souls*, pp. 236–37.

57. Ibid., p. 238.

58. Ibid., p. 242.

59. Ibid., pp. 242–43.

60. Ibid., p. 243.

61. Ibid., p. 243.

62. Ibid., pp. 243–44.

63. Ibid., p. 244.

64. Ibid., p. 244.

65. Ibid., pp. 244–45.

66. *Traité de la Verité de la Religion Chrétienne*, trans. Pierre Lejeune (Utrecht, 1692), p. 124. "La transpiration continuelle des particules qui composent le corps, & ausquelles d'autres particules succédent aussi continuellement, le change pour le moins autant, que cet accident dont nous parlons."

67. Ibid., p. 346. "Rien de ce que nous voyons n'est stable & perpétuel: dans le moment même que je parle de cette vicissitude, je sais que je l'éprouve."

68. *The Resurrection of the (Same) Body Asserted, from the Traditions of the Heathens, the Ancient Jews and the Primitive Church* (London, 1696), pp. 184–221.

69. *Works of Dr. John Tillotson*, sermon 193 (London, 1820).

70. Athenagoras, Pouderon, *L'authenticité du traité sur la résurrection*, pp. 60–63.

71. *Dictionnaire philosophique* (Paris, 1964): "C'est pourquoi on a dit que nous étions tous anthropophages. Rien n'est plus sensible après une bataille; non-seulement nous tuons nos frères, mais au bout de deux ou trois ans, nous les avons mangés quand on a fait les moissons sur le champ de bataille."

72. "Lettre au Marquis de la Farre," in Fontenelle, *Oeuvres complètes*, vol. 3 (Paris, 1989), pp. 461–62. The hypothesis of "proportionally reduced" resurrected bodies is also sarcastically evoked by Voltaire in the article on "Resurrection" in the *Dictionnaire philosophique*. Fontenelle and La Farre touched on another, related difficulty of the theory of the resurrection of the body, namely whether the world is large enough to accommodate the bodies of all men who have ever lived. This is a problem already analyzed by Jewish sages; see, for example, Menasesch ben Israel, *De resurrectione mortuorum* (Amsterdam, 1636).

73. "États et empires de la Lune, " in *Libertins du XVIIIe siècle*, ed. Jacques Prévot (Paris, 1998), pp. 986–87. This type of discussion between a Christian and a nonbeliever has its origins in the patristic texts, for example the fifth-century dialogue between a Christian and a pagan philosopher. After the emergence of Islam, the Muslim is the interlocutor in John Damascene's *Controversy between a Muslim and a Christian* or in Michael II Paleologus's *Discussions with a Muslim* (circa 1390); some of these texts contain examinations of the doctrine of resurrection. For the anti-Christian Jewish polemical texts that mention the logical difficulties of Christian dogma, see Daniel J. Lasker, "Averroistic Trends in Jewish-Christian Polemics in the Late Middle Ages," *Speculum*, vol. 55, no. 2 (Apr. 1980), pp. 294–304.

74. *A Modest Enquiry into the Mystery of Iniquity* (London, 1664), p. 169.

75. Voltaire comments on the medieval theories in the *Essai sur les moeurs*. The Scholastics did not confuse the ritual consumption of the blood and flesh of Christ with ordinary cannibalism, due to the unique status of the body of Christ. In the seventeenth century, the Nonconformist theologian John Owen will claim that this consumption is spiritual: "Many were offended, as supposing that he [Jesus] had intended an oral, carnal eating of his flesh, and drinking of his blood; and so would have taught them to be cannibals. Wherefore, to instruct his disciples aright in this mystery, he gives an eternal rule of the interpretation of such expressions, verse 63, "It is the spirit that quickeneth; the flesh profiteth nothing: the words that I speak unto you, they are spirit, and they are life." To look for any other communication of Christ, or of his flesh and blood, but what is spiritual, is to contradict him in the interpretation which he gives of his own words." See *Sermons of John Owen* (Edinburgh, 1965), p. 560.

76. *A Comical and True Account of the Modern Canibals's Religion, by Osmin True Believer, to which is added a Select Piece, call'd The Story of Stories, taken from the Canibals's Chronicle* (London, 1734), p. 10.

77. Ibid., p. 18.

78. Ibid., p. 19.

79. Ibid., p. 20.

80. Ibid., p. 21.

81. Ibid., p. 22.

82. Similar arguments can be found in the article on "Transubstantiation" in the *Dictionnaire philosophique.* Kames too indulges in scatological humor. Priests traffic the excrements of the Dalai Lama, which are kept in golden boxes by the faithful. "Like the cross of Jesus, or the Virgin's milk, we may believe, there never will be wanting plenty of that precious stuff to answer all demands," the Scottish philosopher observes. "The priests out of charity will furnish a quota, rather than suffer votaries to depart with their money for want of goods to purchase." *Sketches of the History of Man* (Edinburgh, 1774), vol. 2, p. 423.

83. *Dialogues and Natural History of Religion* (Oxford University Press, 1993), pp. 167–68.

84. *Lettres juives, ou correspondence philosophique, historique et critique* (Paris, 1742), vol. 2, p. 240.

85. On anthropophagy and the criticism of Catholic rites in Psalmanaazaar, see Frank Lestringant and Noah Guynn, "Travels in Eucharistia: Formosa and Ireland From George Psalmanaazaar to Jonathan Swift," *Yale French Studies*, no. 86, *Corps Mystique, Corps Sacre: Textual Transfigurations of the Body From the Middle Ages to the Seventeenth Century* (1994), pp. 109–25. Psalmanaazaar passed for a Japanese traveller; he was in fact French, likely a Huguenot fleeing after the revocation of the Edict of Nantes. He even secured a fellowship at Christ Church, Oxford, in order to teach Formosan; somehow he was able to dupe everybody from 1703 to 1728.

86. See, for instance, *Description dresée sur les mémoires de George Psalmanaazaar contenant une Ample relation de l'Ille Formose en Asie* (Paris, 1739), pp. 66–67.

87. *La contagion sacrée, ou histoire naturelle de la superstition* (London, 1770), vol. 1, pp. 17–18, vol. 2, p. 38.

88. *Système de la nature, ou les loix du monde physique & du monde moral* (London, 1781), vol. 2, pp. 12, 245.

89. *Dictionnaire philosophique*, "Spinosa était non-seulement athée, mais il enseigna l'athéisme . . . ce ne fut pas lui qui déchira les deux frères de Wit en morceaux, et qui les mangea sur le gril."

90. *The History of the American Indians; particularly Those Nations adjoining to the Mississippi, East and West Florida, Georgia, South and North Carolina, and Virginia: containing an Account of their Origin, Language, Manners, Religious and Civil Customs, Laws, Forms of Government, Punishments, Conduct in War and Domestic Life, and Habits, Diet, Agriculture, Manufactures, Diseases and Method of Cure, and other Particular,* (London, 1775), p. 391.

91. *The Life and Strange Surprizing Adventures of Robison Crusoe* (London, 1719), p. 257. Of religion on Robinson's island, see Timothy C. Blackburn, "Friday's Religion: Its Nature and Importance in Robinson Crusoe," *Eighteenth-Century Studies*, vol. 18, no. 3 (spring 1985).

92. See Didier Masseau, *Les ennemis des philosophes: L'antiphilosophie au temps des lumières* (Paris, 2000), pp. 43, 124.

93. *Recherches philosophiques sur les Américains, ou Mémoires intéressants, pour servir à l'Histoire de l'Espèce humaine* (London, 1771), vol. 2, pp. 109–10: "les Juifs modernes circoncisent d'une façon très dégoûtante, & qui seroit seule en état d'inspirer de l'horreur pour leurs absurdités religieuses."

94. Ibid. "le Circonciseur fait quelques grimaces, applique sa langue sur les parties génitales du Néophyte, fait entrer ces parties dans sa bouche, & se met à les sucer de toutes ses forces."

95. *Oeuvres* (Paris, 1990), vol. 1, p. 563.

96. *Recherches philosophiques sur les Américains*, vol. 1, p. 256. In a footnote, he attributes this theory to Cluvier (*Commentaires sur l'ancienne Germanie*).

97. *Le spectacle de la nature ou entretiens sur les particularités de l'histoire naturelle* (Paris, 1752), vol. 5, p. 77.

98. *Histoire naturelle du genre humain, ou Recherches sur ses principaux fondemens physiques et moraux; précédées d'un Discours sur la nature des êtres organiques et sur l'ensemble de leur physiologie. On y a joint une Dissertation sur le sauvage de l'Aveyron* (Paris, an IX [1801]), vol. 2, pp. 40, 45.

99. *The New Science* (Cornell University Press, 1984), p. 517.

100. "Et en effet, pourquoi les Juifs n'auraient-ils pas été anthropophages? C'eût été la seule chose manqué au peuple de Dieu pour être le plus abominable peuple de la terre."

101. *Encyclopédie ou Dictionnaire raisonné des sciences, des arts et des métiers* (Paris, 1751), vol. 1, p. 498. "L'anthropophagie n'a point été le vice d'une contrée ou d'une nation, mais celui d'un siècle. Avant que les hommes eussent été adoucis par la naissance des Arts, & civilisés par l'imposition des lois, il paroît que la plupart des peuples mangeoient de la chair humaine. On dit qu'Orphée fut le premier qui fit sentir aux hommes l'inhumanité de cet usage, & qu'il parvint à l'abolir."

102. *Totem and Taboo* (London, 1999), pp. 1–2. For Freud's theory of primitive society, see Robert A. Paul, "Freud's Anthropology: A Reading of the 'Cultural Books,'" in J. Neu (ed.), *The Cambridge Companion to Freud* (Cambridge University Press, 1992).

103. *Totem and Taboo*, p. 141. See also Claude Rawson, "Unspeakable Rites: Cultural Reticence and the Cannibal Question," *Social Research*, vol. 66, no. 1 (spring 1999).

104. *Totem and Taboo*, p. 110.

105. Ibid., p. 141.

106. Ibid. On the sacrifice, see Colin Davis, "Fathers, Others: The Sacrificial Victim in Freud, Girard, and Levinas," *Cultural Values*, vol. 4, no. 2 (Apr. 2000); and Robert A. Paul, "Did the Primal Crime Take Place?" *Ethos*, vol. 4, no. 3 (autumn 1976).

107. *Totem and Taboo*, p. 142. On totemism, see Robert Alun Jones, *Secret of the Totem: Religion and Society from McLennan to Freud* (Columbia University Press, 2005).

108. *Totem and Taboo*, p. 145.

109. Ibid., p. 144.

CHAPTER 6 A QUESTION OF TASTE

1. On the "forbidden experiment," see Roger Shattuck, *The Forbidden Experiment: The Story of the Wild Boy of Aveyron* (Kodansha Globe, 1997).

2. *Histoire naturelle du genre humain, ou Recherches sur ses principaux fondemens physiques et moraux; précédées d'un Discours sur la nature des êtres organiques et sur l'ensemble de leur physiologie. On y a joint une Dissertation sur le sauvage de l'Aveyron* (Paris, an IX [1801]), vol. 2, p. 50.

3. "Of Custom, and that we should not easily change a Law received," *Montaigne's Essays*, trans. Charles Cotton (London, 1743), vol. 1, p. 110.

4. *Lectures on Jurisprudence*, ed. R. L. Meek, D. D. Raphael, and P. G. Stein (Oxford University Press, 1978), p. 334.

5. *Relation historique de l'Ethiopie Occidentale* (Paris, 1732), vol. 2, pp. 295–96. "Ils mangent des corps infectez de ces maux, ils boivent un sang corrompu; le leur ne doit-il pas contracter la même corruption."

6. *Histoire naturelle du genre humain, ou Recherches sur ses principaux fondemens physiques et moraux; précédées d'un Discours sur la nature des êtres organiques et sur l'ensemble de leur physiologie. On y a joint une Dissertation sur le sauvage de l'Aveyron* (Paris, an IX [1801]), vol. 1, p. 260.

7. *Recherches philosophiques sur les américains* (London, 1771), vol. 1, p. 193. ". . . ce qui paroît prouver que cette peste tire son origine de l'abus de manger des hommes."

8. Ibid., p. 193. ". . . à l'isle de S. Dominique, où les Naturels n'étoient pas Anthropophages, la contagion vénérienne sévissoit plus qu'ailleurs: ce qui ruine absolument cette hypothese, puisqu'en ce sens le siége, ou le principal foyer de la maladie, auroit dû être dans les Isles Caraïbes, & non dans les Antilles."

9. Jean Astruc (1684–1766), physician to the French court, published *De morbis veneris libri sex* (Paris, 1736). Astruc rejects Fioravanti's theory on p. 40.

10. *Recherches philosophiques sur les américains* (London, 1771), vol. 1, p. 194. "tous les animaux qui s'entredévorent, & qui sont Anthropophages dans leur espèce, ne souffrent rien de la qualité de cette nourriture si analogue à leur propre espèce." On the moral implications of such experiments, see Anita Guerrini, "The Ethics of Animal Experimentation in Seventeenth-Century England," *Journal of the History of Ideas*, vol. 50, no. 3 (Jul.–Sep. 1989).

11. See Richard J. Evans, *Rituals of Retribution: Capital Punishment in Germany, 1600–1987* (Oxford University Press, 1996), pp. 90–93. According to Evans, the custom was also practised in Denmark; however, in Catholic areas it was exceptional, such as at the execution of Louis XVI on the guillotine, when handkerchiefs, rags, and even a pair of dice were dipped in the royal blood. The origins of the ritual are unknown; rites in which the blood of a sacrificial victim is drunk are mentioned by Frazer in *The Golden Bough*; the latter also describes how the gall of executed bandits was eaten to give courage.

12. *Dissertations sur les Apparitions des Anges, des Démons & des Esprits, et sur les Revenans et Vampires de Hongrie, de Bohème, de Moravie, & de Silesie* (Paris, 1751), vol. 1, p. 466. See also Marie-Helene Huet, "Deadly Fears: Dom

Augustin Calmet's Vampires and the Rule over Death," *Eighteenth-Century Life*, vol. 21, no. 2 (May 1997).

13. *Histoire générale des Antilles habitées par les françois* (Paris, 1667), vol. 2, p. 389.

14. *An Essay on the Principle of Population; or, A View of its Past and Present Effects on Human Happiness*, 6th ed. (London, 1826), vol. 1, pp. 25, 47, 139, 167.

15. *De esu carnium*, 995d. *Moralia*, trans. Harlod Cherniss and William C. Helmbold (Harvard University Press, 1957), vol. 12, p. 555.

16. Porphyry, *De vita Pythagorae*, 43–44. *Porphyrii philosophi platonici Opuscula tria*, ed. August Nauk (Leipzig, 1860), pp. 31–32.

17. *De esu carnium*, 997e. *Moralia*, vol. 12, p. 569.

18. *Three Early Modern Utopias*, ed. Susan Bruce (Oxford University Press, 1999), p. 81.

19. *Of the Origin and Progress of Language* (Edinburgh, 1774), vol. 1, p. 396.

20. Ibid., pp. 396–97.

21. *Nouveau voyage de la Terre Australe, par Jacques Sadeur* (1693), pp. 125–26.

22. *Histoire universelle* (Paris, 1737), vol. 1, p. 18. "Ils alloient chacun de leur côté manger sans aprêt dans les champs les fruits & les herbes qui y naissant sans culture."

23. *First Treatise of Government*, cap. 4, 27, in *Two Treatises of Government* (London, 1824). For later developments, see Anita Guerrini, "A Diet for a Sensitive Soul: Vegetarianism in Eighteenth-Century Britain," *Eighteenth-Century Life*, vol. 23, no. 2 (May 1999).

24. *Discours sur l'origine & les fondements de l'inégalité parmi les hommes* (Amsterdam, 1755), p. 196. "Les Frugivores vivant entre eux dans une paix continuelle, il est clair qu'elle auroit eu beaucoup plus de facilité à subsister dans l'État de Nature, beaucoup moins de besoin & d'occasions d'en sortir."

25. Louis-Sébastian Mercier, *L'Homme Sauvage* (Neuchatel, 1784), p. 32. "Une herbe du bon goût, le fruit du cacoyer, des racines succulentes, quelquefois du gibier."

26. *Oeuvres complètes* (Paris, 1793), vol. 27, p. 259. "L'estomac ni les intestins de l'homme ne sont pas faits pour digérer de la chaire crue, en général son goût ne la supporte pas . . . les sauvages mêmes grillent leurs viandes. A l'usage du feu, nécessaire pour les cuire, se joint le plaisir qu'il donne à la vue, et sa chaleur agréable au corps. L'aspect de la flamme qui fait fuir les animaux, attire l'homme."

27. Jean Arbuthnot, *Essai sur la nature et le choix des alimens, suivant les différentes constitutions* (Paris, 1741).

28. *Émile, ou de l'Education* (Amsterdam, 1764) p. 286–87. "Des fruits, des herbes, & enfin quelques viandes grillées, sans assaisonnement & sans sel, firent les festins des premier hommes. . . . Conservons à l'enfant son goût primitif le plus qu'il est possible."

29. Ibid., p. 292. "Des nourritures végétales, telles que la laitage, la pâtisserie, les fruits, &c. Il importe sur tout de ne pas dénaturer ce goût primitif, & de ne point rendre les enfants carnassiers."

30. Ibid. "Cette observation est de touts les lieux & tous les temps: la barbarie Angloise est connue. . . . Tous les sauvages sont cruels . . . cette cruauté vient de leurs aliments. Ils vont à la guerre comme à la chasse, & traitent les hommes comme les ours. . . . Les grands scélérats s'endurcissent au meurtre en buvant du sang."

31. "Of Custom and Law," *Montaigne's Essays*, trans. Charles Cotton (London, 1743), vol. 1, p. 111.

32. *Of the Origin and Progress of Language*, 2d ed. (Edinburgh, 1774), vol. 1, pp. 224–26.

33. *The Tatler*, March 21, 1709. *The Tatler; corrected from the Originals*, ed. A. Chalmers (London, 1817), vol. 4, p. 19. See also Tristram Stuart, *The Bloodless Revolution. A Cultural History of Vegetarianism from 1600 to Modern Times* (W.W. Norton, 2007).

34. De Léry, *Histoire d'un voyage faict en la terre du Brésil* (Geneva, 1580), pp. 220–23.

35. *The History of Barbados, St Christophers, Mevis, St Vincents, Antego, Martinico, Monserrat, and the rest of the Caribby-Islands* (London, 1666), pp. 332–33.

36. *Histoire des avanturiers filibustiers, qui se sont signalez dans les Indes* (Paris, 1699), vol. 1, p. 465. "Les Crocodiles n'attaquent jamais les hommes blanc, pourveu qu'il y en ait de noirs avec eux."

37. *Of the Origin and Progress of Language*, 2d ed. (Edinburgh, 1774), vol. 1, p. 384.

38. "Du temps de Cromwell une chandelière de Dublin vendait d'excellentes chandelles faites avec de la graisse d'Anglais."

39. "Au bout de quelque temps un des ses chalands se plaignit de ce que sa chandelle n'était plus si bonne. 'Monsieur, lui dit elle, c'est que les Anglais nous ont manqué.'"

40. *The Life and Strange Surprizing Adventures of Robinson Crusoe of York, Mariner*, 3d ed. (London, 1719), p. 195

41. Ibid., pp. 146, 149.

42. *Occasional Reflections upon Several Subjects, with a Discourse about such Kind of Thoughts* (Oxford, 1848), p. 349.

43. Ibid., pp. 349–50.

44. Ibid., p. 350.

45. Ibid., p. 350.

46. See J. E. Tiles, *Moral Measures: An Introduction to Ethics East and West* (London, 2000), p. 1.

47. Herodotus, *Istorii*, ed. and trans. Adelina Piatkowski and Felicia Ştef, 4 vols., bilingual ed. (Bucharest: Teora, 1998–99), III, 38; On Herodotus, see François Hartog, *The Mirror of Herodotus: The Representation of the Other in the Writing of History* (University of California Press, 1988); see also Richard Handler, "Of Cannibals and Custom: Montaigne's Cultural Relativism," *Anthropology Today*, vol. 2, no. 5 (Oct. 1986).

48. *Le spectacle de la nature ou entretiens sur les particularitès de l'histoire naturelle* (Paris, 1752), vol. 5, p. 77.

49. *An Essay Concerning Human Understanding* (Oxford University Press, 1979), I, 2, 4. On the debate around innate ideas, see, inter alia, Douglas Greenlee, "Locke and the Controversy over Innate Ideas," *Journal of the History of Ideas*, vol. 33, no. 2 (Apr.–Jun. 1972).

50. *An Essay Concerning Human Understanding*, I, 2, 27.

51. Ibid., I, 3, 2.

52. Ibid., I, 3, 9.

53. Ibid., I, 3, 9.

54. *La Philosophie du bon-sens, ou réflexions philosophiques sur l'incertitude des conoissances humaines, à la usage des Cavaliers & du Beau-Sexe* (The Hague, 1746), vol. 2, p. 9. Chapter 3, "'Qu'il n'est aucune règle de Morale qui soit innée.' Les Caribes engraissent leurs enfans pour les manger. . . . Plusiers peuples du Pérou font leurs concubines des femmes qu'ils prennent à la guerre; ils nourissent délicatement jusqu' à treize ans les enfans qu'ils en ont, & les mangent alors. . . . Les Druses, peuple du Mont Liban, épousent leurs propres filles."

55. Ibid., p. 12.

56. *Histoire des avanturiers filibustiers* (Paris, 1690), vol. 2, pp. 318–19. "Ainsi les Indiens ont leurs coûtumes, qui ne doivent pas nous sembler plus estranges."

57. Le Baron de Grimm and Denis Diderot, *Correspondance littéraire, philosophique et critique, adressée à un Souverain d'Allemagne* (Paris, 1813), vol. 2, p. 468. "Nous les appelons Sauvages, parce que leurs moeurs diffèrent des nôtres, et que nous regardons nos moeurs comme la perfection de la politesse. Ils ont précisément la même opinion des leurs."

58. *Robinson Crusoe*, p. 202.

59. Ibid.

60. *Against the Ethicists*, trans. Richard Bett (Oxford University Press, 1997), pp. 37–41. On Sextus and scepticism, see Alan Bailey, *Sextus Empiricus and Pyrrhonean Skepticism* (Oxford, 2002). On the connections between scepticism and Montaigne, see William M. Hamlin, "On Continuities between Skepticism and Early Ethnography; Or, Montaigne's Providential Diversity," *Sixteenth Century Journal*, vol. 31, no. 2 (summer 2000); and Zachary S. Schiffman, "Montaigne and the Rise of Skepticism in Early Modern Europe: A Reappraisal," *Journal of the History of Ideas*, vol. 45, no. 4 (Oct.–Dec. 1984); see also Luciano Floridi, "The Diffusion of Sextus Empiricus's Works in the Renaissance," *Journal of the History of Ideas*, vol. 56, no. 1 (Jan. 1995); and Richard H. Popkin, "Sources of Knowledge of Sextus Empiricus in Hume's Time," *Journal of the History of Ideas*, vol. 54, no. 1 (Jan. 1993).

61. *Against the Ethicists*, p. 69.

62. Ibid., p. 72.

63. Ibid., pp. 193–94.

64. Ibid., pp. 195–96.

65. Ibid., p. 118. On the connection between natural law theories and scepticism, see J. B. Schneewind, "Natural Law, Skepticism, and Methods of Ethics," *Journal of the History of Ideas*, vol. 52, no. 2 (Apr.–Jun. 1991).

66. *Montaigne's Essays*, trans. Charles Cotton (London, 1743), vol. 1, p. 118.

67. Ibid., p. 115.

68. Ibid., pp. 117–18.

69. Ibid., "Of the Education of Children," p. 170.

70. Ibid., p. 170.

71. Ibid., p. 171.

72. Ibid., "Of Cannibals," p. 233.

73. John Austin, *The Province of Jurisprudence Determined* (London, 1832), p. 107. On Austin, see Wilfrid E. Rumble, *The Thought of John Austin: Jurisprudence, Colonial Reform, and the British Constitution* (Dover, NH, 1985); and Constance I. Smith, "Locke and John Austin on the Idea of Morality," *Journal of the History of Ideas*, vol. 23, no. 1 (Jan.–Mar. 1962).

CHAPTER 7 THE ANTHROPOPHAGUS IN THE CITY

1. Quoted in Isaac Kramnick, "An Augustan Reply to Locke: Bolingbroke on Natural Law and the Origin of Government," Political Science Quarterly, vol. 82, no. 4 (Dec. 1967), p. 577. See also A. John Simmons, "Locke's State of Nature," *Political Theory*, vol. 17, no. 3 (Aug. 1989), on the erroneous belief that Locke's theory of the state of nature excludes social organization.

2. Thomas Hobbes, *The Questions Concerning Liberty, Necessity, and Chance Clearly Stated and Debated* (London, 1656), 139; see also Gordon J. Schochet, who writes that for Hobbes, "the state of nature no longer appears to have been altogether individualistic; rather it was composed of familial social units that faced each other as autonomous entities" ("Thomas Hobbes on the Family and the State of Nature," *Political Science Quarterly*, vol. 82, no. 3 [Sep. 1967], p. 442). A reading of Hobbes's arguments in the context of the influence of patriarchalism is Richard Allen Chapman, "Leviathan Writ Small: Thomas Hobbes on the Family," American Political Science Review, vol. 69, no. 1 (Mar. 1975).

3. See, for instance, Aristotle, *The Politics and the Constitution*, ed. Stephen Everson (Cambridge University Press, 1996), 1253b1: "Seeing then that the state is made up of households, before speaking of the state we must speak of the management of the household." Departures from this standard view were rather rare; for one example, see Cary J. Nederman, "Private Will, Public Justice: Household, Community, and Consent in Marsiglio of Padua's Defensor Pacis," *Western Political Quarterly*, vol. 43, no. 4 (Dec. 1990). See also T. R. Stevenson, "The Ideal Benefactor and the Father Analogy in Greek and Roman Thought," *Classical Quarterly*, n.s., vol. 42, no. 2 (1992).

4. *Three Early Modern Utopias*, ed. Susan Bruce (Oxford University Press, 1999), p. 69.

5. "une patrie est un composé de plusiers familles." *Dictionnaire philosophique* (London, 1745), p. 279.

6. "Adam and the patriarchs who had absolute power of life and death . . . within their houses or familie. . . . All the duties of a king are summed up in an universal fatherly care of his people," in Filmer, *Patriarcha and Other Political Works* (Oxford, 1949), pp. 63, 76. Numerous authors, from Bodin to Bossuet,

made similar claims. See also Mark Hullilung, "Patriarchalism and Its Enemies," *Political Theory*, vol. 2, no. 4 (Nov. 1974).

7. See Gordon J. Scochet, *Patriarchalism in Political Thought: The Authoritarian Family and Political Speculation and Attitudes, especially in Seventeenth-Century England* (New York, 1975); and Mark Hulliung, "Patriarchalism and Its Early Enemies," *Political Theory*, vol. 2, no. 4 (Nov. 1974); the social background of the doctrines on patriarchal power is discussed by Gordon J. Schochet, "Patriarchalism, Politics, and Mass Attitudes in Stuart England," *Historical Journal*, vol. 12, no. 3 (1969); Steven Ozment, *When Fathers Ruled: Family Life in Reformation Europe* (Harvard, 1983); and Alan Macfarlane, *Marriage and Love in England: Modes of Reproduction 1300–1800* (Oxford, 1987).

8. *The six bookes of a common-weale* (London, 1606), p. 1. See also Henry Heller, "Bodin on Slavery and Primitive Accumulation," *Sixteenth Century Journal*, vol. 25, no. 1 (spring 1994).

9. On the Roman and Greek practices of child exposure, the most extreme manifestation of patrimonial power, see W. V. Harris, "Child-Exposure in the Roman Empire," *Journal of Roman Studies*, vol. 84 (1994). See also Antti Arjava, "Paternal Power in Late Antiquity," *Journal of Roman Studies*, vol. 88 (1998).

10. *The History of Barbados* (London, 1666), pp. 328–29.

11. *Relation historique de l'Ethiopie occidentale* (Paris, 1732), vol. 2, p. 294. "On leur ouvre le ventre, on arrache ces petites créatures qui n'ont pas encore vû le jour; on les devore: c'est, pour ces inhumaines, un morceau délicat."

12. *Oeuvres* (Dresden, 1756), vol. 5, part 1, p. 158.

13. *An Inquiry into the Nature and Causes of the Wealth of Nations* (Oxford University Press, 1976), vol. 1, pp. 88–90.

14. *Histoire naturelle et morale des Iles Antilles de l'Amerique* (Rotterdam, 1658), p. 488.

15. Charles D. Tarlton, "A Rope of Sand: Interpreting Locke's First Treatise of Government," *Historical Journal*, vol. 21, no. 1 (Mar. 1978), defends the *First Treatise* as being of wider significance that the criticism of Filmer.

16. Sir Robert Filmer, *Patriarcha and Other Writings* (Cambridge University Press, 1991), p. 237. On Filmer's theory of the descent from Adam, its sources and significance, see W. H. Greenleaf, "Filmer's Patriarchal History," *Historical Journal*, vol. 9, no. 2 (1966).

17. *First Treatise of Government*, in *Two Treatises of Government* (London, 1824). I, 9.

18. *Second Treatise of Government*, II, 56. See also Iain W. Hampsher-Monk, "Tacit Concept of Consent in Locke's Two Treatises of Government: A Note on Citizens, Travellers, and Patriarchalism," *Journal of the History of Ideas*, vol. 40, no. 1 (Jan.–Mar. 1979); and Melissa A. Butler, "Early Liberal Roots of Feminism: John Locke and the Attack on Patriarchy," *American Political Science Review*, vol. 72, no. 1 (Mar. 1978).

19. *A Methodical System of Universal Law: or, the Laws of Nature and Nations deduced from certain Principles, and applied to Proper Cases* (London, 1763), vol. 2, pp. 48–49.

20. A discussion of Bodin and Hobbes is Preston King, *The Ideology of Order: A Comparative Analysis of Jean Bodin and Thomas Hobbes* (Routledge, 1999).

21. "liberi subjiciuntur patribus, non minus quam servi dominis et cives civitati." *De cive,* in *Opera Philosophica quae Latine scripsit Omnia,* ed. William Molesworth, vol. 2 (London: John Bohn, 1839), chap. 9.

22. A feminist perspective on the relation between Hobbes and patriarchalism is Carole Pateman, "'God Hath Ordained to Man a Helper': Hobbes, Patriarchy, and Conjugal Right," *British Journal of Political Science,* vol. 19, no. 4 (Oct. 1989); the connection between passion and right in the context of seventeenth-century theories of family is analyzed in Victoria Kahn, "'The Duty to Love': Passion and Obligation in Early Modern Political Theory," *Representations,* no. 68 (autumn 1999).

23. *De cive:* "Filium in statu naturali intellegi non posse, ut qui, simul atque natus est, in potestate et sub imperio est ejus cui debet conservationem sui: scilicet, matris, vel patris, vel ejus qui praebet ipsi alimenta; ut capite nono demonstratum est."

24. On the evolution of Western conceptions on the nature of family, see Roderick Phillips, *Putting Asunder: A History of Divorce in Western Society* (Cambridge University Press, 1988); on the rise of the contractualist idea of family, see Mary Lyndon Shanley, "Marriage Contract and Social Contract in Seventeenth-Century English Political Thought," *Western Political Quarterly,* vol. 32, no. 1 (Mar. 1979).

25. On the history of the concept and institution of slavery, see Robin Blackburn, *The Making of New World Slavery. From the Baroque to the Modern Age* (London, 1997); M. L. Bush, *Servitude in Modern Times* (New York, 2000); David Brion Davis, *The Problem of Slavery in Western Culture* (Oxford University Press, 1988); William D. Phillips, *Slavery from Roman Times to the Early Trans-Atlantic Trade* (Minneapolis, 1995); and William L. Westermann, *The Slave Systems of Greek and Roman Antiquity* (Philadelphia, 1955).

26. On the conception of the Stagirite regarding slavery, see Wayne Ambler, "Aristotle on Nature and Politics: The Case of Slavery," *Political Theory,* vol. 15, no. 3 (Aug. 1987).

27. *Politics,* 1265b25.

28. See Glenn Burgess, "The Divine Right of Kings Reconsidered," *English Historical Review,* vol. 107, no. 425 (Oct. 1992):

29. The concept of "Oriental despotism" is studied by Karl A. Wittfogel, "Results and Problems of the Study of Oriental Despotism," *Journal of Asian Studies,* vol. 28, no. 2 (Feb. 1969); see also Eric Voegelin's *Order and History,* in *Collected Works* (University of Missouri Press, 2001); Thomas Kaiser, "The Evil Empire? The Debate on Turkish Despotism in Eighteenth-Century French Political Culture," *Journal of Modern History,* vol. 72, no. 1, *New Work on the Old Regime and the French Revolution: A Special Issue in Honor of François Furet.* (Mar. 2000); Joan-Pau Rubiés, "Oriental Despotism and European Orientalism: Botero to Montesquieu," *Journal of Early Modern History,* vol. 9, no. 1–2 (2005); and Asli Çirakman, "From Tyranny to Despotism: The Enlightenment's

Unenlightened Image of the Turks," *International Journal of Middle East Studies*, vol. 33, no. 1 (Feb. 2001).

30. André Thévet, *Les singularités de la France antarctique, autrement nommée Amerique, & de plusiers Terres & Isles découvertes de notre temps* (Paris, 1558), p. 29.

31. The text of the edict is given in William D. Phillips, *Slavery from Roman Times to the Early Transatlantic Trade* (Minneapolis, 1985), p. 27.

32. *Moeurs des sauvages Amériquains, Comparées aux moeurs des premiers temps* (Paris, 1724), vol. 2, p. 307. "Barbarie que j'avouë être sans égale, audessus de laquelle rien ne peut aller, & qui met le comble à la brutalité de ces Anthropophages."

33. P. de Charlevoix, *Histoire et description generale de la nouvelle France avec le journal historique d'un voyage fait par ordre du Roi dans l'Amérique Septentrionale* (Paris, 1744) p. 34. "Son corps fut ensuite coupé par morceaux, qu'on fut manger aux Esclaves."

34. *An Essay of the Principle of Population*, 6th ed. (1826), vol. 2, pp. 50–51.

35. The literature on the topic of Just War is considerable and expanding; see, inter alia, J. T. Johnson, *The Just War Tradition and the Restraint of War* (Princeton University Press, 1981); and Michael Walzer, *Just and Unjust Wars: A Moral Argument with Historical Illustrations*, 3rd ed. (New York, 2000).

36. *De cive*, 8, 10. "Eodem modo acquiritur jus in animalia ratione carentia, quo in personas hominum; nimirum viribus et potentiis naturalibus."

37. Ibid. "Siquidem enim in statu naturali, propter bellum, omnium in omnes, subjugare vel etiam occidere homines cuique licitum sit, quoties id suo bono conducere videbitur; multo magis idem licitum erit adversus belluas."

38. *History of Barbados* (London, 1666), p. 326.

39. *Histoire des Yncas, Rois de Perou* (Amsterdam, 1704), vol. 1, pp. 50–51.

40. Ibid., pp. 44–45.

41. *Relation historique de l'Ethiopie* occidentale (Paris, 1732), vol. 2, pp. 292–93. "Si on trouve du sang liquide dans quelques uns, on le boit à longs traits . . . mais si tout le sang est déja coagulé, ils s'en frottent tout le corps . . . ils sont un sabat effroyable: les bètes féroces les plus affamées, n'oferoient en approcher . . . ils cassent les os, pour sucer la moëlle. . . . Cinq hommes des plus fortes, prenent celui qu'ils veulent tuer, par les pieds, par les bras, par la tête; & pendant qu'un sixiéme donne quelques coups de haches sur les jointures, ils tirent ce corps de toutes leurs forces, le déchirent, & le démembrent; & chacun emporte le morceau qui lui est échû."

42. G. T. Raynal, *Histoire philosophique et politique des établissemens et du commerce des Européens dans les deux Indes* (Geneva, 1780), p. 29. "Le sort des prisonniers de guerre a suivi les différens âges de la raison. Les nations les plus policées les rançonnent, les échangent ou les restituent, lorsque la paix a succédé aux hostilités. Les peuples à demi barbares se les approprient et les réduisent en esclavage. Les sauvages ordinaires les massacrent, sans les tormenter. Les plus sauvages des hommes les tourmentent, les égorgent et les mangent: c'est leur exécrable droit des gens."

43. *The Six Bookes of a Commonweale* (London, 1606), p. 35.

44. *Two Treatises of Government* (London, 1824), II, 85. On Locke's attitudes toward slavery, see James Farr, "'So Vile and Miserable an Estate': The Problem of Slavery in Locke's Political Thought," *Political Theory*, vol. 14, no. 2 (May 1986). Lockean arguments resurfaced as late as the nineteenth century in the debate on American slavery; see Robert J. Loewenberg, "John Locke and the Antebellum Defense of Slavery," *Political Theory*, vol. 13, no. 2 (May 1985).

45. *Two Treatises of Government*, II, 23.

46. Ibid., II, 172.

47. Ibid., II, 91.

48. Ibid., II, 137. On the significance of Locke's theory, see Robert A. Goldwin, "Locke's State of Nature in Political Society," *Western Political Quarterly*, vol. 29, no. 1 (Mar. 1976).

49. *De l'esprit des lois* (Paris, 1834), book 15, cap. 2, "Origine du droit de l'esclavage chez les jurisonsultes romains." An analysis in Diana J. Schaub, "Montesquieu on Slavery," *Perspectives on Political Science*, vol. 34, no. 2 (spring 2005).

50. *The Social Contract*, trans. Maurice Cranston (Harmondsworth, 1968), p. 51.

51. Ibid., p. 54.

52. Jacobi, letter to La Harpe, 5 May 1790, quoted in Luc Ferry and Claudine Germé, eds., *Des animaux et des hommes* (Paris, 1994), p. 391.

53. See, inter alia, Stephen R. Haynes, *Noah's Curse: The Biblical Justification of American Slavery* (Oxford University Press, 2002).

54. See Allen H. Gilbert, *Machiavelli's Prince and its Forerunners: The Prince as a Typical Book* de Regimine Principum (New York, 1968).

55. On ideas of tyranny, see Roger Boesche, *Theories of Tyranny from Plato to Arendt* (Pennsylvania State University Press, 1995); and Sian Lewis, ed., *Ancient Tyranny* (Edinburgh University Press, 2006).

56. See J. L. Stocks, "Plato and the Tripartite Soul," *Mind*, n.s., vol. 24, no. 94 (Apr. 1915).

57. *Republic*, 575a, in *Opera*, ed. John Burnet, vol. 4 (Oxford: Clarendon Press, 1978).

58. Ibid., 576b. "ton kakiston. estin de pou, hoion onar diêlthomen, hos an hupar toioutos êi."

59. Ibid., 578b.

60. Ibid., 579a–b.

61. Ibid., 565e–566a. "All' adikôs epaitiômenos, hoia dê philousin, eis dikastêria agôn miaiphonêi, bion andros aphanizôn, glottêi te kai stomati anosiôi geuomenos phonou sungenous, kai andrêlatêi kai apokteinuêi kai huposêmainêi chrêon te apokopas kai gês anadasmon, ara tôi toioutôi anankê dê to meta touto kai heimartai ê apolôlenai hupo tôn echthrôn ê turannein kai lukôi ex anthrôpou genesthai?"

62. On *miasma*, see Margaret Visser, "Vengeance and Pollution in Classical Athens," *Journal of the History of Ideas*, vol. 45, no. 2 (Apr.–Jun. 1984). The politics of strong emotions in Plato is studied by Christina Tarnopolsky, "Prudes, Perverts, and Tyrants: Plato and the Contemporary Politics of Shame," *Political Theory*, vol. 32, no. 4 (Aug. 2004).

63. *De officiis*, trans. Walter Miller (Harvard University Press, 1913), III, 32. "Etenim, ut membra quaedam amputantur, si et ipsa sanguine et tamquam spiritu carere coeperunt et nocent reliquis partibus corporis; sic ista, in figura hominis, feritas et immanitas beluae a communi tamquam humanitatis corpora segreganda est."

64. *The Six Bookes of a Commonweale* (London, 1606), p. 212.

65. Algernon Sidney, *Court Maxims* (Cambridge University Press, 1996), p. 11.

66. *Two Treatises of Government*, II, 93.

67. Ibid., II, 228.

68. Jean-Vincent Gravina, *L'Esprit des loix romanes* (Amsterdam, 1766), pp. 332–33.

69. John Trenchard and Thomas Gordon, *Cato's Letters, or Essays on Liberty, Civil and Religious, and other Important Subjects* (Indianapolis, 1995). Letter no. 72, dated April 7, 1722.

70. G. T. Raynal, *Histoire philosophique et politique des établissemens et du commerce des Européens dans les deux Indes* (Paris, 1820), vol. 5, p. 24. "Quand vous aurez autorisé l'homme à manger la chair de l'homme, si son palais y trouve la saveur, il ne vous restera plus qu'à rendre la vapeur du sang agréable à l'oderat des tyrans."

71. See Chantal Thomas, *The Wicked Queen: The Origins of the Myth of Marie Antoinette* (New York, 1999), pp. 126, 132.

72. *De ira*, II, 7–8, in in *Opera Philosophica*, ed. Emil Ferdinand Vogel (Leipzig: Nauck, 1830). "Inter istos quos togatos vides, nulla pax est: alter in alterius exitium levi compendio ducitur. Nulli nisi ex alterius damno quaestus est; felicem oderunt, infelicem contemnunt: maiore gravantur, minori graves sunt . . . omnia perdita ob levem voluptatem praedamque cupiunt. Non alia quam in ludo gladiatorio vita est, cum iisdem viventium pugnantiumque. Ferarum iste conventus est: nisi quod illae inter se placidae sunt morsuque similium abstinent, hi mutua laceratione satiantur. Hoc uno ab animalibus mutis differunt: quod illa manuescunt alentibus, horum rabies ipsos, a quibus est nutrita, depascitur."

73. Quoted in J. F. C. Fuller, *The Conduct of War, 1789–1961* (New York, 1992).

74. On the French critics of despotism and the theories of population decline, see David B. Young, "Libertarian Demography: Montesquieu's Essay on Depopulation in the Lettres Persanes," *Journal of the History of Ideas*, vol. 36, no. 4 (Oct.–Dec. 1975); the connection between morals and science of population is discussed in Sylvana Tomaselli, "Moral Philosophy and Population Questions in Eighteenth Century Europe," *Population and Development Review*, vol. 14, *Supplement: Population and Resources in Western Intellectual Traditions* (1988).

75. On perceptions of the Irish, see Kathleen M. Noonan, "'The Cruell Pressure of an Enraged, Barbarous People': Irish and English Identity in Seventeenth-Century Policy and Propaganda," *Historical Journal*, vol. 41, no. 1 (Mar. 1998); on the Irish vs. Indians, see Ronald Takaki, "The *Tempest* in the Wilderness: The Racialization of Savagery," *Journal of American History*, vol. 79, no. 3, *Discovering America: A Special Issue* (Dec. 1992).

76. For a reading of Swift in the context of the population theories of the period, see Peter M. Briggs, "John Graunt, Sir William Petty, and Swift's Modest Proposal," *Eighteenth-Century Life*, vol. 29, no. 2 (spring 2005). For an analysis of the sources of Swift's pamphlet, see Claude Rawson, "'Indians' and Irish: Montaigne, Swift, and the Cannibal Question," *Modern Language Quarterly*, vol. 53, no. 3 (Sep. 1992).

77. See Ian Campbell Ross, "'A Very Knowing American': The Inca Garcilaso de la Vega and Swift's Modest Proposal," *Modern Language Quarterly*, vol. 68, no. 4 (Dec. 2007).

78. See Robert Mahoney, "The Irish Colonial Experience and Swift's Rhetorics of Perception in the 1720s," *Eighteenth-Century Life*, vol. 22, no. 1 (Feb. 1998).

79. *L'Homme aux quarante écus* (Geneva, 1768), p. 17. "Il y aurait le double de pauvres; ou qu'il faudrait avoir le double d'industrie & gagner le double sur l'étranger; ou envoyer la moitié de la nation en Amerique; ou que la moitié de la nation mangeât l'autre." The success of Voltaire's book was sensational: ten editions in one year, condemned by Parliament in 1768, and placed on the Index in 1771.

80. "Il est arrivé aux hommes ce qui arrive aujourd'hui aux éléphants, aux lions, aux tigres dont l'espèce a beaucoup diminué. Dans les temps où une contrée était peu peuplée d'hommes, ils avaient peu d'arts, ils étaient chasseurs. L'habitude de se nourrir de ce qu'ils avaient tué, fit aisément qu'ils traitèrent leurs ennemis comme leurs cerfs et leurs sangliers. C'est la superstition qui a fait immoler des victimes humaines, c'est la nécessité qui les a fait manger."

81. *The Social Contract*, trans. Maurice Cranston (Harmondsworth, 1968), p. 129.

82. *Histoire naturelle du genre humain, ou Recherches sur ses principaux fondemens physiques et moraux; précédées d'un Discours sur la nature des êtres organiques et sur l'ensemble de leur physiologie. On y a joint une Dissertation sur le sauvage de l'Aveyron* (Paris, an IX [1801]), vol. 1, pp. 100–101.

83. *Essay on the Principle of Population*, in *The Works of Thomas Robert Malthus*, vol. 1, (London 1986). On the development of the theories of population, see Philip Kreager, "Early Modern Population Theory: A Reassessment," *Population and Development Review*, vol. 17, no. 2 (Jun. 1991). On Malthus, see Patricia James, *Population Malthus: His Life and Times* (Routledge, 1979).

84. *Essay on the Principle of Population*, vol. 1, p. 66.

85. In the modern city, there is also the option of consuming the animals of the public zoo; see Rebecca L. Spang, "'And They Ate the Zoo': Relating Gastronomic Exoticism in the Siege of Paris," *MLN*, vol. 107, no. 4, French Issue (Sep. 1992).

86. On the imagery of hunger, see, inter alia, Piero Camporesi, *Bread of Dreams: Food and Fantasy in Early Modern Europe* (University of Chicago Press, 1995).

87. Cf. Frank Lestringant, *Cannibals: The Discovery and Representation of the Cannibal from Columbus to Jules Verne* (University of California Press, 1997).

88. Isaac de la Peyrere, *Rélation d'Islande* (Paris, 1663), pp. 23–24. "Des filles qui sont fort beles dans cete Isle, mais fort mal vestües, vont voir ces Allemans; & ofrent à ceux qui n'ont pas de fame, de coucher auec eux, pour du pain, pour du biscuit, & pour quelqu'autre chose de peu de valeur. Les Peres mesmes presantent leurs filles aux Estrangers."

89. John Shefferius, *The History of Lapland* (Oxford, 1674), p. 61.

90. *An Account of Denmark, as it was in the Year 1692* (London, 1738), p. 57. On English reactions on the reality of poverty in the seventeenth century, see Lotte Mulligan and Judith Richards, "A 'Radical' Problem: The Poor and the English Reformers in the Mid-Seventeenth Century," *Journal of British Studies*, vol. 29, no. 2 (Apr. 1990).

91. Malthus, *Essay on the Principle of Population*, vol. 1, p. 50.

92. See Jeremy Waldron, *God, Locke, and Equality: Christian Foundation in Locke's Political Thought* (Cambridge University Press, 2002)

93. See, inter alia, Thomas A. Fudge, "'Neither mine nor thine': Communist Experiments in Hussite Bohemia," *Canadian Journal of History*, vol. 33, no. 1 (Apr. 1998); Edward L. Surtz, *The Praise of Pleasure: Philosophy, Education, and Communism in More's Utopia* (Cambridge University Press, 1957).

94. William Arens, *The Man-Eating Myth: Anthropology and Anthropophagy* (Oxford University Press, 1980), p. 27. The idea of cannibals' unusual longevity has ancient origins. Ktesias of Knidus claims that the cynocephali live between 150 and 200 years.

95. *Les Voyages de Jean Struys en Muscovie, en Tartarie, en Perse & en plusieurs autres Pays étrangers* (Lyon, 1682), vol. 3, p. 369. "Ils ne possedent rien en propre & ce qu'ils volent aux Etrangers ils le portent de bonne foi dans la masse commune ou ils ont tous le même droit." For egalitarianism and anarchy in the savage societies of the New World, see, inter alia, Janet Whatley, "Savage Hierarchies: French Catholic Observers of the New World," *Sixteenth Century Journal*, vol. 17, no. 3 (autumn 1986); Henry S. Baudet, *Paradise on Earth. Some Thoughts on European Images of Non-European Man* (Yale University Press, 1965).

96. *Montaigne's Essays*, trans. Charles Cotton, 6th ed. (London, 1743), pp. 238–39. See also Michael Wintroub, "Civilizing the Savage and Making a King: The Royal Entry Festival of Henri II (Rouen, 1550)," *Sixteenth Century Journal*, vol. 29, no. 2 (summer 1998).

97. *Histoire Philosophique et politique des établissemens et du commerce des Européens dans les deux Indes* (Paris, 1820), vol. 8, pp. 111–12. "Tous les hommes parlent de la liberté; les sauvages seul la possèdent. Ce n'est pas simplement la nation entière, c'est l'individu qui est vraiment libre. Le sentiment de son indépendance agit sur toutes ses pensées, sur toutes ses actions. . . . Il ne pourrait qu'haïr un maître et le tuer."

98. On Lahontan and Gaudeville, see Jonathan Irvine Israel, *Radical Enlightenment: Philosophy and the Formation of Modernity, 1650–1750* (Oxford University Press, 2001), pp. 579–82. On French representations of New World Indians in the Enlightenment, see Cornelius J. Jaenen, "'Les Sauvages Ameriquains': Persistence into the 18th Century of Traditional French Concepts and

Constructs for Comprehending Amerindians," *Ethnohistory*, vol. 29, no. 1 (winter 1982).

99. Charles de Rochefort, *Histoire naturelle et morale des Iles Antille*, pp. 405, 401, 442, 491.

100. *Discours sur l'origine et les fondamens de l'inegalié parmi les hommes* (Amsterdam, 1755), p. 5. "Tous, parlant sans cesse de besoin, d'avidité, d'oppression, de désirs, & d'orgueil, ont transposé à l'état de Nature, des idées qu'ils avoient prises dans la société; ils parloient de l'Homme Sauvage, & ils peignoient l'homme Civil."

101. Ibid., p. 6. "Commençons donc par écarter tous les faits, car ils ne touchent point à la question." On the significance of the theory of the state of nature in Rousseau, see John T. Scott, "The Theodicy of the Second Discourse: The 'Pure State of Nature' and Rousseau's Political Thought," *American Political Science Review*, vol. 86, no. 3 (Sep. 1992).

102. *Discours sur l'origine et les fondamens*, p. 29. " boivent les Liqueurs Européenes comme de l'eau." On the background of the European perceptions on alcohol consumption in Amerindian societies, see Frederick H. Smith, "European Impressions of the Island Carib's Use of Alcohol in the Early Colonial Period," *Ethnohistory*, vol. 53, no. 3 (summer 2006), pp. 543–66.

103. *Discours sur l'origine et les fondamens*, p. 209. "monstrueux mélanges des alimens."

104. Ibid., p. 210. "La Nature nous fait payer cher le mépris que nous avons fait de ses leçons."

105. Ibid., p. 211. "Soit par ces goûts brutaux & dépravés qui insultent son plus charmant ouvrage, goûts que les Sauvages ni les animaux ne connurent jamais."

106. *Recueil des pièces curieuses sur les matières les plus interesantes* (London, 1749), p. 189.

107. Ibid. "Tous les biens appartiennent à la Republique, et qu'elle, comme bonne Mère de ses Peuples, les dispense à chacun suivant le besoin qu'il en a; De cette manière personne ne sera reduit à la mendicité, & personne n'aüira du superflu. Selon ces maxims on peut établir & conserver un Gouvernement Populaire; Mais si on ne les fuit pas, & qu'on permette dans la Société l'Introduction de ces parloes Meum & tuum, sa ruine est inévitable. C'est pourquoi l'on ne doit jamais tolerer ces expressions; Mon bien, mon Père, ma Mère, mes Enfans, mes Frères, & mes Soeurs, parce qu'elles sont incompatibles avec la Nature du Gouvernement Democratique."

108. *Histoire des avanturiers filibustiers* (Paris, 1699), vol. 1, pp. 173. "Quand deux d'entr'eux rencontrent une belle femme; pour éviter la contestation qu'elle seroit naître, ils jettent à croix pile à qui se sort échoit l'épouse, ensuite ils couchant tous deux alternitivement avec elle." Exquemelin explains the origin of the word *buccaneer* as originating from the Caribs' practice of chopping up their prisoners of war and smoking [*boucaner*] their flesh; the buccaneers are supposed to have done to animals "what the Indians did to people" ("ils font aux animaux, ce que les Indiens font aux hommes," see pp. 101–2).

109. See Christopher Hill, *Liberty against the Law* (London, 1996), p. 119, and Christopher Hill, "Radical Pirates?" in Margaret Jacob and James Jacob (eds), *The Origins of Anglo-American Radicalism* (London, 1984).

110. On communist utopias in Russian folklore, see Richard Stites, *Revolutionary Dreams: Utopian Vision and Experimental Life in the Russian Revolution* (New York, 1989), pp. 15–16.

111. *Recherches philosophiques sur le droit de propriété considéré dans la nature, pour servir de premier chapitre à la* Théorie des loix *de M. Linguet. Par un jeune philosophe* ([Paris], 1780), pp. 65–66. "Oui, l'homme, les animaux, tous les corps dans la nature ont droit sur tout. Ils ont droit les uns sur les autres. L'homme a droit sur le boeuf, le boeuf sur l'herbe, l'herbe sur l'homme. C'est un combat de propriétés, qui sembleroit tender à la destruction de la nature, mais qui la vivifie, la renouvelle, en détruisant ses formes." On Brissot de Warville, see Robert Darnton, "The Brissot Dossier," *French Historical Studies*, vol. 17, no. 1 (spring 1991).

112. *Histoire naturelle, générale et particulière* (Paris, 1758), vol. 7, p. 7. "Ainsi la mort violente est une usage presque aussi nécessaire que la loi de la mort naturelle; ce sont deux moyens de destruction & de renouvellement, dont l'un sert à entretenir la jeunesse perpétuelle de la Nature, & dont l'autre maintient l'ordre de ses productions, & peut seul limiter le nombre dans les espèces."

113. Ibid., p. 66. "Les hommes doivent-ils se nourrir simplement de végétaux Peuvent-ils se nourrir de leurs semblables? Les animaux, les végétaux ont-ils le meme droit sur nous? Jusqu'où doit s'étendre la propriété des êtres?"

114. Ibid., pp. 66–67. "Je n'ai qu'un seul mot pour résoudre ces questions, qui paroissent si problématiques; & ce mot est dicté par la nature meme: Les êtres ont droit de se nourrir de toute matiere propre à satisfaire leurs besoins."

115. Ibid., p. 72. "Tous les êtres ont une répugnance invincible à déchirer, à dévorer ceux de leur espece."

116. Ibid., p. 73–74. "Je le conduirois chez les anthropophages; & là, spectateur de ces festins de chair humaine, où la gaeté même préside, je lui demanderois ce qu'est devenue dans tous ces êtres, cette répugnance prétendue pour la chair de leurs semblables. . . . Je le conduirois enfin chez ces Caraïbes, qui n'ont aucune repugnance à dévorer les membres encore palpitans de leurs enfans qu'ils ont engraissés."

117. Ibid., p. 74. "Tandis que ces sauvages anthropophages, qui ne sont point gâtés par nos institutions sociales, ne sont que suivre l'impulsion de la nature?"

118. Ibid., p. 86. "Point de propriété exclusive dans la nature. Ce mot est rayé de son code."

119. Ibid., p. 87. "La faim, voilà son titre. Citoyens depravés, montrez un titre plus puissant." Warville may have been inspired by Beccaria's treatise on crimes and punishment. Beccaria, discussing theft and the right of property, argues that the latter is "a terrible right, which is perhaps not necessary." *Traité des délits et des peines* (Philadelphia, 1765), p. 107. Le droit de propriété (droit terrible, et qui n'est pas peut-être pas nécessaire).

120. *Histoire naturelle, générale et particulière*, p. 80. "Il seroit dangereux d'en faire l'application dans nos sociétés. On pardonne au révérend P. Jean, de manger une cuisse de suicide Anglois. Il étoit dans les déserts de la Sibérie, prêt à périr de faim. Mais malheur à celui qui, dans la société, auroit quelque goût pour la chair humaine! La loi le puniroit sévérement."

121. On Restif and Hupay, see James H. Billington, *Fire in the Minds of Men: The Origins of Revolutionary Faith* (New York, 1979), particularly p. 79. According to Billington, Hupay composed a *Republican Koran* during the Revolution.

122. *Le militaire philosophe* (London, 1768), p. 12. "Il faut encore que je vous supplie de n'être pas choqué des termes forts qui pourrront peut-être m'échapper en parlant de votre Religion. Je joue un personnage libre, indifférent, dégagé de tous les égards politiques; en un mot, je joue le rôle d'un sauvage, qui n'a l'esprit imbu d'aucun préjugé superstitieux."

123. For example, in *Père Duchesne*: "Républicains, guillotinez-moi ce Jean-foutre de Louis XVI et cette putain de Marie Antoinette en quatre jours si vous voulez avoir du pain, par un commissaire national [Republicans, guillotine for me that Jean-fucker Louis XVI and that slut Maire Antoinette within four days and you will have bread, by a national commissar]." For a history of blasphemy, see David Nash, *Blasphemy in the Christian World* (Oxford University Press, 2007).

124. See Stites, *Revolutionary Dreams*, p. 106.

125. *Histoire naturelle et morale des Iles Antilles*, pp. 386–87. "Ils disent que nous venons nus au monde, & que c'est folie de cacher le corps qui nous a esté donné par la nature."

126. See Louis B. Wright, "The Noble Savage of Madagascar in 1640," *Journal of the History of Ideas*, vol. 4, no. 1 (Jan. 1943).

127. See Stites, *Revolutionary Dreams*, p. 313.

128. See *Revue de l'ordre social*, 1850, no. 1, p. 6; I am grateful to Alistair Ian Blyth for this reference.

129. See *Letter of Amerigo Vespucci*, p. 10, in *Voyages of Amerigo Vespucci* (London, 1885).

130. Restif de la Bretonne, *Le pornographe, suivi en annexe de Etat de la prostitution chez les anciens* (Brussels, 1879). The exigencies of naturalness cause Restif to demand that prostitutes should be forbidden from wearing makeup. See also Susan P. Conner, "Public Virtue and Public Women: Prostitution in Revolutionary Paris, 1793–1794," *Eighteenth-Century Studies*, vol. 28, no. 2 (winter 1994–95).

CHAPTER 8 THE AGENT OF ABSOLUTE CRUELTY

1. [Thomas Northmore], *Memoirs of Planetes, or a Sketch of the Laws and Manners of Makar, by Phileleutherus Devoniensis* (London, 1795), p. 6.

2. *The Life and Strange Surprizing Adventures of Robinson Crusoe of York, Mariner* (London, 1719), p. 182.

3. *A Voyage to Guinea, Brasil, and the West-Indies; In His Majesty's Ships the* Swallow *and* Weymouth, *giving a Genuine Account of the several Islands*

and Settlements, 2d ed. (London, 1737), pp. 23, 133. See also Katherine George, "The Civilized West Looks at Primitive Africa, 1400–1800: A Study in Ethnocentrism," *Isis*, vol. 49, no. 1 (Mar. 1958), pp. 62–72. On the mythology of cannibalism in the Pacific, see Gananath Obeyesekere, *Cannibal Talk: The Man-Eating Myth and Human Sacrifice in the South Seas* (University of California Press, 2005).

4. *Histoire naturelle du genre humain, ou Recherches sur ses principaux fondemens physiques et moraux; précédées d'un Discours sur la nature des êtres organiques et sur l'ensemble de leur physiologie. On y a joint une Dissertation sur le sauvage de l'Aveyron* (Paris, an IX [1801]), vol. 2, p. 50.

5. *Yverdon Encyclopaedia:* "ceux qui ne touchoient qu'aux appendices du corps humains, tels étoient les Topinambours & les Tapuiges, qui au témoignage de Pison, dévoroient la tunique & une partie du cordon ombilical des enfans nouvellement nés; les Péruviens, qui arrosoient de sang humain leur pain sacré."

6. *Histoire générale des Antilles habitées par les françois* (Paris, 1667), p. 409.

7. *Oeuvres de Buffon* (Paris, 1839), vol. 3, p. 327.

8. *Robinson Crusoe*, p. 266. In *Farther Adventures* (9, 67), Defoe tells the story of a French maid about to eat her mistress due to starvation; instead, she bites her own arm.

9. *Histoire de la conquete de la Mexique, ou de la Nouvelle Espagne* (Paris, 1591), p. 306. "On ne dira point leurs Fêtes, leurs Sacrifices, leurs Ceremonies, leurs Sorcelleries, & leurs autres superstitions, parce qu'on les recontre à chaque pas, avec une ennüieuse répétition, dans, les Histoires de Indes; outré que c'est une instruction peu necessaire, & qui n'a ni agrément, ni utilité."

10. *Histoire naturelle et morale des Iles Antilles de l'Amérique* (Rotterdam, 1658), p. 403.

11. Section 334. *The New Science*, trans. Thomas Goddard Bergin, Max Harold Fisch (Ithaca, 1984), p. 97.

12. *The Intelligencer*, 13/1728.

13. *A Discourse on Inequality*, trans. Maurice Cranston (Harmondsworth, 1984), p. 159

14. *Histoire naturelle du genre humain*, vol. 2, p. 49.

15. Reginald Scot, *The Discoverie of Witchcraft* (New York, 1972), pp. 18–19.

16. Robert Bolton, *Mr. Boltons Last and Learned Worke of the Four Last Things* (London, 1633), 6

17. Edward Calamy, *The Happiness of Those Who Sleep in Jesus* (London, 1662), 9–11.

18. William Bates, *A Funeral Sermon Preached Upon the Death of...Dr. Thomas Manton* (London, 1678) 2; Matthew Fowler, *God's Esteem of the Death of His Saints* (London, 1656) 19. More recently, the article "Resurrection" in the *Routledge Encyclopedia of Philosophy* ignores the cannibal, although it contains what is otherwise a typical list of the difficulties of resurrection. A. Olding, "Resurrection Bodies and Resurrection Worlds," *Mind*, n.s., vol. 79, no. 316 (Oct. 1970), pp. 581–85, offers another skeptical treatment of the logical possibility of resurrection of the body; see also John B. Cobb, Jr.,

"The Resurrection of the Soul," *Harvard Theological Review*, vol. 80, no. 2 (Apr. 1987), pp. 213–27.

19. Dobson, *Sermon Preached at the Funeral of the Honorable the Lady Mary Farmor*, 5–6.

20. See William M. Spellman, "Between Death and Judgment: Conflicting Images of the Afterlife in Late Seventeenth-Century English Eulogies," *Harvard Theological Review*, vol. 87, no. 1 (Jan. 1994), pp. 49–65.

21. *Les droits de l'homme et du citoyen, telles qu'ils sont prescripts par la loi naturelle* (Amsterdam, 1715). This is the third edition of the translation and commentary by Barbeyrac. The discussion of the lifeboat can be found at pp. 125–27.

22. The first edition dates from 1714.

23. Section 337. *The New Science*, trans. Thomas Goddard Bergin, Max Harold Fisch (Ithaca, 1984), p. 99.

24. *Two Treatises of Government* (London, 1824), II, 41. This theory is borrowed by Adam Smith in the *Wealth of Nations*.

25. *Encyclopédie, ou dictionnaire raisonné des sciences, des arts et des métiers* (Paris, 1751), vol. 1, p. 498. "Quelques médecins se sont ridiculement imaginés avoir découvert le principe de l'anthropophagie dans une humeur acre, atrabilieuse, qui logée dans les membranes du ventricle, produit par l'irritation qu'elle cause, cette horrible voracité qu'ils assurent avoir remarquée dans plusiers malades."

26. *Leviathan,* ed. Richard Tuck (Cambridge University Press, 1996), part 1, cap. 13. Cf. also *De cive* (10, 1): "Extra civitatem, imperium affectuum, bellum, metus, paupertas, foeditas, solitudo, barbaries, ignorantia, feritas: in civitate imperium rationis, pax, securitas, divitiae, ornatus, societas, elegantia, scientiae, benevolentia."

27. *Leviathan*, part 2, cap. 21.

28. Cap. 13.

29. Part 2, cap. 21.

30. *A Dialogue between a Philosopher and a Student of the Common Laws of England* (Chicago, 1971), p. 18.

31. See Samuel I. Mintz, *The Hunting of Leviathan: Seventeenth-Century Reactions to the Materialism and Moral Philosophy of Thomas Hobbes* (Cambridge University Press, 1962).

32. *Second Treatise of Government*, in *Two Treatises of Government* (London, 1824), sections 16 and 180. A general commentary on rejection of the theory of natural state in the late eighteenth century is in H. V. S. Ogden, "The State of Nature and the Decline of Lockian Political Theory in England, 1760–1800," *American Historical Review*, vol. 46, no. 1 (Oct. 1940). See also J. M. Dunn, "'Bright Enough for All Our Purposes': John Locke's Conception of a Civilized Society," *Notes and Records of the Royal Society of London*, vol. 43, no. 2, Science and Civilization under William and Mary (Jul. 1989).

33. Section 92.

34. Sir Robert Filmer, *Patriarcha and Other Writings* (Cambridge University Press, 1991), p. 188.

35. Ibid.

36. Ibid.

37. Part III, section 1.

38. *Of the Origin and Progress of Language*, 2d ed. (Edinburgh, 1774), vol. 1, p. 222.

39. *A Methodical System of Universal Law* (London, 1763), vol. 2, p. 69.

40. Francis Hutcheson, *On Human Nature* (Cambridge University Press, 1993), pp. 143–44.

41. *Essai sur les mœurs*, in *Œuvres de Voltaire* (Paris, 1829), Introduction, section 7, "Des sauvages."

42. *The Glasgow Edition of the Works and Correspondence of Adam Smith* (Oxford University Press, 1976), p. 115. On Smith's reaction to Hobbes and his critique of egoism, see David Levy, "Adam Smith's 'Natural Law' and Contractual Society," *Journal of the History of Ideas*, vol. 39, no. 4 (Oct.–Dec. 1978).

43. *An Inquiry into the Nature and Causes of the Wealth of Nations* (Oxford University Press, 1976), p. 89.

44. *Essay on the Origin of Languages*, "la guerre et les conquêttes ne sont que des chasses d'hommes. Après les avoir conquis, il ne leur manquait que de les dévorer: c'est ce que leurs successeurs ont appris à faire."

45. Ibid., "un homme abandonné seul sur la face de la terre . . . devait être un animal féroce. Il était prêt à faire aux autres tout le mal qu'il craignait d'eux."

46. Ibid., "la même cause qui empêche les sauvages d'user de leur raison, comme le prétendent nos juristconsultes, les empêche en même temps d'abuser de leurs facultés."

47. Ibid., "L'homme sauvage, quand il a diné, est en paix avec toute la nature, et l'ami de tous ses semblables. S'agit-il quelquefois de disputer son repas, il n'en vient jamais aux coups sans avoir auparavant comparé la difficulté de vaincre avec celle de trouver ailleurs sa subsistance; et comme l'orgeuil ne se mêle pas du combat, il se termine par quelques coups de poing; le vainqueur mange, le vaincu va chercher fortune, et tout est pacifié."

48. John Austin, *The Province of Jurisprudence Established* (London, 1832), pp. 1–2. On the concept of law, see Robert N. McLaughlin, "On a Similarity Between Natural Law Theories and English Legal Positivism," *Philosophical Quarterly*, vol. 39, no. 157 (Oct. 1989).

49. Austin, *Province of Jurisprudence Established*, p. 111.

50. Ibid., pp. 97–98

51. Ibid., p. 189.

52. Ibid., pp. 192.

53. *De beneficiis*, 4, 20, in *Opera Philosophica*, ed. Emil Ferdinand Vogel (Leipzig: Nauck, 1830). "Ut aves, quae laceratione corporum aluntur, lassa morbo pecora et casura e proximo speculantur, ita hic imminet morti, et circa cadaver volat."

54. *Three Early Modern Utopias*, ed. Susan Bruce (Oxford University Press, 1999), pp. 21–22. On More and the influence of travel relations in America, see Alfred A. Cave, "Thomas More and the New World," *Albion: A Quarterly Journal Concerned with British Studies*, vol. 23, no. 2 (summer 1991).

55. Quoted in Paul Lawrence Rose, *Revolutionary Antisemitism in Germany from Kant to Wagner* (Princeton University Press, 1990), p. 50.

56. *An Essay on the Nature and Immutability of Truth in Opposition to Sophistry and Scepticism* (London, 1773), p. 467.

57. *The Ecclesiastical History* (Oxford University Press, 1995), vol. 5, p. 141.

58. *Histoire d'un voyage faict en la terre du Brésil, autrement dite Amerique* (Geneva, 1580), pp. 228–30. On the reception of de Léry in the eighteenth century, see Frank Lestringant, "The Philosopher's Breviary: Jean de Léry in the Enlightenment," *Representations*, no. 33, Special Issue: The New World (winter 1991); see also Andrea Frisch, "In a Sacramental Mode: Jean de Léry's Calvinist Ethnography," *Representations*, no. 77 (winter 2002). At the execution of Ravaillac, cannibalism was alleged by eye witnesses; see Orest Ranum, "The French Ritual of Tyrannicide in the Late Sixteenth Century," *Sixteenth Century Journal*, vol. 11, no. 1 (spring 1980).

59. *Dialogues and Natural History of Religion* (Oxford University Press, 1993), p. 163.

60. *Sketches of the History of Man* (Edinburgh, 1774), vol. 1, pp. 245–50.

61. *Moeurs des sauvages amériquains, comparées aux moeurs des premiers temps* (Paris, 1724), vol. 2 p. 291. "Ils regardent avec raison, comme quelque chose de plus barbare & de plus féroce, la brutalité des Duels."

62. "Les peuples du Canade et les Cafres, qu'il nous a plu d'appeler sauvages, sont infiniment supérieurs aux nôtres."

63. *Observations de Jean-Jacques Rousseau de Genève sur la réponse qui a été faite à son Discours, Oeuvres completes*, ed. V. D. Musset-Pathay (Paris, 1823), vol. 1, p. 120. "Offrons quelques aliments à ces tigres, afin qu'ils ne dévorent pas nos enfants."

64. *Oeuvres completes*, ed. V. D. Musset-Pathay (Paris, 1824), vol. 2, p. 454. "Je vois les peuples se former, s'étendre, se dissoudre, se succéder comme les flots de la mer; je vois les hommes, rassemblés sur quelques points de leur demeure pour s'y dévorer mutuellement, faire un affreux désert du reste du monde, digne monument de l'union sociale et de l'utilité des arts."

65. Histoire des Yncas, Rois de Perou (Amsterdam, 1704), vol. 1, pp. 50–51.

66. *Les voyages de Jean Struys* (Lyon, 1682), p. 358.

67. See Sade, *Aline et Valcour, ou le roman philosophique*, in *Oeuvres* (Paris, 1991), vol. 1, pp. 556–57.

68. *Robinson Crusoe*, p. 218.

69. Adam Smith, *Lectures on Jurisprudence* (Oxford University Press, 1978), pp. 214–15, and *An Inquiry into the Nature and Causes of the Wealth of Nations* (Oxford University Press, 1976), vol. 2, p. 269. On theories of primitive society and development of property in the Scottish Enlightenment, see Paul Bowles, "The Origin of Property and the Development of Scottish Historical Science," *Journal of the History of Ideas*, vol. 46, no. 2 (Apr.–Jun. 1985). The violent expansion of European states is analyzed in Janice E. Thomson, *Mercenaries, Pirates, and Sovereigns* (Princeton University Press, 1994).

70. *Histoire philosophique et politique* (Amsterdam, 1772), vol. 6, pp. 15–16.

71. *Works of the Right Hon. Edmund Burke* (London, 1884), vol. 1, p. 10. For a general history of evil, see Susan Neiman, *Evil in Modern Thought* (Princeton University Press, 2002).

72. Kant, *Political Writings*, trans. H. B. Nisbet, 2d ed. (Cambridge University Press, 1991), pp. 102–3. See also Leonard Krieger, "Kant and the Crisis of Natural Law," *Journal of the History of Ideas*, vol. 26, no. 2 (Apr.–Jun. 1965).

SELECT BIBLIOGRAPHY

Acosta, Joseph. *Histoire naturelle et morale des Indes, tant Orientales qu'Occidentales*. Paris, 1598.

——. *De procuranda indorum salute*. Madrid, 1984.

Adair, James. *The History of the American Indians; particularly Those Nations adjoining to the Mississippi, East and West Florida, Georgia, South and North Carolina, and Virginia: containing an Account of their Origin, Language, Manners, Religious and Civil Customs, Laws, Forms of Government, Punishments, Conduct in War and Domestic Life, and Habits, Diet, Agriculture, Manufactures, Diseases and Method of Cure, and other Particulars*. London, 1775.

Arbuthnot, Jean. *Essai sur la nature et le choix des alimens, suivant les différentes constitutions*. Paris, 1741.

Arens, William. *The Man-Eating Myth: Anthropology and Anthropopha*. Oxford, 1980.

——. *La Philosophie du bon-sens, ou réflexions philosophiques sur l'incertitude des conoissances humaines, à la usage des Cavaliers & du Beau-Sexe*. The Hague, 1746.

Arnauld, Antoine. *Écrits sur le système de la grâce générale*. Paris (?), 1715.

Atkins, John. *A Voyage to Guinea, Brasil, and the West-Indies; In His Majesty's Ships the* Swallow *and* Weymouth, *giving a Genuine Account of the several Islands and Settlements*. 2d ed. London, 1737.

Atkinson, Geoffrey. *The Extraordinary Voyage in French Literature from 1700 to 1720*. Paris, 1922.

——. *Les relations de voyages du XVIIe siècle et l'évolution des idées: Contributions à l'étude de la formation de l'esprit du XVIIIe siècle*. Paris, n.d.

——. *Le sentiment de la nature et le retour à la vie simple, 1690–1740*. Paris, 1960.

——. *The Sentimental Revolution: French Writers of 1690–1740*. Seattle, 1960.

Auguet, Roland. *Cruelty and Civilization: The Roman Games*. London, 1972.

Augustine. *City of God*. Translated by Henry Scowcroft Bettenson. Harmondsworth, 2003.

——. *The Enchiridion on Faith, Hope, and Love*. Translated by Thomas S. Hibbs. Washington, DC, 1996.

Austin, John. *The Province of Jurisprudence Established*. London, 1832.

Bacon, Francis. *The New Organon*. Translated by Michael Silverhome. Cambridge, 2000.

Basil of Caesarea. *Sur l'origine de l'homme*. Paris, 1970.

Bauman, Richard A. *Crime and Punishment in Ancient Rome*. London, 1996.

Baxter, Richard. *A Holy Commonwealth*. Cambridge, 1994.

Beaglehole, J. C., ed. *The Journals of Captain Cook on his Voyages of Discovery*. Cambridge, 1967.

Beattie, James. *An Essay on the Nature and Immutability of Truth in Opposition to Sophistry and Scepticism*. London, 1773.

Beccaria, marquis of. *Traité des délits et des peines*. Philadelphia, 1765.

Berman, David. *A History of Atheism in Britain from Hobbes to Russell*. London, 1990.

Billington, James H. *Fire in the Minds of Men: The Origins of Revolutionary Faith*. New York, 1979.

Blackburn, Robin. *The Making of New World Slavery: From the Baroque to the Modern Age*. London, 1997.

Blackstone. *Commentaries on the Laws of England*. London, 1793.

Blair, Ann. *The Theater of Nature: Jean Bodin and Renaissance Science*. Princeton, 1997.

Boas, George. *Essays on Primitivism and Related Ideas in the Middle Ages*. Baltimore, 1948.

———. *The Happy Beast in French Thought of the Seventeenth Century*. Baltimore, 1993.

Bodin, Jean. *The Six Bookes of a Commonweale*. London, 1606.

Boemo [Boemus], Giovanni. *Gli costumi, le leggi, e l'usanze di tutte le genti*. Venice, 1558.

Boesche, Roger. *Theories of Tyranny from Plato to Arendt*. Philadelphia, 1996.

Boucher, Philip P. *Cannibal Encounters: Europeans and Island Caribs, 1492–1763*. Baltimore, 1992.

Bowerstock, G. W. *Martyrdom and Rome*. Cambridge, 1995.

Boyle, Robert. *Occasional Reflections upon Several Subjects, with a Discourse about such Kind of Thoughts*. Oxford, 1848.

———. *Selected Philosophical Papers of Robert Boyle*. Indianapolis, 1991.

Branham, R. Bracht, and Marie Odile Goulet-Cazé, eds. *The Cynics: The Cynic Movement in Antiquity and its Legacy*. Berkeley, 1996.

Bretonne, Restif de la. *Le pornographe, suivi en annexe de État de la prostitution chex les anciens*. Brussels, 1879.

Bruce, Susan, ed. *Three Early Modern Utopias*. Oxford, 1999.

Buckle, Stephen. *Natural Law and the Theory of Property: Grotius to Hume*. Oxford, 1991.

Buckley, Michael J. *At the Origins of Modern Atheism*. New Haven, 1987.

Buffon. *Histoire naturelle, générale et particulière*. Paris, 1758.

———. *Oeuvres de Buffon*. Paris, 1839.

Burke, Edmund. *Works of the Right Hon. Edmund Burke*. London, 1884.

Burlamaqui, J. J. *Principes du droit naturel et politique*. Geneva and Copenhagen, 1764.

Burnet, Thomas. *A Treatise concerning the State of Departed Souls, Before, and At, and After the Resurrection*. 2d ed. corrected.Translated from Latin by Mr. Dennis. London, 1739.

Burns, J. H., ed. *The Cambridge History of Political Thought: 1450–1700*. Cambridge, 1991.

Bush, M. L. *Servitude in Modern Times*. New York, 2000.

Bynum, Caroline Walker. *The Resurrection of the Body in Western Christianity, 200–1336*. New York, 1995.

Calmet, Dom Augustin. *Dissertations sur les Apparitions des Anges, des Démons & des Esprits, et sur les Revenans et Vampires de Hongrie, de Bohème, de Moravie, & de Silesie*. Paris, 1751.

Campbell, Mary Baine. *Wonder and Science: Imagining Worlds in Early Modern Europe*. Ithaca, 1999.

Camporesi, Piero. *Bread of Dreams: Food of Fantasy in Early Modern Europe*. Cambridge, 1989.

———. *The Incorruptible Flesh: Body Mutation and Mortification in Religion and Folklore*. Cambridge, 1988.

Camus, Jean-Pierre. *L'Amphithéâtre sanglant*. Paris, 2001.

Carlino, Andreea. *Books of the Body: Anatomical Ritual and Renaissance Learning*. Chicago, 1999.

Carlson, Marvin. *Theories of Theatre: A Historical and Critical Survey from the Greeks to the Present*. Ithaca, 1986.

Carlton, Eric. *Massacres: A Historical Perspective*. Hants, 1994.

Célestin, Roger. *From Cannibals to Radicals: Figures and Limits Exoticism*. Minneapolis, 1996.

Chalmers, A., ed. *The Tatler; corrected from the Originals*. London, 1817.

Chambers, F. R. S. *Cyclopaedia, or, an Universal Dictionary of Arts and Sciences*. 5th ed. London, 1743.

de Charlevoix, Pierre François Xavier. *Histoire et description générale de la nouvelle France avec le journal historique d'un voyage fait par ordre du Roi dans l'Amérique Septentrionale*. Paris, 1744.

Chinard, Gilbert. *L'Amérique et le rêve exotique dans la littérature française au XVIIe et au XVIIIe siècle*. Paris, 1913.

Clark, Stuart. *Thinking with Demons: The Idea of Witchcraft in Early Modern Europe*. Cambridge, 1999.

Clarke, Samuel. *A Discourse concerning the Being and Attributes of God, the Obligations of Natural Religion and the Truth and Certainty of the Christian Revelation.* London, 1738.

Collier, Jane. *The Art of Ingeniously Tormenting.* London, 1753.

La Condamine, Charles-Marie de. *Histoire d'une jeune fille sauvage, trouvée dans les Bois à l'âge de dix ans.* Paris, 1754.

———. *Relation abrégée d'un voyage fait dans l'intérieur de l'Amérique méridionale, par M. De La Condamine.* Paris, 1778.

Cooper, Frederick, and Ann Laura Stoller, eds. *Tensions of Empire: Colonial Cultures in a Bourgeois World.* Berkeley, 1997.

Corbin, Alain. *The Village of Cannibals: Rage and Murder in France, 1870.* Cambridge, 1992.

Crook, Peter. *Darwinism, War, and History: The Debate over the Biology of War, from the* Origin of the Species *to the First World War.* Cambridge, 1994.

Crosby, Alfred. *Ecological Imperialism: The Biological Expansion of Europe, 900–1900.* Cambridge, 1986.

Crucé, Emeric. *The New Cyneas.* Philadelphia, 1909.

Cumberland, Richard. *Traité philosophique des lois naturelles, ou l'on recherché et l'on établit, pas la nature des choses, la forme de ces loix, leur principaux chefs, leur ordre, leur publication & leur obligation: on y réfute aussi les Elémens de la Morale & de la Politique de Thomas Hobbes.* Amsterdam, 1744.

Cummins, John. *The Voyage of Christopher Columbus: Columbus' Own Journal of Discovery Newly Restored and Translated.* London, 1992.

d'Argens, Boyer. *Lettres juives, ou correspondence philosophique, historique et critique.* Paris, 1742.

Daston, Lorraine, and Katharine Park. *Wonders and the Order of Nature, 1150–1750.* New York, 1998.

Davis, David Brion. *The Problem of Slavery in Western Culture.* Oxford, 1988.

Dawson, Doyne. *Cities of the Gods: Communist Utopias in Greek Thought.* Oxford, 1992.

Defoe, Daniel. *The Strange and Surprizing Adventures of Robinson Crusoe of York, Mariner.* 3d ed. London, 1719.

Demeunier, Jean-Nicolas. *L'esprit des usages et des coutumes des deferens peuples.* Paris, 1785.

van Delft, Louis. *Littérature et anthropologie. Nature humaine et charactère à l'âge classique.* Paris, 1993.

Deslandes, Andre-François. *Réflexions sur la mort des grands hommes qui sont morts en plaisantant.* Rochefort, 1755.

Detienne, Marcel, and Jean-Pierre Vernant, *La cuisine du sacrifice en pays grec.* Paris, 1979.

Diderot, Denis. *Oeuvres Complètes*. Paris, 1876.

———. *Opuscules philosophiques et littéraires, la plupart posthumes ou inédites*. Paris, 1796.

Dodds, Muriel. *Les récits de voyage sources de "L'Ésprit des lois" de Montesquieu*. Paris, 1929.

Doueihi, Milad. *A Perverse History of the Human Heart*. Harvard, 1997.

Downing, F. Gerald. *Cynics and Christian Origins*. Edinburgh, 1992.

Duchet, Michele. *Anthropologie et histoire au siècle des lumières*. Paris, 1971.

Dudley, E., and M. E. Novak, eds. *The Wild Man Within*. Pittsburgh, 1972.

Durand, Gilbert. *Les structures anthropologiques de l'imaginaire*. Paris, 1992.

Ehrard, Jean. *Encyclopédie, ou dictionnaire raisonné des sciences, des arts et des métiers*. Neufchastel, 1765.

———. *L'idée de la nature en France à l'aube des Lumières*. Paris, 1970.

Enders, John. *The Medieval Theater of Cruelty: Rhetoric, Memory, Violence*. Ithaca, 1999.

Evans, Richard J. *Rituals of Retribution: Capital Punishment in Germany, 1600–1987*. Oxford, 1996.

Exquemelin, Alexandre-Olivier. *Histoire des avanturiers filibustiers, qui se sont signalez dans les Indes*. Paris, 1699.

Faussett, David. *The Strange and Surprising Sources of Robinson Crusoe*. Amsterdam, 1994.

Favre, Robert. *La mort dans la littérature et la pensée françaises au siècle des lumières*. Lyon, 1978.

Ferguson, Adam. *An Essay on the History of Civil Society*. 6th ed. London, 1793.

———. *Essays on the Intellectual Powers, Moral Sentiment, Happiness and National Felicity*. Paris, 1805.

Ferry, Luc, and Claudine Germé, eds. *Des animaux et des hommes: Anthologie des texts remarquables écrits sur le sujet, du XVe siècle à nos jours*. Paris, 1994.

Fiddes, Nick. *Meat: A Natural Symbol*. London, 1988.

Fido, Martin. *Bodysnatchers: A History of Resurrectionists, 1742–1832*. London, 1988.

Filmer, Sir Robert. *Patriarcha and Other Writings*. Cambridge, 1991.

Fontenelle, Bernard. *Oeuvres complètes*. Paris, 1989.

———. *A Plurality of Worlds*. Translated by Mr. Glanvill. London, 1702.

Formey, Jean Henry Samuel. *Conseils pour former une Bibliothèque peu nombreuse, mais choisie*. Berlin, 1746.

———. *Principes du droit de la nature et des gens. Extrait du grand ouvrage latin de M. de Wolff*. Amsterdam, 1758.

———. *Questions de droit naturel: Sur le Traité du droit de la Nature de M. le Baron de Wolff*. Bern, 1762.

Foucault, Michel. *Les anormaux. Cours au Collège de France 1974–1975*. Paris, 1999.

———. *Folie et déraison: Histoire de la folie à l'âge classique*. Paris, 1961.

———. *Surveiller et punir*. Paris, 1975.

Franklin, Julian H. *Remarques sur la politesse des sauvages de l'Amerique septentrionale*. Passy, 1784 (?).

Frazer, J. G. *The Collected Works*. Vols. 1–2. *The Golden Bough: A Study in Comparative Religion*. Richmond, 1994.

Freud, Sigmund. *Totem and Taboo*. London, 1999.

Fuller, J.F.C. *The Conduct of War, 1789–1961*. New York, 1992.

Garnsey, Peter. *Ideas of Slavery from Aristotle to Augustine*. Cambridge, 1996.

Geary, Patrick J. *Furta Sacra: Thefts of Relics in the Central Middle Ages*. Princeton, 1990.

Gent, Lucy, and Nigel Llewellyn. *Renaissance Bodies: The Human Figure in English Culture, c. 1540–1660*. London, 1995.

Geremek, Bronislaw. *Poverty: A History*. Oxford, 1994.

Gierke, Otto. *Natural Law and the Theory of Society*. Cambridge, 1958.

Gilbert, Allen H. *Machiavelli's Prince and its Forerunners:* The Prince *as a Typical Book* de Regimine Principum. New York, 1968.

Gilles of Rome [Aegidius Romanus]. *On Ecclesiastical Power*. Woodridge, 1986.

Glacken, Clarence J. *Traces on the Rhodian Shore: Nature and Culture in Western Thought from Ancient Times to the End of the Eighteenth Century*. Berkeley, 1967.

Godwin, Barbara. *Justice by Lottery*. Harvester, 1992.

Goldman, Lawrence R., ed. *The Anthropology of Cannibalism*. Westport, 1999.

Gonthier, Nicole. *Le châtiment du crime au Moyen Âge: XIIe–XVIe siècles*. Rennes, 1998.

Gravina, Jean-Vincent. *L'Esprit des loix romanes*. Amsterdam, 1766.

Greene, John C. *The Death of Adam: Evolution and Its Impact on Western Thought*. Ames, 1996.

Gregory, Brad S. *Salvation at the Stake: Christian Martyrdom in Early Modern Europe*. Harvard, 1999.

de Grimm, Le Baron, and Denis Diderot, *Correspondance littéraire, philosophique et critique, adressée à un Souverain d'Allemagne*. Paris, 1813.

Gross, Jean-Pierre. *Fair Shares for All: Jacobin Egalitarianism in Practice*. Cambridge, 1997.

Grotius, Hugo. *Mare Liberum/De la liberté des mers*. Paris, 1990.

———. *Of the Rights of War and Peace*. London, 1715.

———. *Traité de la verité de la religion chretienne*. Utrecht, 1692.

Hanke, Lewis. *All Mankind is One: A Study of the Disputation between Bartolomé de la Casas and Juan Gines de Sepulveda in 1550 on the Intellectual and Religious Capacity of the American Indians*. De Kalb, 1974.

———. *Aristotle and the American Indians: A Study in Race Prejudice in the Modern World*. Chicago, 1959.

———. *The Spanish Struggle for Justice in the Conquest of America*. Boston, 1965.

Hannaford, Ivan. *Race: The History of an Idea in the West*. Baltimore, 1996.

Hastings, Hester. *Man and Beast in French Thought of the Eighteenth Century*. Baltimore, 1996.

Heineccius, Johann Gottlieb. *A Methodical System of Universal Law, or the Laws of Nature Deduced from Certain Principles and Applied to Proper Cases*. London, 1763.

Hill, Christopher. *Histoire de l'Académie Royale des Sciences et Belles Lettres: Année MDCCLIV*. Berlin, 1756.

———. *Histoires prodigieuses extraictes de plusiers auteurs*. Paris, 1598.

———. *Liberty against the Law: Some Seventeenth-Century Controversies*. London, 1996.

Hobbes, Thomas. *A Dialogue between a Philosopher and a Student of the Common Laws of England*. Chicago, 1971.

Hochstrasser, T. J. *Natural Law Theories in the Early Enlightenment*. Cambridge, 2000.

d'Holbach, Baron. *La contagion sacrée, ou histoire naturelle de la superstition*. London, 1770.

———. *Système de la nature, ou les loix du monde physique & du monde moral*. London, 1781.

———. *Système social, ou principes naturelles de la morale et de la politique avec un examen de l'influence du gouvernement sur les moeurs*. London, 1773.

Hsia, R. Po-Chia. *The Myth of Ritual Murder: Jews and Magic in Reformation Germany*. New Haven, 1998.

Hume, David. *Dialogues and Natural History of Religion*. Oxford, 1993.

———. *An Enquiry Concerning the Principles of Morals*. London, 1751.

———. *Essays and Treatises on Several Subjects*. London, 1788.

———. *Philosophical Works*. Vol. 4. Edinburgh, 1827.

Hutcheson, Francis. *On Human Nature*. Cambridge, 1993.

Israel, Jonathan Irvine. *Enlightenment Contested: Philosophy, Modernity, and the Emancipation of Man, 1670–1752*. Oxford, 2006.

———. *Radical Enlightenment: Philosophy and the Formation of Modernity, 1650–1750*. Oxford, 2001.

Jacob, Margaret, and James Jacob, eds. *The Origins of Anglo-American Radicalism*. London, 1984.

Janson, H. W. *Apes and Ape Lore in the Middle Ages and Renaissance*. London, 1952.

Jaume, Lucien, ed. *Les déclarations des droits de l'homme. Du débat 1789–1793 au Préambule de 1946*. Paris, 1989.

Johnson, David. *The Rhetoric of* Leviathan: *Thomas Hobbes and the Politics of Political Transformation.* Princeton, 1986.

Johnson, Harold J., ed. *The Mediaeval Tradition of Natural Law.* Kalamazoo, 1987.

Jordan, William Chester. *The Great Famine: Northern Europe in the Early Fourteenth Century.* Princeton, 1996.

Jüttner, Siegfried. *Neue Bilder vom Menschen in der Literatur der Europäischer Aufklärung.* Frankfurt, 1998.

Kames, Lord [Henry Home]. *Sketches of the History of Man.* Edinburgh, 1774.

Kant, Immanuel. *Political Writings.* 2d ed. Translated by H. B. Nisbet. Cambridge, 1991.

Kors, Alan Charles, and Edward Peters, eds. *Witchcraft in Europe, 400–1700: A Documentary History.* Philadelphia, 2000.

Kyle, Donald G. *Spectacles of Death in Ancient Rome.* London, 1998.

Labat, Jean-Baptiste. *Relation historique de l'Ethiopie Occidentale.* Paris, 1732.

———. *Voyage du Père Labat aux Iles de l'Amérique.* The Hague, 1724.

Lachiver, Marcel. *Les années de misère: La famine au temps du Grand Roi, 1680–1720.* Paris, 1991.

Lactantius. *The Divine Institutes.* Washington, 1964.

Laertius, Diogenes. *Lives of Eminent Philosophers.* Translated by R. D. Hicks. Cambridge, MA, 1925.

Lafitau, Joseph-François. *Moeurs des sauvages amériqains, comparées aux moeurs des premiers temps.* Paris, 1724.

Lahontan, baron de. *Nouveaux voyages de M. le Baron de Lahontan dans l'Amérique septentrionale.* The Hague, 1704.

Laursen, John Christian. *The Politics of Skepticism in the Ancients: Montaigne, Hume, and Kant.* Leiden, 1992.

Léry, Jean de. *Histoire d'un voyage faict en la terre du Brésil, autrement dite Amérique.* Geneva, 1580.

Lescarbot, Marc. *Histoire de la Nouvelle-France.* Paris, 1617.

Lestrignant, Frank. *Cannibals: The Discovery and the Representation of the Cannibal from Columbus to Jules Verne.* Berkeley, 1997.

Locke, John. *Political Essays.* Edited by Raymond Geuss, Quentin Skinner, and Mark Goldie. Cambridge, 1997.

———. *Some Thoughts concerning Education.* Oxford, 1997.

Magnus, Olaus. *A Description of the Northern Peoples* [*Historia de gentibus septentrionalibus*]. London, 1988.

Malthus, Thomas Robert. *An Essay on the Principle of Population; or, A View of its Past and Present Effects on Human Happiness.* 6th ed. London, 1826.

Mandrou, Robert. *Magistrats et sorciers en France au XVIIe siècle: Une analyse de psychologie historique.* Paris, 1968.

Maravall, José Antonio. *Culture of the Baroque: Analysis of a Historical Structure*. Manchester, 1986.

Mariana, P. Jean de. *Histoire generale d'Espagne*. Paris, 1725.

Marshall, P. J., and Glyndwr Williams. *The Great Map of Mankind: British Perceptions of the World in the Age of the Enlightenment*. London, 1982.

Masseau, Didier. *Les ennemis des philosophes: L'antiphilosophie au temps des lumières*. Paris, 2000.

McMinn, Joseph. *Swift's Irish Pamphlets: An Introductory Selection*. Gerald's Cross, 1991.

M D [Jean-Louis-Hubert-Simon Deperthes]. *Histoire des naufrages, ou recueil des relations le plus interressants des naufrages, hivernemens, délaissemens, incendies, famines, & autres evènemens funestes sur mer; qui ont été publiées depuis le quinzième siècle jusqu'à present*. Paris, 1789.

Meek, Ronald L. *Social Science and the Ignoble Savage*. Cambridge, 1976.

Merback, Mitchell B. *The Thief, the Cross, and the Wheel: Pain and the Spectacle of Punishment in Medieval and Renaissance Europe*. London, 1999.

Mercier, Louis-Sébastian. *L'Homme Sauvage*. Neuchatel, 1784.

Mintz, Samuel I. *The Hunting of Leviathan: Seventeenth-Century Reactions to the Materialism and Moral Philosophy of Thomas Hobbes*. Cambridge, 1970.

Molesworth. Robert. *An Account of Denmark, as it was in the Year 1692*. London, 1738.

Momigliano, Araldo. *The Classical Foundations of Modern Historiography*. Berkeley, 1990.

[Monboddo, Lord]. *Of the Origin and Progress of Language*. 2d ed. Edinburgh, 1774.

Montaigne, Michel de. *Essais de Montaigne*. Edited by Charles Louandre. Paris, 1854.

———. *Montaigne's Essays*. Translated by Charles Cotton. London, 1743.

Montesquieu, Charles-Louis de Secondat, baron de. *De l'Esprit des Lois*. Paris, 1834.

More, Henry. *An Account of Virtue*. London, 1690.

———. *An Explanation of the Grand Mystery of Godliness*. London, 1660.

———. *A Modest Enquiry into the Mystery of Iniquity*. London, 1664.

[Morelly]. *Code de la nature, ou le veritable esprit de ses loix, de tout tems négligé ou méconnu*. Par-tout, 1755.

Morgan, David. *The Mongols*. 2d ed. Oxford, 2007.

Muratori, Ludovico Antonio. *Relation of the Missions of Paraguay, wrote Originally in Italian*. London, 1759.

Musurillo, Herbert, ed. *The Acts of the Christian Martyrs*. Oxford, 1972.

[Naigeon, Jacques André], *Le militaire philosophe*. London, 1768.

Newman, Lucille, ed. *Hunger in History: Food Shortage, Poverty, and Deprivation*. Oxford, 1995.

Nicole, Pierre. *Traité de la grâce générale*. N.p., 1715.

Niderst, Alain. *Fontenelle*. Paris, 1991.

[Northmore, Thomas]. *Memoirs of Planetes, or a Sketch of the Laws and Manners of Makar, by Phileleutherus Devoniensis*. London, 1795.

Ockham, William of. *A Short Discourse on Tyrannical Government*. Cambridge, 1992.

Ogilby, James. *Africa; being an accurate description of the regions of Aegypt, Barbary, Lybia and Billedulgerid, the Land of Negroes, Guinee, Aethiopia and the Abyssines*. London, 1670.

Origen. *Traité des principes*. Paris, 1978.

Ozment, Steven. *When Fathers Ruled: Family Life in Reformation Europe*. Harvard, 1983.

Padgen, Anthony. *The Fall of Natural Man: The American Indian and the Origins of Comparative Ethnology*. Cambridge, 1982.

Paré, Ambroise. *Deux livres de chirurgie*. Paris, 1573.

[de Patot, Simon Tyssot]. *Voyages et Avantures de Jacques Massé*. Bordeaux, 1710.

de Pauw, Cornelius. *Recherches philosophiques sur les américains, ou Mémoires intéressants pour servir à l'Histoire de l'Espèce Humaine*. London, 1771.

————. *Récherches philosophiques sur les greques*. Berlin, 1788.

Pearce, Roy Harvey. *The Savages of America: A Study of the Indian and the Idea of Civilization*. Baltimore, 1953.

de la Peyrere, Isaac. *Rélation d'Islande*. Paris, 1663.

Phillips, William D. *Slavery from Roman Times to the Early Transatlantic Trade*. Minneapolis, 1985.

Pick, Daniel. *Faces of Degradation: A European Disorder, c. 1848–c. 1918*. Cambridge, 1989.

Pipes, Richard. *Property and Freedom*. New York, 2000.

de la Placette, Jean. *Essais de morale*. 2d ed. Amsterdam, 1716.

Platt, Peter P., ed. *Wonders, Marvels, and Monsters in Early Modern Culture*. Newark, 1999.

[Pluche, Noel-Antoine]. *Le spectacle de la nature ou entretiens sur les particularités de l'histoire naturelle*. Paris, 1752.

Plutarch. *Moralia*. Vol. 12. Translated by Harlod Cherniss and William C. Helmbold. Cambridge, MA, 1957.

[de Poincy, Louis]. *The History of the Caribby-islands, viz. Barbados, St Christophers, St Vincents, Martinico, Dominico, Barbouthos, Monserrat, Mevis, Antego &c in all XXVIII: in two books. The first containing the natural; the second the moral history of those islands, rendered into English by John Davies*. London, 1666.

[Polo, Marco]. *La description géographique des provinces et villages les plus fameuses de l'Inde Orientale*. Paris, 1556.

Pontas, Jean. *Dictionnaire de cas de conscience.* Paris, 1730.

Porphyry. *Porphyrii philosophi platonici Opuscula tria.* Edited by August Nauk. Leipzig, 1860.

Pouderon, Bernard. *Les apologistes gréques du IIé siècle.* Paris, 2005.

Praz, Mario. *La chair, la mort et le diable dans la littérature du 19e siècle: La romantisme noir.* Paris, 1977.

Prévot, Jacques, ed. *Libertins du XVIIIe siècle.* Paris, 1998.

Pufendorf, Samuel. *Les devoirs de l'homme et citoyen, tels qu'ils lui sont prescrits par la loi nauturelle.* Translated by J. Barbeyrac. Paris, 1822.

———. *Le Droit de la Nature et des Gens, Système Général des Principes les plus importans de la Morale, de la Jurisprudence, et de la Politique.* 5th ed. Translated by Jean Barbeyrac. Amsterdam, 1734.

———. *The Law of Nature and Nations; The Second Edition, carefully Corrected, and Compared with Mr. Barbeyrac's French Translation.* Oxford, 1710.

[Radicati, Alberto]. *A Comical and True Account of the Modern Canibals's Religion, by Osmin True Believer, to which is added a Select Piece, call'd The Story of Stories, taken from the Canibals's Chronicle.* London, 1734.

———. *Recueil des pièces curieuses sur les matières les plus interesantes.* London, 1749.

Rawson, Elizabeth. *The Spartan Tradition in European Thought.* Oxford, 1969.

Raynal, Thomas. *Histoire philosophique et politique des établissemens et du commerce des Européens dans les deux Indes.* New ed. Paris, 1820.

Rediker, Markus. *Between the Devil and the Deep Blue Sea: Merchant Seamen, Pirates, and the Anglo-American Maritime World, 1700–1750.* Cambridge, 1987.

Régnier-Bohler, Danielle. *Croisades et Pélerinages. Récits, croniques et voyages en Terre Sainte.* Paris, 1997.

Reinier, Louis. *Discours d'Athenagore sur la resurrection des morts.* Breslau, 1753.

Rey, Roselyne. *The History of Pain.* Cambridge, MA, 1995.

Richardson, Ruth. *Death, Dissection, and the Destitute.* London, 1987.

Robertson, William. *The History of America.* 3d ed. London, 1780.

de Rochefort, Charles. *Histoire Naturelle et Morale des Iles Antilles de l'Amerique.* Rotterdam, 1658.

Roger, Jacques. *The Life Sciences in Eighteenth-Century French Thought.* Stanford, 1997.

Romm, James S. *The Edges of the Earth in Ancient Thought: Geography, Exploration, and Fiction.* Princeton, 1992.

Rose, Paul Lawrence. *Revolutionary Antisemitism in Germany from Kant to Wagner.* Princeton, 1990.

Rose, R. B. *Gracchus Boeuf: The First Revolutionary Communist.* London, 1978.

Rossi, Paolo. *The Dark Abyss of Time: The History of the Earth and the History of the Nations from Hooke to Vico*. Chicago, 1994.

Rousseau, J. J. *Discours sur l'origine et fondemens de l'inégalité parmi les hommes*. Dresden, 1755.

———. *A Discourse of Inequality*. Translated by Maurice Cranston. Harmondsworth, 1984.

———. *Emile, ou de l'Èducation*. Amsterdam, 1764.

———. *Oeuvres completes*. Edited by V. D. Musset-Pathay. Paris, 1823.

———. *The Social Contract*. Translated by Maurice Cranston. Harmondsworth, 1968.

Rowe, Christopher, and Malcolm Schofield. *The Cambridge History of Greek and Roman Political Thought*. Cambridge, 2000.

de Sade, marquis. *Oeuvres*. Paris, 1990.

Sadeur, Jacques [Gabriel de Foigny]. *Nouveau voyage de la Terre Australe*. Paris, 1693.

Sanborn, Geoffrey. *The Sign of the Cannibal: Melville and the Making of a Post-colonial Reader*. Durham, 1998.

Scattola, Merio. *Das Naturrecht vor dem Naturrecht: Zur Geschichte des "ius naturae" im 16. Jahrhundert*. Tubingen, 1999.

Schaack, Michael J. *Anarchy and Anarchists: A History of the Red Terror and Social Revolution in American and Europe*. Chicago, 1989.

Schmale, Wolfgang, ed. *Human Rights and Cultural Diversity*. Goldbach, 1993.

Schoefield, Malcolm. *The Stoic Idea of the City*. Cambridge, 1991.

Scochet, Gordon J. *Patriarchalism in Political Thought: The Authoritarian Family and Political Speculation and Attitudes, especially in Seventeenth-Century England*. New York, 1975.

Scot, Reginald. *The Discoverie of Witchcraft*. New York, 1972.

Selden, John. *Of the Dominion, or Ownership of the Sea [Mare Clausum]*. London, 1652.

de Sepulveda, Juan Gines. *Democrates Segundo, o de las justas causas de la guerra contra los indios*. Madrid, 1984.

Sextus Empiricus. *Against the Ethicists*. Translated by Richard Bett. Oxford, 1997.

Shattuck, Roger. *The Forbidden Experiment: The Story of the Wild Boy of Aveyron*. New York, 1980.

Shefferius, John. *The History of Lapland*. Oxford, 1674.

Siculus, Diodorus. *Histoire universelle*. Paris, 1737.

Sidney, Algernon. *Court Maxims*. Cambridge, 1996.

Simpson, A. W. Brian. *Cannibalism and the Common Law: The Story of the Last Voyage of the "Mignonette" and the Strange Legal Proceedings to which it Gave Rise*. Chicago, 1984.

Skinner, Quentin. *Reason and Rhetoric in the Philosophy of Hobbes*. Cambridge, 1996.

Smith, Adam. *An Inquiry into the Nature and Causes of the Wealth of Nations*. Oxford, 1976.

———. *The Glasgow Edition of the Works and Correspondence of Adam Smith*. Oxford, 1976.

———. *Lectures on Jurisprudence*. Edited by R. L. Meek, D. D. Raphael, and P. G. Stein. Oxford, 1978.

———. *The Theory of Moral Sentiments; or, An Essay towards an Analysis of the Principles by which Men naturally judge concerning the Conduct and Character, first of their Neighbours, and afterwards of themselves*. 10th ed. London, 1804.

Smith, Bernard. *European Vision and the South Pacific, 1768–1850: A Study in the History of Art and Ideas*. Oxford, 1960.

Smollett, Tobias. *The History and Adventures of an Atom*. Athens, 1989.

Snowden, Frank M. *Blacks in Antiquity: Ethiopians in the Greco-Roman Experience*. Harvard, 1970.

[Solis, Don Antoine de]. *Histoire de la conquête de la Mexique, ou de la Nouvelle Espagne*. Paris, 1591.

Sorell, Tom. *Moral Theory and Anomaly*. Oxford, 2000.

Stanford, Craig B. *The Hunting Apes: Meat Eating and the Origins of Human Behavior*. Princeton, 1999.

Stephanus Brutus Junius. *Vindiciae contra Tyrannos: Or concerning the Legitimate Power of the People over a Prince*. Cambridge, 1994.

Stites, Richard. *Revolutionary Dreams: Utopian Vision and Experimental Life in the Russian Revolution*. New York, 1989.

Strauss, Leo. *The Political Philosophy of Hobbes: Its Basis and its Genesis*. Chicago, 1977.

[Struys, Jean]. *Les Voyages de Jean Struys en Moscovie, en Tartarie, en Perse, aux Indes & au plusiers autres Païs étrangers*. Amsterdam, 1682.

Stube de Piemont, F. H. *Ebauche des loix naturelles et du droit primitif*. Amsterdam, 1765.

Swift, Jonathan, and Thomas Sheridan. *The Intelligencer*. Oxford, 1992.

Talmon, J. L. *The Myth of the Nation and the Vision of the Revolution: The Origin of Ideological Polarization in the Twentieth Century*. London, 1981.

Tannahill, Ray. *Food in History*. London, 1988.

du Tertre, Jean-Baptiste. *Histoire générale des Antilles habitées par les françois*. Paris, 1667.

Thévet, André. *Les singularités de la France antarctique, autrement nommée Amérique, & de plusiers Terres & Isles découvertes de notre temps*. Paris, 1558.

Thomas, Chantal. *The Wicked Queen: The Origins of the Myth of Marie Antoinette*. New York, 1999.

Thomas, Hugh. *The Slave Trade: The History of the Atlantic Slave Trade, 1440–1870*. New York, 1997.

Tierney, Brian. *Rights, Laws, and Infallibility in Mediaeval Thought*. Aldershot, 1997.

Tiles, J. E. *Moral Measures: An Introduction to Ethics East and West*. London, 2000.

Trenchard, John, and Thomas Gordon. *Cato's Letters, or Essays on Liberty, Civil and Religious, and other Important Subjects*. Indianapolis, 1995.

Tropp, Martin. *Images of Fear: How Horror Stories Helped Shape Modern Culture, 1818–1918*. Jefferson, NC, 1990.

Turnbull, George. *Discourse upon the Nature and Origin of Civil Laws*. London, 1740.

Tyson, Edward. *Ourang-Outang, Sive Homo Sylvestris*. London,1699.

de Vattel, Emerich. *Questions de droit naturel, sur le Traité du droit de la Nature de M. le Baron de Wolf*. Bern, 1762.

le Vayer, François Mothe. *Œuvres*. Dresden, 1756.

de la Vega, Garcilasso. *L'Histoire des Yncas, Roys de Perou*. Amsterdam, 1704.

Verlinden, Charles. *L'esclavage dans l'Europe medievale*. Ghent, 1977.

Viagrello, Georges. *A History of Rape: Sexual Violence in France from the 16th to the 20th Century*. Cambridge, 2001.

Vickers, Ilse. *Defoe and the New Sciences*. Cambridge, 1996.

Vico, Giambattista. *The New Science*. Translated by Thomas Goddard Bergin and Max Harold Fisch. Ithaca, 1984.

Vitalis, Orderic. *The Ecclesiastical History*. Oxford, 1995.

de Vitoria, Francisco. *Political Writings*. Translated by Jeremy Lawrance. Cambridge, 1991.

Voltaire [François-Marie Arouet]. *Candide, ou l'Optimisme*. Paris, 1759.

———. *Dictionnaire philosophique*. London, 1745.

———. *Essai sur les Moeurs et l'esprit des nations*. Stuttgart, 1829.

———. *L'Homme aux quarante écus*. Geneva, 1768.

———. *Oeuvres*. Paris 1829.

———. *La Philosophie de l'Histoire*. Autrecht, 1765.

Vyverberg, Henry. *Historical Pessimism in the French Enlightenment*. Harvard, 1958.

———. *Human Nature, Cultural Diversity, and the French Enlightenment*. New York, 1989.

[de Warville, Brissot]. *Recherches philosophiques sur le droit de propriété consideré dans la nature pour servir de premier chapitre à la Théorie des loix de M. Linguet, par un jeune philosophe*. Paris, 1780.

Wolf, Christian. *Principes du droit de la nature et des gens*. Amsterdam, 1758.

Wolf, Larry. *Inventing Eastern Europe: The Map of Civilization on the Mind of Enlightenment*. Stanford, 1994.

Wolff, Christian. *Principes du droit de la nature et des gens*. Amsterdam, 1758.

Wolpe, Hans. *Raynal et sa machine de guerre: "L'Histoire de deux Indes" et ses perfectionnements*. Stanford, 1957.

Yack, Bernard. *The Longing for Total Revolution: The Philosophical Sources of Social Discontent from Rousseau to Marx and Nietzsche*. Princeton, 1996.

Youlton, John W. *Thinking Matter: Materialism in Eighteenth-Century Britain*. Oxford, 1983.

INDEX